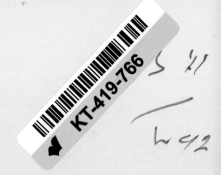

MARGOT
AT WAR

MARGOT AT WAR

LOVE AND BETRAYAL IN DOWNING STREET 1912–16

Anne de Courcy

Weidenfeld & Nicolson
LONDON

First published in Great Britain in 2014
by Weidenfeld & Nicolson

3 5 7 9 10 8 6 4 2

© Anne de Courcy 2014

A CIP catalogue record for this book
is available from the British Library.

ISBN (hardback): 978 0 297 86983 2
ISBN (trade paperback): 978 0 297 86986 3

Typeset by Input Data Services Ltd, Bridgwater, Somerset

Printed and bound by CPI Group (UK) Ltd, Croydon, CR0 4YY

The Orion Publishing Group's policy is to use papers
that are natural, renewable and recyclable and made
from wood grown in sustainable forests. The logging and
manufacturing processes are expected to conform to
environmental regulations of the country of origin.

Weidenfeld & Nicolson
The Orion Publishing Group Ltd
Orion House
5 Upper Saint Martin's Lane
London, WC2H 9EA

An Hachette UK Company

www.orionbooks.co.uk

CONTENTS

List of Illustrations   vii

Introduction   1

Part One: 1912   7

Part Two: 1913   103

Part Three: 1914   133

Part Four: 1915   227

Part Five: 1916   307

Aftermath   341

Acknowledgements   355

Bibliography   357

Index   361

ILLUSTRATIONS

SECTION ONE

Margot Asquith ice skating, c.1912 (*Ullstein bild/Topfoto*)

Margot photographed by Frederick Hollyer, c.1890 (*Victoria and Albert Museum*)

Sketch by Margot of William Gladstone felling a tree at Glen (*Bonham Carter Trustees/Bodleian Library, MS. Photogr. c.120, fol.84*)

Glen House (*Bodleian Library, MS. Photogr. c.121, fol.6*)

Wilfrid Scawen Blunt (*Bodleian Library, MS. Photogr. c.121, fol.30*)

Margot at a foxhunt meet in Melton Mowbray, Leicestershire (*Bodleian Library*)

Asquith photographed by his son Raymond, c.1890 (*Bodleian Library*)

Margot at the corner of 20 Cavendish Square (*Bodleian Library, MS. Photogr. c.120, fol.46*)

Asquith in the study at 20 Cavendish Square (*Bodleian Library*)

Chalk portrait of Margot by John Singer Sargent, 1897 (*National Portrait Gallery, London*)

Elizabeth Asquith with her governess Anna Heinsius, 'Frau', and dog, Tony (*Bodleian Library*)

Margot, Elizabeth and Asquith on their way to the Wee Free Church in Scotland, 1904 (*Bodleian Library*)

Katherine and Raymond Asquith, 1913 (*National Portrait Gallery, London*)

Violet Asquith and Venetia Stanley at Penrhos, 1907 (*Anthony Pitt-Rivers*)

Herbert 'Beb' Asquith (*Mary Evans*)

Arthur 'Oc' Asquith, 1918 (*National Portrait Gallery, London*)

Cyril 'Cys' Asquith (*Bodleian Library*)

Cynthia Asquith and Venetia Stanley holding her pet monkey, Fluto (*Anthony Pitt-Rivers*)

Puffin Asquith playing with a model aeroplane in the garden at 10 Downing Street, c.1910 (*Mary Evans*)

Margot talking to a chauffeur (*Bodleian Library, MS. Photogr. c.120, fol.59*)

LIST OF ILLUSTRATIONS

SECTION TWO

Maud Allan in costume as Salome, c.1908 (*Mander & Mitchenson Archive/ University of Bristol/ArenaPAL*)

10 Downing Street, 1904 (*London Metropolitan Archives, City of London SC/PHL/01/465-111*)

The Great Dining Room at 10 Downing Street, c.1904 (*London Metropolitan Archives, City of London, SC/PHL/01/465/79/112*)

The drawing room at 10 Downing Street, 1900 (*London Metropolitan Archives, City of London, SC/PHL/01/465/79/96*)

Suffragettes accosting Asquith as part of their 'Pestering the Politicians' policy, 1908 (*Stapleton Historical Collection/Heritage Images/Topfoto*)

Duff and Lady Diana Cooper

David Lloyd George and Edwin Montagu en route to the House of Commons to present the Budget, 1914 (*Topfoto*)

Crowds in London watch the declaration of war being read aloud by a city councillor, 4 August 1914 (*akg-images*)

Winston Churchill and his wife Clementine arriving for the launch of HMS *Iron Duke*, 1912 (*Mirrorpix/Bridgeman*)

Sir John French with Asquith, 1914 (*John Frost Newspapers/Mary Evans*)

Margot and Violet in 10 Downing Street, 1914 (*Bodleian Library, MS. Photogr. c.120, fol.58*)

The Wharf, Sutton Courtenay, 1915 (*Illustrated London News/Mary Evans*)

Asquith and Lloyd George at The Wharf, May 1915 (*Bodleian Library*)

The wedding of Violet and Maurice 'Bongie' Bonham Carter, 30 November 1915 (*Illustrated London News/Mary Evans*)

Venetia, 1915 (*Illustrated London News/Mary Evans*)

Elizabeth pictured in The Tatler, 1915 (*Illustrated London News/Mary Evans*)

Article from The Bystander breaking the news of Raymond's death at the Battle of Flers-Courcelette on 15 September 1916 (*Illustrated London News/Mary Evans*)

Asquith and Sir Edward Grey at the Ministry of Foreign Affairs in Paris, March 1916 (*Roger Viollet/Topfoto*)

Margot and Puffin outside the Royal Courts of Justice (*Topfoto*)

Lytton Strachey and Margot, 1923 (*National Portrait Gallery, London*)

Margot as Elizabeth I at Worcester College, Oxford, 1923 (*Topfoto*)

Margot and Violet at the Royal Academy of Arts, 1924 (*Topfoto*)

Margot and Asquith at The Wharf, January 1925 (*Bodleian Library, MS. Photogr. c.120, fol.74*)

INTRODUCTION

Most books have at least one *raison d'être*. Mine is a fascination with Margot Asquith – her originality, wit, chic, vitality, the intensity of her emotions, often so forcefully expressed – and the drama of her last five years as Prime Minister's wife during a time that is one of the most important in our history.

Margot was someone who had created herself and her own path through life. She was largely self-educated, with a passion to learn more. In an era when 'Society' was narrow, close-knit and aristocratic, Margot, a tradesman's granddaughter, surmounted by sheer force of personality the invisible stockade that surrounded this elite to arrive at its inner heart, dispensing en route with any of its conventions – such as chaperonage – that she considered meaningless.

But what she really enjoyed was the conversation of the highly intelligent; and by the time she was twenty-five, she was friends with most of the cleverest men in the country. Gladstone, who wrote a poem to her, sat her on his knee; Oscar Wilde dedicated a story to her; admirers wrote to her daily; the great Benjamin Jowett, Regius Professor of Greek and Master of Balliol College, Oxford, advised her on what to read and whom to marry. No beauty in an age of 'beauties', she compensated for her lack of looks by superb, stylish clothes. Although she was so sought after, suitors courted her unavailingly – for nine years she was deeply in love with a glamorous ne'er-do-well with whom she saw no future but whom she could not bring herself to leave.

By now, as 'the fabulous Miss Tennant', she was so well known that when a rumour swept London that she was going to marry Arthur Balfour, soon to be Prime Minister, he denied it with the words: 'No, that is not so. I rather think of having a career of my own.' Her impact on the politician H.H. Asquith, then the Liberal Party's rising star and a married man with five children, was

I

immediate, so that within months of his wife's death from typhoid he was pursuing her passionately.

His courtship of her reveals a man far different from the cool, bland, almost dull, imperturbability usually presented as his persona. His letters are those of someone intensely romantic, besottedly in love, raised to the heights then agonised as she blew first hot, then cold. 'Upon my knees, which I bend too rarely to God, I implore you to think twice and thrice before you shut the door . . . for your love is life, and its loss black despair,' he wrote after one of her rejections.

By the time she married him, Asquith had become Home Secretary, the man tipped to be a future prime minister. Margot's gift for friendship and her constant entertaining introduced the entire Asquith family to a life in which politicians, aristocrats, literati and churchmen gathered daily round the luncheon or dinner table. It was a world where politics was entertainment as well as government, with the wives, daughters, friends and sisters of politicians spending their afternoons in the Ladies' Gallery and discussing the speeches afterwards at the various dinner parties they would be attending.

In these intimate gatherings, as in bedrooms and drawing rooms all over London, secrets were told, decisions were taken, allegiances subtly shifted and gossip passed round, with the running of the country largely in the hands of this small, powerful group. Although there were no women politicians, female influence could be powerful. Lady Campbell-Bannerman (the wife of Asquith's predecessor as Prime Minister) refused to let her husband accept a peerage; Margot herself often wrote to ministers in her husband's Government to congratulate, chide or give her own views; Clementine Churchill tried to intervene on behalf of Winston when she felt he had been unfairly treated.

The two years immediately before the 1914–18 war (the fifth and sixth of Asquith's premiership), where my story of the Asquiths begins, are as important as any in British history. Though for the privileged the glossy surface of life seemed unaltered, just as ice can crack beneath an unbroken covering of snow so huge changes were in motion to alter entirely the world as they knew it.

The year 1912 saw the fledgling Welfare State and a Labour Party emerging as a political force. There was constant industrial unrest as workers fought against their poor pay and conditions.

The suffragette movement had turned to militancy: who now could imagine a prime minister beaten about the head, as Asquith was, by women armed with hunting crops or attacked on a golf course by two who tried to strip him?

Though the vote was still elusive, there was a steady flow of women away from domestic service and into offices, where the new fashions – skirts had risen above the ankle for the first time in centuries – enabled them to climb the stairs of omnibuses and, if suffragettes, to flee their pursuers more successfully. Widening horizons still further was the steady increase in newspaper readership, though nobody, if the evidence I have collected from diaries and letters from around the country is to be believed, saw the war coming. Instead, all attention was focused on the question of Home Rule for Ireland, almost as bitterly divisive in the political classes of England as it was in Ireland.

The violent emotions that accompany profound social change were reflected in the personal lives of those inside No. 10. Against the background of a Government beset by troubles and the looming possibility of a civil war, Asquith fell in love. The object of what became an obsessive passion was his daughter Violet's best friend, Venetia Stanley, a young woman aged twenty-five to his sixty. When Margot discovered her Henry's new attachment her diary is filled with misery. To add to the torrent of emotion coursing through Downing Street, one of Asquith's Private Secretaries was also in love with Venetia, another with Violet, while Violet and Venetia were themselves locked in a friendship with near-erotic undertones. To add to Margot's difficulties, her relationship with her husband was already complicated by Violet's jealous, almost incestuous adoration of her father and insistent, constant presence ('I have only been alone with Henry and my children three weeks in nineteen years,' Margot wailed to a friend).

The outbreak of war only increased Asquith's passion for Venetia, and the letters multiplied. Picture the Prime Minister, sitting in Cabinet as great questions of strategy are discussed, while young men are dying in their thousands in the trenches, when a messenger brings in a letter. It is from Venetia. Immediately he opens it, reads it with the utmost concentration, picks up his pen and writes several pages – quite probably containing a Cabinet secret – with equal concentration while discussion continues around him, sends for the messenger and dispatches his answer. Then, and only then, does he rejoin the discussion.

Looked at closely, almost everything about those few years seems strange to us. It was a war that for the first seventeen months was run almost entirely on a voluntary basis (except for the requisition of horses). Much war work was done by children: Girl Guides worked in soup kitchens, filled sandbags, padded splints for broken limbs; Boy Scouts acted as messengers in the War Office.

Attitudes sometimes make one gasp: what shocked onlookers at Victoria Station, when two young women motorcyclists were departing for the Front as dispatch riders, was not the thought that they were going into danger and possible death but the fact that they were wearing leather breeches *without a covering skirt*. Well-born young women, off to within miles of the Front to nurse horrific cases of gangrene, amputation and the bloodiest of wounds – a duty they mostly performed heroically – were not allowed to travel across the Channel without a chaperone; when Lady Sackville thought her estate carpenters were in danger of being conscripted she wrote to Lord Kitchener, the Secretary of State for War, to ask him to exempt them and by implication her footmen too, as 'parlour-maids are so middle class'.

Yet the old order was changing fast, although few of those who had, for so long, led a life gilded and supported by privilege seemed to realise it. Just as mechanisation was affecting warfare, so a new breed of politician was thrusting forward – Lloyd George is the prime example – conscious of the power of image, of the need to appeal directly to the ordinary men and women of the country, and of the ability of the rapidly growing press to further both those aims. Modernisation was encroaching on all sides, in everything from reading material and attitudes to the growing demands of the workers (and the increased free time allowed them). For women, this meant not only clothes that were actually easier to wear and better adapted to a freer, more active lifestyle than that allowed by the lavish, corseted, petticoated Edwardian dresses but also a chance to fulfil roles that were useful as well as decorative.

To anyone who has been through, or read about, more recent wars it seems extraordinary that a large part of the country was so little affected by it in 1914, or determined to remain so – not least the Prime Minister. Downing Street, though at the heart of government and privy to all the most terrible secrets of war, was still run like an Edwardian mansion. The prime ministerial timetable included luncheon parties almost every day, a leisurely drive with Venetia every Friday afternoon, weekends in the country, bridge every night after dinner with the prettiest young women available and a determined air of leisure once the House or Cabinet had been left behind. Nemesis, when it finally came, was swift. It was, indeed, the end of an era.

PART ONE

1912

ONE

Nothing like it had ever been seen in No. 10 Downing Street before. There were gasps from the smartly dressed audience, their chairs pushed back against the panelled walls, as the young woman, in a flimsy dress of diaphanous chiffon, a garland of flowers round her dark hair, her feet and legs bare, glided into the grand drawing room. They watched transfixed as, with graceful, swaying movements of arms and torso, she began her 'nymph' dance to Mendelssohn's 'Spring Song'.

For this was the famous Maud Allan, whose daring 'Salome' performance topped the bill at the Palace Theatre in Shaftesbury Avenue. Her finale, carrying on a platter a wax model of St John the Baptist's head to which she gave a lingering and sensual kiss on the lips, was a sensation – not least for the way she was dressed.

'The dancer has her breasts covered with two closely fitting shields; these cover the nipple & part, not all of each breast. Except for necklaces & a few ornamental looking cords to holding the breast shields in position the body is completely naked to a level with the points of the hips,' salivated one newspaper, adding that 'no shoes, stockings, or drawers are worn'.

So daring was Maud's dancing that the Manchester authorities had banned her entire show. The young P.G. Wodehouse was moved by this to write a ditty on the subject (sung to a popular tune):

> There's a girl who can dance in a way
> That astonishes people, they say.
> They see her Salome,
> And gasp out, 'Well, blow me!
> That's pretty remarkable, eh?'
> The name of this damsel is Maud,
> She's succeeded at home and abroad;

But the hawk-eyed committee
Of Manchester city
Are not among those who applaud.

That afternoon in 1908 Maud was performing her sensational dance in Downing Street at the invitation of her friend Margot Asquith, whose husband, H.H. Asquith, had become Prime Minister a few weeks earlier. In that era, when convention ruled and scandal attached itself like a burr to anyone stepping outside the norm, inviting a young woman, banned for obscenity in one of Britain's major cities, to dance half naked within the residence of the Prime Minister was a daring thing for even Margot to do.

But then, Margot was no ordinary Prime Minister's wife – nor, in his way, was Asquith an ordinary Prime Minister.

As 1912 opened, it seemed as if the golden Edwardian summer would stretch on for ever. Even a different monarch had done little more than make the Court a duller and less licentious place. The sense of entitlement in the upper classes was almost palpable. For as long as most people could remember, the British Empire had been the greatest power on the globe. The South African War, so far away, had lasted a mere two years and had barely impinged on the consciousness of many, let alone modified the style of living of the grandest Edwardians. It seemed that nothing ever would – could – alter this.

But Britain was on the cusp of social and political changes that would irrevocably affect national life. Many came from government; many from those it ruled – and these would produce a new kind of government that responded to the wishes of the people rather than the decisions of a privileged elite, and a new kind of politician, not only aware of this 'people power' but able to harness it.

At the heart of government was its best-known family: the Prime Minister, Herbert Henry Asquith, who had helped to bring about some of these changes but would in turn be their victim; his wife Margot, an extraordinary figure in her own right; their two children and Asquith's own five children by his first wife. Three others were almost as family: the Prime Minister's two Private Secretaries, Maurice ('Bongie') Bonham Carter and Edwin Montagu, and his daughter Violet's best friend, the Hon. Venetia Stanley. Within months, all of them would be linked in an emotional cat's cradle.

No. 10 Downing Street was the official residence of the Prime Minister and his family but Asquith and his wife, the former Margot Tennant, lived in an ambiance that we would hardly recognise. Security was virtually non-existent. To modern eyes, the thought that any determined person could simply stride through the front door seems almost unbelievable. As Margot recorded in her diary: 'I never knew what prevented anyone coming into this house at any moment: some would say after lunching with us that nothing had.'

These luncheon parties had been given almost daily by Margot since the Asquiths' marriage seventeen years earlier; they were preferred to dinners by Asquith, who did not enjoy all-male conversations except in the House and disliked the custom of women leaving the men to their port and retiring to the drawing room. What he liked in the evening was having a few friends to dinner, with general conversation followed by several rubbers of bridge.

On most days the Downing Street dining table would be surrounded by a mixed collection of guests: Members of Parliament, young women, perhaps one or two of the Asquith sons, Violet, women friends of Margot and literati like Robbie Ross (Oscar Wilde's literary executor and his lover) or Eddie Marsh – arts patron, civil servant, friend to poets and Private Secretary to Winston Churchill.

Two of the most regular guests, so much so that they became part of the close family circle, were Bongie and Montagu, in 1912 aged respectively thirty-two and thirty-three. Bongie had been at Balliol with Asquith's two eldest sons, Raymond and Beb, through whom he had met Violet during her coming-out year in 1905; shortly thereafter he had become her father's Private Secretary. Montagu had been elected as MP for Chesterton in 1906, spotted by Asquith as a rising young politician and co-opted to work for him.

Asquith, who often had no idea who would be there until he walked in from the Cabinet Room, would preside benignly at these gatherings – although sometimes he had a brisk way with bores, generally cutting them off short before they were launched into full flood. 'I don't know whether you are aware, Mr Asquith,' began one rash luncheon guest, 'that under the American constitution . . .' Sensing a tedious monologue, the Asquith guillotine came down. 'The worst in the world, of course,' interjected the Prime Minister immediately, removing the sting by warmly ushering the visitor into the next room to join the rest of the group.

Asquith's political career and most of the family well-being were reliant on his wife's wealth: when he became Prime Minister in 1908 his income had dropped to the ministerial salary of £5,000. He was now sixty (he was born on 12 September 1852). He had fallen in love wth his first wife, Helen Melland, the daughter of a Manchester doctor, when he was only eighteen and they married when they were little more than boy and girl. Their five children were Raymond, Herbert ('Beb'), Arthur ('Oc'), Violet and Cyril ('Cys'); in 1912 aged respectively thirty-four, thirty-one, twenty-nine, twenty-five and twenty-two.

Unlike most of the men in Margot's circle, who were Eton alumni from aristocratic or upper-middle-class families, her husband came from a Yorkshire mercantile and Congregational background and had been educated at the City of London School, which he left at eighteen having won a classical scholarship to Balliol. Four years later he was awarded the Craven Scholarship and became President of the Oxford Union, then as now a breeding ground for politicians.

Shortly after graduating he was elected a Fellow of Balliol, and read for the Bar, to which he was called in 1876. His ability to assimilate facts almost instantaneously, combine widely differing strands of reasoning into one cohesive whole and then present this as a compelling argument, coupled with his habit of working until three every morning, led quickly to success at the Bar and, later, to his mastery of the House of Commons, which he entered in July 1886, becoming Home Secretary only six years later. His gift of lucidity was such that it was said that he could drive a Roman road through any subject, while the calm assurance of his manner underlined the authority that emanated from him in debate.

Winston Churchill – when President of the Board of Trade, his first post as a Cabinet minister in the Asquith Government – described him to the diarist and Egyptologist Wilfrid Scawen Blunt as 'a very simple-minded man, very ingenuous, but he has a wonderful talent for work, and the clearest possible head for business. He will sit up playing bridge and drinking late at night, and yet in the morning he will come to his office or the House and enter into the most complicated business with his head entirely clear and work on for six or seven hours. He will attend committees and give full attention to every point of discussion, and draft amendments in his perfectly clear handwriting without altering a word, clause after clause, and he is far and away the best speaker in the House.'

He was good company. The German Ambassador, Prince Lichnowsky, accurately summed up the impression he made. 'A jovial *bon viveur*, fond of the ladies, especially the young and pretty ones, he is partial to cheerful society and good cooking . . . Formerly a well-known barrister with a large income, and for a number of years in Parliament, then a minister under Mr Gladstone, a pacifist like his friend Grey,* and favouring an understanding with Germany, he handled all questions with the cheery calm and assurance of an experienced man of business, whose good health and excellent nerves had been steeled by devotion to the game of golf.'

Asquith who, according to Wilfrid Scawen Blunt, had lived during his first marriage in a 'small house in Hampstead with a garden behind where they kept chickens . . . and went in and out to his chambers daily on the top of an omnibus,' had had no trouble adjusting to Margot's infinitely grander life when they married, taking to rich food and – especially – drink rather than the simpler fare he had been used to, and relishing after-dinner bridge and the conversation of beautiful women rather than the everydayness of family life.

The Prime Minister's zest for enjoyment, noted Lichnowsky, was shared by his wife. Other than this Margot, about to celebrate her forty-eighth birthday, was not like her husband in any way. In an age of languid, marmoreal beauties, she was slim, with an excellent figure, active and fit from days spent roaming the wild countryside round Glen, the Tennants' Scottish home and, later, in the hunting field. Her strong points physically were an abundance of dark brown hair, a pearly complexion, dark eyes and unquenchable vitality, but it was her original and charismatic personality that made the over-riding impression. At the age of only nineteen she had been viewed by many as the most distinctive young woman in London. When she was still unknown, Lord Pembroke, placed beside her at a dinner party and later to fall in love with her, had scribbled a note to his hostess asking, 'Who is this girl with the red heels?'

* Sir Edward Grey, Britain's Foreign Secretary.

Socially, she cared little for conventions she found meaningless. As a young girl she had scandalised London Society by ignoring the iron but unspoken law of chaperonage – even, to the horror of the older generation, travelling alone by train. More than anything else, though, it was her extraordinary frankness that surprised, fascinated, appealed and sometimes appalled. It was, as Desmond MacCarthy wrote, a 'dangerous, graceless, disconcerting, invigorating, merciless, shameless, lovable candour'. What other young woman of twenty-two would have dared say to Lord Randolph Churchill after his sudden, surprise resignation as Chancellor of the Exchequer, 'I am afraid you resigned more out of temper than conviction, Lord Randolph'? In an era of frozen gentility, her speciality was going too far. Together with her wit, brilliance, warmth and penchant for entertaining, it was a quality that ran like an electric current through Society.

Margot was the eleventh of twelve children (though four died young). She was inseparable from her younger sister Laura until Laura, who married in 1885, died a year later in childbirth. She also had three half-sisters: after the death of her mother Emma in 1895 her father had remarried in 1898 at the age of seventy-five a young woman of thirty, Marguerite Miles, who had caught his eye when they were both dining with Lord Burnham, owner of the *Daily Telegraph*. They went on to have three daughters.

Thanks to her upbringing in this big, sociable family she had none of the usual maidenly hesitation or reserve when talking to men – if she liked one he would be asked to one of the large and agreeable luncheon parties at her father's London house.

By the time she was twenty-five this frank and open approach had made her the close friend of most of the leading intellectual and social figures of the day, who wrote to her, sent her books, flowers, love letters and poems. Oscar Wilde dedicated his short story 'The Star Child'* to her, she enjoyed *tête à têtes* with Gladstone (who also wrote a poem to her), she danced in a scarlet frock and black lace petticoat for an enchanted officers' mess and Harry Cust, editor of the *Pall Mall Gazette* and lover of numerous Society women, declared: 'In spite of the sores and the bores and the flaws in it/My own life's the better for small bits of yours in it.'

* From *A House of Pomegranates*, published in 1891.

Aged only twenty-two she had suffered a damaging blow to her appearance that could have caused her a miserable loss of confidence. On an April day in 1886, as her diary records at the time: 'I was riding down a green slope in Gloucestershire while the Beaufort hounds were scattered below vainly trying to pick up the scent; they were on a stale line and the result had been general confusion. It was a hot day and the woods were full of primroses. The air was humming with birds and insects, nature wore an expectant look, and all the hedgerows sparkled with the spangles of spring.'

Margot rode down to a gap in a fence that divided her from the others, kicked her horse over it and woke up in a nearby cottage with a tremendous headache. She had been concussed: a branch had caught her in the face, her nose and upper lip were badly torn and her nose broken. The doctor who was sent for stitched her up without anaesthetic (chloroform, then) as there was no time to fetch it; and her nose remained crooked (by the time she eventually gave up hunting, in 1905, she had broken both collarbones, several ribs, both kneecaps and dislocated her jaw).

Without conventional beauty, she pinned her faith on style and elegance – all her life her clothes would be beautiful and expensive, with the simplicity that comes from perfect cut, emphasised by overtones of drama. They gave her pleasure and confidence, they were her armour against the all-powerful sway of the beauties and, as she once said: 'Clothes are the first thing that catch the eye.' It was this ethos that made her say to her three young half-sisters, who found her lightning mind and outspoken tongue intimidating: 'Oh darlings, you dress like parsons' daughters. Can't you be more chic?'

When she married Asquith, Margot faced the formidable prospect of becoming stepmother to five children – five children for whom their dead mother had created a close family circle with herself at the centre. As her friend Benjamin Jowett, the Balliol scholar and tutor, theologian and Platonist, wrote to her: 'The real doubt about the affair is the family; will you consider this and talk it over with your mother? The other day you were at a masqued ball, as you told me – a few months hence you will have, or rather may be having, the care of five children, with all the ailments and miseries and disagreeables of children and not your own, although you will have to be a mother to them, and this state of things will last during the greater part of your life.'

Margot herself was deeply worried. 'I had no reason to think I was maternal,' she wrote, 'and I was haunted by the thought that if I married him I might ruin his career' – she was aware that many of Asquith's friends thought her highly *mondaine* way of life and unfettered speech would spell disaster to this rising star of the Liberal Party. She also realised that his children would, naturally, be prejudiced against the idea of a stepmother. 'I felt I was not worthy to undertake the care and guidance of exceptionally clever children brought up in different surroundings from my own.'

When she became their stepmother she found them daunting, Raymond and Violet in particular regarding her from a position of lofty, almost disdainful intellectual superiority. 'I do not think if you had ransacked the world you could have found natures so opposite in temper, temperament, and outlook as my stepchildren when I first knew them,' she wrote.

Certainly Raymond's brilliance had never been in doubt. Aged seven, he described the discarded skin of a python seen at the zoo as 'an outworn fetter broken and cast off by its soul'; from then on his academic progress was triumphant, concluding with a slew of Oxford's glittering prizes and a first-class honours degree, after which he followed in his father's footsteps and became a barrister. A schoolboy of almost sixteen when his new stepmother flashed like a glittering dragonfly into his life, both his good looks and his aloof, rather cynical persona were already evident.

Margot had worked hard at being a good stepmother, her natural warmth penetrating even Raymond's hard outer carapace – he had become aware of the good qualities that lay beneath the ebullience that the Asquith children found so hard to take (Violet thought Margot's habit of thanking the servants after they had performed some task 'undignified' in the wife of a senior politician). When he was knocked over by a huge wave on the Aberdeenshire coastline and got up half stunned, with his face and knee streaming with blood, it was Margot who knew what to do. 'Margot is always splendid on these occasions,' he wrote to a friend. 'She took me back to the house and covered me with ice and raw beef.' And when at Oxford, he told her that if he got into any difficulty he would certainly consult her, 'for I think you know more of the world and take a saner view of it than almost anyone else'.

Her great generosity was also welcome. When Raymond wanted

to marry Katharine Horner, the daughter of Frances Horner, one of Margot's oldest friends – and Asquith's confidante in his pursuit of Margot – it was Margot who made this possible by settling £400 a year on Raymond, then a young barrister earning far too little to marry on. She also paid for the entire wedding, held from 20 Cavendish Square on 23 July 1907.

She did the same for Asquith's second son, Beb, who married Lady Cynthia Charteris in 1910 – Cynthia too adopted the habit of semi-sneering comments about Margot while blithely accepting her generosity. Cynthia, the daughter of Margot's friends Lord and Lady Elcho (later Wemyss), had been brought up in aristocratic surroundings, and her mother Mary had expected her to marry the heir to some large estate. Beb, a mere barrister from a family outside the sacred circle, was frowned on for some time, and the couple's meetings had to be in secret, until finally Cynthia's family gave way. Margot and Asquith gave Cynthia a diamond tiara as a wedding present as well as helping them financially, but though this meant they had enough to live on, and the leisure for Beb to pursue his real interest, poetry, by the standards of their friends they were poor.

It was not long before Margot won over the two youngest boys, Cys, then a lively little boy with a mop of red curls, and Oc – his father's favourite and soon Margot's. 'The reason Oc is the most loved of my stepchildren is that he is far the most human of them,' she wrote in her diary later. 'He has a rich nature and a real sense of responsibility. He is absolutely unselfish. He knows the precise value of brains and puts them in proportion. He can give up and serve others. He isn't self-enfolded . . .'

By 1912 the twenty-five-year-old Violet was the only one of Asquith's children by his first wife still living at home, and her relationship with Margot was one of the most powerful ingredients in the emotional cross-currents that would soon envelop Downing Street.

She was the closest of his first five children to her father and with her he was much more demonstrative than with his sons, allowing his natural affection to show. After the death of her mother when she was four, Asquith had had the small girl's bed brought into his own room in his London flat, and as she grew older would talk to her of his political concerns when he came in at night. Sometimes she would wake him early to continue these talks, often having to shake him hard as he slept deeply after a late night at the House. Several years of this night-time intimacy formed the basis of a relationship that had become almost incestuous in its closeness. The loss of her mother, the sudden, unexpected ejection from her father's bedroom after several years and the arrival of a new stepmother led to a lifelong jealousy of Margot in Violet and, in Margot, of rivalry with her stepdaughter as both sought to be the closest to Asquith.

Margot was determined to give Violet as good an education as possible – then, this meant a good governess – but what served Violet best of all was her own fierce intelligence, her literary appetite and the constant encounters with Asquith and Margot's political and literary friends. 'Happy child! You are seeing life from the stage box,' said one of them, the author Henry James.

When Violet was eighteen (in 1905), Margot took great pains over her coming-out, arranging for her father Sir Charles Tennant and his second wife Marguerite to give a ball for Violet, and Margot's niece Frances Tennant, in their large house at 40 Grosvenor Square. It was a lavish occasion: the big double drawing room, cleared for dancing, was swathed in roses, Violet's dress came from Worth and on the morning of the ball Sir Charles sent both girls a diamond necklace. Violet commented later that it made her feel conspicuous (young girls normally wore pearls).

Of Margot's own children by Asquith, only two survived. Her first pregnancy set the pattern for those that followed. Her labour was protracted, she suffered great pain, and her baby had to be sacrificed to save her life. Margot herself did not recover consciousness until the following day. For both Asquiths, the loss of this little creature, their first child together, was a profound grief. At once, Asquith wrote to his wife, immured in her room: 'Darling sweetheart and wife, I have just read for the first time your inexpressibly dear and touching love-letter written more than three weeks ago. I have resisted the temptation of opening it all this time; somehow I dared not, until all was over. But I am rewarded for my patience, for it is to me the dearest tribute that has ever been paid to me by woman or man, and I shall carry it with me as a blessing and an inspiration until I die . . .

'To me, from the first hour I knew you until now, you have been the best that I have known. I have loved and love you truly and loyally and with all my nature: and now we are more bound together than ever by the hopes and the fears and the loss which we have shared. God make us ever more and more to each other and help us both to do and to bear.'

Margot was so ill that word got round that she was dying. Once, Asquith opened the front door to find two of her former suitors, Peter Flower and Evan Charteris, on the doorstep. 'Henry said it was curious to see these two men who hated each other united for a moment in a common fear.' The mutual dislike was not surprising. Peter Flower, the younger brother of Lord Battersea, was Margot's first great love, whom she had met when she was nineteen. She was struck at once by his good looks and unforced elegance. Seconds later, she became aware that these were as nothing compared to the extraordinary, almost animal, grace and vitality that he exuded. But as she was quickly to learn, in marital terms – the subliminal perspective from which most single young women viewed most men in those days – he was a complete waste of time.

He was thirteen years older than Margot, and a man with an appalling reputation. Numerous husbands had threatened to horse-whip him, he borrowed money from his friends and seldom paid them back – from time to time he would disappear to India to hunt big game when creditors became too pressing or emotional affairs too difficult to handle – and he was an inveterate gambler. Nor did he have any of Margot's intellectual interests (he had never been known to read a book in his life) and he could be rude, bad-tempered and unpleasant. Yet his charm, looks and sheer masculinity made him fatally attractive to women.

To Margot, his mixture of passion, daredevilry and tender emotion was irresistible. Once he sprang across the area at the front of 40 Grosvenor Square and into the open window of the library when she did not open the door quickly enough. Once she outfaced a current mistress, the beautiful Lady Randolph Churchill. Another night, having left a ball together, they quarrelled so badly that Margot walked home by herself, to be confronted by her furious father, who asked her what she thought she was doing walking the streets alone at two in the morning in nothing but a ball dress – she had flung Peter's sheltering coat back at him. The two of them were drawn to each other like magnets but both realised the other could not – or would not – change.

Charteris (the sixth son of the tenth Earl of Wemyss) had fallen in love with her with little encouragement. 'Oh Margot how I loved your letter,' he wrote to her soon after they had met. 'It seemed like a break in the cloud that parting from you always makes for me . . . I leave you <u>all all</u> mine [love], keep it will you and be sometimes glad perhaps you've got it . . . and say you love me, ever so little.' In many ways he was a paler copy of Peter Flower, one of a type that physically attracted her, good-looking, keen on a country, sporting life, but though he was delightful company even Margot quickly re-alised that if they married she would soon become bored with him; nor would he have been able to stand up to her.

His love was almost abject. 'I've given you all the devotion that I had to give, accepting the fact that you only cared for me in the second degree – and now at the end of it I tell you I want you to marry me, that all my happiness and my future are involved with you, that I wish only to be in love with you and with you for the rest of life and win from you slowly the love that you have never given me . . . you have driven me more than once to petty infidelities but in not one of them have I ever forgotten or denied that I loved you more than any woman that ever has been or will be for me.'

When she told Evan Charteris that she was going to marry Asquith it was the end of his hopes. Frantically he wrote to her: 'I never thought in my heart that it was possible you should marry Asquith – or possible even that you should marry anyone but me – for you see you are so different to other women . . .' Nevertheless, soon after Margot turned him down, the susceptible Charteris was at the feet of Margot's friend Lady Desborough.

Margot took some time to recover from her difficult labour. Hard and miserable as the experience had been, it did not put her off the idea of more children. She came from a large family and expected to have one herself, so she did not hesitate to become pregnant again. Both Asquiths were delighted when a healthy little girl with large blue eyes arrived in February 1897. She was christened Elizabeth ('"Eli" = Hebrew for God, "Shabeth" = covenant, therefore Eliza-beth means "God is my Covenant"', wrote Margot in her diary). Three years later another baby arrived – a daughter, as Margot had hoped – who lived for only seven hours, Asquith sobbing on his knees by the cradle. Again Margot was very ill; so much so that she had to be sent off to Switzerland for two months, where the fresh air, walking and skating helped her convalesce.

Their son Anthony was born in November 1902. Almost from birth he was called Puffin, after Violet had so nicknamed him because of his prominent nose, or Honeypuffin; according to Margaret's baby book, Asquith sometimes called him Mr Puffindorf. Five years later, and in the seventh month of her pregnancy ('I dreaded more than I can describe another dead baby') Margot had her last child, a boy. Although so premature, he seemed healthy. He was wrapped in cotton wool and put in his father's dressing room to sleep, with a nurse watching; Asquith, like the doctors, happy and smiling, left Margot's room as she drifted off to sleep. Next morning she was woken by her doctors, followed by a miserable-looking Asquith. Before she could speak the senior doctor said: 'Did you hear us come down early? Your baby died at six this morning.'

Margot's grief was wild, savage and uncontrollable. This third death plunged her into a black pit of despair, a post-natal depression augmented by her physical debilitation. At best, she never ate much; when feeling ill or nervous she seemed to subsist mainly on cups of tea and occasional biscuits. She was white, exhausted, very thin and utterly miserable.

It was a time when large families were commonplace from royalty downwards; Margot herself was one of twelve children, with Asquith's five not considered in any way out of the ordinary, and few doctors then would have attempted to counsel a woman to limit the size of her family to the two or three more usual twenty years later.

However, Margot had had only two living children out of five pregnancies and five births. Each pregnancy was difficult; during them she would suffer and lose weight (of one she wrote: 'I am a very bad subject – I am so small up to now that I sometimes think it must be a bluebottle'). After the last, her emotional and physical trauma was such, and her health had become so precarious, that both Asquiths were told by the doctors that she must not have any more. Contraception was, generally speaking, in its infancy and the method most of her friends relied on, *coitus interruptus* (known in Margot's circle as 'leaving church before the sermon') was not foolproof.

There was only one thing to do, she was told: close the bedroom door. This decision spelled the end of marital relations for the Asquiths.

TWO

Margot's first impressions of No. 10 Downing Street were unfavourable. 'I looked at the dingy exterior and wondered how we would live there,' she mused, as she sat in their car while Asquith entered to tell the mortally ill Sir Henry Campbell-Bannerman that he had seen the King and accepted his invitation to form a government.

'Leaning back, I watched the evening sky reflected in the diamond panes of the Foreign Office windows, and caught a glimpse of green trees. The door opened and the Archbishop came out . . . as I reflected on the dying Prime Minister I could only hope that no sound had reached him of the crowd that had cheered his successor.'

After the Liberal landslide of 1906, with 397 Liberal MPs elected and a majority of 125 over all other parties combined, the leader of the party, Sir Henry Campbell-Bannerman, had moved into No. 10 Downing Street. Asquith, as his Chancellor, could have had the use of No. 11, but he and Margot preferred to stay in the large and comfortable house in Cavendish Square that Margot's father had given them as a wedding present, decorated by Margot with what her stepdaughter Violet was later to call her 'impeccable eye'.

It was big enough to accommodate all five of the younger Asquith children and their three governesses, as well as the fourteen servants needed to run an establishment unwieldy by any standards – the kitchen and stables were in nearby Henrietta Place and the various courses for luncheon or dinner, carried in a specially heated trolley, used to rumble along a subterranean tunnel connecting the old-fashioned kitchen and the panelled dining room, while Margot's love of having friends and relations to stay meant that cans of hot water had to be carried upstairs several times a day. But it had walls frescoed by Sir James Thornhill and a beautiful staircase.

Margot painted the drawing room blue and, unusually for that era, the hall was white, though as she pointed out to a friend who commented on it, 'Not white, darling – skull-coloured!'

This was not a mere figure of speech; in her bedroom she had a human skull, found by the son of the shepherd on her father's estate at Glen, who presented it to her. 'My faithful and silent companion,' she wrote of it when the Asquiths moved to Downing Street. 'It has always been with me, just to remind me to <u>live</u> not to exist . . .'

Asquith was particularly fond of his study, which Margot had carefully furnished to make him as comfortable as possible, with a large desk and red leather armchairs, of which his favourite was placed in front of the fire in winter and in summer by the window, overlooking a paved courtyard.

When Sir Henry Campbell-Bannerman died in 1908 (the only Prime Minister to die in No. 10) and Asquith succeeded him, the Asquith family perforce had to leave Cavendish Square for No. 10 Downing Street, which seemed to both of them an awkward and unprepossessing dwelling. Although the Board of Works had tried to make this historic house as easy to live in as possible, it was shabby, with faded chintzes from top to bottom, and an unloved, uncared-for appearance.

Of Asquith's immediate predecessors both Sir Henry and Lady Campbell-Bannerman had been too ill to take an interest in the decor while Balfour, as a bachelor, had done little, though his unmarried sister Alice, who ran his household, had very definite ideas about the garden. She had had the previous large expanse of gravel turfed over – though leaving wide gravel paths – the plane trees pollarded and the 'miserable shrubs' with which it was filled rearranged so that there was room for herbaceous borders. These were filled with irises, tulips, pinks and daffodils, with jasmine and clematis against the walls and plantings of annuals such as white tobacco plants, nasturtiums, mignonette and wallflowers. But the house itself was another matter.

It was a challenge for Margot to make No. 10 into a warm, welcoming and elegant dwelling.

Margot's father, the Liberal MP Sir Charles, had made his fortune through the family chemical works and from gold – he had overheard the casual gossip of a retired Anglo-Indian about an abandoned gold mine, had concluded from it that there must be more gold in the mine and then bought up most of the shares for a pittance. The mine was opened up, the gold was there and the Bart, as Sir Charles was known when he became a baronet in 1885, sold the shares for around £7 each and bought the 4,000-acre Scottish estate of Glen in Peeblesshire. He was a collector of great taste and had had most of the 5,000 volumes in his large library beautifully rebound in morocco leather; his collection of pictures* included ten Reynolds, six Romneys, five Gainsboroughs (all portraits), five landscapes by Turner, three by Constable, two by Bonington and ten by Morland. He also had a fine collection of Meissen and Chinese porcelain.

Brought up among these exquisite paintings, furniture and china, Margot was used to surroundings that were charming and comfortable. Her first step was to bring to No. 10 some of her own pictures, rugs and furniture.

'It is an inconvenient house with three poor staircases,' she wrote, 'and after living there a few weeks I made up my mind that owing to the impossibility of circulation I could only entertain my Liberal friends at dinner or at garden parties.' In the spring, the screams of peacocks in St James's Park often disturbed sleepers.

Telephones had been put in – adjacent to the Cabinet ante room, with its pegs for ministers' coats, was a small telephone room. A lift had been installed in the central well of the house to make things easier for Charlotte Campbell-Bannerman, but the house was too rambling 'and one almost needed a map to find one's way. Having no bump of locality, soon after our arrival I left the drawing room by one of the five doors and found myself in the garden instead.'

Even more inconvenient was the siting of No. 10's solitary bathroom: it was on the first floor, just by the Prime Minister's bedroom, its only access through his sitting room (which had in fact been partitioned earlier in order to create this bathroom). This meant that the family had to creep in and out when they could in order not to disturb him. One of the first things the Asquiths did on arrival at No. 10 was to arrange for the installation of a bathroom on the attic floor† where most of the servants lived.

---

* Death duties made it necessary to sell most of them in the 1920s.
† According to architects' plans held in the National Archives.

Asquith, who missed his agreeable Cavendish Square study, by day worked mainly in the Cabinet Room when it was otherwise unoccupied. Late at night or in the early hours he would sit at his large desk near the window of one of the big rooms on the first floor that overlooked Horse Guards Parade, red boxes interspersed with a collection of tiny silver figures and crystal animals given him by friends.

The life inside No. 10, through the heavy, green-painted* oak front door, was invisible as the windows facing the street were those of the least important rooms, give or take a brief glimpse of the hall through the two ground-floor windows. The large windows in the basement looked into the kitchen quarters.

Those above belonged to the room over the front door, given to Violet when the family moved in. Violet, who had come out three years earlier, went to dances night after night and although her room was dark and gloomy – it never got the sun – its great virtue was that it could be reached by a separate staircase just past the messengers so that when, as often, Violet came in late from dancing she could slip upstairs to bed without disturbing the rest of the family. 'I remember going to the window very drowsily in the morning and seeing the young men I had danced with hanging up their bowler hats and umbrellas across the road in the Foreign Office.'

For her own bedroom Margot had chosen one of the three drawing rooms on the first floor. Here she wrote the many letters that most well-to-do women spent hours on in the morning; on her writing desk were photographs of her children and friends, a new and an old Bible, the prayer book Laura had left her, pieces of china and other odds and ends. It had four large windows, two overlooking St James's Park and two with a view over the garden – always full of birds – to Horse Guards Parade. Its walls were covered with Lincrusta, put in by Alice Balfour and hated by Margot, who did her best to disguise it by painting it a pale warm green.

'There is a fine old mantelpiece,' she wrote, 'but the effect of this is ruined by a brass fender and prominent grate, put in by C.B. to give out more heat. Both he and Lady C. B. died in this room. Some of my friends ask me if I mind about this, but I say it would take a

---

* Originally made of black oak and believed to date from Robert Walpole's time, the famous Downing Street door was painted green during Asquith's premiership, after which it reverted to black.

very modern structure to find a room that no one had died in, and I like old houses.'

On the walls were pastels and watercolours of the children and on either side of the fireplace two small chairs embroidered by her mother, 'on which are laid my underclothes for night and morning'. On one of the 'hideous' Ministry of Works chests of drawers were two telephones, one external, one to her maid's room; on the other stood a crucifix, a Dresden china box holding a handkerchief belonging to her first love and a few love letters from him and others.

Into attic and basement rooms (the Asquiths installed four new attic bedrooms) squeezed the seventeen servants – their number supplemented by charwomen – thought necessary to look after the family: the butler, twenty-seven-year-old Philip Nye; the housekeeper, Rosa Hodges; Florence the cook; three footmen; three housemaids; three kitchen maids; an odd-job man and a hall boy; Margot's French lady's maid Madeleine Trotte; Violet's lady's maid Annie (at thirty the oldest of the servants) and Elizabeth's German governess Anna Heinsius, always known as Frau.

There was a hall porter, uniformed in a blue frock coat with crimson and gold embroidered crowns on the lapels, who was supposed to check visitors but, recorded Margot, 'he was over-anxious and appeared flurried when spoken to. Poor man, he was never alone; he sat in his hooded chair,* snatching pieces of cold mutton at odd hours; tired chauffeurs shared his picture paper, and strange people – not important enough to be noticed by a secretary or a messenger – sat watching him on hard sills in the windows; or, if he were left alone for a moment, the baize doors would fly open and he would find himself faced by me, seeing a parson, a publican or a protectionist out of the house. But our porter was not a strong man, and any determined Baronet with hopes of favours to come about the time of the King's birthday could have penetrated into No. 10.'

Despite its importance, the house itself was curiously anonymous. While anyone could walk along Downing Street, Margot found herself constantly amazed that so few taxi drivers seemed to have any idea of its whereabouts. Nearly always, she had to tell them the way if she did not wish to get taken to Down Street,

* A leather hooded chair by Chippendale, with a drawer beneath the seat where once hot coals were placed to keep the occupant warm – it was originally used by attendants outside the front door.

Piccadilly by mistake. 'Even the Press while trying to penetrate the Prime Minister's heart, was unable to divulge the secret of his home. Liver-coloured and squalid, the outside of No. 10 gives little idea to the man in the street of what it is really like.'

THREE

It was sometimes lucky that the man in the street – or rather the woman in the street – was vague as to the location of No. 10. As the inhabitants of Downing Street sipped their tea on the afternoon of 1 March 1912, members of the Women's Social and Political Union, popularly known as suffragettes, were about to unleash mayhem only a few hundred yards away. Dedicated to gaining women the vote, the WSPU knew that, standing firmly in their path, immovable as a rock, was Asquith. Now, for the first time since the suffrage movement had begun, they struck without warning.

Earlier that afternoon, around 150 well-dressed women, in stylish velvet or broadcloth *tailleurs*, with tightly corseted waists, fur stoles flung nonchalantly around their shoulders and large hats bedecked with feathers, had drifted into Oxford Street, Regent Street, the Strand and Piccadilly. Those who noticed them might have picked up a hint of their purpose from the colours of their clothes. Many wore dresses, scarves or hat trimmings in purple, white and green – the colours of the WSPU, signifying respectively dignity, purity and hope – with jewellery of pearls, amethysts or emeralds.

At exactly 5.45, hammers were pulled out of sable muffs or satin handbags and the crash and tinkle of broken glass resounded as, in twos and threes, these elegant women broke shop windows, among them two of London's most famous department stores, Marshall & Snelgrove and Liberty's, as well as offices, like those of the Canadian Pacific Railway and the Grand Trunk Railway. It was clear that they had been told which targets to aim for and also how to use their hammers: all of them struck the glass of the windows so that neither they nor any passers-by were wounded by shards of falling glass.

Their leader Mrs Pankhurst, swathed in long skirts and a befeathered hat, drove in a taxi to Downing Street, where she hurled stones at the Prime Minister's windows. The police were quickly on the scene and 124 of them were arrested, including Mrs Pankhurst's daughter Sylvia, and a number sent to prison.

In that class-ridden society, where clothes were an indicator of status, to be dressed as only the rich could afford was to disarm suspicion and command respect. But after this, the police began to eye even the most richly dressed Society women with suspicion, as a high proportion of suffragettes were from the upper classes.

The campaign for female suffrage had been raging since the previous century. As the vote stood in 1912 most – but not all – men over twenty-one had the franchise (roughly speaking, it was householders or those who paid rent of £10 or more a year; this covered both lodgers and shopkeepers). No woman, however, even if she owned vast estates, was allowed to vote.

It was a question that split families: when Constance Lytton, daughter of the first Earl of Lytton, became a suffragette (the term was used to denote an active, or militant, female suffragist), she was supported by one sister, but another wrote to an aunt: 'We cannot disguise from ourselves that our old Constance has gone forever. I feel, whatever it may be in the future, for the moment she has passed out of the lives of her family.'

Reasons against giving women the vote ranged from a hatred of change, the fact that as men were physically stronger and had to enforce the laws they should therefore be the ones to make them, self-interest – a fear that women would vote for such social reforms as temperance or even a ban on alcohol – to the more bizarre reaches of physiology (roughly summed up as 'once a month women go mad'). One Parliamentarian, pointing out that there were 1,300,000 more women than men in the country, objected to the political voting power being placed in the hands of women: 'The government of the country would therefore be handed over to a majority who would not be men, but women,' thus summing up the amorphous general fear of his own sex that men might lose their power.

Women were told they were creatures of impulse, that their proper sphere was the home, that they were incapable of balanced judgement, and even – from the former Viceroy, Lord Curzon – that it would damage British prestige in India. They were told that because they did not fight in wars or go down coal mines they should not be allowed to vote; it was understood (among the opponents of suffrage) that they lacked the ability to reason; simultaneously it was thought they might vote as a sex and elect only female Members to the House of Commons.

The earlier suffragists, under Mrs (later Dame) Millicent Fawcett, had employed only constitutional means to strive for the vote. But their moderation meant that progress was painfully slow and many women felt that the time for talk had passed and action was required. Thus in 1903 Mrs Emmeline Pankhurst founded the WSPU with the significant words: 'We shall work not by means of any outworn missionary methods but by political action.' These more militant women, led by Mrs Pankhurst and her two daughters, Sylvia and Christabel, became known as suffragettes.

Everyone knew that Asquith was the main opponent of female suffrage – even at the age of fifteen, he had led the opposition to it in a school debate on the subject – and soon he became a focus for the suffragettes' hostility. He was fully supported by both Margot and Violet – two of the most intelligent and liberal-minded women in London – thanks to their joint belief that the man they idolised was always right. It must be remembered, too, that then even to believe in the suffrage required independence of mind: for centuries, indeed for most of recorded history, women had been brought up to be, and to believe themselves to be, subordinate to men. It was an attitude so traditional, so hallowed by time, and so expected, that many women were as anti-suffrage as most men.

Sometimes protesters chained themselves to the railings of No. 10. Once, when Margot's youngest half-sister, 'K', a particular friend of Puffin's, was staying at No. 10 the house was picketed by suffragettes. K and Puffin ran up to the third-floor nursery, seized a large teddy bear and hurled it out of the window onto the surprised suffragettes below – one of the few occasions on which there was a physical response from anyone in Downing Street.

Asquith would always remain silent and as dignified as possible if assaulted as when, on Sunday, 5 September 1909, he was attacked by three suffragettes, one of whom struck him repeatedly as he left Lympne church (the Asquiths had rented Lympne Castle, in Kent, for their weekends and holidays). Not content with that, they followed him to Littlestone Golf Club and attacked him again as he left the clubhouse after playing his Sunday afternoon round of golf.

Golf clubs were the perfect target for the suffragettes, and their favoured tactic of etching 'Votes for Women' with acid on the courses meant high visibility among those who could help them or who might sympathise. For among politicians golf was the favourite game – in fact, it could have been designed for them, offering as it did not only fresh air and exercise but the chance to chat privately on sensitive subjects without any danger of being overheard (caddies always kept a discreet distance). It had been brought to prominence by the former Prime Minister Arthur Balfour, who was, although never more than a good average player, such a passionate advocate of the game's charms* that he was called by some 'the father of English golf'.

Many of the women arrested and sent to prison went on hunger strike – only to be force-fed by prison doctors, a brutal system that involved holding a prisoner down and forcing a tube into her mouth, held open by a wooden or steel gag, and down her throat. Constance Lytton, imprisoned in Holloway in early 1912, had been on hunger strike for four days when she suffered force-feeding; she had to lie in her vomit-covered clothes all night as the wardresses said it was too late to get her a change of clothing. She lost weight at the rate of 2lb a day, and became so emaciated that after her release she often had to eat her meals kneeling, as sitting in a chair was too painful.

A Conciliation Bill, which would have given women limited franchise, had come before Parliament in 1910 but did not go through: Asquith, along with most of his party, believed that as the million-odd women who would gain the vote were necessarily well-off to rich, they would vote Conservative – and the Liberals would lose the next election.

The suffragettes, provoked, decided on direct action. One evening two large stones were hurled through the window of the Asquiths' dining room at No. 10, where they were sitting with guests, after Asquith had refused to receive a suffragette deputation at the House of Commons. There were battles with the police, the women's long skirts hindering them in their struggles, with showers of hairpins

* He was Captain of the North Berwick Club from 1891–2 and of the Royal and Ancient Club of St Andrews a few years later.

tumbling out of elaborately done coils and puffs of hair as they tried to wrestle themselves away.

This violence encouraged some and enraged others of their supporters, such as H.G. Wells, who wrote in *The Freewoman* of 7 December 1911: 'I am one of those people who agree with the end and detest the means of the current suffrage agitation . . . At present women are not regarded as citizens; they do not regard themselves as citizens; they behave accordingly, and most of the trouble of life ensues . . .'

While the beleaguered Government tried to restore normality the suffragettes stepped up their campaign. Window-smashing increased, usually of Government offices after some rebuttal in the House of Commons. Fines and imprisonments were now commonplace. Here, too, gender played a part: while men supporters were given the less harsh treatment of political prisoners (they could write articles or books, and were allowed frequent visits and other freedoms), women suffragists were treated as common criminals.

A third (and, as it happened, final) Conciliation Bill, the Parliamentary Franchise (Women) Bill, was debated on 28 March 1912. This, too, was defeated, though narrowly – by 222 votes to 208 – largely because the Irish Parliamentary Party, believing that time given over to debating votes for women would delay the chances of Irish Home Rule, voted against it. However, as the eight members of the Government who had voted against the Bill would have overturned the result had they voted the other way, Asquith once again got the blame. It was, however, just one of the problems he had to face in this year that would bring such difficulties in its train.

FOUR

A door in the hall of No.10 Downing Street connected to the residence of the Chancellor of the Exchequer at No. 11. On becoming Prime Minister Asquith had offered the Chancellorship to David Lloyd George (who was then forty-five years old to Asquith's fifty-six), and the Lloyd Georges had straight away moved in from Chelsea. 'I shall be proud to serve under your Premiership and no member of the Government will render more loyal service to his chief,' was Lloyd George's warm acceptance.

The two men could not have been more different. Margot's slightly mystified description of her husband after a few years of marriage gives a little of the impression the famous Asquith reserve must have made on others. 'When he arrives after having been away from me and after writing me love letters that any woman would be proud to receive he shows no trace of any emotion whatever on his face or in the solidity of his person. He has no buoyancy, no impulse, no gift of expressing delight whatsoever – this prevents him ever being a lover in my sense of the word. He has no play and appears to take everything for granted. The train has brought him and <u>there</u> he is.

'This curious simplicity does not mean coldness; it is a want of quick sensibility to others and an utter unconsciousness of self. I sometimes wonder if he notices whether I receive him warmly or coldly. He says he does but I should like to <u>feel</u> it. He is curiously slow at seeing the nuances of intimate easy talk and so I can't leave things silhouetted . . . his mind has little or no shorthand of a social kind, half frivolous half domestic. He has no temper, no mischief, no repartee, no abandon or recklessness, very little that is accident and nothing that is uncertain. What he has got is infinite sympathy, tenderness and consideration for other people's feeling, common sense that amounts to genius, personal humility, detachment and breadth, unconscious nobility of character in the way of unselfishness, truth-fulness, generosity and fearlessness – all the things one would most wish to impress on one's children.'

Many of Lloyd George's characteristics, however, were traits one would not necessarily wish to impress upon one's children. A compulsive womaniser and morally dubious despite his Calvinistic Welsh background, he was a brilliant orator, good-looking, enor-mously energetic, charismatic, with a political approach at the opposite end of the spectrum from that of Asquith. He was passion-ate rather than restrained, appealing to the emotions of his hearers rather than to their reason; for him, none of the cool logic that had made Asquith such a force at the Bar; instead there were fervent outpourings, spiked with memorable phrases, and an awareness of image, to which the growing power of the press could be harnessed – something to which Asquith gave little thought. This conscious-ness of the need to create a recognisable persona would become part of the future political landscape.

As Chancellor, Lloyd George was determined to help the poor and unfortunate. 'He wanted the poor to inherit the earth, particu-larly if it was the earth of rich English landlords,' commented the journalist and historian George Dangerfield, who described him as 'a man set apart from his other colleagues on the Asquith cabinet . . . when he first exploded into politics, an angry little solicitor from an uncouth, starved district in Wales, he brought with him some-thing alien and dangerous'. His personality was magnetic; women crowded to the Strangers' Gallery in the House of Commons to hear him and few were better than the Chancellor at the well-aimed, memorable shaft.

'A fully-equipped Duke costs as much to keep up as two Dread-noughts – and they are just as great a terror and last longer,' was his response to the Duke of Northumberland who, having told the House of Lords that safeguarding the rights of property was more important than improving working-class houses, had just been ordered to demolish twenty-two of his own cottages as unfit for human habitation.

But already the seeds of suspicion as to Lloyd George's integrity had been sown in Margot's mind. The list of those to serve in the new Cabinet had been prematurely published in the *News Chron-icle*, and the evidence for this leak pointed (accurately) to Lloyd

George. Margot at once wrote to Churchill (the new President of the Board of Trade and therefore a Cabinet minister), with whom Lloyd George was dining that evening, to tell him this, saying 'Lloyd George's best chance, if he is a good fellow, <u>which</u> I take <u>your</u> word for, is not to lie about it when Henry speaks heavily to him but to give up the whole Press campaign.' She added that Henry 'was perfectly furious'. It was an early and fairly mild example of a habit that grew on her: attempting to support or protect her husband in ways that were all too easily described as 'meddling'.

Asquith did indeed speak to Lloyd George – or rather, he asked Churchill to do so – but in much more tactful and moderate terms. Margot, however, was not prepared to let the subject go. That night she gave one of her regular dinner parties, attended by various Asquith supporters and her husband's great friend Richard Haldane, Secretary of State for War and author and implementer of the important and highly effective Haldane Reforms of the Army. Encouraged by the reaction of the others, Margot returned to the topic of Lloyd George and his indiscretion, warning one of the guests that the new Chancellor would be a danger to 'our' Cabinet and begging him 'to keep Henry up to the mark'.

Unfortunately Asquith, the last man to encourage factions, overheard this and gestured peremptorily for her to leave the room. Margot, conscious that she should not have interfered, crept out meekly. The upshot was that when Lloyd George crossly denied that he had had anything to do with this unauthorised disclosure, Asquith asked him to put this in writing – and then let the matter drop. Between the two men it was merely a warning shot across the bows, meant, and received, as such. For Margot, it was the start of an increasing perception of Lloyd George as someone disloyal and, eventually, treacherous.

For two members of their respective families, however, this closeness was a boon. Although the garden of No. 11 belonged to No. 10, the Chancellor was allowed the use of it. Lloyd George and his wife of twenty years, Margaret Owen, had four children, two boys and two girls. Of these the youngest, Megan, was the same age as Puffin Asquith, now a sunny-natured little boy with fair curly hair, and the two soon became inseparable, with the communicating door in constant use. If Puffin did not run into No. 11 Megan would come into No. 10. They would usually have their tea together and, if Lloyd George was home for this, it included hymn-singing.

The two children, both five when their families first moved to Downing Street, would often divert themselves by going up and down in the lift of No. 10. It was a wheezy lift; its gates clattered as the children went in and out, and the whine of their endless journeys distracted the ministers, the secretaries and even the messengers. But into the Cabinet Room, secured by double doors so that the sound of the discussions, and dissensions, should not be overheard, the noise was unable to penetrate.

Once, the children became trapped in it, and it was only after both houses and the garden had been thoroughly searched and family and staff members had run into Downing Street and Horse Guards Parade shouting their names that someone pressed the button for the lift, saw it was no longer working, and they were found. Thereafter they took to playing in the garden with Puffin's model aeroplanes, which had to be launched by hand. Often these would land in Horse Guards Parade and the policemen on duty who wearily had to bring them back umpteen times would remark with increasing asperity: 'I believe this is yours, sir?' as they handed them to Puffin.

In 1911, Asquith and Lloyd George had won a battle that marked a seismic change in the country's political structure. It had taken some time to come about. But first came an (unsuccessful) and far less popular measure.

This was the Licensing Bill, argued for passionately by Asquith – ironically, in view of the fact that he was sometimes seen swaying at the Dispatch Box. On one occasion in April 1911, when Asquith appeared on the front bench too drunk to speak, Churchill wrote to his wife: 'Thursday night the PM was vy bad & I squirmed with embarrassment . . . [He] entrusts me with everything [in the House] after dinner. Up till that time he is at his best – but thereafter it is an awful pity & only the persistent freemasonry of the House of Commons prevents a scandal . . .'

The Bill's aim was to curb the number of pubs and drinking dens and to regulate the trade – the national alcohol bill was £200 million (twice that of the United States) and pubs were open from 6 a.m. until 11 p.m. It was a measure greeted warmly by Margot, who had worked in the East End, starting a crèche in Wapping with her sister Laura; and every summer for years had taken fifty-odd factory girls in three large wagonettes, accompanied by a brass band, for a jaunt to the country. She was, therefore, well aware that when people lived on the narrowest of margins, drink could ruin poor families – in this part of London, the average working-class family spent around a quarter of its weekly income on drink. Her stepdaughter Violet, then twenty-two, was equally enthusiastic. 'I delight in the boldness of the Licensing Bill.'

When the Bill was thrown out by the Lords, exercising their power of veto,* both women urged Asquith to 'do something' so that Liberal ideals might be maintained. But he replied simply: 'My time will come.' Neither they nor the Lords knew then how soon, and how deadly, his retaliation would be.

The Liberals had long been aware that (apart from drink) the greatest cause of poverty was old age. A mere ten years earlier, surveys had shown that a quarter of the population was living in poverty, with more than half of these at subsistence level – enough money for food, rent, fuel and clothes but not enough for 'luxuries' such as public transport – and the rest of this group, ten per cent of the total population, below even this.

In large towns slums proliferated, with crammed tenements, beggars – often children – pubs that soaked up wages that should have gone to a household, and with tuberculosis a constant hazard, let alone ills such as scabies, impetigo and vermin infestation caused by lack of washing facilities.

Poverty was also widespread in rural communities. George Wyver, the son of a stonemason, who had been left orphaned at the age of four after both his parents died of consumption, was sent to the Poor Law (Workhouse) School but was so unhappy there he managed to persuade his older brother John – who had been keeping himself as a labourer since the age of fifteen – to take him away and help him find a job. Opportunities for a nine-year-old were limited, but 'he [John] secured me a job at 1.5d per hour and for a 56 hour week was 7s per week. We lodged with agricultural labourers in the village of Stoke near Rochester and I gave my brother 6s 6d and

---

* Then, even if a Bill had passed the necessary third reading in the House of Commons, if the Lords threw it out it did not become law.

kept 6d myself 3d save and 3d spend. Lodgings were very cheap about 3s per week and you found your own food. If you boarded with the people you could have board and lodgings for about 10s to 12s per week.'

In the poorest labourers' cottages conditions were minimal, with a sack for a hearth rug on bare bricks, a table and a couple of chairs and sometimes – in these simple one-up, one-down dwellings – a stepladder instead of stairs. Under the table might be a pail of water, fetched from the well shared with several other cottages. Better-furnished ones would have pictures and texts on the walls with a 'piece rug' (made from scraps of the family's worn-out clothing) on the hearth. Sanitation, always outdoor, usually consisted of a board with a hole cut in it over a deep trench or vault, emptied from time to time. If the weather cut earnings, it was a case of finding what you could – scaring crows for eight pence a day or leading horses along roads for sixpence.

When working life and therefore earning was over, those who had been unable to save and who had no relatives to care for them often wound up in the workhouse. Women fared particularly badly: about three-quarters of the recipients of 'outdoor relief', as it was called, were female.

These workhouses were harsh, depressing places, designed to scare off anyone who was able-bodied enough to work: clothes were confiscated and a prison-style uniform issued, married couples were not allowed to share a room and the food was so scanty – the standard dinner was 6oz bread and 2oz cheese – that malnutrition was common. The average life expectancy was fifty for a man and fifty-four for a woman.

Asquith had announced the Government's intention to introduce an Old Age Pensions Act in May 1908 and Lloyd George became the driving force – he had long been an opponent of the Poor Law (one of its regulations stated that conditions in workhouses should be lower than those for the poorest labourer) and he was determined to take action that would, in his words, 'lift the shadow of the workhouse from the homes of the poor'.

The Act, which became law on 1 January 1909, was the first step in the development of today's welfare state. From its inception, half a million or so people over seventy became entitled to five shillings a week non-contributory pension, to be collected from post offices.

They had to be British citizens, with no criminal record and known never to have been work-shy – in other words, the 'deserving poor'.

Lottie Martin, the daughter of a Nottinghamshire foundry worker, described its effect. 'It was a wonderful step forward. Previously a person had to be very nearly destitute to be able to apply to the local council for help, and then relief was only given if they had no children in a position to help. Often the younger people would help their parents, to the detriment of their own families or because of the disgrace everyone attached to receiving relief. Many were too proud to apply for Parish help and only had the few shillings from their children and a little food from their neighbours . . . a lump of coal from one, a candle or two or even a meal would be offered. But not all old people were lucky enough to have kind people around them and invariably these products of a world that worked them hard for small wages ended their days at Basford Workhouse, to die the death of a pauper.'

The Government also introduced the National Health Insurance Bill: for a maximum of four pence a week every employed person could be insured against sickness costs. It drew immediate and furious opposition from the British Medical Association. At their annual general meeting in July 1912 the incoming president, Sir James Barr, condemned the Bill as: 'the most gigantic fraud which had ever been perpetrated on the public since the South Sea Bubble'. What he wanted instead was 'improvement of the race' through eugenics.

The Eugenics movement, its aim being to encourage marriage between the healthy and intelligent and discourage it between the disabled and handicapped, had been growing in strength for some time. The Eugenics Education Society (founded in 1907 to campaign for marriage restrictions for the weak) had attracted some of the cleverest thinkers in England, especially those on the left. The socialists Sidney and Beatrice Webb (the founders of the Fabian Society and the London School of Economics), Harold Laski and John Maynard Keynes were among them, while George Bernard Shaw wrote: 'The only fundamental and possible socialism is the socialisation of the selective breeding of man' and the philosopher Bertrand Russell proposed that the state should issue colour-coded 'procreation tickets' to prevent the gene pool of the elite being diluted by inferior human beings.

Sir James Barr was an ardent campaigner for sterilisation of the physically or mentally handicapped. 'The race must be renewed from the mentally and physically fit,' he told the BMA. 'Moral and physical degenerates should not be allowed to take any part in adding to it.' Fortunately these words fell on deaf ears.

To pay for its reforms the Government had come to power promising to cut naval expenditure – the whole ethos of the Liberal Party was anti-war – although British defence policy was to ensure that the strength of the British Navy equalled that of the next two largest navies* combined.

No one was more envious of this mighty maritime force than Queen Victoria's grandson, Kaiser Wilhelm II of Germany. This man, born in 1859 and brought up under the strictest discipline, physically handicapped (he had been born with a withered arm and imperfect balance) and riddled with complexes, had as a little boy visited Plymouth and Portsmouth, where the glories of Britain's Navy made an indelible impression on him. As he wrote in his autobiography: 'I had a peculiar passion for the navy. It sprang to no small extent from my English blood. When I was a little boy . . . I admired the proud British ships. There awoke in me the will to build ships of my own like these some day, and when I was grown up to possess as fine a navy as the English.'

Ever since, he had dreamed of German naval might. As ruler of a militaristic country unhappy with its position vis-à-vis the other great powers, he was determined to rely on strength rather than diplomacy and with his fierce mustachios,† fondness for glittering uniforms and rigid, imperious stance was both symbol and figurehead for this ambitious nation. Bellicose to his fingertips, he wished to increase the strength of the German armed forces, with a navy that could match the British Royal Navy. In 1900, with the Second Naval Law that doubled the size of the German fleet, he had begun German naval expansion and, with it, an arms race.

The naval race between Britain and Germany generated huge public support in both countries and was the single greatest cause of

---

* At the time this policy was enshrined in law with the Naval Defence Act of 1889 these were the French and Russian navies.

† They were kept in shape with pomade, and so famous that a whiskery South American monkey was named the Emperor Tamarin after him (or them).

Anglo-German antagonism. As an island, Britain had always relied entirely on her Navy to protect her from invasion where Continental nations depended on their armies.

From the British point of view, the build-up of the German navy could have only one object in view – to be in a position to wrest control of the seas from Britain. So when the Kaiser claimed to be 'Admiral of the Atlantic' it was hardly surprising that the *Daily Mail* declared in 1907: 'All the fine words in the world cannot disguise the fact that the naval competition between England and Germany is intense, and that Germany is now building a great fleet with the express object of meeting the British Navy at sea.'

Thus when the British Government commissioned four new Dreadnoughts (instead of the six originally planned) the cry rose, 'We want eight and we won't wait!', fostered by the Conservatives and, behind the scenes, the First Sea Lord, Sir John ('Jackie') Fisher. Asquith proposed a compromise that satisfied everyone: four Dreadnoughts to be laid down in 1909–10 and a further four later.

To pay for the new social provisions the Chancellor had to raise more in taxes. Necessary as these were, the Budget had a secondary purpose – to serve as a statement of intent (later it became known as the People's Budget). On 29 April 1909, in a speech so lengthy that there had to be a pause for half an hour while he recovered his voice, Lloyd George introduced it. At the time he described it as a 'war Budget' against poverty, which he hoped, as a result of it, would become 'as remote to the people of this country as the wolves which once infested its forests'.

It was an extraordinarily strategic Budget that could have been – some said specially was – designed to raise the hackles of the House of Lords and the wealthy, with its raising of income tax, introduction of a new 'super tax' and even a tax on petrol. From the start it aroused controversy, so much so that the King informed Lloyd George that he regretted attempts 'to inflame the passions of the working and lower orders against people who happen to be owners of property'.

Lloyd George was not to be diverted. At a large meeting on the Budget in Limehouse, in London's East End, on 30 July 1909 he launched a series of well-aimed shafts at rich employers who grudged paying tax to support the poor that rendered some of the great landowners and coal-mine owners apoplectic with fury.

It was powerful, inflammatory stuff, received with cheers and laughter by the audience of workmen and dockers and it provoked an immediate and furious response from those who would be taxed to pay for the new provisions. To Lloyd George, this was meat and drink.

But for Asquith, let alone the King, it was too much. When Edward VII, on board the royal yacht, the *Victoria and Albert*, based at Cowes, invited the Prime Minister (staying on the *Enchantress*, the 3,000-ton Admiralty yacht, to view the Naval Review at Portsmouth) to visit him, the King wasted no time saying what he thought.

Asquith had, of course, known the King for some time and grown to respect him as an accomplished performer of the duties of a constitutional monarch. Edward VII's public behaviour upheld the dignity of the Crown and his exquisite manners set those around him at ease, although his approach to religion was simple. (His instructions to the Archbishop of York, Cosmo Lang, had been nothing if not straightforward: 'Keep the parties in the Church together and prevent the clergy wearing moustaches.') He was affable, gregarious and pleasure-loving, and although he enjoyed racing and had no hesitation in chasing pretty women – his popularity had even survived a couple of scandals (including appearances in the witness box) – these were weaknesses that endeared him rather than otherwise to the male half of his subjects.

To the Prime Minister, much more germane than his private life was Edward's ability to establish excellent relationships with most of the crowned heads in Europe (to most of whom he was related). The King could speak French and German as fluently as English and was a reasonable hand at Italian and Spanish so that his personal diplomacy was invaluable to the Government, notably in the Entente Cordiale* in the third year of his reign. In sum, the two got on well.

Eventually, the Finance Bill (to give it its correct name) was passed by the House of Commons on 4 November 1909, after a mammoth total of 554 divisions including many all-night sittings – for several of these Asquith came across from Downing Street to take over from the Chancellor for the last hour or two before breakfast.

---

* A series of agreements between Britain and France that signalled the end of almost a thousand years of intermittent conflict.

It went through with its main clauses intact, from the raising of income tax and estate duties to the new system of land-taxing, and was sent straight up to the House of Lords. Here, as everyone knew, it would be turned down – and then what?

As expected, it was turned down: the first time a fiscal Bill had been rejected by the Lords. It was, realised everyone in government and many outside it, a declaration of war. Battle lines had been drawn and the inference was obvious: what had been a conflict over finance had become a struggle over democracy. As no government could carry on without the finance it needed, Asquith immediately called a general election. The following Saturday, Trafalgar Square was packed with supporters demonstrating against the Lords.

Parliament was prorogued; Asquith, Lloyd George and Churchill nailed their colours to the mast by all publicly declaring that they would not again hold office in a government where the Peers could overrule the people; both the Liberal and Labour parties felt it intolerable that a government with a sizeable majority could be thwarted by an Upper Chamber consisting mainly of the Opposition.

All of them, though, were aware of – to use a modern expression – the Catch-22 situation that thus arose: as any Bill had to go through the Upper House, with its power of veto, the Peers therefore had the right not to pass a Bill that curbed their powers.

The only solution to this would be to ask the King to create so many new Liberal Peers that they would swamp the Tory majority in the Upper House, a delicate procedure and one likely to cause great dismay in the King. When Asquith tackled him about it during a visit to Balmoral – at least 300 would be needed – the King was only willing to say that he would consider it if Asquith won an election on that premise.

Thus the general election of 15 January–10 February 1910[*] was virtually a referendum on the Budget. It resulted in a hung Parliament, with 274 Liberal seats to 272 for Arthur Balfour's Conservatives (although the Conservatives polled more votes), leaving Asquith dependent for a majority on the eighty-two Irish Nationalist members, whose ultimate aim was Home Rule. It was touch and go. 'For the moment, we do not know how the Irish will vote, but

* Elections then lasted three weeks.

if they join the Tories against us we shall resign,' wrote Margot in her diary.

Now another factor intervened.

The King at sixty-nine had been plagued by bronchitis for years. This did not affect his appetite: he ate and drank copiously of the rich food which was served at grand Edwardian dinner tables. A typical dinner given for his male friends that March, in which he did full justice to the menu even though in failing health, included turtle soup, salmon, grilled chicken, saddle of mutton, snipe stuffed with *foie gras*, asparagus, fruit, a large iced concoction and a savoury. All his regular hostesses knew that in addition they had to provide a cold chicken for the royal bedside table in case he felt hungry in the night. He also smoked heavily – his average was twenty cigarettes and twelve cigars a day.

In March his bronchial trouble worsened but the rich dinners continued. On 7 March he set off for the Continent, suffering heart pain and indigestion in Paris, but pressed on to Biarritz, where he was holidaying with his mistress Mrs Keppel (a great friend of Margot's). He had visited this chic seaside resort on France's Atlantic coast for a month every spring for the past five years to enjoy its milder climate. But this year the weather could hardly have been worse – there was thick snow in the grounds of his hotel on 1 April – and he had another attack of bronchitis that kept him indoors for a week.

Queen Alexandra, Edward's deaf, beautiful Danish queen who for a long time had been no more than an affectionate consort, urged him to join her on her Mediterranean cruise for his health's sake – neither of them would have considered her visiting him because of the presence of his recognised but unacknowledged mistress. But he did not want either to leave Mrs Keppel or be too far from home while the Government was in such turmoil. As his continued ill health had gone unreported, he was the subject of criticism for staying in France whilst political tensions were so high.

Meanwhile, Asquith had to parry questions in the Commons on the Government's intentions. 'We had better wait and see,' he said in answer to one from the Conservative Viscount Helmsley on 3 March, repeating his 'wait and see' phrase several times in the following weeks. Originally hissed ('like an otter', according to Margot) as a threat, it would come back later to haunt him.

The King returned on 27 April, going straight to Sandringham, where in bitter wind he made his usual inspections of the estate and farm, soggy from five days' rain, discussing with his head keeper the prospects of partridges the following year for the famous Sandringham shoot.

The next day the Budget was passed in the Commons, but the battle with the Peers was to continue.

Early on the morning of 6 May the Asquiths' friend Frances Horner, mother of Raymond Asquith's wife Katharine, telephoned to ask Margot if she was worried, as she feared the King was seriously ill. Margot seized *The Times*, read the bulletin about the King's bronchitis signed by his two doctors ('The King has suffered an attack of bronchitis and has been confined to his room for two days'), dressed hurriedly and went straight to Buckingham Palace, where she knew the most recent bulletin would be posted on the railings in front. It read: 'No progress; condition causes grave anxiety.'

She remembered that when she had last seen him three months earlier she had noticed how short of breath he was – they had sat next to each other most of the evening. Back in Downing Street, she found Sir Charles Hardinge (the former British Ambassador to Russia, who had just been appointed Viceroy of India). He said he had left Lord Knollys in tears and suggested she sent a telegram to Asquith (he was on the *Enchantress*, sailing to Gibraltar to inspect the fortifications there). 'Advise your returning immediately. The King seriously ill: all London in state of well-founded alarm: Margot', she wrote. Her message was dispatched from the Admiralty in cypher.

In her diary she scrawled: 'It is like a dream and all London is holding its breath with anxiety. When I think what his death means I can hardly hold back my tears. I went out and ordered a black dress and hat at Jays [department store].'

As the day progressed, the forecourt of the entrance in Buckingham Palace Road was filled with streams of cars and carriages holding ambassadors, churchmen, dignitaries of all sorts as well as those who simply wanted to show their devotion to this popular monarch. The fitful sunshine disappeared and a cold drizzle fell from the heavy skies. The streets emptied, with only a few cars and cabs instead of the usual throng driving to plays or restaurants, theatres were almost empty and there were none of the usual long queues for the cheap seats in music halls.

That night, when Margot said her prayers with Elizabeth and Puffin, they prayed out loud that God would save the King. After dining out, she made a detour to Buckingham Palace before going back to Downing Street. She went to bed but could not sleep.

At midnight there was a knock on her bedroom door. It was the head messenger, who walked in and said: 'His Majesty passed away at 11.45.' 'So the King is dead!' said Margot, and burst into tears.

Asquith, with the *Enchantress* now steaming home from Gibraltar, received a message from George V, the former Prince of Wales and now the new King, in the early hours of Saturday, 7 May. 'I went up on deck and I remember well that the first sight that met my eyes in the twilight before dawn was Halley's comet blazing in the sky . . . I felt bewildered and indeed stunned . . . we had lost, without warning or preparation, the Sovereign whose ripe experience, trained sagacity, equitable judgement and unvarying consideration counted for so much.

'For two years I had been his Chief Minister, and I am thankful to remember that from first to last I never concealed anything from him. He soon got to know this, and in return he treated me with a gracious frankness which made our relationship in very trying and exacting times one, not always of complete agreement, but of unbroken confidence.'

The grief at the death of the King was genuine and unforced. Vast, silent, black-clad crowds lined the route as the coffin passed, drawn by black horses and accompanied by guardsmen slow-marching with rifles reversed. Men and women wore black for months, coachmen tied black ribbons to their whips; one woman even sewed black ribbons to her daughter's underwear.

The habits and attitude of the new King, George V, and his Queen, Mary – formerly Princess May of Teck – were as unlike as possible those of Edward VII and Alexandra. George's tastes were simple, the collecting of stamps rather than new and beautiful mistresses, or as he himself put it: 'I'm not interested in any wife except my own.' What appealed to him was the life of a simple country gentleman, rather than the louche, scented glamour and intrigues of his father's Court. 'He is simple and not at all magnificent,' thought Margot, who had known him all her life, adding, 'He speaks no language well and in a very loud voice.'

He was reserved, so shy that while in public he looked almost glum ('We sailors never smile on duty'), in private he was only able to express his deep feelings for his wife by letter. It was a trait shared by Queen Mary, who was, however, artistically well educated; her knowledge of the fine arts would later lead to great improvements in the look and furnishing of the royal palaces. Accustomed to the sophistication and presence of Edward VII, the ministers who first came in contact with him were apt to underestimate him, sometimes a touch patronisingly. 'The King is a very jolly chap but thank God there's not much in his head,' wrote Lloyd George to his wife. 'They're simple, very very ordinary people, and perhaps on the whole that's how it should be.'

For although rigidly determined that no aspect of royal protocol should be ignored in public, in private the King was unassuming and genial. To one new, youthful and shy lady-in-waiting who hung back to allow her sovereign to precede her out of the room after dining *en famille* with the King and Queen at Windsor, he said, gesturing her to pass in front of him: 'I may be a king but I am also a gentleman.'

To everyone's relief the King and Queen did not cancel Royal Ascot, which fell only a month after Edward's death (although the royal box was empty). Later it became known as 'the Black Ascot' – everywhere there were long black dresses trimmed with black fringes; black lace parasols cast a sombre shadow on the faces beneath; the hats, wider than ever, were lavishly surmounted by black ostrich, osprey and paradise feathers, the whole often veiled in black tulle. One observer, looking at all the black-plumed hats, thought it looked at first glance as if 'an immense flight of crows had just settled'.

The first time Margot met George V after he became King was at Windsor in November where, according to protocol, 'I curtseyed very low and kissed his hand. He didn't like this but he smiled rather sweetly. I've always liked him very much.' The King, seemingly abashed at having his hand kissed by a woman he had known since boyhood, pulled it away, saying: 'How absurd!' 'Not at all, Sir,' Margot replied. 'I like doing the right thing when I can.' The shy Queen did not get the same approbation. 'She is very stiff and dull.'

During conversation after dinner it became clear that the King disapproved heartily of the suffragettes. 'In a loud cheery voice he explained how he would chop all their hair off, give them hard labour and then, with a slight lowering of the voice, repeated what his father had thought so witty.' The suffragettes, he told Margot, were known as 'the unenjoyed'. She was not amused, writing: 'I have no great taste for stale jocularities and no available social laughter but I did my best.'

For Parliament, Edward VII's death had meant an immediate cessation of hostilities. The Budget for 1909–10, so bitterly contested the year before, went quietly through with a sizeable majority.

Asquith was still determined to break the absolute power of the Lords and, if possible, the deadlock resulting from the January election. When Margot, in Scotland with the children, received a telegram from him saying '*tout est fini*' she knew immediately that there would be another election, and returned to London at once.

That November Asquith went to Buckingham Palace to see the King, taking with him a paper on the various points he wished to raise, most notably on obtaining a pledge from the King that if necessary he would create 300 new Liberal Peers. In his own mind, Asquith was certain that the mere threat of this flood would force the Lords to back down.

The King, though unhappily, gave his promise. 'After a long talk,' he wrote in his diary that evening, 'I agreed most reluctantly to give the Cabinet a secret understanding that in the event of the Government being returned with a majority at the General Election, I should use my Prerogative to make peers if asked for. I disliked having to do that very much.'

But as the King realised, there was no alternative: if he had not agreed, Asquith – as he told Margot – would have resigned. 'If the King refuses to exercise his prerogative, I resign at once and explain the reasons for my resignation by reading this paper in the House of Commons. If we are beaten in the General Election the question will never arise, and if we get in by a working majority the Lords will give way, so the King will not be involved.'

A fortnight later, Parliament was dissolved. The election took place from 3–19 December 1910 (the last British election to be held over several days) on the issue of the Lords' veto. The result was as if the previous eleven months might not have been. The number of seats won by each party had barely changed, with the Liberals achieving only one more than the Conservatives. Again, Asquith needed the support of the Irish Nationalists to be sure of a majority.

The only real difference after the election was the growing unpopularity of the House of Lords. To Asquith and Lloyd George this was a powerful weapon indeed although it took until mid-May 1911 to pilot the Parliament Bill through the House of Commons, as the attempt to curb the powers of the Lords was seen as treachery by many – though by no means all – of Asquith's political opponents, and virtually all those in Society.

On 24 July there was an unprecedented scene in the House of Commons. Asquith was cheered on his way by crowds in the streets as he drove with Margot, cool and elegant in grey chiffon and a large black hat, in an open car to Parliament. Once inside, it was a different story. He was shouted down by the Opposition so forcibly by catcalls, cries of 'Who killed the King?' and even 'Traitor!' when he rose to speak that after half an hour he gave up, threw his papers onto the table in front of him and sat down, saying that he declined 'to degrade himself further'.

Margot, furious and upset, scribbled a note and had it sent down to Sir Edward Grey. Grey, a baronet from Northumberland who had become an intimate of the Asquiths when, aged forty-three, he was appointed Foreign Secretary. He was a hard and conscientious worker driven by conviction rather than ambition and, as all those who knew him well understood, his real passion was the rivers and wildlife of his native county rather than the cut and thrust of daily politics. As Margot also knew, Grey was respected by the House.

'They will listen to you,' she wrote, 'so for God's sake defend him from the cats and the cads.' Grey rose and in the shortest speech ever made in the Commons said: 'If arguments are not listened to from the Prime Minister, there is not one of us who will attempt to take his place.' There was silence until F.E. Smith, brilliant advocate and Parliamentarian and one of the chief shouters, rose, when there was further uproar; finally the Speaker suspended the sitting. Margot was so grateful to Grey that when she came across him alone afterwards she kissed his hand, whereupon his eyes filled with tears. (Of F.E. she said later: 'He's very clever but sometimes his brains go to his head.')

Asquith, with the King's pledge in his pocket, was straightforwardly confident of victory – and certain of it when, in August, Lord Morley, at the instigation of the King, read out a statement saying that 'His Majesty would assent . . . to a creation of Peers sufficient in number to guard against any possible combination of the different parties in opposition by which the Parliament Bill might be exposed a second time to defeat.'

That night, the Lords caved in – by a vote of 131 to 114 diehards. It was victory, a victory that meant 'Government by the People' was no longer a phrase but a reality. It was apocalyptic also in another sense: it was the beginning of the invisible, irrevocable decline of the old order, the final long-drawn-out ending of the Edwardian era, of government by the aristocracy, of a way of life that had once seemed changeless and immutable – and of the tightly meshed cohesion of that social grouping known as the Souls.

FIVE

The Souls had really originated with the two youngest Tennant sisers. In her teens and early twenties, Margot and her beloved younger sister Laura had been at the centre of a group of friends of both sexes, many of whom came to stay at Glen. Margot described Glen as 'a place buried in the restful hills where the echoes of the burn are never heard, except by the peewit and the curlews and the moor mists wreathed round the sun', and she was never happier than when staying there. It was so cold that as children she and Laura had to pile on layers of garments and wore chamois leather 'lung protectors' and flannel petticoats all year long.

The girls' father, Charles Tennant, had had the moderately-sized Georgian house enlarged into a turreted castle. At times as many as fifty guests, all with valets, ladies' maids and grooms, stayed there. The young men would enjoy the excellent shooting and fishing, the girls would tramp over the moor together, and late at night all of them would congregate in the little room where Margot and Laura slept for hours of chat and discussion.

When Laura, who had married Alfred Lyttelton, one of the friends who came to stay at Glen, died in childbirth the friends who had been visiting for some years came at first to talk with Margot about her sister or simply to see her. After the statutory six months of mourning had passed the invisible ley lines of friendship re-established themselves, but this time with Margot at their centre. The group found they preferred each others' company to that of anyone else – and the entity later known as the Souls was born.

Save for the Tennant girls, the Souls were drawn from the same aristocratic milieu as the rest of Society, with the same large country houses, the same troops of servants ministering to their every need, the same luxurious standard of living taken completely for granted. Yet they could not have been more different from what was then known as the Marlborough House Set (Marlborough House was where Edward VII had lived when Prince of Wales). The Souls' distinguishing feature was the value they placed on intelligence, with wit following a close second. They valued art, music, philosophy and fine writing, and regarded philistinism as a deadly sin. Their conversation was spiced with quotations, epigrams, sparkling *mots*.

Another prized Souls' quality was sensitivity, both in speech and letters. They wrote to each other constantly in terms of affection so extravagantly expressed that often they seemed like love letters (when they *were* love letters, this florid romanticism was the perfect cover). Letters in any case were an important part not only of any courtship but also of daily life: one could almost say that these Edwardians grew up with a pen in their hands. Unselfconsciously the men wrote poems to the women they admired; if to another man, often a comic verse about him in the visitors' books of their hostesses to commemorate a stay.

The real catalyst for their coagulating as a group was Margot's strong belief in friendships and determination to acquire as many as she could, especially from among the most brilliant men of the time. Where other young single women would have been too modest, demure or timid to initiate overtures, Margot had no such scruples. She made her admiration, interest and wish for friendship with such a man perfectly plain, often beginning with an invitation to a luncheon party in her father's large house in Grosvenor Square. She also made it clear that this was no sexual ploy; and almost always the men, flattered and intrigued by her genuine feelings, responded warmly.

It was an age when everyone, from the poorest to the richest, made his or her own entertainment. Where others would play billiards, bridge or act in charades, the Souls' post-prandial favourites were on a loftier intellectual level. Most of the games were introduced by Margot and Laura, who had played them at Glen as they grew up. One, Styles, was to write a sonnet or prose paragraph in the style of a particular author, such as Shakespeare, Milton, Meredith or Browning – often this meant that female Souls, less well educated than their husbands, brothers or lovers, spent hours reading such authors before one of their regular house parties.

Another favourite game, which lingered on well into the twentieth century, was Clumps, an early version of Twenty Questions; rather than confining themselves to simple factual answers, the Souls extended it to include concepts, situations and quotations such as 'the eleventh hour', 'women and children first' or 'to be or not to be'.

Acting games were popular, from charades to Dumb Crambo – a kind of *tableau vivant* in which the players dressed up to represent a well-known saying or episode, such as Napoleon crossing the Alps. Other Tennant games were Epigrams and Character Sketches – when completed, these were handed to an umpire, who had to read them aloud and the party then guessed the authorship of each one. Among their umpires were Bret Harte and, later, George Curzon, Harry Cust, George Wyndham and Lionel Tennyson. When together, the Souls went on playing these games for years.

Millicent, the beautiful Duchess of Sutherland, was a founder Soul. She believed in equality between the sexes, read a lot, wrote poetry and short stories and held famous receptions at Sutherland House. Others at the heart of the group were Henry Manners, Marquis of Granby* and his wife Violet, Lord and Lady Elcho and Lord and Lady Pembroke. Pre-eminent among them, though, was Arthur James Balfour, Chief Secretary for Ireland during Lord Londonderry's viceroyalty and later Prime Minister – 'to each is dear Arthur the dearest' said Curzon, himself famed for his wit and brilliance, while Margot wrote admiringly of his 'cool grace'.

The lofty intellectual and spiritual plateau on which the Souls resided did not prevent them from indulging in numerous, though discreet, love affairs. Mary Elcho, a noted hostess whose daughter Cynthia was to marry Beb Asquith, had a long *amitié amoureuse* with Balfour and a love affair with Wilfrid Scawen Blunt (by whom she also had a baby), Violet Manners with Harry Cust, Ettie Grenfell with one of the youngest Souls, Evan Charteris – after Margot had definitively turned him down – and Harry Cust with almost everyone.

Margot, who for years adored Curzon – both she and Laura were a little in love with him – talked of his 'enamelled self-assurance'. This brilliant and controversial man was all his life adored by some and hated by others. Sometimes this enmity was aroused by a seeming arrogance: a spinal injury in his late teens meant that he had to wear a steel corset which gave him an impression of stiffness and

---

* Who succeeded to the dukedom of Rutland in 1906.

hauteur. This did not deter Margot, who turned to him – as did her other sisters – when she wanted to improve her mind. No thought that he might be otherwise occupied deterred her. She started one letter: 'I know you are always busy, so am I,' before going on to ask his help with an essay she had to write on Tennyson's *Maud*, set by a lecturer in classes she and her sister were attending. 'Either call round tonight or tomorrow night between 6 and 7 or write me one or two hints and criticisms on Maud,' she ordered, adding only as an afterthought: 'Do you mind being thus bothered?'

Curzon did not mind. He wrote frequently to his 'loving little Margie', his '1st girl', as when he set off in the autumn of 1889 on his long journey through Persia (his departure was known as 'the passing of a Soul') and his sympathy and understanding meant much to her. The idea that this closeness could ever founder would have been inconceivable to both of them then. It was a Soul tenet that politics should not interfere with private friendships; Conservative and Liberal Souls had always mingled freely and cheerfully. Curzon, for instance, although deeply Conservative, much enjoyed staying in the fiercely Liberal Glen household.

After the 1885 election, when Gladstone introduced his first Home Rule Bill (which was defeated), divisions were so deep and feelings so fierce that, except for the Souls, members of the two parties viewed each other over an unbridgeable chasm in private as well as public life.

As Margot wrote later: 'Our decision not to sacrifice friendship to public politics was envied in every capital in Europe. It ... gave men of different tempers and opposite beliefs an opportunity of discussing them without heat and without reporters.' As well as the Liberals Gladstone, Asquith, Chamberlain and Lords Harcourt and Rosebery, Conservatives like Curzon, Balfour, Lord Salisbury and Lord Hartington (first a Liberal, later a Unionist) all came to the Tennant house in Grosvenor Square and later to other 'Soul' houses.

When this attitude eventually changed, the effect was equally cataclysmic on several of the Souls' careers. The conflict over the Parliament Bill was a death blow to their legendary political impartiality: the links that had held them together for so long snapped, their leaders turning on each other with a fury fuelled by a bitter sense of betrayal. No longer did friendships cross party lines with impunity although – being the Souls – this did not always come into the open. Arthur Balfour felt betrayed by his friends, not only by Asquith, who had failed to inform him that he had extracted guarantees to create Peers from George V, but also by his fellow Tory and fellow Soul George Curzon, who worked against him in the House of Lords canvassing Peers to vote in favour of the Parliament Bill. Against both, Balfour's revenge would be belated but deadly.* In the early halcyon days such a thought would have been just as great a treachery.

But now, the policies that Asquith and his Liberal Government were trying to push through rebounded to a considerable degree on his personal life and that of his family. One of those most affected when the Parliament Bill went through was Asquith's daughter Violet, who as a good-looking girl in her early twenties could have expected to be bombarded with invitations. 'Social ostracism was practised against us very rigidly on two occasions,'† she wrote later. 'We were pariahs and outcasts. Yet you are never very lonely at Downing Street, even when you are cut by fashionable society. I mean we didn't suffer.'

This blacklisting was largely because what was called Society, drawn from probably around 2,000 families – many of them related, some linked by marriage, others by long-standing friendships – was almost entirely Conservative. Many were aristocratic and owners of thousands of acres. With the system of primogeniture, these estates remained intact (over ninety per cent of Britain was in these private hands) and Society small, and its members wanted to preserve this status quo. Margot and Asquith, by contrast, both came not only from different backgrounds but from a different, Liberal tradition.

There was, of course, a certain mingling. With land came power: it was almost impossible for a non-landed person to obtain a peerage. Thus the first stage in the rise of a man made rich through his own hard work and business acumen, like Margot's father, was the purchase of a large estate, after which often came ennoblement and therefore a seat in the House of Lords – Margot's brother Edward

* Curzon's last hope of becoming Prime Minister was spiked by Balfour, who advised George V against appointing 'dear George' in succession to Bonar Law in 1923, while he revenged himself against what he saw as Asquith's betrayal by joining in the coup against him in 1916.
† The other was the battle over Home Rule for Ireland.

had been raised to the peerage as Lord Glenconner only a year earlier, in 1911.

Britain was largely ruled by this elite. Many eldest sons of Peers sat in the House of Commons as a kind of apprenticeship on their way to the Lords, from which had been drawn most prime ministers in the nineteenth century, while until the previous year the Lords themselves, with their right of veto over any Bill passed in the House of Commons, had the final say on any legislation. It was a time when 'the ruling classes' really *were* the ruling classes, and Asquith's victory was in direct opposition to this entrenched Conservative viewpoint.

It did, however, all reflect a groundswell of change that had already begun to make itself felt – although, unlike most changes hitherto, this stemmed from the bottom upwards. The labour market, particularly for women, was offering new opportunities and directions. This was most visible in the decline in numbers of those going into domestic service, then much the largest employer of women.

Servants were the fuel on which both ducal mansions and the suburban villas of prosperous grocers ran – Margot had crammed seventeen into Downing Street. All had their respective roles, which sometimes governed their sleeping quarters – the sexes were rigorously separated and small fry like boot boys often slept in some cupboard in a basement.

Housemaids rose at five or six in order to light fires well before breakfast, then scurried off to bring up morning tea and hot water. They made beds, cleaned rooms, black-leaded grates – a house with eight servants might burn half a ton of coal a day – and scrubbed the front steps, often the only welcome breath of fresh air they drew all day. Parlour maids opened shutters, laid downstairs fires, set and cleared away tables, polished furniture and cleaned the silver.

It was the aim of many to become a lady's maid, one of the most enviable domestic posts. A good lady's maid's position was inviolable: she did everything for her mistress, from packing and unpacking to listening to confidences and dressing and undressing her – when Violet Asquith's maid became ill she had to ask Asquith's valet to undo her dress. Alice Keppel's maid drew her bath, scented it with two rose-geranium bath salt cubes, laid out her underclothes under a lace cover, knelt on the floor to put on her stockings, laced her into her stays, did her hair, pinned her veil on to her hat, buttoned up her gloves, put her powder and cigarettes and money into her bag as well as doing all the washing, ironing and mending of her clothes.

For many it was impossible to think of life without several servants around at all times. 'If you leave us in your little house with a cook and housemaid it is enough if we bring a man & maid,' wrote Margot Asquith to her stepmother, who was lending Asquith and Margot a small house in Scotland for a holiday.

Grander houses employed men as well as women. At Welbeck (the stately home of the Dukes of Portland) the duties of footmen who waited at table included daily changing of livery, from the morning's black trousers and white shirt to afternoon and evening garb of short scarlet coat, scarlet waistcoat, purple knee breeches, white stockings, black pumps with bows and a square white bow tie. In Curzon's house, if there were more than fourteen to dinner – a frequent occurrence – his footmen wore knee breeches; a dinner party of twelve, he believed, was a mere domestic occasion and did not warrant them.

Footmen, who were expected to be tall and good-looking, were also the servants who historically had carried notes and messages around, so being 'good with the telephone' – by 1912 there were half a million subscribers throughout the country – was quickly becoming one of a footman's duties.

Most houses, especially those in remote areas, were still lit by gas, as electricity was expensive and many kept a servant especially to deal with this. William Heath, the chauffeur-groom to Thomas Cochrane, son-in-law of the sixth Earl of Glasgow, at his Scottish estate of Crawford Priory in Fife, where the house was lit by gas, described the time-consuming process needed to keep the lamps (lit by matches) functioning – this included removing sludge from the cylinders and taking it into the woods to bury it deep.

Heath's own job spanned the transition from carriage to car, from horse to machine.* His employer kept four cars, the most elegant in Heath's view being the black Thornycroft; like the carriages it had superseded, its doors were embellished with the family crest.

---

* Horses were still very much in evidence in the years just preceding the Great War. They pulled the massive coal carts and the heavy, beautifully painted brewers' drays and delivery vans from shops and department stores.

Although covered by the roof, the driver's compartment was otherwise open to the weather. The right-hand gear and brake levers, a large serpentine horn, headlamps and wheel hubs were all of brass and the mudguards were made of black patent leather stretched over a metal frame. As with carriages, next to the chauffeur's seat was another for the footman.

Heath's dark blue livery also had hints of the coachman – wide breeches like a groom's finishing in polished black leather gaiters, a tight double-breasted jacket with a high collar and brass buttons bearing the family crest, and boots. Only the cap struck a new note: peaked and military, with a cockade. The final touch was a pair of large black gauntlet gloves.

During the first few years of the century cars* were slowly beginning to replace horses (although there were still around 7,000 horse-drawn hansom cabs in London). They were kept in 'motor stables' and driven by 'motor servants', albeit wearing the breeches and gaiters of the former coachmen, which in many cases they were. By August 1905 the Asquiths had begun seriously to debate selling their carriage horses; they took the plunge the following year, investing the £200 the animals fetched in a £450 car. 'The horses [are] sold,' wrote Violet in her diary in June 1906. 'In their stead we have a large red cheap slow uncomfortable motor.'

The King favoured claret-coloured Daimlers and Mercedes and hated being overtaken. Cars were still purely the preserve of the rich (the ultimate Edwardian motoring status symbol would be the 1911 Rolls-Royce Silver Ghost, costing £1,154 – more than most people earned in ten years). Unheated and at the beginning lacking both hood and windscreen, cars demanded special clothing, goggles, dustcoats and motoring veils for women, rubber capes to keep the rain out for both sexes, furs or leather for winter.

Less grand households might not have had a car but were equally well looked after by those they employed. In her autobiography, the famous crime writer Agatha Christie reminisced: 'Servants did an incredible amount of work. Jane cooked five-course dinners for seven or eight people as a matter of daily routine. For grand dinner parties of twelve or more, each course contained alternatives – two soups,

---

* By 1912 there were 88,265 cars in the country, 52,600 goods vehicles and 69,501 motorcycles.

two fish courses, etc. The housemaid cleaned about forty silver photograph frames and toilet silver ad lib, took in and emptied a hip bath (we had a bathroom but my mother considered it a revolting idea to use a bath others had used), brought hot water to bedrooms four times a day, lit bedroom fires in winter, and mended linen etc., every afternoon. The parlour-maid cleaned incredible amounts of silver and washed glasses with loving care in a papier-mâché bowl, besides providing perfect waiting at table.'

The long and the short of it was that everyone who could afford a servant kept one. Apart from anything else, in that highly class-conscious society it was the sign of middle-classdom: to be middle-class you had to have at least one servant. The lot of a servant girl – and it always was a girl – in a one-servant household was deeply unenviable. Lottie Martin, the daughter of a foundry worker living in Beeston, Nottinghamshire, whose family could not afford further education, had to leave school on her thirteenth birthday and became 'a little drudge', on the go from earliest morning until late at night, in the household of the local chemist, and with little free time.

For those who did not have servants, much of the heavy work fell on the daughters of the house. This was especially so in the country. In the Devonshire Arms – half farm, half pub, in the small, isolated Peakland village of Sheldon – the diary of Maria Gyte, wife of the owner, describes what had to be done, all by her two daughters: meals to prepare for a large household as well as for the men who worked the farm and those who came to the inn, fires to be laid, lamps trimmed, housework and laundry done, the dairy whitewashed, rooms papered and decorated, cheese made from surplus milk.

In country villages, household work often included not just the routine preparation of food after purchase but often help with its slaughter by those who were going to eat it. Many families kept a pig and the autumn pig-killing by the village pig-killer – usually of a sow that had had a couple of litters – was one of the highlights of the village year as it meant plentiful, delicious meat for a week or so. The bristles were burnt off, the pig hung up, and the offal and lean meat cut out and sent round to neighbours or relatives, who would do the same when they killed a pig. The sides were often smoked in someone's smoke loft, or hung in the chimney over a wood fire. Finally, what remained of the carcass was salted and the fat rendered down.

Unsurprisingly, as alternatives to domestic service began to appear, young women jumped at them. Shops, factories, stores and offices were advertising for female staff – the first female typist had appeared fifteen years earlier, in 1897. *The Freewoman*, which billed itself as a 'Weekly Feminist Review', commented in December 1911 that 'the feature of the week which we consider of the greatest importance to Feminists is the fact that a woman has been appointed Insurance Commissioner at a salary of £1,000 a year, no diminution of salary being made on account of her sex. This is a landmark.' It was.

Working outside the home meant both independence and much more free time. Even the tanning factory, which became Lottie Martin's next job, was preferable to her former domestic slavery although the work was hard and dirty, the working day, which began at 7 a.m., lasted ten hours, and the girls standing at the long benches hammering the leather were sent home if they talked to one another. Once out of the factory, though, they could let themselves go.

'The Wakes, which was the first Sunday nearest to the 11th of July, was a great occasion, full of frivolity,' wrote Lottie. 'We would do the Turkey Trot and run one another around with confetti and tickler brushes. On the Sunday the men's clubs would walk to the parish church attended by the Silver Prize band, many of the marchers never entering the church again until the following year when the proceedings were repeated. On the Monday, the church Sunday Schools would walk from the old cross which stood where the war memorial is now. Before starting off they would invariably sing "Stand Up for Jesus" and "Onward Christian Soldiers", then follow the procession along with drays decorated with Biblical scenes for which the best had a prize.'

Several inter-related factors had encouraged this shift away from domestic service. One was much better transport. With London's railways now almost completely electrified, commuting was far easier. Within London there was the General Omnibus Company, their buses carrying advertisements of the day for salt or soap, tobacco or tea. An open staircase at the rear led to a roofless upper deck, where the seats were made of slats of wood, with a leather apron for use in wet weather. More modestly there was the Tube, often with the same wooden slatted seats, and of course the trams. 'The latter clanged their way along the busy thoroughfares, on which lay the intricate tracery of tram lines,' wrote John James Heath, whose father Bill had worked as chauffeur-groom to Lord Cochrane.

Another reason for the swing away from servitude was the Balfour Act of 1902, which had brought in secondary education by raising the school-leaving age from ten to twelve – an extra two years that had the effect of increasing the reading population. Along with this was the burgeoning of the popular press, which offered new ideas and possibilities, largely thanks to the newspaper genius Alfred Harmsworth (who had been raised to the peerage as Lord Northcliffe in 1905).

In 1896 he had founded the *Daily Mail*, an instant hit that held the world record for daily circulation until his death in 1922. It cost a halfpenny at a time when other London dailies cost one penny, and was more populist in tone and more concise in its coverage than its rivals. Just as importantly – especially at that time of budding female emancipation – from its first beginnings it was aimed largely at women, the only national newspaper to be so. Northcliffe's dominance of printed media was increased in 1903 when he founded the *Daily Mirror* and went on to buy and restore to health two ailing newspapers, the *Observer* and *The Times*.

Then there was the dramatic change in women's fashions. Gone was the S-bend corset mandatory for the voluptuous Edwardian beauty, which pushed the bust upwards and outwards, made the hips slant backwards and held the body in a rigid stance. Gone were the layers of frilly petticoats – sometimes up to half a dozen – the sweet-pea pastels, the laces and the feather boas, the whole apparatus of excessive, uncompromising, time-consuming femininity. Instead there was a new, upright, pared-down silhouette, with long tailored jackets and skirts unimpeded by petticoats, which allowed much greater freedom of movement – and a far less inflexible approach to the business of being female. With the narrower skirts came large muffs and the first handbags – there was no room for the numerous pockets of earlier times.

Unlikely or frivolous as this may sound, this profound change in female fashion helped accelerate the shift away from the domestic. In these outfits the new breed of young women workers had no trouble in striding along the streets to work without hems trailing in the mud; versions were worn by skiers (with gaiters or breeches underneath) or, tailored in leather, sported by young women motorcyclists. For suffragettes, the new fashion was a boon – after setting pillar boxes on fire or throwing stones they could dash away and mingle in crowds before the arrival of the police.

Another great appeal of work outside the domestic sphere was the chance to have what were called 'followers'. The teenage Lottie enjoyed walking over the fields with her friends to the nearby village of Long Eaton, where they would pair off with the local boys who would walk them back again. Sometimes one of the boys would play his mouth organ and, recalled Lottie 'we girls would sing along with such tunes as "Moonlight Bay", "Beautiful Doll", "You Made Me Love You" and "If You Were the Only Girl in the World"'.

In domestic service, by contrast, many households had refused to allow their servants to entertain admirers even to a blameless cup of tea in a busy kitchen – 'no followers' was a common demand from would-be employers – and some even sacked them if they wished to marry, or indeed if they did marry. As Lady Emily Lutyens wrote to her husband, the architect Edwin Lutyens, her friend Lady Battersea 'was in great distress about her maid, having been found to have been married to a footman. The maid had a babe and had to produce to Lady B her marriage certificate. The maid had to go and the footman was sacked.' Office work held no such draconian threat; and also gave a girl not only more opportunities to meet a potential boyfriend but more free time to spend with him. The only problem here was that, as the 1911 census had revealed, there was a 1.3 million 'surplus' of women (the excess of women over men had been known since the middle of the last century).

These could turn to another branch of the press – the Lonely Hearts papers. Like the national papers, they too had boomed, with the *Matrimonial Times* relaunching in 1904, the Sheffield-based *International Matrimonial Gazette* going national in 1909 and the launching of the *Matrimonial Mascot* in 1910.

Of these, much the most successful was the *Matrimonial Times* ('A Larger Circulation than any other Matrimonial Paper in the World!') which cost a whopping 6d compared to the penny cost of *The Times*. Many of its advertisements were from maidservants who had little chance of meeting a member of the male sex unless it was a whistling errand boy with a delivery. 'Domestic Servant desires a matrimonial alliance with a respectable, steady, sober, quiet, hard-working, industrious man in constant employment. Only those with honourable intentions need reply', ran a typical one.

At first, most of those in the upper echelons of society barely noticed the diminution of the servant class, hedged about as they were with power, wealth and, often, titles and great lands. In any case they would have had first choice of what was going because the larger the house, the greater the kudos, the better the conditions and the more company their potential servants would have.

In the country, 'the big house' was the natural focus and employers had often known many of their servants from their birth in the nearby village. This was particularly true in Scotland, with its clan system, where everyone knew almost everything about everyone else. At Glen, when the great Gladstone, four times Liberal Prime Minister of England and known as the Grand Old Man, came to stay (he sat for the neighbouring constituency of Midlothian), he was venerated by Margot's father – but the whole household knew that his grandfather was a dishonest baker, spelling his name Gladstalnes but known locally as 'licht baps' for selling his bread at false weights. (Margot's mother imparted this information to Wilfrid Scawen Blunt when he came to stay at Glen, and Blunt jotted it down in his diary.)

Margot herself had no trouble finding servants, as she paid generously and had the advantage of a sizeable staff. Brought up in a big country house where, thanks to a large family whose friends constantly came to stay, lunch and dinner for twenty was commonplace, she continued this tradition when she married.

No. 10 was in fact run like a country house, filled not only with members of the family but also with constant lunch and dinner guests. It was a household of considerable glamour – the Prime Minister, urbane and charming, Margot, impeccably dressed, entering to shriek a greeting across the room before lighting a cigarette and firing off her darting shafts of conversation, perhaps a couple of Asquith's tall, good-looking and clever sons, the slender, brilliant and witty Violet with one of her train of admirers, several leading politicians, a peer, a literary figure or two, a couple of pretty young women irresistibly drawn to the house. In modern parlance, the Asquiths knew everyone: Asquith had achieved the country's top job while Margot had been one of the few women to break through the invisible stockade behind which the aristocracy lived.

For that day and age, it was an extraordinary achievement. The small inner ring of aristocratic families who composed Society and whose children were therefore included in every invitation to the Season's balls and dinners were those who had been linked throughout generations by marriage and birth and complicated lines of cousinage. Most of them knew each other and, if they did not, they knew all about each other and where each fitted into the cat's cradles of relationships. It was a tight, exclusive little world.

By contrast, Margot's great-grandfather was a Glasgow chemist who had discovered dry bleaching powder (which revolutionised the industry) and, as an entrepreneur of supreme ability, had made a huge fortune. Although her father had a large estate in Scotland and a house in Grosvenor Square, was a former MP and had been created a baronet, he was still considered as 'in trade'. As Violet said many years later: 'Society used to be like a walled city, with entrances and exits, and you needed a passport to get in.' Margot had not been born with that passport.

Thus, after Margot's presentation as a debutante and the ball given for her by her father, invitations tailed off. But that year her brother Eddy took her to Royal Ascot where, through one of his friends, she was presented to the Prince of Wales (the future Edward VII). Politely he asked this stylish young woman if she would back her fancy for the Wokingham Stakes and have a small bet with him as to the winner.

Margot, who, as an expert rider, had acquired much knowledge of horses, seized her chance. She told the Prince that she could not accept his bet unless she saw the horses; accordingly, they went down to the rails and watched the runners gallop past. As they did so, Margot picked out the horse she thought would win; when it duly did so the Prince, impressed, asked her to lunch and next day gave her a gold cigarette case with a diamond and sapphire clasp as her 'winnings'. After this, barriers breached by the royal accolade, invitations to all the great houses poured in and she was 'made' socially.

The Asquiths' social landscape, therefore, was wide and deep, peopled with a regular cast of close friends, promising acquaintances and political grandees. Among their most frequent guests was Asquith's (junior) Parliamentary Private Secretary, Edwin Montagu, the second son of the immensely rich Lord Swaythling, the Jewish former MP and founder of Samuel Montagu and Company, one of England's largest and most respected financial institutions. Edwin Montagu belonged, of course, to the Liberal Party, as did most influential Jews at that time – it was the party of the middle class, private enterprise, reform and the rights of the individual, whereas Tories stood for the aristocracy and landowners, the Anglican Church and time-honoured English tradition.

Montagu had been President of the Cambridge Union and had been elected Liberal MP for the West Division of Cambridgeshire at twenty-seven, in the 1906 election.* He was described by one man who knew him as 'an imposing, almost fearsome figure, with an overlarge head, a dark, saturnine pock-marked complexion, black moustache. His mouth was large, sensual and slightly twisted. A gleaming monocle in his eye gave an impression of fierceness which bore no relation to his character.'

He had a huge, ungainly body, a deep, soft voice and dark eyes that sparkled with humour and kindliness. He loved the open-air life, had a great knowledge of ornithology and was happiest shooting or merely watching wild birds on the Norfolk Broads. Although he was an entertaining companion his friends would joke about his glooms and his hypochondria. Duff Cooper remembered him as 'very nervous. Whenever he talked about the future he would interject: "But I, of course, shall be dead by then."'

Although anti-Semitism was still fairly widespread it was generally latent and, in the upper classes at least, found its outlet largely in general – though usually unspoken – prejudice. It had not prevented Asquith from making the young Montagu his protégé almost as soon as they met, and facilitating his political rise (as it had not prevented Lord Derby from helping the late Prime Minister Disraeli). In turn, Montagu's intelligence, hard work and vision were of enormous help to the Prime Minister.

Within a year of becoming Asquith's Private Secretary he had become an habitué of the Asquith family; as Asquith's protégé he

* Chaim Bermant, *The Cousinhood.*

was spending more time with them than with his own family. Margot was particularly fond of him, and treated him as a confidant. They exchanged letters – hers beginning 'Dearest Mr Montagu' – and he would often bring her flowers.

He was a constant at many of her dinner parties, with their mixture of the social, the literary and the political, as with this description (by Beatrice Webb, economist, social reformer and watchful observer of her surroundings) of one of them. It consisted of the Russian Ambassador, the Desboroughs (Ettie Desborough was one of Margot's fellow Souls and a great friend; her husband Willie was a noted athlete and a politician), the Conservative politician and former First Lord of the Admiralty Lord Goschen, Lord and Lady Islington, who had just returned from New Zealand where he had spent two years as Governor, Mrs Lowther (the Speaker's wife), Lord Hugh Cecil, known to his friends as 'Linky' and leader of the Hughligans, a group of radical young Tory MPs, Margot's friend Mrs Lester, one or two aristocratic young men, Violet and Raymond. For Beatrice Webb's austere tastes, it was a little too much.

'The large garish rooms, the flunkeys and the superlatively good dinner gave a sort of "Second Empire" setting to the entertainment. Lady Desborough, Margot, Mrs Lester and Lady Dickson-Poynder [Islington] were all very decolletée and highly adorned with jewels. The conversation aimed at brilliancy – Margot sparkling her little disjointed ways, kindly and indiscreet, Lady Desborough's somewhat artificial grace, Lady Dickson-Poynder's pretty folly, Mrs Lester's outré frankness lending a sort of "staginess" to the talk. We might all have been characters brought on to illustrate the ways of modern society . . . '

One subject that did not figure in the conversation in 1912 was the possibility of war. It was true that Germany was known to be bitterly jealous of Britain's colonies and influence, and had been building up her naval strength. But to the population at large, ignorant of diplomatic and other exchanges, she did not seem to pose a threat. And was not the Royal Navy, the country's bulwark against invasion, twice the size of the next two largest navies put together?

True, there had been the threat of war between Germany and France the previous year, caused by the Agadir Crisis, but this had been averted – in part thanks to a powerful, assertive speech by Britain's Chancellor, Lloyd George.

This potential conflict had been sparked by the threatening arrival of the German gunboat *Panther* at the Moroccan port of Agadir (under French control) on 1 July 1911. Three weeks later, on 21 July, Lloyd George delivered his speech at the Mansion House. After describing Britain's contribution to liberty, he continued: 'I would make great sacrifices to preserve peace.' But if peace could only be preserved, he said, by Britain allowing herself to be treated where her interests were vitally affected as if she were of no account, 'then I say emphatically that peace at that price would be a humiliation intolerable for a great country like ours to endure'.

It was an unmistakable warning against further German expansion and Germany backed off. A Franco-German accord was signed and all seemed calm again.

But for Germany this humiliation was another augmentation of her festering discontent. Or as the well-known commentator on foreign affairs Dr E.J. Dillon, writing in the *Contemporary Review* of January 1912, put it: 'The root of the antagonism between Germany and Great Britain is this: we want to keep what we have, and, therefore, we favour the maintenance of the *status quo*; whereas our Continental cousins crave for what they have not got, and are minded to wrest it from the hands of those who possess it.' Unfortunately, few were listening to him.

~~~

SIX

Lloyd George had not only set out Britain's attitude to the possibility of German aggression in Morocco in his stirring speech; he had also used the crisis to effect an end to one of the most damaging strikes in British history.

As 1912 opened, Britain was seething with the industrial disturbances that had begun the previous year or so with a wave of country-wide strikes, walkouts and riots, a period that became known as the Great Unrest. Competition from the expanding industries of America and Germany had resulted in a drop in wages over the past ten years; the unions had grown in strength and the Liberal Government was short of money for its promised reforms. The mounting tension was exacerbated by the boiling heat (on 9 August the temperature was 95 in the shade).

In Liverpool's Central Station, as angry workers gathered, a cart of herrings was attacked and the fish hurled everywhere; in London, tension and nervousness were such that gunmakers sold out of revolvers. Then – far worse – came the news that the four railway unions were preparing to call their men out at a mere thirty hours' notice. Such a thing had never happened before and it was certain to paralyse the country and cripple its economy.

Unofficial strikes had erupted in various parts of the country throughout July and early August and Asquith had met various union leaders, offering them a Royal Commission to inquire into their grievances; this, however, was rejected, as the leaders felt it would drag on interminably while poor wages needed dealing with immediately.

The Government had to act. But when Asquith dealt with the union leaders, his usual emollient negotiating skills left him and he stated uncompromisingly that he would not hesitate to 'employ all the forces of the Crown' to prevent a stoppage. Angered at this threat, the leaders called the men out at midnight on 17 August, bringing the North and the Midlands to a standstill. The thousands of men already out were promptly joined by many thousands more.

The worst of the confrontations was in the steel town of Llanelli, Carmarthenshire. Here, what had begun as a peaceful strike had started on the afternoon of Thursday, 17 August 1911, in protest at average wages of £1 per week (this was about twenty per cent below the norm for skilled workers). Troops were called in and during the following day and night violence erupted; shops were vandalised and looted, train tracks, the railway station and town hall wrecked, two of the strikers shot and four people died when rioters, not knowing that it contained explosive detonators, set fire to a freight wagon in a siding.

In Liverpool, with a gunboat standing by on the Mersey, the Army shot dead two strikers following three days of guerrilla warfare in the streets of the city centre; the strikers mounted mass pickets and the strike committee issued permits for the movement of bread and milk. By now almost every provincial port was closed. Against this vast, unofficial army, no strike-breaking organisation was effective and eventually the shipping industry employers gave in to demands for higher wages. Then the London docks joined in.

Taxi drivers struck, women working in sweatshops struck. Even schoolchildren struck – in a total of sixty-two towns up and down the country, ranging from Portsmouth and Southampton to London, Liverpool and Glasgow. The first child strike took place in Hull in early September at St Mary's Roman Catholic School, when twelve of the older boys led the younger boys out at break. Soon there were crowds of boys outside other Hull schools, howling 'Come out!' and 'Blackleg!' at the boys going in for afternoon lessons.

In Liverpool the boys copied the way their fathers had been organised by electing a strike committee – among its demands were the abolition of the cane, a penny a week for monitors and an extra half-day's holiday a week. Most of the child strikers were dragged back to school by their mothers – but a glance at their thin, sunken faces shows the extent of the poverty they suffered.

It was clear that only force – which a Liberal Government, dedicated to improving conditions for the poor, would have deplored using – could have defeated those taking part in the Great Unrest. It had to be brought to an end and concessions made.

At this point Lloyd George deployed not only his sympathy for the workers but his talent for negotiation, offering the employers the face-saving excuse that, with the threat of war conveyed by the Agadir Crisis, the matter must be settled quickly for the sake of the nation's safety. With this to persuade them, the employers accepted that there must be conciliation and concessions while the union leaders, glad to resume control over their unruly followers, concurred. (Lloyd George had also introduced salaries for MPs, called 'allowances', of £400 p.a. to keep the rapidly rising Labour Party on side and, in a time of industrial turmoil, out of the hands of the unions that had been bankrolling them.)

By the end of 1911 there had been 872 different strikes, most spontaneous reactions by workers across the country to the dreadful working conditions imposed upon them, and many begun in defiance of their national union leaders.

But the unrest was not over: 1912 was welcomed with more strikes – in January the miners voted four to one for a national strike and on 1 March the first ever national miners' strike began. Its effect was dramatic and the reactions extreme. 'The greatest catastrophe that has threatened the country since the Spanish Armada,' said *The Times*. There were calls for siege rations, martial law and even a stockpile of revolvers.

Margot felt deeply for the workers, realising that for many the simple act of surviving was a daily battle. 'I don't mind prophesying that there will be terrible awakenings in a few years to the absolute necessity of giving a minimum – or, better still, a <u>living</u> – wage to every worker in our islands,' she wrote. 'The facts and figures that came to my knowledge (and Henry's) of the real conditions and wages, not even so much of the miners as of the carters and porters in the docks, made me ill and I was sleepless for three nights running. Puffin, Elizabeth and I prayed every night about it.'

Within a month the Government had rushed a Minimum Wage Bill through Parliament, providing for arbitration to settle the level of minimum wages, district by district. Although this was rejected, there was now much less enthusiasm for the strike and it was called off.

Turbulence also threatened in Downing Street. Violet's constant presence in her marriage made Margot so miserable that she wrote wretchedly to a friend: 'Don't show or tell anyone about my letter to you as in some ways I think I might be a little blinded by Violet. I feel as if by now the end of my keen youth must be over, I ought to have my own husband and my own children in a house of my own – I have only been alone with Henry and my children three weeks in nineteen years. This has got on my nerves; it is really physical and the more I control the longing or the showing of it, the iller I feel. We are always à trois – in shops, in the hills, on official occasions, round the fire and at the altar. I long to take the communion service with Henry alone – I long to talk to him, to be with him – it would be so easy if she would marry . . .'

For Violet's worship of her father had intensified rather than abated as she grew older. Usually it took the form of trying to be with him as much as possible – preferably without Margot – so much so that Margot found it almost impossible to be alone with her own husband. Violet would frequently 'tag along' if Margot and Asquith planned an outing together; often Asquith would simply take her on some tour without telling Margot of the proposed expedition.

Of all his children, she was much the closest to him. With her there were none of the emotional constraints he felt with his sons; he was flattered by her passionate interest in politics and open adoration of himself and proud of her fair-haired looks, gentle voice, slender figure, incisive intelligence and popularity. For her, he was and would always remain the supreme being, far and away the most important person in her life, to whom no other man could come close.

Margot, who always did her best to be fair-minded over her stepchildren, wrote in her diary that 'Violet is not pretty but everyone is in love with her. I never saw a more conspicuous instance of how little beauty matters than in Violet. She is not even soignée or prettily arranged. She has very dirty ribbons and waistbelts half below her sash, her shirts crooked, her cuffs and collars never really nice very little natural taste but somehow her vitality, her wonderful manners keenness and sweetness of nature all triumph over her torn and dirty clothes, not a very good complexion and not pretty teeth just as if they were unnoticeable trifles. She has lovely hair and a pretty figure.' Margot, who had always had to rely on elegant clothes and personal style rather than looks, took a polished finish more seriously than most.

Despite their joint adoration of Asquith, both women went about pleasing him in entirely different ways. Where Margot's efforts on her husband's behalf went into trying to promote him and his interests, Violet would focus on those small attentions that made his life pleasanter, such as a novel for him to read in the train.

Margot, who wanted a happy family life, felt she could hardly complain to this devoted father about his daughter's loving attentiveness without sounding either unreasonable or shrewish. If Margot were temporarily absent – as when she planned a health holiday in the south of France – Violet would go with him to Archerfield, a beautiful Adam house in Scotland about twenty miles from Edinburgh and North Berwick, lent to Margot by her brother Frank after the death of their father. Here Violet would eat the hearty breakfast that the housekeeper had prepared for their arrival, and in fine weather they would play golf on the excellent and famous North Berwick links that stretched down to the sea (the course had been described by *Country Life* as 'the best private golf course in the world').

When London was afflicted with one of its regular, terrible 'pea-souper' fogs, Margot and the children took refuge in Archerfield – for anyone with a cough the London fogs, weighted with dirt, soot and coal dust, were a serious bar to recovery. Their full, choking horror was recorded by John James Heath. As a little boy, one day he was out walking in London with his father when one of the worst pea-soupers closed down. 'Street lights appeared little more than a murky pinkish haze. Horses and cabs jangled by, their lights doing nothing to guide their way. The few motor cars daring to traverse the roadway were blowing their horns to make their presence known.

'As we walked on, I became aware of a thick choking feeling in my chest. Gradually the atmosphere was getting thicker and thicker, I looked up at Dad. He was fading from sight, I could hear his voice but his face I could not see. He gripped my hand more tightly but I could see little beyond his elbow. I could hear people shuffling by but they were formless and shadowy. The heavy blanketed silence was all the more evident when I noticed the lack of human voices. That same silence was however frequently broken by gasping coughs and clearing of throats. I became conscious of a clinging coldness and a numbness in my limbs; a feeling like drowning as the air became too thick to breathe. I gripped Dad's hand even tighter; neither of us spoke.'

Thus when Asquith wrote that January, 'We have thick fogs here every other day. I am writing now (2.30 p.m.) by electric light, with yellow darkness outside,' both he and Margot were delighted that she had taken the children to the purer air of Scotland. Violet, who had as usual seized every chance to be on her own with her father, stayed in Downing Street. This time, however, her tenaciousness rebounded: she was so badly affected that she had to be dispatched to St Moritz to recover.

Normally, Violet's tactics were effective. She would encourage her father to join her and her friends, to laugh and joke and play bridge with them, treating him as one of themselves in a way Asquith found highly flattering and enjoyable. It may not have been done consciously but it had the effect of keeping him away from Margot – and of preventing her from seeing the beginnings of a folly that would turn into an obsession.

Part of the trouble was that the two women were incompatible characters – each was irritated by and jealous of the other. Violet, clever, graceful, cool, charming, logical, could not empathise with Margot's intuitive stabs at life, calling the Asquith reserve into play so successfully that Margot, who was very responsive to affection, felt that Violet seldom showed any and probably rather despised her. 'I can't do anything with her because she thinks I am not clever enough about life,' mourned Margot.

To Margot, it must have seemed at the time the classic situation of the stepmother with a stepdaughter so jealously guarding her own access to a beloved parent that she was forced into second place. The truth – that she was being replaced as confidante by a much younger woman – would come as a shock that was profound, humiliating and devastating.

SEVEN

Asquith and Margot had met when they sat next to each other at a dinner party in the House of Commons in March 1891 – Asquith and his friend and fellow barrister Richard Haldane used to entertain together frequently at the Savoy Hotel or the House of Commons. Asquith, then aged thirty-nine, was instantly taken with the twenty-seven-year-old Margot. After dinner, they strolled together on the terrace and Asquith, fending off everyone else, guided her to the darkest corner where, as Margot wrote in her diary, 'we gazed into the river and talked far into the night'.

'I was deeply impressed by his conversation and his clear Cromwellian face,' she recorded of her first meeting with this stocky, blue-eyed figure (though her judgement of him as exceptional did not prevent her noticing that he was unfashionably dressed). It was an apt description. Asquith's mind was concise, ordered and armoured against most eventualities, and he was upright and honourable to an almost Puritan degree: although the friendship developed quickly, neither would have dreamed of embarking on an affair, though later he told a mutual friend that when he, a married man with five children, had first met her, 'Margot took possession of me . . . The passion which comes, I suppose, to everyone once in life, visited and conquered me.'

Soon Margot was asking Asquith to her father's house at 40 Grosvenor Square. Asquith, a robust, full-blooded man who had hitherto led a life that alternated between quiet domesticity and work, took at once to this exciting new milieu of excellent food and wine, intimate political gossip of a high order, pretty women, clever men and sophisticated conversation. For him Grosvenor Square was the gateway into a wider world – one where decisions that influenced thousands could be taken in seemingly casual conversations or where an ambassador might unbutton himself to a trusted opposite number over the after-dinner port.

Although Margot had discounted his wife in this friendship, she was careful to abide by the conventions. 'I do hope, Mrs Asquith, you have not minded your husband dining here without you,' she said to Helen Asquith the first time her husband brought her to Grosvenor Square. 'But I rather gathered that Hampstead is too far away for him to get back to you from the House of Commons.* You must always let me know and come with him whenever it suits you.' Once, but only once, she was able to persuade both Asquiths to come with her to Taplow Court, home of Lord and Lady Desborough, for one of their weekend house parties.

For Helen preferred life at home in the midst of her family and discussion of their family doings to going out. 'She is more wrapped up in her children than any woman I know,' Asquith told Frances Horner, then his closest woman friend. Or as Margot put it: 'She lives in Hampstead and has no clothes.' With Mayfair and Belgravia as London's social heartlands and dining out an almost nightly ritual, this was an effective shorthand for describing a social non-starter.

This acceptance by Helen that while her husband might be cut out for great things, not to speak of a more dashing social life, she did not care to join him meant that there was no barrier to the growing friendship and closeness between Margot and H.H.

Margot, however, was becoming aware that the current between them held, on Asquith's side, deeper feelings than simple friendship – feelings that never could or would be acknowledged by this faithfully married man. The situation suited her: although his friendship was becoming a vital part of her life, she was not remotely in love with him.

Then, on 11 September 1891, everything changed. Helen died of typhoid while on holiday with the Asquith children on the Isle of Arran. A single dash marks Asquith's diary for that day.

Asquith wasted no time in laying siege to Margot. His courtship of her brought Margot abruptly to the central dilemma in her romantic life: she was attracted by men who were good-looking, high-spirited, brave and loved the 'outdoor' life as she did – the

---

* Hampstead is roughly four miles from Grosvenor Square and all transport was then of course horse-drawn.

sportsmen she met out hunting or in shooting parties – but who did not satisfy the intellectual side of her nature, with its intense search for knowledge. She was equally drawn to clever men of affairs whose intellectual vigour and clarity of thought she admired deeply and whose minds were so well furnished that she knew a lifetime of interest would lie ahead – but she seldom found them physically attractive.

But the years were passing and none of the suitors who had pursued her had come near to luring her into marriage, though Margot's powers of attraction seemed undimmed. When she was twenty-six her brother-in-law Alfred Lyttelton, while on one of his numerous visits to Glen, wrote to a friend: 'Swain after swain comes, pays his court, sighs, goes, and sends presents, leaving us all wondering . . .'

Margot was now so well known, and the power of her personality so famous, that there was much speculation in the press about whom she would marry. She had been talked about from the start and her behaviour had often made news. As a debutante, she had persuaded her father to buy her the best horse money could buy, and on this beautiful animal – a bright bay with black points – wearing a perfectly tailored habit, she rode in Rotten Row every morning. It was the time of the beauties: people would stand on chairs in the park to see them pass, shops put their photographs in their windows. Soon Margot, perfectly turned out and an exquisite rider, was also one of the sights. At one house party she danced a 'furious cancan' on the landing as they all went up to bed. It is difficult to think of any other young Victorian woman who would have been able to dance, or who would have dared to perform, this risqué dance in mixed company as a goodnight entertainment – unchaperoned as usual.

Her name was linked with numerous eligible men, many well known in the political world. She had come nearest to marriage with Alfred (later Lord) Milner, a shy and sensitive man of thirty-eight, who had never been attracted to a woman before (not as unusual as it sounds in that day and age, with colonial service taking many men away from female company for years). Although perfectly at ease in the company of men, especially clever men, women were to him almost a different species; he was easily embarrassed and any rebuff would send him curling back into his shell.

Margot, by contrast, wore her emotions on her sleeve, often

discussed them with her friends and, as did her fellow Souls, wrote letters in extravagant, highly romanticised terms that usually meant little beyond a genuine liking. When she sent him a lock of her hair, and a book with a poem written in her own hand on the flyleaf, he must have thought she was in love with him. And when he asked if he could dedicate his latest book to her this was, in his terms, a declaration of intent. When he joined Margot and her mother Emma in Egypt for a holiday, with Emma's very clear approval, he thought his chance had come.

One marvellous evening, as the hot daylight was fading, they rode together near the Pyramids (then some way outside Cairo). It could have been a scene out of a romantic novel: the glamorous setting, the couple on two beautiful Arab horses, Margot in a tight white jacket that showed off her slight but excellent figure, the warm air, the illimitable vista of the desert. Milner clearly decided to seize the moment. Stopping his horse, he dismounted, lifted Margot off her Arab mare, kissed her passionately and proposed to her.

She was not as overwhelmed as he had hoped she would be. The kiss had shaken her and she temporised. She was not sure that she wanted to marry him – but she did not want to lose him. She wrote to him warmly, then a few days later, on the way home, she wrote gently rebuffing him.

By now Asquith was open in his pursuit of her. 'You tell me not to stop loving you,' he wrote, 'as if you thought I had done or would or could do.' For him it was the start of two years of alternating hope and shattering disappointment as when, on the day before he left for his constituency to fight the 1892 general election, Margot told him that she would definitely never marry him. It brought an anguished response from Asquith: 'Upon my knees, which I bend too rarely to God, I implore you to think twice and thrice before you shut the door . . . for your love is life, and its loss black despair.' He was to go through many such miserable moments as Margot blew first warm and then icy cold. 'O! Margot – love of my life – if you had the least idea how I love you . . .' he wrote in the middle of the election.

It was, in those days, unthinkable that a woman who could, should not marry. Girls from Margot's background were sheltered and protected almost as if growing up in a seraglio, with female independence unknown. They passed from the care of a father to that of a husband or, if they remained unmarried – the worst fate that could befall – lived as a less-regarded family member in the house of parents or brother. Thus, as the only 'career' open to a woman was marriage, the acquisition of a husband was vital. Even Margot, unconventional though she was, realised this.

She slowly came to an anguished decision. In her diary, signalling the path she must already have subconsciously chosen, she wrote mournfully: 'I feel condemned to marry the best man I know.' She told her 'oldest and most treasured' friend, George Curzon, of Asquith's courtship and her romance with the attractive Evan Charteris. Curzon told her to take Asquith. 'The latter [Charteris] gives her the élan and fascination of youth, looks and physical charm, things that will last a maximum of ten years,' Curzon wrote to a friend. 'The other will give her devotion, strength, influence, a great position, things that last and grow. Therefore I said take him, for though you will lose the fugitive you will gain the permanent.'

Above all she recalled her feelings for the charismatic Peter Flower and the magnetic attraction between them. The strongest bond of all was the physical attraction. She told one friend:[*] 'I slept with him every night – every night of my life – everything except the thing itself.' Of him she wrote mournfully: 'I know that I shall never again be in love, never again feel the thrill that praise, blame or kisses have had for me nor the intoxicating excitement of provoking the very passion that one chides, the same reckless challenge, the same shy scruples.'

Asquith's pursuit of Margot was greatly disapproved of by some of his friends. When the novel *Dodo*, by E.F. Benson,[†] came out in 1893, its eponymous heroine's personality modelled on the more frivolous and superficial aspects of Margot's, Asquith was greeted one day by Lord Rosebery with the words: 'My dear Asquith, I advise you to read *Dodo* – there is a great deal of truth in it.' It was true that the flamboyant Dodo, who like Margot cut a swathe through London Society, also had Margot's chic, frankness and wit – 'It's all very well to talk of love in a cottage but just wait till the chimney begins to smoke' – but she was depicted as selfish,

[*] To Florrie Bridges; from Cynthia Asquith's diary of 5 November 1916.
[†] The son of the Archbishop of Canterbury.

vain, incurably self-centred and relentlessly frivolous. What Asquith thought of this advice was shown by his reaction when he found the book left prominently by his bed when staying with a friend: he picked it up and hurled it straight out of the window.

'She does not love me, at least not in the way I love her,' he wrote to a friend. 'Her passion long since went elsewhere; and whomever she marries her husband will have to win his way. I am under no illusions but I love her, and my love for her is the best thing in my life.' But when he held her in his arms her diary wails that her heart felt leaden; after he had gone, she recorded, 'the fearful struggle between what I <u>know</u> to be great and good and above all passionately devoted <u>to me</u> and what I am equally sure attracts me . . . All the passion and concentrated devotion in the world does not make up for the thrill of light that fills one's soul at the touch of what one loves.'

Eventually she agreed to marry him. Joyfully and immediately, he dashed off a note to Grosvenor Square: 'Almost for the first time in my life I feel as if I could not distinguish dreams from realities. The thing has come about which I have most longed for, waited for, prayed for, willed as I never did with any other aim or object in my life.' But the mutual attraction between her and Evan remained so strong that a few weeks later they were told to leave St Paul's Cathedral by a verger when they were discovered canoodling in a dark corner at the start of matins – something unimaginable with Asquith.

Her friends were discouraging about her decision to marry. 'In their delight at my parting from Peter [Flower],' she wrote, they 'had missed no opportunity of bringing Henry and me together [but they] were overcome with anxiety that so famous a man as the Home Secretary should contemplate marrying so frivolous a person as myself – and I was cautioned – by all but Arthur Balfour, Jowett, George Curzon, George Pembroke, St John Midleton, Lady Manners, Mr Gladstone and my sister Charty – to give up any such notion. I was told that I was not marrying Henry but his five children, and that I had not the discipline, education, or selflessness to take such a hazard. I was well aware that what they said was true.'

Nor was the proposed match viewed enthusiastically in the hidebound circles of the Court. Asquith, unfamiliar with Court etiquette, wrote to ask Queen Victoria's Private Secretary, Sir Henry Ponsonby, whether he need seek royal consent to the marriage. The Queen noted grimly on the back of his letter: 'How curious . . . that *he* should ask if my consent is required to his marriage. If this *was* required the Queen wd not give it as she thinks *she* is most unfit for a C. Minister's wife. V.R.I.'

Finally, on 4 April 1894, their engagement was announced. The prospect of an imminent physical relationship with a man for whom she felt no flicker of attraction filled Margot with despair. Her diary of that time is full of agonised notes: 'I must not be a fool and think the end of the world has come because I am engaged to be married'; 'The strain even to be decently civil when I saw Henry made my knees perspire'; 'Everything is easy when one is in love and nothing comes without effort if one is not,' and 'I find myself constantly wishing I were dead'.

It was the wedding of the year: the fabulous Miss Tennant was giving up her single status to become the wife of the man whom the whole political world thought would become Prime Minister, a marriage that seemed a fitting crown to her dazzling single life. Yet as she emerged from her father's house to an admiring throng so deep that she was made a quarter of an hour late at the church, only Margot knew that the chain round her neck was from Evan Charteris, and the lock of hair in the little black velvet heart hanging from it had been cut from Peter Flower's head. Four past and future prime ministers – Gladstone, Rosebery (Gladstone had resigned that March after differences with his Cabinet), Balfour and the bridegroom – signed the register at St George's, Hanover Square, where they were married on 10 May 1894. Here the crowds outside were even thicker, so that driving the bridal couple to the reception at 40 Grosvenor Square was almost impossible.

At first everything pointed to disaster, with Margot appearing to feel that she had made a terrible mistake. At the wedding reception she hid under the stairs in tears, where she was comforted by Curzon and Balfour. On their wedding night, waiting for Asquith in their bedroom, she 'thought with a certain lingering of how Peter and Evan when they had said goodnight to me in past days of delicious love-making had noticed and admired my nightgown and the general externals of my hair and appearance . . . I must not look back. I wondered calmly if I would be good enough to go through with the undertaking of marriage calmly and without too much effort.'

When Asquith, in an Indian dressing gown, got into bed with her, 'he put his arms round me and I lay very tired with my head on his shoulder and felt him shudder under my more restrained embrace. I lay quite still and silent and then I said: "I think we will go to sleep. I will put out the candle."' She put out the only light, a candle, and Asquith, accepting this postponement of married life, kissed her hands and hair, 'and we retired to opposite sides of the bed ... He breathed deeply and I felt an immense dreariness mixed with great gratitude to him for his fine control and understanding.'

As a description of someone repelled by the idea of a lifetime of physical intimacy with a person to whom she was not attracted, little could be more telling. Fortunately this sexual revulsion did not last: many years later Margot was to write, 'No woman ever had such passion, sympathy, tenderness and fun with her husband as I've had.' At the time, she was determined to put the dangerous aspects of the past out of her mind: one of her first acts of married life in their beautiful eighteenth-century house in Cavendish Square was to burn hundreds of the letters she had received from other men – some had written to her daily. The only ones saved from the bonfire were those from Peter Flower and Evan Charteris. 'There are too many and they are so beautiful – such words of love ...'

Learning to call Asquith 'Henry' (she did not like the name 'Herbert', by which he had been known to his wife and intimate friends) rather than 'Mr Asquith' had been the next step, then came meeting his children. It was her first encounter with the impenetrable Asquith reserve, reinforced, unsurprisingly, with a natural suspicion of this dragonfly stranger who was to take their mother's place.

She could have been describing the spirit that created the Souls when she wrote: 'Tennants believed in appealing to the hearts of men, firing their imagination and penetrating and vivifying their inmost lives ... The Asquiths – without mental flurry and with perfect self-mastery – believed in the free application of intellect to every human emotion: no event could have given heightened expression to their feelings. Shy, self-engaged, critical and controversial, nothing surprised them and nothing upset them ... They rarely looked at you and never got up when anyone came into the room. If you had appeared downstairs in a ball-dress or a bathing gown they would not have observed it and would certainly never have commented upon it if they had.'

But she was determined – not to be a mother to them but to try and provide the comfort and affection of a close and loving relation. As she put it in a charming letter to the eldest boy, Raymond, 'I only want to say one thing. You must not think that I could <u>imagine</u> even a possibility of filling your mother's (and my friend's) place. I only ask you to let me be your companion . . . if need be your helpmate. There is room for everyone in life if they have the power to love.'

The promise to be the children's helpmate was most often to be fulfilled financially: Margot was both rich and generous. Less tangible was another benefit: through Margot, to whom all doors had been open since her 'Soul' days, whose friends were writers and intellectuals as well as aristocrats, the Asquith children, from middle-class, professional stock, were enabled to lead a social life to which they could otherwise not have aspired.

When the doctors had given their uncompromising verdict after Margot's last, dangerous pregnancy in 1907 that her bedroom door must remain closed to her husband, Asquith was a vigorous man of only fifty-five, in excellent health, who loved his wife deeply and to whom sex was important. To be told that his marriage bed was no longer open to him at a time when its comforts could have done much to alleviate the unavoidable strains of a high office in politics must have been a bitter deprivation. It says much for the love both felt for each other that for a number of years the closeness and confidence they shared was untouched.

It was not, of course, the end of the story. Asquith's need for sex did not disappear but expressed itself by touching and fondling, or attempting to fondle, a nearby attractive woman with anything from a clasp of the arm or a grasp of the knee to an attempted kiss. In the family and among intimates this was an unspoken secret: in Cynthia Asquith's diary, for example, references to such behaviour are inked out. Those who knew him before and during his marriage testify to endless examples of what would today be called 'inappropriate touching' – if the word had been invented then he would have been known as a groper – and he had a penchant for peering down 'Pennsylvania Avenue', as a woman's cleavage was then known.

For Margot, for whom sex with her husband had been a process of adjustment rather than passionate attraction, the cessation of marital relations was no such deprivation. Emotionally and cerebrally, she remained as closely tied to him as ever while understanding – with a touch of guilt – his enjoyment of feminine company and therefore viewing with indulgence what she called his 'little harem', the five or six pretty and clever young women by whom he loved to be surrounded. One of them would soon not merit this tolerance.

From 1907 Venetia Stanley, as Violet's closest friend, had been one of the Downing Street intimates. Venetia, tall, dark and handsome rather than pretty – her contemporaries found her looks rather masculine – was the youngest of the seven children of Lord and Lady Stanley of Alderley and Sheffield, one of Britain's oldest aristocratic families. She was highly intelligent – she steeped herself in the classics and modern literature – and indifferent to convention (her father was outspoken, caustic, radical and a freethinker).

Her home, Alderley Hall, was a huge grey stone house in Cheshire, facing north over its rolling deer park. Here visitors came and went constantly and often there were house parties of twenty or more. Sometimes these were alarmed by two of the menagerie of animals kept by Venetia: a monkey called Fluto that would lie in wait on the top of bookcases or pelmets and drop on unwary passers-by, and Lancelot the bear cub that roamed the grounds, banged on doors and sometimes lumbered into the kitchen in search of food (Venetia was eventually ordered by her father to get rid of it to a zoo).

Along with a number of other young men and women, largely the children of the 'Souls', she was a member of what became known as 'the Coterie' – or to those who disliked what they stood for, 'the Corrupt Coterie'. They smoked, drank – in an age when most young women drank little if at all – and took drugs, then easily obtainable over the counter, and largely considered themselves free from the normal constraints of behaviour.

Raymond Asquith, tall, physically attractive, with grey eyes and auburn-brown hair of a colour best described as bronze, was the undoubted male leader of this gilded band. 'Whatever Raymond thought and did was followed by the other young Olympians,' wrote Lady Ottoline Morrell, wife of the MP Philip Morrell, describing 'the armour of sceptical cleverness that had been hardened and polished by Oxford and by the smart set in London who flattered and admired him'.

One of these was Lady Diana Manners, daughter of the Duchess of Rutland (much later, it emerged that this child of Violet Rutland had in fact been fathered by Harry Cust, not the Duke). Diana was the beauty of the age, courted by all the young men, a leading member of the Coterie, avid for notice and perfectly prepared to be outrageous. The newspapers loved her. 'Lady Diana Manners came and plumped herself down next to me at supper and behaved as if she was eating in a pigsty,' wrote Edward Cazalet, a Cambridge undergraduate invited to most of the smartest dances. '[She] took six plovers' eggs, messed about with them on her plate, and stirred her champagne with her fork! . . . most peculiar!'

Others of the Coterie were less flamboyant but most, thanks to the intellectual standards of their parents, had an independent cast of mind, although being a 'Soul' child brought with it expectations that could weigh heavily. 'I must frankly confess that the afterglow of the tradition of the Souls somewhat clouded my very early youth,' Violet Asquith was to write many years later (in October 1947, in *The Listener*). 'For we were constantly told by my stepmother . . . how lamentably we fell short of all their standards – in wit, in point, in intellectual ambition, in conversational skill and social competence, yes, even in our after-dinner games.'

This did not stop Violet and Venetia, who had met in their debutante years, forming an instant bond, an affection that was close and intense, with a faint subtext of lesbianism – even accounting for the fashion for expressing oneself extravagantly that they might have inherited from their 'Soul' parents, these phrases breathing devotion could easily have been written by a lover. Of the two, Violet was the star; in the circles in which Venetia was born and moved plenty of other girls, like herself, had fathers who were Peers but to be the daughter of a prime minister lent an added lustre. Margot called Venetia 'Violet's squaw', writing in her diary that 'Violet is much more refined and has done a lot for Venetia but Venetia's slavish love, encouraging and feeding Violet's natural egotism has been very bad for Violet. They are both without reverence of any sort; natural mockers and materialistic.'

But the friendship was close and genuine. 'Oh my darlingest, I could not possibly give you any idea of how terribly I want you,' wrote Venetia to Violet early in their friendship. 'I suppose whenever I had gone after being so much with you I should have found it quite crushingly drear and terrible ... I can think of nothing but you and at every instant wonder what you can be doing and whether you are having fun and also whether there is even an instant when you think it would be rather fun if I were there.'

'Goodbye darling,' wrote Violet on 27 July 1907, from 20 Cavendish Square. 'I wish you weren't gone. When I see you again it will be in air and peace and joy – how glorious to think of. I feel momentarily in utter collapse of spirit from balls and tears and lashers but Wed. is coming and the end of all tension. Write to me very often and don't stop loving me. Yr. V.'

'I think about you incessantly,' wrote Venetia from Penrhos, the Sheffield house on Anglesey. 'Your two letters have been the only good moments in this last most tedious week. I read them over and over again ... The thought of having you here shines out radiantly ... I think of you all day and try hard to imagine what you are doing. You will find me very exacting and unreasonable but if you only knew how an envelope changes my day. Darling, I love you.'

Venetia responded in similar, quasi-amorous vein: 'My most beloved I simply can't give you the faintest, foggiest notion of what a huge difference the arrival of your letter this afternoon made ... I can't bear to think that it will be more than a month before I see you again.' One letter concluded: 'I do want you so, SO much. Your V.'

They poured out secrets to each other, discussing 'dentists' (tête-à-tête assignations, often secret), men, books, politics, parties and their social round. But Violet did not appear to notice – and certainly did not comment on – the fact that more and more frequently Venetia became one of any party that accompanied Asquith. These drives, walks or lunches in company did not disturb Margot, who had a busy life of her own and was well aware of her husband's predilection for the company of the young. Her focus was much more on Violet's steady interposing of herself between Margot and her husband. Asquith was well known to enjoy the company of pretty young women. As Diana Manners, one of the group of whom he was especially fond, pointed out: 'Mr Asquith was interested in his daughter's friends and I was one.'

Venetia had also become friends with Edwin Montagu, an even more constant habitué of Downing Street. She would often ask him to stay. 'My dear Mr Montagu, Could you come and stay at Penrhos on Friday July 14, or could you get away on Wednesday and come for the Prince of Wales' Investiture at Caernarvon?' runs one of the notes in her small, rather masculine hand. 'The Prime and Violet are coming . . . I know it's fearfully far for such a short time but it would be very nice if you could come. Yrs Venetia Stanley.'

Often he was there when only she and her family were at Alderley; frequently she would send for him to lunch or dinner with her in London; often she told him, when he was unable to come, that she was 'sad'.

The previous year, 1911, Montagu's father, Lord Swaythling, had died, leaving Montagu a rich man with an annual income of £10,000 – subject to one proviso. The terms of his father's will stipulated that he married only a woman of the Jewish faith. Montagu, who knew of his father's fierce determination that his son should not marry 'outside', had already unenthusiastically proposed to a cousin, by whom he had been firmly rejected. Although attracted by Venetia, as he never thought of forfeiting his new fortune his flirtatious friendship with her remained unchanged for some time.

But his feelings had gradually grown warmer. By October 1911 the formal 'Dear Miss Stanley' had given way to 'My dear Venetia (I have somehow slipped into addressing you by the most beautiful name in the world, which happens to be yours) – if you dislike it you will of course some time or other say so (please don't) – it is I suppose because I think of you thusly).' He had begun to hint at this without crossing the boundary line of friendship. 'I *was* disgusted not to see you last night. I went out to my usual solitary dinner at the Reform and returned just after you left. I loathe to think of you in London for a whole week and not to be able to see you at all!'

At the end of December 1911, when staying at Archerfield with the Asquith family, Montagu had written: 'I want you now, very much indeed. That is literally true.' But afraid, perhaps, of having said too much, he allowed a lighter note to creep in, adding: 'But there is a more urgent negative quality which you possess that makes my longing for you more intense. It is that you don't play golf. I am rather lonely! Not that I'm not enjoying myself hugely but I would enjoy company for my solitary walks to the sea while everybody else plays holes and talks about them. It's a good party, the Prime as you say in very best form (but getting oh so venerable . . .).'

Asquith, venerable or not, would also have wished for her company. Both were now beginning their courtship of this striking woman, now twenty-four, an age when the need for marriage must have begun to obtrude itself on her thoughts – though not, as she had indicated, to Montagu. So she was able comfortably to ignore phrases like 'I want you more' in the letters he now regularly wrote to her, and to which she replied in bland conversational terms; and to allow him to call her 'Venetia' while replying to 'Dear Mr Montagu'. The trouble was that she did not – to put it in modern terms – fancy him.

Asquith, however, began to claim more of Venetia's time. Often they took drives in his new Napier on Friday afternoons to the more rural parts of London – Richmond, Roehampton or Hampstead. They would meet from time to time at luncheon or dinner parties. Sometimes he would call on her in the early evening at her parents' house in Mansfield Street and she would often visit the Asquiths in Downing Street – they had let their house in Cavendish Square to Lady Cunard. (Maud Cunard had been seen by a workman on a ladder in bed with the conductor Thomas Beecham early one morning at her husband Sir Bache's Leicestershire house, Nevill Holt, and had fled to London to lead a single life.)

By early January 1912 Asquith's focus on Venetia had become so obvious that Margot had begun to think that it was more than simple predilection. When he and Montagu together left for a holiday in Sicily she wept, writing in her diary that she was 'jealous of those who had gone with him'. She certainly did not mean Montagu: as usual jumping to an intuitive conclusion (and, as quite often, a correct one), she guessed that he would invite Venetia and Violet to join them. Violet, she knew, was always trying to turn her father's attention away from Margot and towards herself; and so close were she and Venetia that they were known as 'the Inseparables'. Their friendship was in any case the perfect cover for the growing intimacy between Asquith and his daughter's friend.

Margot's surmise was correct: Asquith had persuaded Venetia to leave a skiing trip in Switzerland to come with Violet to join him and Montagu in Sicily. Their arrival was slightly delayed owing to Violet's tonsillitis and before they arrived Asquith had written reassuringly to Margot: 'the children are beautiful, but I haven't seen one woman at whom one would be tempted to look twice'.

Once Venetia was there, it was different: it was during these holiday weeks amid the ancient Greek temples, lavender and orange
groves of that beautiful island, lying on the grass soaking up the
sun in the Greek theatre in Taormina, playing auction bridge in
the evenings in an intimate foursome, driving around the ruins of
Messina* by moonlight, that the relationship between the fifty-nine-
year-old Prime Minister and the twenty-four-year-old Venetia began
to develop into something more than friendship, although looking
back on it, Asquith wrote merely: 'The first stage of our intimacy (in
which there was not a touch of romance and hardly of sentiment)
came to its climax when I went to Sicily with Montagu . . . at the
beginning . . . of 1912. Violet and Venetia joined us there and we
had together one of the most interesting and delightful fortnights
in all our lives.'

What he was well aware of, no doubt with a touch of guilt, was
how unhappy Margot was; and from Taormina he wrote to reassure her. 'Why should you think that anything you have written has
"alienated" me? It could not, even for a moment, and even tho' I
thought some things you said (or suggested) a little less than just,
I love you always wherever I am; and you well know no-one ever
does or ever could take your place.' He ended his letter, 'ever with
all my heart your own'.

The party returned on 1 February, after a calm and moonlit crossing, to run straight into a mêlée of waiting suffragettes at Charing
Cross – cheerfully Asquith, implacably opposed to their tactics, told
Margot that 'Violet had the satisfaction of crunching the fingers of
one of the hussies'.

A few weeks after their return Asquith realised that he was no
longer simply attracted to Venetia and fond of her, he was in love
with her. The Asquiths had been lent a house at the edge of the New
Forest, near Lymington, and Venetia was a weekend guest there. On
Sunday morning, while the others were out in the garden, Asquith
and Venetia were sitting in the dining room chatting and laughing in
their usual way when, he wrote: 'in a single instant, without premo-
nition on my part or any challenge on hers, the scales dropped from
my eyes; the familiar features and smile and gestures and words
assumed an absolutely new perspective; what had been completely

* In December 1908 an earthquake had shattered the town.

hidden from me was in a flash half-revealed, and I dimly felt, hardly knowing, not at all understanding it, that I had come to a turning point in my life'. He was then sixty, she twenty-five.

For Asquith it was a revelation; from then on, Venetia moved from being a charming but reasonably peripheral figure to the centre of his life.

EIGHT

For Easter 1912 the Asquiths escaped to Ewelme Down,[*] in Oxfordshire, a house lent them by a friend, Frank Lawson. As Margot
immediately realised, at forty-eight she was alone with her husband
and their two children for only the second time in her married life.
But it was not the second honeymoon she had hoped for: Asquith
was working on the draft of his Home Rule speech, to be delivered
two days later, and both were suffering in health and, in Margot's
case, emotionally – the 'private misery' of which she wrote in her
diary was her first suspicions of her husband's feelings for Venetia.

With Margot, emotional traumas were invariably reflected physically. She had begun to sleep abominably, she was thin, ill with
colitis and exhausted. But when Asquith came into her bedroom
and, after asking how she was, sat down suddenly and said 'I don't
feel well', she was horrified and her own troubles fled from her
mind. 'This from him was like my saying I felt I was dying.'

She looked up to see him gazing at her and exhaustion written,
as she put it, like a railway map over his whole face. When she
sprang up and ran to him he told her that he had felt giddy for the
past three weeks. Next day she sent him to the doctor, who prescribed rest – the strain of the past few months, with the strikes,
attacks by the suffragettes, battles in Parliament, the tension over
the forthcoming Home Rule Bill and the management of his own
party, coupled with drinking too much, had all combined to attack
a constitution that was still robust. Fortunately, he took note of the
doctor's advice not just to rest but to drink less.

The Asquiths returned to London for the first reading of the
Home Rule Bill, when Asquith made a speech lasting one hour and

---

[*] Built two years earlier by the well-known architect Walter Cave, a friend of the
Asquiths.

fifty-seven minutes. 'I wish you'd been there,' wrote Montagu to Venetia. 'It was a great day. The Prime expounded with great vigour and often with a first class phrase. A really good Bill. It was delightful to find his voice was very strong and that he lasted without much effort for two hours . . .'

Afterwards, Asquith was reassured by the doctor that in his sixtieth year he had the arteries of a young man and that his blood pressure had dropped almost to normal. Margot's relief was such that her own health improved, although she was chagrined not to be invited with him to go to stay at Balmoral – the reason was that the King wished to discuss the Home Rule Bill with his First Minister in an informal setting and in complete confidence. In other words, it was a business meeting although, as a concession to the Prime Minister, a bridge table was arranged for after dinner. Otherwise, the visit was the opposite of everything Asquith enjoyed: inside, this baronial castle on the banks of the Dee was dark, draughty and cold – though whatever the temperature, women had to dine décolletée – with dark wood panelling, tartan decor, stags' heads on the walls and simple food and drink. As Asquith did not shoot, the excellent stalking passed him by.

His Home Rule speech was one to which he had given much thought. For, bad as the industrial troubles were at the beginning of 1912, they paled beside the burning question of Home Rule, which was proving so divisive that a civil war between Ulster and the rest of Ireland seemed more likely than any other kind.

The Liberals had been committed to Home Rule for Ireland since 1886, when Gladstone was converted to it and a Home Rule Bill introduced (Ireland had, after all, been a separate kingdom less than a hundred years earlier, until the passing of the Act of Union in 1800). This and a Home Rule Bill of 1893 were killed off by the House of Lords with their power of final veto. The Lords, largely Conservative, believed that decentralising control from London could be the first step towards a weakening of their own power.

With the Liberal landslide of 1906, Home Rule could have become law – except that it was not part of the Liberal Party's election platform (Asquith himself was lukewarm about it then). Indeed not all Liberals supported the idea, many viewing it as initiating a possible break-up of the United Kingdom, and it would inevitably have been again rejected by the Lords.

After the 1910 elections, which wiped out the Liberal majority in the House of Commons, the Liberals were dependent on the support of the Irish Nationalists and, to a lesser degree, Labour, to remain in power. Asquith quickly came to an understanding with John Redmond, leader of the Irish Nationalists, that if Redmond supported his move to break the power of the Lords he, Asquith, would then in return introduce a new Home Rule Bill.

When the Parliament Act of 1911 curbed the power of the House of Lords, allowing them only the chance to delay legislation, it was payback time. A third Home Rule Bill was tabled, scheduled if successful to become law in 1914. To achieve this, Asquith would need all his powers of irrefutable logic and persuasiveness to convince a divided House.

What bedevilled matters was that Ulster and the rest of Ireland were, in many respects, two separate nations, split along lines of race, origin and – most crucially – religion. The South was Celtic, native Irish and Catholic; Ulster people were of largely Scots extraction, descendants of immigrants who had arrived during the 'Plantation of Ulster' in the 1600s. They considered themselves entirely British and were not only Protestant but fiercely anti-Catholic. To them, as to many of their British supporters, the modicum of Irish independence proposed was not so much Home Rule as Rome Rule and in April 1912, in the Balmoral district of Belfast, 100,000 men and women demonstrated against it, under the largest Union Jack flag ever made until then (it measured forty-eight feet by twenty-five feet).

Their leader, Sir Edward Carson, had been supported on the platform by Andrew Bonar Law, the leader of the Opposition and son of an Ulsterman, who promised them, in a near-treasonable utterance, that if Ulster refused to accept the passing of the Home Rule Bill, they would not lack 'help from across the water'.

It seemed an insoluble problem and over the coming months goodwill, time and energy – the first in notably short supply – would be needed if it were to be successfully concluded. But the difficulties attendant on it did not prevent Asquith, newly aware that he was in love, writing to Venetia in terms that could still – just – be described as the friendship of an older man for a young woman whom he knew well and liked immensely. 'I missed you more than I can say,' ended a little note on 26 March. 'When shall I see you again?' and a few days later: 'I want to see you (& *must*) before you go . . . HHA'.

Opposition to the Home Rule Bill was furious and strident, with Ulster, fiercely British, adamantly refusing to become part of an independent Catholic South. In a rousing speech Bonar Law reminded the House that Ulstermen had said they would never accept the Bill's provisions – and that he believed them.

Only coercion, he said, could deliver all of Ireland into a Home Rule Parliament; only force – which would probably mean bloodshed – could divide Ulster from the union with Britain. Did the Government plan to hurl the full majesty and power of the law, supported by the bayonets of the British Army, against a million Ulstermen marching under the Union Jack and singing 'God Save the King'? As Bonar Law knew, it was an unanswerable question, and he sat down amidst cheers.

The Government was in a quandary. The Irish leader, John Redmond, demanded that the Home Rule Bill, giving Ireland its own parliament, should cover the whole of Ireland while Ulster, backed by the Conservative Opposition who wanted to defeat the Home Rule Bill, refused to become part of a united Ireland. Asquith, a believer in the soothing effects of the passage of time, hoped that between the tabling of the Bill in 1912 and its estimated passing into law in 1914 the Ulster Protestants would gradually drop their opposition.

It was a vain hope. From the start it was clear that Ulster was determined to remain independent of the South, if necessary forming her own provisional government. Ulstermen were equally prepared to defend their position by force – certain in the knowledge that no British government, let alone the peace-loving Liberals, would, or could possibly, physically attack part of the British Isles for wanting to remain British.

Four days after Asquith's speech in Parliament, and temporarily putting a stop to the intense rivalries and emotions roused by the Irish Question, was what became the most notorious maritime tragedy of the century – the sinking of the *Titanic*, the largest passenger steamship in the world, on her maiden voyage.

Billed as 'unsinkable', she had set sail from Southampton on 10 April 1912, with 2,224 passengers and crew. On 14 April, at 11.40 at night, she collided with an iceberg and sank two hours and forty minutes later. Only 712 people survived.

This fast, elegantly furnished, luxurious ship had attracted some of the best-known personalities of the Edwardian era – all, of course, travelling first-class. Among them were John Jacob Astor IV ('the richest man in America') and his bride Madeleine, returning from their Paris honeymoon; the pioneer of investigative journalism, social activist, and editor of London's *Review of Reviews* William T. Stead; millionaire industrialist Benjamin Guggenheim and his mistress; Wimbledon champion Karl Behr; film actress Dorothy Gibson; and Sir Cosmo and Lady Duff Gordon, better known as the highly successful and fashionable dressmaker Lucile.

The whole country was overwhelmed by the disaster and by the needless waste of life that came to light when many lifeboats were found to be half-empty. 'When we read of that challenging, luxurious ship at bay in the icefields and the captain sending his un-answered signal to the stars, we could not sit through dinner,' wrote Margot that night in her diary.

The packed memorial service for the *Titanic* in St Paul's Cathedral evoked overpowering emotions. After St Chrysostom's Liturgy ('Give rest, O Christ, to Thy servants with Thy saints'), sung by a male choir, came the Dead March with its roll of drums reverberating through the dome. One man dropped to the ground and several women had to be led out fainting. The last words of the service, from the hymn 'Eternal Father', were 'Oh hear us when we cry to Thee/for those in peril on the sea'.

The tragedy did not deflect passions over the Home Rule question. Families were riven by it and friendships broken. At least three of Asquith's own Cabinet – Churchill, the Chancellor Lloyd George and the Foreign Secretary Sir Edward Grey – were opposed to the Bill, and opposition in Ulster grew ever more bitter as the months passed.

As the year drew on, the suffragettes stepped up their activities. In June Margot, as ever totally protective of her husband, boxed the ears of one importunate lady in the resplendent setting of an India Office reception. At a Nottingham meeting, where both of them stayed with Sir Jesse Boot,* fear of assault by suffragettes was such

---

* Later the first Lord Trent, and the man who transformed the company set up by his father into a national chain of chemists.

that there was wire netting over the windows, the car and even the bath, largely to prevent injury or damage through the hurling of stones and bricks. Wilfrid Scawen Blunt, once a would-be lover of Margot's and invited to her Downing Street garden party that summer, wrote that 'of course, I did not go. Precautions have to be taken against the suffragettes, who come on these occasions to knock Asquith about.'

The following month two women were apprehended by a police constable outside the country house of Lewis Harcourt, one of the Cabinet's leading 'Antis' [against female suffrage], with materials to set the place on fire and a note which declared the intention 'to do something drastic'. Five days after this, on 18 July 1912, one suffragette, Mary Leigh, who had already been arrested nine times and spent over fifteen months in jail, hurled a hatchet into a carriage in which Asquith and Redmond were riding in Dublin – the first time a British prime minister had visited the city. She missed, and they were unhurt. She escaped and the same evening she and another girl tried to set fire to the Theatre Royal just after Asquith had left.

When the architect Edwin Lutyens went to stay with Lord Stamfordham, the King's Private Secretary, at Balmoral, where – as he wrote to his wife that September – he was 'met at Ballater by a royal carriage with two hired horses', he learned that on the previous night all the flags on the golf course had been destroyed 'and suffragette flags put in with mottoes on them. They evidently thought Asquith or Churchill was at the Castle. The men seemed amused and rather shocked at the cheek of doing it in the King's own garden but the womenkind are furious against their sisters! One woman has been turned out of the Ballater golf club for having accosted Asquith while he was playing.'

None of these problems, however, distracted Asquith from his pursuit of Venetia. 'I am going to lunch on Friday with Winston and Clementine,' he told her on 10 June. 'Winston said he would ask you, which I thought an excellent idea, as afterwards we might take the air in the new Napier. Do see that this comes off and if he fails through forgetfulness be bold and propose yourself.'

Winston Churchill, then aged thirty-eight, had recently been made First Lord of the Admiralty – Asquith had offered him the post in October 1911 when he was staying with him in Scotland. One evening, as they walked near the Firth of Forth in the twilight, two battleships, immense in the gathering gloom, glided into view. It was enough for Churchill. 'I accepted with alacrity,' he wrote afterwards.

A passionate romantic – he loved the poetry of Byron – Churchill was above all a doer. He had fought with the Bengal Lancers on the Indian Frontier, travelled along the Nile, fought in the South African War, where he had been captured, and escaped, over hundreds of miles of Boer territory. He had been a war correspondent and by the time he was twenty-five had written, as he put it, 'as many books as Moses'. Violet Asquith, who had been in love with him and was devastated when he married the beautiful Clementine Hozier in 1908, remained a great friend and his most ardent supporter.

As First Lord, he was immensely efficient and far-sighted ('He has a great belief in submarine warfare as the weapon of the future,' wrote Wilfrid Scawen Blunt after a long and convivial evening with him), throwing all his energies into his work, spending much of his time from then on in the Admiralty yacht *Enchantress* and inspecting every kind of naval establishment in Britain and the Mediterranean to check that the Navy was in a permanent state of preparedness.

Another lunch party was organised on 21 June, the day after which Churchill wrote to his wife, 'The naughty old sage [Asquith] took Venetia for a long motor drive in the country yesterday after Auction Bridge . . .' By July the drives had settled into a Friday routine ('I shall call for you tomorrow [Friday] about 3.30'), and later in the year: '. . . but what about the afternoon? Shall we go for a little spin, or will you come to Downing Street and have a talk? or shall I come to you? The whole of this catechism needs a detailed reply.'

Few other young women would have gone – or been allowed to go – on such frequent long, solitary drives with an older married man. But Venetia was strong-willed and unconventional, born with the social self-confidence of a rich aristocrat, a member of the free-thinking Coterie and, like most of her friends of a similar age, at twenty-five felt she had outgrown the need for chaperonage.

For younger women this rule was still firmly in place, recognised by both sexes alike. 'Our dance is on the 13th December, just a month hence. <u>Do</u> come to it if you possibly can. Let me know as soon as possible if you can come also if you want to bring a chaperone or use one of the available ones here,' wrote an admirer to the twenty-year-old Evie Davies, the daughter of a regular soldier stationed at Woolwich Arsenal. And again, a few weeks later, 'Look here! If my married sister comes would you be able to do a night show on Tuesday night instead of Wednesday? <u>Do</u> try and do this as it would be much more cheery than the afternoon.'

Even the more liberated just-twenty Lady Diana Manners was still forbidden to be alone with a man except by chance in the country. 'A married woman must bring me home from a ball. For walking and shopping and even driving in a taxi, a sister or a girl was protection enough. I could go to the Ritz but to no other London hotel.' The actress Ruth Draper (then in her late twenties) had been brought up never to pass gentlemen's clubs without lowering her eyes, even in a taxi.

The young, unmarried girl was sacrosanct; no man, unless he wished to face social ostracism, would allow himself to seduce a young, single girl of marriageable age. If a girl was 'ruined', she *was* ruined, with all prospects of a good marriage – perhaps any marriage – gone, and with it all that made life enjoyable for a woman; and the man who had ruined her was marked down as a cad.

Once married, however, and having presented her husband with an heir, and if possible a 'spare', if her husband was complaisant she was free to indulge in a clandestine affair. Of course, not everyone did, as many marriages were for love; equally, parents frequently urged their children into marriages made for dynastic reasons – as the Queen had done with the Prince of Wales – and here the temptation to stray was naturally greater.

Nor would most girls have known what it was they were being shielded from unless they had been enlightened by an older married sister or friend – no parent would have dreamed of discussing sex with a young unmarried daughter. Adelaide Stanley (Venetia's niece) talked of her mother's 'terrified shirking of all responsibility for imparting biological facts'. Sometimes this could prove almost catastrophic. 'When I think of the things I have never been told it's a wonder I am as I am,' lamented Evie in her diary that year. 'It's wrong and to think I should never have been told – it's awful . . . Nothing has ever been explained to me. How can any girl of spirit be expected to grow up properly? To think that all these months I have known nothing and in my blind ignorance and innocence have been living and trying to form my ideas of life and people.

'I have never been taught to love my body. The horror, the disgust, the struggling against it on finding out. The helplessness of it all. It seems as though the whole world has fallen away from under my feet. I understand nothing and nobody. I can't think one way or another. It means an entirely new adjustment of everything – my life, my ideas, my ideals, my judgements.'

Although without benefit of the chaperone – the requisite married woman – sexual intercourse was almost as tightly regulated among what were called the working classes. Girls were strictly brought up and young men knew exactly how far they could go – to be an unmarried mother meant shame and ignominy heaped on you and your child, and no decent man wanted to be the cause of that, although 'spooning' was considered normal between courting couples.

'I'm just longing to see you, Dolly dearest, for then we will cuddle close together and have a nice long spoon and a talk together for I have plenty to tell you and I shall have plenty of kisses from you, dearest, after so long a time,' wrote twenty-year-old Arthur Moore, the son of the night porter at the City Carlton Club, to his sweetheart Dolly Anderson. 'How fine it would be to cuddle together, our arms entwined, my lips pressed to yours in one long sweet kiss.' (The two were later married.)

NINE

The furore engendered by the tabling of the Home Rule Bill did not die down. Ulster's determination not to be swallowed up by a more independent Ireland grew steadily, led largely by Sir Edward Carson, a man of brilliance and boundless energy. On 28 September 1912 he was the first of almost half a million to sign the Ulster Covenant (immortalised in Kipling's poem 'Ulster') that bound its signatories to resist Home Rule.

The Home Rule Question dominated after-dinner conversation at Windsor Castle, where the Asquiths stayed the night in November. Margot had been talking to her friend Sir John Fortescue, the Castle's Librarian and Archivist, as they sat and smoked cigarettes 'on a back stair. However after a time he took me into a vast drawing room. The King came straight out of the smoking room's open doors and sat next to me in the bay window and we talked for an hour and ten minutes. I am truly fond of him but of course he has known me since he was a "middy"* so we talk without respect. He opened on H. Rule etc and all its horrors! And in a kind of voice as if it would never pass because <u>he</u> would prevent it.'

Margot, of course, opposed these views. 'I said to him: "You see sir you only see fashionable Tories and not very clever ones." "Not at all! I see them all. I'm devoted to my Prime Minister but he is making <u>a great mistake</u>."' The argument continued for a long time until eventually Margot concluded it by saying: 'It is me who have contradicted you and disagree with your views, who must ask forgiveness – but let us be quite open and simple on priorities or we shall have a formal dull friendship.' She rose and curtseyed and at

---

* George V had become a midshipman, the lowest officers' rank in the Royal Navy, in 1879, when he was just fifteen.

the same time the King stood up, 'to the great relief of all the party who jumped up and scattered to bed'.

At the same time, the suffragettes were introducing a new and unpopular tactic. On the evening of 26 November 1912 WSPU members poured acid, ink, tar and lampblack into pillar boxes in the City of London, the West End and many provincial cities, destroying thousand upon thousand of letters, documents and other correspondence – in Newcastle alone, 2,000 letters were destroyed or damaged. The evening was dark, the women – if seen – would simply have appeared to be posting a letter, so that not a single one was caught. Mrs Pankhurst, however, made it clear that the destruction was organised by the WSPU.

That December, two venturesome women tried to force their way through the double front doors of the house of the Home Secretary, Herbert Gladstone. They were spotted by Beb Asquith, who had been playing golf with Gladstone that afternoon; but before he could reach them one of them managed to head-butt Gladstone in the midriff. As Beb and Gladstone were describing the scene over dinner that night at Walmer Castle on the Kent coast,* there was a crash of broken glass as a large piece of granite was hurled through the window, mercifully missing Asquith but breaking a plate and sending a fountain of soup over the woman opposite him. Although there was a hue and cry, the two suffragettes escaped in a boat they had moored in the nearby canal, slipping away in the darkness while their pursuers searched the wood beside it.

Meanwhile, another emotional triangle was forming, again with Asquith as its pivot. In the summer of 1912, Venetia seemed to be encouraging Edwin Montagu (now Under-Secretary of State for India). She was allowing him to call her 'My dearest Venetia', to drop in phrases like, 'you knew how I longed for a letter from you and swore when it didn't come, if you knew how glad I am to get it, you would not have grudged writing it'. Her letters were short and impersonal, yet she was seeing him more frequently, and issuing more invitations to him than ever ('Are you doing anything

---

* Official residence of the Lord Warden of the Cinque Ports. Lord Brassey, the Warden and Liberal supporter of Asquith, allowed the Prime Minister to use it whenever he wanted. Originally built in Henry VIII's reign as part of a chain of coastal artillery defences, the Castle looked out over the Channel.

Thursday evening, will you dine here? Anyway let's do something either Saturday or Sunday if you do decide to throw over Lady Airedale').

Nor did she hesitate to rap him over the knuckles if she thought he was lacking in attentiveness. Once, when he apparently failed to answer a summons, she rebuked him crisply: 'I wonder what your reason is for completely ignoring invitations. I can think of several. First, that you have forgotten. Second, that you're too indolent, and third that you don't want to come either tomorrow or at a future date. If the third is the reason your method is to be recommended not for its civility but for its thoroughness, for I can promise you that in future you won't have to bother even to remember not to answer. VS.'

This combination of hands-off imperiousness and apparent pleasure in his company – and Montagu was charming, witty, clever and cultured – had the effect that by the end of July Montagu was trying to discuss marriage with her. It was unavailing; by 4 August she had turned him down, making it clear that her rejection was because she did not want to sleep with him since she found him sexually unattractive.

Montagu had no reason to keep his feelings for Venetia, and his pursuit of her, secret from Asquith, since he believed the Prime Minister was simply a friend who enjoyed her company – and indeed, may have imagined that Asquith, so fond of him, might further his own suit. But Asquith, who had previously regarded Montagu as out of any running where Venetia was concerned because of his Jewish faith, now seems to have become jealous, regarding Montagu as a competitor. It is from this period that he began referring to him to Venetia as 'the Assyrian' and calling attention to his Jewishness from time to time with phrases like 'the silken tents of Shem' as a synonym for Montagu's luxurious house at 24 Queen's Gate, its windows hung with silk curtains. 'I know (for he spent Monday night here),' he wrote on 14 August, 'that the Assyrian has been coming down among you like a wolf on the fold. Did the sheen of his spear dazzle your vision? And what happened? Tell me all about it.'

Montagu was not deterred by Venetia's refusal, pleading with her all August to reconsider his proposal. She had said she might accept him but only if their relationship could be what she called 'a compromise affair' – that is, friendship, but no sex; he, of course, did not want this but was still anxious to marry her; however often she rejected him, he kept coming back, pleading to see her before he left for India, for which he departed on 4 October.

Nevertheless, while he was away she wrote him long, chatty letters. 'I spent most of last week in London staying at Downing Street,' she told him in answer to one received from him just before he reached Bombay. 'I saw not very much of the P.M. Do you remember my saying how much he varied in his liking for me, and that sometimes he quite liked me and at others not at all, well this was one of the not at all times. He was horribly bored by my constant presence at breakfast, lunch and dinner. He seemed much better tho' and said his shoulder didn't hurt him at all and he was playing golf regularly. I was very glad to see the old boy again, he is quite one of my favourite people.'

Whether Venetia genuinely felt she was out of favour or whether her remark was meant to allay any suspicions Montagu might have as to her developing relationship with the Prime Minister is impossible to know. What is certain is that Margot was acutely aware of an intangible difference in the emotional atmosphere of No. 10; and this affected her own behaviour. 'My darling,' she scribbled in a pencil note to her husband as he was attending the Opening of Parliament on 30 December, 'do write just one line, quite short. You've made me so unhappy at having been sulky to you tonight. Forgive me.'

Asquith returned the same note, with his answer on it. 'Darling – Why should you be unhappy? I love you and only you. Your H.'

His reply was, as Margot had asked, brief – but hardly true. Venetia had asked him to stay, for the first time, at Alderley. For Asquith it was like visiting the promised land: happily he abandoned any thought of spending the time with his wife and young family. His visit took place from 3–5 January 1913. 'You don't need to be told how much I enjoyed my time with you,' he wrote afterwards. 'I purposely keep back, when we are together, so much more, I dare say, than you suspect.'

PART TWO

1913

TEN

On 2 January 1913 Margot took her sixteen-year-old daughter Elizabeth, along with her German governess, to stay for a few weeks in Switzerland, herself returning to Downing Street on 26 January. It was a Sunday and Asquith was away for the weekend, so she asked herself to dine with Lloyd George. 'He was delighted if I didn't mind a cold meal and a few men. Of course I liked a few men. I put on a teagown – blue tunic, black satin skirt – and walked into the next door house. It took me a little while to realise I was in the middle of a woman suffrage lot who had met to talk over a possible compromise.' (The suffragettes were stepping up their campaigns against property; and the antipathy of the public to the force-feeding of suffragette hunger strikers was embarrassing the Government. Many of the Liberals, as with this group, sympathised with women's desire for the vote.)

Nor would Margot have known of another aspect of her next-door neighbour's ménage that was almost exactly a mirror image of her own. That January, the Chancellor had finally managed to persuade Frances Stevenson – a young woman originally hired to tutor his daughter Megan during the summer holidays of 1911, aged a mere twenty-four to his fifty, an age gap similar to that between Asquith and Venetia – to become his mistress. Although Frances had found the charismatic Chancellor a fascinating personality from the start, and was delighted when he offered her work, it was not until a year later that they had admitted their feelings for each other.

Margaret Lloyd George, who had stood by her husband through several of his previous philanderings, accepting his robust denials of anything untoward, had no idea of his relationship with Frances – already more profound than any of his previous affairs. In any case, Margaret spent much of her time at the family home in Criccieth, north Wales, while two of Lloyd George's staff helped him and

Frances, now Lloyd George's personal secretary, conduct their clandestine affair. As Frances worked in Lloyd George's office, and was only admitted to No. 11 secretly, no one at No. 10 had any idea either.

The Government was beset on all fronts. Ulster's determination to resist the Government's policy of Home Rule was taking forceful shape. Three days before the third reading of the Bill Sir Edward Carson founded the Ulster Volunteer Force, which brought together several different loyalist militias to resist Home Rule. The Bill, passed by the House of Commons, then moved on to the House of Lords, which was against it almost to a man, rejecting it for a second time on 30 January 1913 by 326 votes to 69.

Although it seemed that at last female suffrage, which had been slowly gathering support, might be making progress, when the Conciliation Bill was reintroduced in 1912 it had been defeated on its second reading. A rumour had swept the House that Asquith would resign if it were passed, so many Liberals sympathetic to the cause instead voted against it.

A few days later, on 28 March, a letter several columns long from the distinguished bacteriologist Sir Almroth Wright, justly famous for his invention of the anti-typhoid injection, appeared in *The Times*. In it he denounced the whole idea of giving women the vote, based on what he described as their psychological instability. Think, he demanded of his readers, of 'the serious and long-continued mental disorders that develop in connection with the approaching extinction of a woman's reproductive function'. The mind of woman was always threatened with danger, he thundered, there were 'periodically recurring phases of hypersensitiveness, unreasonableness and loss of sense of proportion'. He concluded that peace would come again only when the present surplus of women (around 1.5 million) had gone abroad and found husbands there.

After this, furious letters poured in to *The Times*, the best being Clemmie Churchill's. 'After reading Sir Almroth Wright's able and weighty exposition of women as he knows them the question seems no longer to be "Should women have votes?" but "Ought women not to be abolished altogether?"'

Predictably, the suffragettes stepped up their campaigns. From then on, no holds were barred: street lamps were broken, keyholes stopped up with lead pellets, house numbers painted out, reservoirs polluted with dye, telegraph wires snipped with long-handled clippers, municipal flower beds wrecked, railway carriage cushions slashed and envelopes containing snuff and red pepper sent to every Cabinet minister. The glass of the Crown Jewel case in the Tower of London was smashed – the royal palaces were immediately closed to the public – thirteen pictures slashed in the Manchester Art Gallery, deckchairs thrown into the Serpentine and the refreshment pavilion in Kew Gardens burnt down.

The WSPU leader, Mrs Pankhurst, fearless and determined, now decided to strike at the heart of government, choosing as her target the Chancellor. Lloyd George had earlier supported her movement but when in government had done little to help – largely because he judged that, given the franchise, women would use it to vote Tory. To the suffragettes, this was betrayal.

A house was being built for Lloyd George by the wealthy Liberal Sir George Riddell, one of a number Sir George was donating as weekend retreats to prominent Liberals. This was Pinfold Manor at Walton-on-the-Hill. From Lloyd George's point of view, it had everything. Down the road was Walton Heath Golf Club, favoured by many politicians for its proximity to London, and nearby, in a cottage of her own, his secretary and mistress, Frances ('Pussy') Stevenson.

In February 1913, the police were notified of an explosion there at 6.10 a.m. Lloyd George himself was abroad at the time. The authorities soon discovered that, in the weeks leading up to the bombing incident, a number of women had at different times visited nearby Tadworth Village and Walton-on-the-Hill and made inquiries as to the visits of prominent politicians to the nearby Walton Heath golf course and the houses used by them for weekends; also that on the morning of the explosion a car, traceable by its number, had been heard to leave the vicinity of the house at about 4.30 a.m.

The explosion was caused by a five-pound tin of gunpowder, put in a bedroom on the first floor and ignited by a fuse that must have taken around two hours to burn down. The bedroom was wrecked inside and the exterior wall now bulged out about four inches. It was fortunate that not all the explosives detonated as, if they had, some of the workmen arriving on site would have been killed.

Mrs Pankhurst admitted responsibility and was put on trial (under

Section 10 of the Malicious Injuries to Property Act) at a packed Central Criminal Court. When she got out of her car – driven by a female chauffeur – cheers rose from the suffragettes outside. Despite the evidence, she pleaded Not Guilty because, although she accepted full responsibility for the destruction wrought, she said she was neither a wicked nor a malicious woman and that whatever the sentence, she would not submit to it. She was found guilty and sentenced to three years in prison, whereupon the suffragettes in court leapt to their feet and shouted 'Shame!' and her supporters outside began to sing the movement's song, 'Marching On' (to the tune of the 'Marseillaise'). In Plymouth, supporters cut telephone wires in protest at her sentence.

Soon afterwards, the Prisoners (Temporary Discharge for Ill Health) Act, secretly debated by the Cabinet in February, was rushed through Parliament. It meant the end of force-feeding: instead, a suffragette who went on hunger strike was, under the Act, released from prison as soon as she appeared so weak that her health or her life was in danger, and taken to the house of a friend to recuperate. However, after a week during which she was supposed to have recovered, the Act allowed for her to be reimprisoned. Thus it became popularly known as the Cat and Mouse Act as the imprisonment, release and subsequent rearrest of the women resembled a cat playing with a mouse – especially as police waiting to rearrest them would surround the house to prevent them being spirited away by friends.

But the 'mice' soon became adept at disappearing, helped by a network of suffragette supporters. One trick was for a large group of heavily veiled women to visit the house where one of them was in hiding. Suddenly the door would burst open and they would all rush out at once, scattering in different directions. The few police watching front and back doors could not follow them all, nor could they tell from behind the veils which one was the escapee.

Another girl got out of the 'safe house' when a slim fellow suffragette, dressed as an errand boy and carrying a hamper, her face partly disguised by the apple she was munching, entered through the back door on a supposed delivery. A quick change of clothes inside, and the errand boy – this time the 'mouse' – left, with cap at the same angle and still munching 'his' apple.

The Act proved to be counter-productive, as public sympathy

swung towards the suffragettes on account of this harsh and unfair treatment, while the inability of the government to lay its hands on high-profile suffragettes gave rise to mockery.

The pressure of relentless opposition on all fronts had taken its toll on Asquith and Margot was anxious for him to have a real rest. At the beginning of April she had been to the theatre and dinner with Count Mensdorff, the Austro-Hungarian Ambassador, Clemmie Churchill and her own old beau Evan Charteris and on the way home had said to Clemmie: 'Are you going to ask me on the Yacht? I asked Henry if he would like me to come & he said "Yes, but I should like to be invited by Winston".'

Clemmie, in turn, asked her husband: 'Don't you think the simplest way will be to ask the P.M., Margot & Violet and let them settle it between themselves?' Margot, she added, was 'very nice & simple, but she looked rather sad – she said pathetically: "It *is* my turn this year. I have never been on the Yacht!"' Churchill responded by asking Clemmie, just off to spend a weekend at The Wharf, the Asquiths' recently acquired house in Sutton Courtenay on the Thames, not to 'commit yourself and the yacht unnecessarily to Margot, if you can help it'.

Knowing that a trip on the *Enchantress* was in the offing Margot, when asked a few days later to tea by Clemmie, said to her: 'How I wish Henry was going away with you at Whitsuntide [Whit-Sunday was on 11 May]! It would do him so much good.' What she did not know was that Churchill had already invited Asquith on the *Enchantress*, to cruise from Genoa to Malta – and that the Prime Minister had asked if they would invite Violet too.

By the time of the tea party, an embarrassed Clemmie had an awkward five minutes when she found that Margot did not know either that her husband had already been invited – or that both he and her stepdaughter, who had replied by telegram, had accepted. 'She . . . seemed a little hurt when she found Violet was going too & she had been discounted,' Clemmie told her husband. There was a pause and then Margot said: 'Oh, I see,' and changed the subject.

This discovery that, once again, she had been left out of her husband's plans, without a word, in favour of her twenty-six-year-old stepdaughter increased Margot's feeling of isolation. She was not a complainer; instead, she told herself that what she wanted was to finalise everything at The Wharf, so that they could use it as soon as possible.*

The Wharf had been bought by Margot in 1911 as a country retreat that was not too far from London, should Asquith need to return there in a hurry. It was originally two small cottages about eighty feet from the river, set behind an old barn, the three selling for £1,300. Margot was determined to buy them and, with no spare cash at the time, turned for help to the immensely rich and ugly banker J.P. Morgan, who for over twenty years had been fascinated by her.

The Asquiths' friend, the architect Walter Cave (a member of the Arts and Crafts Artworkers' Guild), told her that for £3,000 (to include the purchase price) he could make a charming dwelling from the cottages and barn. Margot was thrilled and went to thank Morgan for his generosity in her newest and nicest summer outfit, a grey dress with long black-fringed sash and a little white hat with black feathers. Morgan was enchanted, pulling Margot out of her chair and saying: 'How will you kiss an ugly old fellow like me?' 'With affectionate coolness,' said Margot firmly. There was a little more byplay, after which Morgan concluded by saying that he realised he could never make her love him but he hoped she would always keep a corner of her heart for him.

The result of this tender exchange was a three-storey house, with tall chimneys, carved wooden pelmets over the windows, trellis-work banisters and rough-cast plaster walls. The ground floor of the barn was converted into a living room; above was a bedroom, quickly commandeered by Margot, who always liked her own size-able space.

Yet again, Violet had managed to take her place. 'Henry and Violet went on the Admiralty yacht from Genoa to Malta,' Margot wrote in her diary on 21 May 1913. 'They returned here 10th. This voyage was a great mistake ... I <u>hated</u> him going away again without me ... as I get older I mind more having so little of him to myself. I never cried more passionate tears or felt iller than I did the days before he went away.'

At the root of her problem was loneliness: Asquith was spending less and less time with her and she in turn was therefore becoming

---

* Then as now, building works over-ran and it was not finally completed until July.

less and less involved in the world of politics that meant so much to her. She loved Asquith deeply, she admired him more than any other man and she minded terribly that, although never less than kind and affectionate, he did not confide in her as he used to, or discuss questions of the day with her with the same interest and fervour. It was as though he was moving away from her even in their own home.

However, she kept up appearances in public, attending the London premiere of Vaslav Nijinsky's *L'après-midi d'un faune,* a ballet like no other, with little actual dancing and only one of the leaps for which Nijinsky, the greatest dancer who ever lived, was famous. Instead there was scandal. At its Paris premiere the year before, the sophisticated first-night audience had first hissed, then applauded, and *Le Figaro* had thundered: 'We are shown a lecherous faun, whose movements are filthy and bestial in their eroticism, and whose gestures are as crude as they are indecent ... the over-explicit miming of this mis-shapen beast, loathsome when seen full-on but even more loathsome in profile,* was greeted with the booing it deserved.'

For his ballet Nijinsky wore a cream bodysuit with brown piebald patches, as might be seen in the coat of an animal. To this were added a short tail, a belt of vine leaves and a cap of woven golden hair surrounding two golden horns. His ears were extended with wax to be more pronounced and pointed, his make-up made his face appear more animal. 'The miracle of the thing lies with the fabulous Nijinsky, the peerless dancer, who as the faun does no dancing,' said the *Daily Mail.* 'It is a full evocation of a being half-boy, half-brute, consummate and uncanny.'

It was not surprising that Margot, with her love of music, the arts and the avant-garde, was there to see this extraordinary, controversial performance. Count Harry Kessler, Anglo-German diplomat, aesthete and diarist, described her at the ballet as 'very much the *grande dame*, with very beautiful pearls, in a very elegant dress of blue-silver brocade ... a little, dark, brisk witty woman with hard lines in a once rather pretty face, not sentiment but all push. She keeps "society" quiet while Asquith and Lloyd George bleed it.'

Meanwhile, feelings over Home Rule became ever more polarised

---

* Much of the ballet was acted in profile, and the writer was seeking to imply that Nijinsky was showing bulging genitalia.

and the industrial unrest continued. The year would see a total of 1,459 separate strikes, with the membership of the recently founded Workers' Union up from 23,000 at the end of 1912 to 91,000 by December 1913. Their numbers were such and public sympathy for their demands so great that the employers had reluctantly been forced to grant a minimum wage.

The next blow came from the suffragettes. In the 1913 Derby, run on Wednesday, June 4, the King had entered his horse Anmer, a bay with a white stripe down his face and two white hind socks. He was ridden by the well-known and successful jockey Herbert Jones, who had often ridden for the King's father, Edward VII, and who had already won two Derbys. He wore the unmistakable royal racing silks – gold-braided purple jacket with scarlet sleeves and black velvet cap with gold rosette and fringed purple bow.

The Derby was a great day out. Londoners of all classes had always flocked to it and from when it was first run in 1780 it had also traditionally been a royal event. On that warm, sunny June day King George V and Queen Mary had both come to watch the race. But, wrote the anonymous correspondent of *The Lady* magazine: 'I wish that fate had taken me away, for the day brought a succession of shocks such as I hope never again to receive on a racecourse, and which make my heart beat faster even now when I think about them.' She was not too upset, however, to note that the Queen wore white, with a hat wreathed in pale pink flowers.

Those who could afford it generally sat in the grandstands or even on top of omnibuses that made alternative makeshift stands in the middle part of the racetrack. The centre of the course had always been free so it was here that the many working-class Londoners came to watch the race, smoking and drinking, and generally enjoying themselves in the fresh air.

Emily Wilding Davison, the militant suffragette who had served a prison sentence the previous year 'for attempting to destroy the contents of Post Office letterboxes', walked through this crowd to make her way to the famous sharp bend of Tattenham Corner. In her pocket was a return train ticket to London and an invitation to a suffragette event that evening; round her waist was tied a furled banner in the purple, green and white suffragette colours. She waited for the race to start, standing quietly behind the barriers.

As the horses rounded Tattenham Corner, Anmer was third from last, galloping at around 35 m.p.h. Emily Davison slipped quickly under the barrier, ran out onto the course before anyone could stop her, and reached out for Anmer's bridle, grabbing at the reins as she was struck by Anmer's chest. The impact lifted her clean off the ground and flung her down unconscious, blood pouring from her mouth and nose. As Anmer somersaulted, Jones came off and the horse partially fell on him.

Jones, who got off comparatively lightly in a potentially lethal situation, did what all jockeys are trained to do. Having come off his horse, he stayed where he was until the back riders had gone past. He was stretchered off the course and taken to the ambulance room at the back of the grandstand, where he was found to have a fractured rib, a bruised face and slight concussion. He stayed the Wednesday night at the Great Eastern Hotel in Liverpool Street, London, but by Friday was back in Newmarket where he was de-scribed as 'quite cheery'.

Anmer also survived his tumble, emerging with only bruised shins. He quickly scrambled to his feet, galloped after the others, and finished the race as a riderless horse.

At first all was confusion, as the crowd swarmed onto the track. Jones later recollected that he saw Emily Davison trying to grab his reins while other spectators claimed that they had heard a woman shout 'Votes for Women!' just before she sprang out in front of the King's horse. Still others believed that she was simply trying to cross the course and had not seen that there were still horses galloping on it – once the race was over, the crowd always surged out onto the course to walk down to the finish.

Emily Davison, who was taken to Epsom Cottage Hospital, was so badly injured that she never regained consciousness. It is prob-able that her heart was damaged in the impact. That Wednesday evening the King asked after her and was told that Mr Mansell Moullin, a consultant surgeon at the London Hospital, had been called in. It was in vain: she died four days later, from massive inter-nal injuries. Queen Mary sent a telegram to Jones, wishing him well after his 'sad accident caused through the abominable conduct of a brutal lunatic woman'.*

---

* Fifteen years later, Herbert Jones laid a wreath at the funeral of Emmeline Pankhurst, in honour of her and Emily Davison.

The Times summed up the accident in a tone of great disapproval. 'She very nearly took Jones's life and her own. Had Anmer brought down the other horses which were close behind him, a scene might have followed of which it is horrible even to think, and nobody could have maintained, had it occurred, that it was not a natural consequence of what she did.' The suffragettes, naturally, saw Emily Davison as a martyr for the cause.

Adding to the Government's difficulties was a looming scandal that would involve some of its most senior members. The first intimation of what became known as the Marconi Affair had begun to trickle out in the summer of 1912. It centred on allegations that highly placed members of the Liberal Party, under Asquith as Prime Minister, had profited by improper use of information about the Government's intentions with respect to the Marconi Company.

The previous year, Asquith and the Cabinet had approved a plan for a chain of state-owned wireless stations to be erected throughout the British Empire; and Asquith had asked the Postmaster General, Herbert Samuel, to find a company to undertake the work. Samuel accepted the tender given by the Marconi Wireless Telegraph Company, considered the best in the field, the chairman of which, Godfrey Isaacs, was a close friend of his and the brother of Sir Rufus Isaacs, the Attorney General in Asquith's Government. Guglielmo Marconi, founder of the company and Nobel Prize-winner for his invention, had been the first man to send wireless signals over water; as the Government realised, the ability to send long-distance transmissions of messages over vast distances was a vital new method of communication.

Although the contract was not made public, Marconi shares had almost trebled by the following March. Rumours began to circulate that Isaacs and Samuel, knowing that the Government was about to issue a lucrative contract, had made a profit from speculating in the company's shares.

Hilaire Belloc, poet, former MP and editor of the political weekly *The Eye-Witness*, suspected that some members of the Government had been buying shares in the company. He wrote to his mother, Bessie Parkes Belloc, that he had heard rumours that 'Lloyd George has been dealing on the Stock Exchange heavily to his advantage with private political information'. After investigations by his reporters,

Belloc published allegations of corruption in *The Eye-Witness*, suggesting that Sir Rufus Isaacs had made £160,000 out of the deal and that Godfrey Isaacs, David Lloyd George and Herbert Samuel had also profited by buying shares based on knowledge of the government contract. In fact, neither Isaacs nor Samuel had bought the British company's shares but that April, Isaacs, Lloyd George, the Master of Elibank (Parliamentary Secretary to the Treasury) and the Liberal Chief Whip had bought shares in the American Marconi Company.

Although it was run quite separately, they kept their transactions secret, believing – accurately – that they would be misconstrued. In January 1913 a parliamentary inquiry was held into the claims made by *The Eye-Witness*, when it was discovered that Samuel, Godfrey Isaacs and the Liberal Chief Whip had all bought shares, as had Rufus Isaacs, who immediately resold 1,000 of them to Lloyd George. By a tragic irony, the sinking of the *Titanic* had increased their value: when the 700-odd survivors were landed in New York, it was because the ship that rescued them, the *Carpathia*, had been alerted by the *Titanic*'s Marconi equipment.

Sir Rufus Isaacs, summoned to appear in the inquiry, was forced to disclose that the American shares had been bought at a favourable price when not yet available to the general public; and that the Master of Elibank had used Liberal Party funds to buy his. This was, of course, a gift to the Unionist opposition, with its built-in question: if they believed in their own innocence, why did they not disclose the purchase of the shares immediately rather than wait until forced to?

The matter culminated in a fierce debate in Parliament on 18–19 June 1913. 'We are now extremely exercised over the "Marconi" Scandal,' wrote Lady Talbot de Malahide (she and her husband had come over from Ireland so that he could vote against the Home Rule Bill when it came up for its second reading in the House of Lords).

But a Unionist vote of censure on Isaacs and Lloyd George was rejected by the Government majority and it was decided that none of them had been guilty of corruption. Instead, the House perforce accepted the ministers' apology. Asquith, privately describing their conduct as 'lamentable' to the King, noted of his Chancellor, so popular with the public, a few days later: 'I think the idol's wings are a bit clipped.'

All of them were cleared but an unsavoury whiff of peculation remained. Although Asquith commented loyally, 'They have done nothing in the least dishonourable but have behaved with an almost incredible lack of judgment,' *The Times*' leading article of 19 June was more forthright. 'A man is not blamed for being splashed with mud. He is commiserated. But if he has stepped into a puddle which he might easily have avoided, we say that it is his own fault. If he protests that he did not know it was a puddle, we say that he ought to know better; but if he says that it was after all quite a clean puddle, then we judge him deficient in the sense of cleanliness. And the British public like their public men to have a very nice sense of cleanliness.'

No sooner had the Government put the Marconi Scandal behind it than the Home Rule Bill, with all its attendant fiercely held and diametrically opposed opinions, its looming threat of civil war and its violent enmities between former friends, came sharply into focus again. 'Home Rule Bill at the House of Lords,' wrote Lady Talbot de Malahide on 14 July 1913. 'We ladies took our places in the Ladies' Gallery to hear the great debate.'

Listening to debates in Parliament was one of the regular entertainments of the well-off, especially of those with parliamentary connections. Married women would go with friends or take their daughters, and comment afterwards on the speeches at dinner parties. With so many politicians, both in the Lords and Commons, drawn from the upper echelons of society, this close connection with what husbands, brothers, sons or friends were saying in Parliament was of immense concern. Margot, to whom the life political – especially as discussed with her husband afterwards – had become an absorbing interest, spent constant afternoons in the Ladies' Gallery.

So high were the passions aroused by the Bill's progress that the next step in another, more serious contest, the naval arms race, did not attract so much notice when Winston Churchill, as First Lord of the Admiralty, announced in the House of Commons two days later: 'We shall receive, in the near future, incomparably the greatest delivery of warships ever recorded in the history of the British Navy . . . and . . . during the next eighteen months a super-Dreadnought of the latest possible type, and of the highest possible cost, every forty-five days.'

Dreadnoughts were then the most expensive, powerful and

revolutionary battleships ever built. When the Liberals came to power the Russo-Japanese war had just concluded, culminating in what the maritime strategist Sir Julian Corbett called 'the most decisive and complete naval victory in history' with the Battle of Tsushima in May 1905, in which the Russian fleet was almost completely destroyed; of the forty-five Russian ships involved, only three managed to return to their home port of Vladivostok. What had ensured the Japanese victory was heavy, long-range gunfire.

In Britain, the importance of this had been immediately realised by the First Sea Lord, the visionary, volatile Admiral Sir Jackie Fisher, who became the driving force behind a new design of warship so revolutionary she immediately made all other battleships obsolescent.

When HMS *Dreadnought*, built at Portsmouth Dockyard between October 1905 and December 1906, glided down the slipway she was not merely an improved version of what had gone before, but the signal for change in the world's navies. Her armoury was massive, with ten twelve-inch guns (the previous record was four), and her gun turrets were placed higher than usual so that long-distance fire was more accurate. She was the first warship to be propelled by steam turbines only (most were still coal-fired) and at twenty-one knots she was faster by three knots than any other warship.

Her impact was so great that her name became generic: all other ships of her class were known as Dreadnoughts and other navies, including that of the Kaiser, scrambled to build their own. The navy with the most Dreadnoughts, it was believed, would be invincible.

Those who did listen attentively to the First Lord's statement might have wondered how a party of which the core principle was peace, and which had come into power in 1906 pledged to reduce naval and military expenditure, now found itself committed to such increased armaments.

'To ignore the preponderant role played by Germany in compelling European people to lay out larger and ever larger sums on dreadnoughts, heavy and mountain guns, fortresses, soldiers and ammunition, is to read contemporary history with one eye shut,' Dr E.J. Dillon had thundered in the *Contemporary Review* the previous September. 'But to put a stop to the world competition for naval and military superiority ought not to be a task beyond the power of European governments. If it has not been seriously tack-led, the reason is to be sought in Germany's refusal to entertain the idea. Nay, more, Germany set an example of increased expenditure which is literally ruinous and will, perhaps, force on a war as the supposed lesser evil.'

Seen through German eyes, this was likely and, for some, desir-able. As Count Harry Kessler had written to a friend during the Agadir Crisis, 'All nations have become what they are by war, and I shouldn't give two pence for a world in which the possibility of war was abolished.'

But when, on 9 November 1908, a bright, clear, windy day, Margot had launched the first of the planned new Dreadnoughts, HMS *Collingwood*, such thoughts were far from everyone's minds. Always one of the first to try out a new fashion, she was dressed for the occasion in one of the new tight skirts* in biscuit-coloured cloth and a matching string blouse, with a black hat. 'I name you *Colling-wood*. God bless you and all who sail in you,' she proclaimed in a loud, clear voice as she successfully broke the ropes that held the ship in place and the great vessel slid without a splash into the sea.

As 'Rule Britannia' was sung to the accompaniment of massed bands, she watched the bluejackets below stuffing small bits of rope into their pockets for luck.

---

* The hobble skirt, designed by the couturier Paul Poiret, was so tight around the hem that women could only take tiny, geisha-like steps. Some employers denounced them as unsafe – stepping off a high pavement was difficult – and sometimes climbing into a cab took so long that, to the mockery of passers-by, traffic jams formed. It was said that shoes wore out quicker because of the number of tiny steps that had to be taken.

ELEVEN

Though still believing that Venetia was just one of the group of young women such as Diana Manners whom Asquith enjoyed seeing, Margot's instinct – an instinct that in some cases had amounted almost to foreknowledge – had made her sense that something was wrong and, as always, her mental state affected her health. No longer did she feel well and happy but ill and nervous.

Venetia was a frequent guest at The Wharf, for Margot entertained there just as much as at Downing Street. It was smaller, of course – there were seven bedrooms – but being newly built there were three bath or shower rooms instead of the more usual single bathroom, with the main bathroom covered in rare pale green and blue glass tiles, and oak floors throughout. Black goatskin rugs were scattered everywhere; Asquith's bedroom had a black silk eiderdown; there was a 'Chinese' bedroom where the theme was black and gold lacquer and a more conventional drawing room with antique walnut furniture and yellow and grey silk curtains. The inevitable after-dinner bridge was played in the library, on a fold-out Chippendale mahogany card table.

Almost all the rooms overlooked the walled garden at the back, which ran down to a small waterway off the Thames, originally cut to serve a paper mill nearby. There was another garden at the front. In the old barn in the garden were guest apartments as well as Margot's top-floor bedroom and a large drawing room on the ground floor that held a grand piano – a joy to the musical Puffin.

The white dining room, with its two garden windows hung with red damask curtains, was rather narrow, but that did not deter Margot from giving her usual large luncheon parties, less formal – and therefore noisier – than her Downing Street entertainments. The real snag was not so much that the rooms were small and low but that the walls were paper-thin, so that by the end of one of the

Asquiths' frequently chaotic weekends, the hosts were usually as eager to escape as the guests.

Violet's infringement on Margot and Asquith's life together was constant. 'Of course I long passionately to have Henry and my own children for the last bit of my youth to myself,' wrote Margot in her diary for August. 'I'm a passionate earthy creature and feel a bitter resentment against fate that I have no calm little inside life with my own. It has helped to make me ill. If Violet doesn't marry I shall feel I have been cheated.'

These emotions were nothing compared to her anguish when she discovered her husband's feelings for Venetia – watching him fall ever more heavily under the spell of another woman was agonising. She felt she had no weapons to win him back: she was twenty-three years older than Venetia nor was she a beauty, while Venetia had youth, looks and the charm of novelty. She felt humiliated and be-wildered and did not know what to do.

She told her friends that the reason she was unhappy was that Puffin, now aged ten, had gone off to school. Asquith had found it difficult to say what sort of schooling would be best for their son for the next few years, and it was she who had taken the de-cision to send him to Summer Fields, in the country-ish outskirts of Oxford – Asquith felt that he was too delicate – thinking that fresh air, exercise and the company of boys of his own age would be better for him than solitary education by a tutor in Downing Street. She drove over on Saturday afternoons from The Wharf to see him and was delighted that he was so happy and improv-ing so greatly in health. But she missed him dreadfully. 'I felt quite sick if I was stupid enough to pass his bedroom door or go through his nursery. I ordered the rocking horse out of my sight and told the housemaids they were not to turn his little dog out of his bedroom.'

Her health failed to improve and her misery increased. 'I guessed what the season would be for me without either Elizabeth or Puffin but I had no idea it would be so bad,' she wrote then. 'Also I wanted to be near Henry and I was never so far away from him. No one so tender and perfect as he is if he realises what is happening but neither he nor Violet had the least idea of my sufferings.'

One night when Asquith arrived home late and went into her room he found her weeping silently into her pillow. He knelt down

Margot ice skating on a lake in 1912. Hats and gloves were worn everywhere except on the beach.

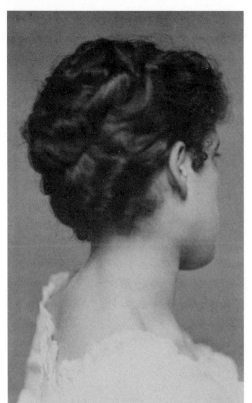

Top left Margot aged twenty-six. Her hair – thick, brown and lustrous – was her chief beauty.

Above Margot's childhood at Glen was both idyllic and extraordinarily sophisticated. She might wander alone on the hills of the 3,500-acre estate all day, or mix with the politicians of her father's circle. Gladstone was a frequent visitor, hence Margot's sketch of him cutting down a tree at Glen *(above right)*.

'The best-looking man I ever saw.' Wilfrid Scawen Blunt was a guest at Glen, where he paid unavailing court to Margot (though later wrote in his diary that he had seduced her) and wrote her a poem about her 'Mocking eyes, beseeching lips.'

Margot *(left)* was an excellent rider. She went hunting for the first time aged seventeen and fell off almost at once, but the thrill of it was a revelation and she went on to ride so daringly that the Master, the Duke of Beaufort, asked her if she would like to wear the blue and buff habit of the Beaufort hunt. She asked him pertly, 'Do you always do this sort of thing when you meet anyone like me for the first time?' To which the Duke neatly replied: 'Just as it is the first time you have ever hunted, so it is the first time I have ever met anyone like you.'

Above left Asquith's son Raymond took this photograph of his father when he was a child.

Above right Margot at the corner of Cavendish Square – the Asquiths lived at No. 20, a beautiful eighteenth-century house bought for them as a wedding present by Margot's father. When Asquith became Prime Minister in 1908, he used its tradesmen's entrance for the only time in his life, slipping out of it to avoid the waiting press at the front.

The Asquiths loved Cavendish Square and only reluctantly moved to No. 10 Downing Street, where Asquith missed his comfortable study *(above)* and Margot her boudoir.

This portrait of Margot three years after her marriage by the fashionable painter John Singer Sargent tactfully overlooks her broken nose but gives a hint of the style and chic – rather than beauty – on which she relied. Even as a young girl she often wore black, then almost entirely the province of married women, and for an early Ascot she wore a grey dress with black spots and a wide black hat trimmed with a huge red rose; for dinner black chiffon instead of the usual pastels.

Top left and above The Asquiths loved Scotland. In 1904, when these pictures were taken (and Asquith was in Opposition), they rented a castle in Ayrshire which had a lovely garden, poor shooting, bathing in an icy river, moderate fishing, two horses, and a pony for seven-year-old Elizabeth. The essential golf links, to which they drove daily, were ten miles away. Elizabeth's German governess, always known as Frau and to whom they were all devoted, came with them *(above)*.

Asquith's eldest son, Raymond, with his wife Katharine. Katharine's mother, Frances Horner, was Margot's greatest female friend among the Souls. She had also been Asquith's confidante in his pursuit of Margot – she was the woman to whom he wrote: 'She does not love me, at least in the way I love her. I am under no illusions, but I love her . . . '

Violet Asquith *(left)* and her closest friend Venetia Stanley at Penrhos, the Stanley house on Anglesey. Asquith spent more and more time at Penrhos as he became infatuated with his daughter's best friend.

Right Margot got on better with some of her stepchildren than others, especially the younger ones: Beb *(top)*, whose heart she won when he was a child with a welcome gift of extra track for his model railway; Oc *(middle)*, her favourite; and the youngest, Cys *(bottom)*, who was closest to his sister Violet.

Venetia Stanley *(left)* talking to Beb's wife, Cynthia. The monkey, Fluto, held by Venetia, was one of her menagerie of animals which included a bear cub that roamed through parts of the house, until finally her father ordered her to get rid of it.

Left When they moved to 10 Downing Street, the Asquiths missed their lovely house in Cavendish Square, which was immediately snapped up by Winston Churchill for his mother. However, the garden of No. 10 proved a boon, especially to Puffin, who spent hours in it playing with his model aeroplane.

Below Margot, seen here talking to a Downing Street chauffeur, preferred being driven to and from No. 10 in the Asquiths' motor as 'few taxi drivers seemed to have any idea of its whereabouts.'

and kissed her as she told him it would be best for her 'as I was so tearful and rotten' to go right away from him for two months. 'He got up and said with such emotion "Has it come to this?" The idea of hurting him deeply was so awful that I said "Oh just to get well ... " He put his arms round me and his eyes were wet as I clasped him to me. His love cheered me ...' Margot had to be content with that, and indeed for a time was. She did her best to be kind and friendly to Venetia when she came to No. 10, but this was made more difficult by her feeling that Violet knew about her father's passion and connived in it.

Asquith knew quite well why Margot was so depressed. His emotion when he found his wife weeping was, perhaps, the first sign of guilt that he showed over his pursuit of Venetia. For he had, during the early months of 1913, been spending a great deal of time with her. He would see her most Friday afternoons and often at weekends, he would stay at Alderley, she would lunch or dine at No. 10 Downing Street; and they met from time to time at dinner parties with friends. This proximity had its effect on Venetia as well as on Asquith: she now told her other admirer, Montagu, how fond she had become of Asquith.

Her very openness about her affection for the Prime Minister, a man for whom Montagu's feelings were equally warm, must have prevented her aspiring suitor from imagining that such affection was in any way romantic. At the same time, she minimised the depth of Montagu's feelings and the increasing closeness of her relationship with him when with Asquith or writing to him.

Montagu had returned from India in March 1913 after an absence of almost seven months. Venetia, after telling him she would be back in London the day after he returned, urged him to visit her that evening – she was dining in Downing Street.

With Montagu's return, Asquith became aware that she was more closely involved with him than he had previously thought ... and jealousy provoked the near-jibes in his letters that now began again, epitomised in this verse (written in April) that he sent to her: 'Venetia, though a Christian child/Sprung from an Aryan stem – /Frequents – too easily beguiled! – /The silken tents of Shem.' It was also another reference to Montagu's Jewishness, which Asquith constantly emphasised, believing that it put Montagu firmly out of bounds to his beloved.

On 7 April he was describing Montagu's visit to The Wharf to Venetia in the same terms. 'The congested Wharf found room for Clemmie Churchill, Robert Ross and the Assyrian. The last named was in an introspective and sombre mood: declared that he had never known what it was to be free from physical & mental pain: and complained that he amused nobody and that nobody amused him. Apart from this he seemed to be in quite good spirits & played Bridge with zest and determination ... It was a lovely windy day and I missed you very much.'

He did not have to miss her for long. During the Easter recess, Asquith went off alone for a visit to Penrhos, the summer home of the Stanleys. It was a large grey stone house with battlemented walls on the island of Anglesey, looking over a narrow strait to green fields. Margot was left in London with the younger children, despondent at the thought of her husband, unhindered by her inhibiting presence, freely rejoicing in Venetia's company. He was seeing her more and more: often at weekends as well as for their regular Friday afternoon drives.

Montagu, too, was spending as much time with her as he could. Soon his old feelings had returned – if they had ever disappeared.

In May 1913 King George and Queen Mary went to Berlin to attend the wedding of Princess Victoria Louise, the Kaiser's only daughter, to the Duke of Brunswick. Although the King did not have the deft graciousness and dignified assurance of his father – the 'Uncle of Europe' – he was determined always to do the right thing and conscientious over even the smallest detail. It was said that at private dinner parties each guest would be brought up to talk to him for exactly three minutes, to be surreptitiously ticked off on a piece of paper by an equerry as they left.

The Queen, shy but imposing, looked magnificent in Indian cloth of gold with a crown of pearls and diamonds, a diamond collar with a large diamond necklace beneath it and various diamond stars. 'Our visit to Berlin has, I think, been a great success in every way,' wrote the King to his equerry Sir Charles Cust, 'and I trust that it may tend to improve the relations between the two countries. Nothing could have exceeded the kindness of the Emperor and Empress ...'

The Germany they did not see on their visit was one in which militarism, order and hierarchy were glorified. Even the Reverend Harold Williams, the mild-mannered Chaplain of St George's, the English church in Berlin, had noticed this although, having come across it in a different context, he saw it as the strong bullying the weak. 'I do not like German bullying,' he wrote in his diary, recording how one day, when he came across a boy hitting a little girl lying in the street whom he had already knocked down, he had given the boy a cuff and told him to stop it. 'I was surprised to find that the Germans to whom I mentioned this disapproved of my action,' he wrote. '"One does not treat German *boys* like that" I was told. I gradually discovered, of course, that bullying is inseparable from German militarism.'

Perhaps as an echo of its military hierarchism, this prosperous nation, after twenty-seven years of peace during which its population had expanded dramatically and in which industries like chemicals, scientific equipment and steel had boomed, was threaded with rules and regulations. Restaurant menus gave advice on how to pour out wine without spilling it, people were not allowed to walk on pavements more than three abreast nor sing nor whistle and even pillar boxes had notices saying, 'Do not forget to stamp and address your envelope'.

Allied to this was immense, heel-clicking formality. Molly Marshall, who spent the years 1910–12 at a Charlottenburg finishing school, described in a letter home the mini-curtseying that was a part of daily life in that eight-boarder household. 'We all have to make "bobs" when we go into meals and when we shake hands with the Frauleins. At first I could not bring myself to do it but now I always do. It is killing though.'

The Kaiser had approved a new Army Law that added eighteen infantry regiments as well as cavalry and heavy artillery to the army; Germany now had a peacetime strength of 870,000 and in war could put five million men in the field.

Everywhere the officer was glorified, holding a privileged position in society, subject only to army law – the judgement of his peers. So intertwined were the ideas of honour and personal combat that, although by 1913 duelling was disappearing, universities encouraged rapier contests, with rapier scars on the face a symbol of prestige, and, it was believed, attractive to women. As a Hamburg paper reported, some enterprising firms offered simulated duelling scars 'without pain or interruption to business' as an allurement to the opposite sex.

Berlin, the capital of this huge, prosperous nation, had grown enormously and the Kaiser, riding in his glittering uniforms on his white charger through his capital, past its squares and gardens, its miles of new wide boulevards and the classical statues depicting his relations, was now the popular icon both of that prosperity and its military image of itself. For his Jubilee in mid-June he was given a silver eagle to go on the bow of his new yacht; there was a massive military parade, bands and homage from the various German princes.

At home, lethargy seemed to have overtaken the Government even while turbulence ruled in the arts. Diaghilev, the Ballets Russes and the exotic designs and brilliant colours of Léon Bakst were effecting a revolution in clothes and decoration among the theatre-going public and through them rippling outwards to the wider world. Even *The Times* noted – a touch grumpily – on 6 July 1913, 'It is difficult . . . to determine how much our almost bare feet and quite bare arms and neck owe to Mr Asquith's indifference to stable government or to the anarchy in the political and artistic world.'

It was true that Asquith had sunk all too readily into the years of good living made possible by his wife's money. 'Henry [Asquith] came yesterday for a bit, he is altered, his face is like a very fat old woman, with long silvery hair,' wrote Mary Elcho when staying with the Asquiths at Walmer Castle that summer. 'But his good temper and spirits were wonderful.' Drink was a continuing problem: the twenty-one-year-old Olwen Lloyd George was once reproved by her mother for saying that Asquith did not know what was going on 'because he had drunk too much and fallen asleep'.

Margot, by contrast, was known as a cultural trendsetter, often seen at first nights at the opera and ballet. The 'finishing' year she had spent in Dresden as a young girl had imbued her with a passion for music and clothes. There, in spare moments she had taken herself to the opera, where her chaperone-less state and penchant for vivid, dramatic garments once led to a misunderstanding – in a scarlet crêpe de Chine dress, black cape and her pearls she was mistaken for a woman of easy virtue by a smart young officer. Asquith did not enjoy music: when, during their courtship, Margot took him to

Wagner's *Die Walküre*, which she adored, he remarked afterwards: 'There was only one person more unhappy than myself there, and that was the horse, when they led him on.'

As for fashion, it had always caused comment. A modest alteration in the female neckline, the introduction of the hitherto-unknown V-neck, now proved controversial; after one doctor's warning against exposing the throat it had been dubbed 'the pneumonia blouse', while beauty writers hastened to say that it should not show a trace of the dreaded sunburn. 'Lemon juice should be applied, then a towel dipped in hot water and wrung out wrapped round the neck.'

But the V-neck was as nothing to the changes brought about by the dressmaker of the moment, Paul Poiret. Poiret's work was so revolutionary that it gave a sartorial shock comparable to the arrival of Christian Dior's New Look in 1947. He often used bright colours such as reds, greens and violets, rather than the soft pastels then favoured, he disposed of the encumbering petticoats and, most noticeably of all, did away with the rigidly structured hourglass corsets that had given the statuesque Edwardian beauties their sculptured opulence. Instead he used flowing drapery, loosely based on classical Greece and Rome, and brought in the first brassiere – a band of grosgrain, reinforced with short whalebone strips and sewn into the garment itself.

Margot had always spent freely on clothes. At sixteen she had accidentally overheard her mother's voice lamenting to a friend: 'Margot, a few years ago, promised to be so pretty and just look at her now!' Hardly any comment could have been more discouraging to a teenage girl soon to embark on a life in which attracting a suitable husband was both goal and focus. Like many women uncertain of their looks, she relied on style and chic for impact.

As a young girl, in defiance of the convention of pastels for anyone of her age, she often wore black, then almost entirely the province of married women: one of her Ascot hats was a wide black straw trimmed with a huge red rose; for dinner it was often black chiffon. Most of these clothes were by the famous dressmaker Worth, then at the zenith of his power, prestige – and price. With her slender figure – she weighed around eight stone – upright carriage and love of strong colours she was ideally suited to wear Poiret's creations, which were even threatening to oust those of the august house of

Worth, which had single-handedly dictated fashion to the wealthy for over fifty years.

So taken was Margot with the new fashions that she invited a group of friends to tea at Downing Street to view them. It turned out to be a political gaffe of the first order, though perhaps she should have foreseen it when a number of women refused to attend for fear of the reaction among Asquith's political enemies, the Conservatives.

Their fears were well grounded. Margot's tea party caused a storm of criticism. 'An Exhibition in Gowning Street!' thundered the Conservative press, 'French Industry Represented by the British Prime Minister!' The Liverpool Drapers' Association sent a telegram of protest to the Prime Minister regretting the unpatriotic use of his official residence to promote a French dressmaker, a meeting was held in Mayfair to discuss some form of practical protest, and the next issue of the *Drapers' Record* featured an article headlined 'Mrs Asquith's Indiscretion', beginning, 'The experience of the past week has shown how strongly the Poiret incident is resented . . .'

In *The Times* was a critical letter from a Conservative MP, to which Margot responded that there had been no exhibition and sale of foreign stuffs or clothes at 10 Downing Street. 'I received in my private rooms at tea from 20 to 25 of my personal friends, and a well-known French costumier, whose models can be bought in any London shop, brought some specimens for the inspection of myself and my guests. It was a purely private occasion.' In the same edition of the paper there were several large display advertisements featuring copies of Poiret tea gowns, in silks and velvets, for six and a half guineas, on sale in London.

In the world beyond Downing Street the constant wrangling between employers and workers, as the latter struggled to improve their conditions, continued. As trade increased, so more labour was needed. 'There was a good demand for labour on many jobs in the London area,' wrote George Wyver, a stonemason who had become a trade union organiser. 'This gave the incentive to the unions to deal with the non-union labour that always develops in bad times, hence the union men on jobs whenever possible against the non-union men.'

For women it was more difficult. The Duchess of Marlborough,

American and with a social conscience awakened after her separation from the Duke, was determined to assist. In November 1913 she helped two influential women trade union officials, Gertrude Tuckwell and Margaret Laurence, organise a meeting at Sunderland House to call public attention to the shameful conditions in which women worked in the 'sweated industries' (usually, at home, often in the tailoring industries, for tiny wages). 'Last week me and my husband sat from 5.30 till 11 at night and made fourteen dozen shirts,' said one female shirtmaker. She earned ten shillings, of which ten pence went on cotton.

Although the suffrage movement continued to gain general support – by 1913 there was an International Woman Suffrage Alliance (it met in Budapest that year) – there was little progress in Britain. When some women did achieve success, it was only after constant struggle and usually in the teeth of bitter hostility and prejudice. In 1912, according to the Abraham Flexner Report, out of a total of approximately 40,000 doctors listed on the British Medical Register, only 600 were women. Education for women was still in its infancy and in general hotly contested by male establishments. Parents were against it as female students were considered bluestockings and unlikely to get married. One approving article in the Oxford University magazine *Isis* referred to a weekly Isis Idol as: 'His dealings with the fair sex are limited to one-time possession of a bicycle named Phyllis.'

So women continued to chain themselves to railings, pollute reservoirs with dye, smash windows, firebomb empty buildings, smash shop windows by using catapults from buses and throw stones. The stone-throwing had two objectives: one was largely a symbolic protest, the other to cut short the struggle with the police – which was often acutely painful to the women concerned – by committing an offence which could not be ignored.

But militancy merely hardened Asquith's obduracy (and indeed put off many supporters). That September of 1913 he was as usual staying in Scotland, and again as usual with Violet. Often they made up a golf foursome with the Labour leader Ramsay Mac-Donald (whom Violet somewhat shamefacedly admitted she found handsome) at the nearby Lossiemouth golf links – Lossiemouth, in Morayshire, was where MacDonald had been born. As they played on one of those early September mornings, two women rushed up and tried to tear off Asquith's clothes. They were only prevented by Violet. For Asquith, the fear of having his clothes ripped off was much more terrifying than the threat of actual violence.

He was attacked again later when driving to Stirling to unveil a memorial to Sir Henry Campbell-Bannerman, his predecessor as Prime Minister. His car was held up by women lying across the road and as it slowed down other women leapt out from behind the hedges that lined the roads on both sides, jumped onto the car's running-boards and belaboured the Prime Minister over the head with dog whips. Today it seems extraordinary that even after repeated physical attacks on both the Prime Minister and members of his Government there was so little security around him (only on formal occasions did two detectives accompany the Asquiths).

Churchill, who dined with Asquith, Violet and Oc, told his wife: 'The suffragette affair on the road to Stirling was horrible and upset Violet a good deal. One of the women slashed Mr Asquith four times with a crop over the head before she was seized. Luckily his face was saved . . . by the brim of his stiff hat. He never seems to defend himself on these occasions but remains calm & stolid & unwinking! About two pints of pepper were thrown into the car but luckily no one's eyes were injured.

'When arrested the three women gave their names of – Violet Asquith, Frances Tennant and Maud Allan! And under those names they have been charged and will appear. Tonight the Prime and Violet are dining here with me & I shall try & get Sir Edward Grey for a 4th for Bridge.' The name Maud Allan was a clear dig at Margot Asquith, also known to be utterly opposed to the idea of female suffrage (from as early as 1909, according to Wilfrid Scawen Blunt's diary entry for 8 March that year, she had been receiving threatening letters, mostly anonymous, from suffragettes, menacing her with bombs and even the murder of her children).

The fissures in London Society continued apace, notably over Home Rule. Even the twenty-one-year-old Diana Manners, then primarily interested in having fun with fellow members of the Coterie, to whom the politics of their parents mattered not a jot, noted that 'This was a time when Conservatives did not speak amicably to Liberals.' She herself would go 'rather surreptitiously' to Downing Street.

Most observers thought the same. In October the American

Ambassador wrote to President Wilson: 'a bishop explained to me at elaborate length why the very monarchy is doomed unless something befalls Lloyd George and his programme. Every dinner party is made up with strict reference to the party politics of the guests. Sometimes you imagine you see something like civil war and money is flowing out of the kingdom into Canada in the greatest volume ever known . . .'

At the end of September Montagu, still pursuing Venetia, once more asked her to marry him and was again turned down, after which he joined Asquith on the *Enchantress* – the Prime Minister's second trip on her that year. Asquith quickly found out about this second rejection and wrote at once to Venetia. 'The personnel of the yacht itself is familiar to you – especially one member of it, whom I need not particularise. The offhand reference in your letter seems inadequate; according to all accounts . . . there was at one moment something very nearly approaching a *crise de coeur*. Why don't you give me a full and veracious narrative of this interesting incident? Was your conscience perchance still suffering from the after-swell which is apt to follow an emotional storm? The other personage in the drama – tho' looking slightly shattered – is as well as could be expected.'

It must have been difficult for Asquith to have avoided a certain amount of private gloating when he heard this news; and a slight note of contentment does seem to seep through his letter. At any rate, he reaffirmed his feelings when he signed his letter of 18 October to Venetia, who was coming to spend some time, ostensibly with Violet, at Archerfield, 'All my love, always'.

It was another of the letters that arrived constantly throughout the whole of the year, written as usual on his prime ministerial notepaper, smallish, long and narrow, folded like a narrow upright card or notelet, with the lion and unicorn of England in white on a small blue oval; written across this were the words 'Prime Minister'.

As for Venetia, she continued to treat Montagu in exactly the same way as before, writing to him, asking him to stay, dining at his house, expecting him to visit her when she wanted. Nor could Montagu keep away, difficult and unsatisfactory though he found the situation. 'There comes a time when my lack of success becomes very hard to bear,' he wrote. 'And the yearning for what I cannot have becomes so poignant that I cannot trust myself to behave naturally.' But he would not, he told her, give up: as long as Venetia was free, Montagu would try to win her.

In November, Margot took her daughter Elizabeth to Paris and installed her in the finishing school where she would stay for the next year. After Margot's return to Downing Street, she and Asquith went to Windsor Castle for one night 'to meet the heir to the throne of Austria, Archduke Franz Ferdinand and his pretty non-royal wife'. Then, never could anyone have guessed the fate that hung over the couple. That night all Margot recorded in her diary was that 'the Austrian ambassador in Paris told me afterwards he disliked her and loved the archduke, that she was an intriguer and an adventuress etc. I told him that I liked her and that it must be awful to live in a court that was hostile.' To the Ambassador she said, undoubtedly stiffly: 'I presume her greatest offence was in marrying him.' To which he replied: 'If not her great offence, his greatest folly.'

After dinner at Windsor the company was taken by the King and Sir John Fortescue 'round the famous pictures, the Waterloo Chamber, indeed every room of importance in the Castle. Lord Crewe and I nearly died of fatigue. I found myself stumbling about over the huge tiger heads covering the floor of one of the rooms (all the tigers shot by the King). I hung behind outside the precious library and flung myself on a sofa.' Even so, it was a sharp contrast to Sandringham, the favourite home of Edward and Alexandra, which Margot, with her finely tuned eye, had found hideous with its yellow oak panelling, bad portraits and chairs and sofas upholstered in Brigade of Guards blue-and-red-striped linen when she and Asquith had stayed there two years earlier.

It was a time when only the rich went abroad for holidays – indeed, the rich were usually the only people who *had* holidays. The Trades Union Congress had first passed a resolution for holidays with pay in 1911, but this was not followed up until later as holidays were seen by employers as merely a way of raising pay for their workers. More relevant still, few of the workers were sufficiently above subsistence level to afford to travel anywhere on holiday.

Villages usually had some kind of 'day', generally run by a local club and involving brass bands, food, drink and a holiday atmosphere. In Preston Candover in Hampshire, Club Day was, said Daisy Thorp, 'a great day to which wagons and caravans came from all around. The band marched in procession to all the large houses nearby, played some tunes and received a donation.' The rest of the day was rather like a fair, with stalls, side shows and a meal in a tent, and dancing to a pianist in the evening in the village hall, the rough board floor strewn with soap flakes to smooth it and an energetic Sir Roger de Coverley as the grand finale.

For some of the more affluent, Switzerland was already a way of life: the mountain air was supposed to have a curative effect on tuberculosis (or 'consumption' as it was often called), so that it was dotted with sanatoria before becoming a winter sports centre. Biarritz was another spot on the social map, as were Cannes, Nice, Dinard and Deauville, while those with a gambling streak flocked to Monte Carlo – but much the favourite winter holiday destinations were the French and Italian Rivieras, with Egypt for winter cruises.

That winter, members of the Asquith family chose both. Cys, who had just achieved a First at Oxford in his Greats Final, was exhausted and stressed, as well as suffering from an unrequited love affair, and was in a debilitated state aggravated by an operation for appendicitis. Margot sent him on holiday to Egypt, accompanied by Violet, to convalesce in an atmosphere well away from anything mentally strenuous.

Margot, so wretched over her husband's infatuation with Venetia that she felt ill, went for a 'rest cure' to Antibes rather against her will as, knowing that Violet would be away, she would be missing one of her few chances to be alone with her husband. What she did not know was that he had already written to Venetia (at midnight on 8 December – presumably before Margot had decided to go to the Riviera) begging her to find a pretext for asking him to come to her. The letter ended 'The whole of my love. Write.'

Margot left London for Antibes on 28 December 1913 and spent the first three days there entirely in bed, 'too exhausted and miserable for words. Henry wrote every day – he was very unhappy about me. He cried the last two nights before I left. I told him everything – but for him, his wisdom, emotion, depth of feeling, and amazing insight into my character and difficulties I should never get well. As it was, I was quite determined to go through with the cure, and the massage (which I loathe), and I did go through with it.' The effect of the cure was that she put back on a much-needed eleven pounds in weight – but at a price.

Margot was subsidising the whole family. As well as the Downing Street establishment, the house in Cavendish Square cost her £700 a year to maintain; she had been giving Raymond an annual £750 and Violet an annual allowance of £100. Charities and presents had mopped up another £950 – Margot was wildly generous. 'My bankers informed me I was heavily in debt,' she recorded in her diary. 'I shall be much more so when I have paid all the operations, nurses, homes, journeys to Riviera and Khartoum hotel bills and doctors all over the world.' But the letters from her husband heartened her. 'Darling, I have only time for one line to tell you how much I miss you and long that this exile of yours will make you really strong and well and happy for years to come. That is my one wish . . . ever your own.'

Accounts of another kind were threatening to cause a split in the Cabinet: the question of the Naval Estimates for 1914–15. Churchill, as First Lord of the Admiralty, was entirely focused on the creation and maintenance of a highly equipped, invincible Navy; Lloyd George wanted less money spent on defence in order to have more for his planned social reforms. Angrily, he gave an interview to the *News Chronicle* on the last day of December 1913, in which he confirmed that there were disagreements within the Cabinet, warned that there would need to be an increase in taxes 'unless there is an effort made to reduce the overwhelming extravagance of our expenditure on armaments' and stuck to his opinion that social services were more pressing.

'The prospects for the world have seldom been more peaceful,' he declared. 'There is scarcely a cloud on the horizon. Never has the sky been more perfectly blue.' But then, earlier in the month, the Imperial Chancellor had said much the same thing when he told the Reichstag of the improvement of Germany's relationship with England, and that there might even be 'a permanent rapprochement between nations of the same stock'.

PART THREE

1914

TWELVE

As the Government's troubles multiplied, so Asquith's outpourings to Venetia grew longer, with scattered sentences more overtly romantic. 'I agree we had a very good time in Sicily. I wouldn't go so far as to say "it answered <u>every</u> requirement". I can imagine even more ideal conditions – but I fear they are not likely to be realised in the way I should picture them.' 'There is nothing as you know that I would not show you, so great and deep is my trust . . . beloved.' 'I shall come for you immediately after lunch tomorrow – say about 1/4 to 3. I <u>so</u> much want and need to see you again beloved.'

It is difficult to believe that Venetia was not playing a game by simultaneously encouraging both Montagu and Asquith. She was well aware of Montagu's feelings for her, she made use of his car and chauffeur, allowed him to entertain her and her friends at his sumptuous house, and beckoned him willingly to her side whenever she felt the need of company.

As for Asquith, she saw him constantly. She had had eight years' experience of the adult world, and was sophisticated and well enough accustomed to male admiration to recognise when it crossed the invisible border between the love of a friend and that between man and woman. She had told Montagu that he repelled her sexually; if she had done the same to Asquith, it is unlikely he would have ended a letter with 'You are constantly in my thoughts – and heart.'

Margot had begun to realise Venetia's growing influence. The only person with whom she felt she could share this worry, who knew all three of them, was Edwin Montagu, so she wrote to him confiding her anxious feelings. As a man who could not then imagine this unlikely pairing, his answer to her was robust.

Dearest Margot . . . Don't you know what you are to him? How amused you can afford to be at all his relations? Those who know you both would laugh at a comparison between your relations with him and those of any other woman in the world. So show him you acknowledge his right to any amusements he chooses in order that he may get every ounce of himself for the struggle. Show him how confident you are of him and yourself and you will prove to be once again the big-minded loving Margot, who has no more loyal admirer and friend than

Yours very affectionately,

Edwin Montagu.

Montagu's confidence in the innocence of the relationship was understandable. Asquith was, after all, a man aged sixty-one to Venetia's twenty-six and the father of her closest friend – someone who in the normal course of events would have been looked on as a kind of honorary uncle, with whom the thought of a physical relationship would have been horrifying.

It was how most young women would have viewed it. Evie Davies, two years younger than Venetia, summed up the feelings – perhaps even her own reaction – that a girl in her twenties would have to an approach from a much older married man. 'What does the average girl, hair just up and no experience, be she 17, 18 or 19, think about love in connection with a middle-age married man? If she thinks about love, it's likely to be very superficial and in quite an un-understanding way, and she would never look for it except in a young and unmarried man. For a girl is very prudish at first, I think, even if she is of a passionate nature . . .'

The Friday drives had now become a ritual, around two hours in the Napier, the glass panel between the chauffeur and the two in the back seat impermeable to conversation, a carriage rug over laps (early cars had no heating) disguising any hand-holding (Asquith frequently referred in his letters to 'the touch of your hand'). For Margot, adoring of her husband, desperately jealous of the younger woman, they were a misery. As she wrote to Montagu, '. . . I told you that every Friday I suffered *tortures*. I had a vile night and when I was struggling to eat my dinner in bed I knew in my bones that Henry was with Venetia.' But she was, she said, far too fond of him to show him how miserable it made her at so difficult a time in his parliamentary career.

It is impossible to know how Venetia viewed Asquith's loving phrases, as none of her letters to him have survived. It is certain that she would have relished the rest of the contents of his letters: the political gossip, the flattery of being privy to who said what to whom during a Cabinet meeting, disclosures of decisions still secret – for instance, that the thirty-five-year-old Montagu was to be promoted to the post of Financial Secretary to the Treasury. She also heard his real views of some of his colleagues.

He was just as frank about them to Margot. Writing to her for her birthday on 2 February, after affectionately saying how glad he was she was so much better, he told her: 'We are bound to be in for a strenuous and rather turbulent time, and I can see that whatever is to be done to steer the ship I shall have to do by myself. LlG has no judgment, Winston is self-absorbed, Grey has very little outlook and Haldane is completely obscured by mists and clouds.'

She arrived back in London on 15 February, the night before the official reception given by the Prime Minister before Parliament returned after the Christmas recess. She felt altogether fitter and enlivened by the after-effects of having her children to herself for such a comparatively long time: Elizabeth for three weeks at Cannes and Puffin for another three weeks at Antibes.

'If Henry had been there I should have had the happiest winter since I gave up hunting,' she wrote in her diary, adding that in order to be on her best form at the party she had dined in bed the night before and on the evening itself put on her best dress: 'The one I wore at Windsor made by Paquin and only cost £20, an embroidered rose pink velvet apron and rose velvet collar on a black and steel dress.' As always, it was up-to-the-minute but she did not really care for the latest fashions. '[They] are meant to be bold and rebellious but they are really confused and grotesque.'

Her wretchedness over her husband's obsession with Venetia was such that she hardly enjoyed anything then. She longed for Venetia to disappear; and only one way seemed possible. 'Oh! If only Venetia would marry,' she wrote to Montagu, her friend and confidant. 'How I loathe girls who can't love but claim and collect alike a cuckoo for their own vanity – Venetia's head is completely turned.' For the unfortunate Montagu, longing only to persuade Venetia to accept him, Margot's letter, written in ignorance of his feelings, must have been an unwelcome touch of irony.

To neither woman, though, did Asquith's letters in those first few months of 1914 contain any reference to a possible threat from Germany.

'Few of us realised in the earlier half of 1914 how near the crash was to us,' wrote H.G. Wells. Not only the Liberals but many Conservatives also felt that Germany had no warlike intentions: there had been co-operation between Britain and Germany over the turbulent Balkans and only eighteen months earlier the Conservative Lord Esher, regarded as an authority on defence matters, had told an audience of Service officers that 'war becomes every day more difficult and improbable'.

When Count Harry Kessler invited George Bernard Shaw to lunch at the German Embassy, Shaw, dressed that February morning in a green summer suit, gave the Ambassador, Prince Lichnowsky, his typically Shavian view that the way to ensure world peace was to 'prepare a new Triple Alliance between Germany, England and France and to make this the basis of the peace of the world. Other countries should be told that war will henceforth be considered as a sort of nuisance and that if anybody embarks on it this Triple Alliance will call him to book.'

Lichnowsky laughed and, recorded Kessler, 'emphasised, as always, how good the relations between England and Germany now were'. The only war that anyone thought could – indeed, might easily – happen was one between Ulster and the South of Ireland, with the enforcement of the Home Rule Bill later in the year.

Meanwhile, domestic issues monopolised the Government's attention. As the row over the Naval Estimates – with the fear of a Cabinet split, the possible resignation of either of the two parties concerned and even the threat of an election – rumbled on, Asquith took an optimistic view. 'I think we shall get through our little troubles on the navy,' he told Margot. 'LlG squeezing in one direction and Winston in the other. Neither of them wants to go and in some odd sort of way they are really fond of one another.' A few days later he noted that 'both LlG and Winston are anxious for an accommodation. When that is settled we shall have to switch on again to Ireland, which keeps the poor little King in a perpetual fluster.'

The cause of tension between the two ministers was basically a fight over the money to be allotted in the 1914 Budget. Not only did around £11 million have to be found for greatly improved social measures such as education and health services, but a deficit of over £5 million resulting from a huge increase in naval expenditure since Churchill became First Lord of the Admiralty in 1911 had to be corrected.

The Navy's primary fuel was coal; Churchill's determination that the Fleet should be as efficient and modern as possible meant that the Government was committed to an expensive programme of converting Britain's warships from coal-burning to using oil as fuel.

Coaling was a long, laborious and filthy process, involving almost all of a warship's crew. After the piling of coal into buckets or sacks – often while having to keep their balance on the side of an ever-decreasing mountain of coal on the quayside – and unloading it into the coal bunkers, they had to clean the ship and scrub their clothes until every vestige of coal dust had disappeared. It was also impossible to refuel at sea, meaning that a quarter of the Fleet might be forced to put into harbour for coaling at any one time.

Oil appeared to offer huge advantages. It produced much more heat than coal so that boilers could be smaller and ships could travel twice as far and go faster. It produced less smoke, so a fleet would not reveal its presence as quickly, could be stored in tanks anywhere – allowing more efficient design of ships – and transferred to boilers through pipes rather than by stokers' shovels, thus reducing manning, the laborious cleaning process and the overall time taken, and refuelling could be done at sea.

Against this was the fact that the oil supplies of the world were in the hands of vast oil trusts under foreign control, whereas there was an inexhaustible supply of British coal with a global network of coaling stations in place. In addition coal was inert, so a shell exploding in a storage bin would not cause so much damage.

As Churchill noted, the advantages conferred by liquid fuel were inestimable. But he also recognised that a switch would be difficult to implement: opposing the transition was the weight of naval tradition, underscored by the loss of the strategic advantage of large coal supplies in Britain.

The cautious approach was not in Churchill's nature. In 1912 Admiral Fisher had written to him saying, 'What you do want is the super-swift – all oil – and don't fiddle about with armour . . . There is only one defence and that is speed!' It chimed with Churchill's own thinking: when he learned that to outmanoeuvre the German fleet Britain's fastest ships would need a speed of twenty-five knots – at least four knots faster than possible at the time – he concluded: 'We could not get the power required to drive these ships at twenty-five knots except by the use of oil fuel.' Oil it would be, so that Britain was ready.

Most of the Liberal Party, on the other hand, did not believe – or want to believe – that there was a chance of aggression from Germany. And in addition to their conviction that those – like Churchill – who thought there was such a chance were sabre-rattling, there was a political imperative: a 'good' Budget would help them win the election scheduled for 1915 and, as far as their Chancellor, Lloyd George, was personally concerned, would help him to live down the Marconi Scandal that had so tarnished his name. The necessary monies for this 'People's Budget' were to come from the better-off, via an extra twopence on income tax – bringing it up to 1s 4d – and increased super-tax and death duties (in the event, the fight-back from the rich of both parties meant that only 1d went on income tax).

The running battle with the suffragettes, now growing increasingly desperate, continued, with Asquith seemingly unwilling to give an inch, despite the fact that most of his Cabinet now opposed his stance. 'I think it disgraceful that millions of women shall be trampled underfoot because of the convictions of an old man who notoriously can't be left alone in a room with a young girl after dinner,' wrote Ethyl Smyth. Smyth, the daughter of a Major-General, was one of those from whom Asquith's predilections were no secret.

She was also a musician, and the composer of 'The March of the Women', which became the anthem of the suffragette movement. (When Emmeline Pankhurst called on WSPU members to break a window of the house of any politician who opposed votes for women, Smyth was one of the 109 members who responded, serving two months in Holloway. When her friend Thomas Beecham visited her there, he found her leaning out of a window conducting the anthem with a toothbrush as suffragettes marched round the quadrangle singing it.)

In March a suffragette damaged Velásquez' painting *The Rokeby*

Venus in London's National Gallery with a meat chopper and one young woman even managed to plead the suffragette cause – for a brief moment – in the august surroundings of Buckingham Palace. On 4 June Lady Blomfield, the widow of a distinguished architect, had arranged to present her two debutante daughters at Court. But they had shown such sympathy with the suffrage movement that she became suspicious that they might somehow disrupt proceedings, so left them behind when she set off.

The moment she had gone, the two immediately changed into their presentation dresses and went off to the Palace, where they explained that their mother had gone on ahead but had taken their tickets with her. With their names on the list they had no difficulty in getting in. One of them, at the moment she had descended in an exquisite curtsey in front of the King, called out: 'Your Majesty – stop forcible feeding!' Courtiers rushed up from all directions and the girl was immediately hustled away. When her mother, who was in another room, heard what had happened she fainted, saying next morning that the episode was 'deeply deplored by the whole family'. The King described it in his diary, adding, 'I don't know what we are coming to.'

An interrupted ceremony was one thing, property damage quite another. More and more, women were turning to arson: in seven months, as many as 107 buildings were set on fire. Between March and July an emaciated Mrs Pankhurst was imprisoned four times, each time going on a protracted hunger strike so that by the end she was mere skin and bones and her flesh shrank, terrifyingly, prompting Asquith to confide in Venetia: 'Another small complication is that Sylvia Pankhurst, whom McK is letting today out of prison – she has been eight days without food or drink – proposes to continue her "strike" to the point of suicide, either at her own home or perhaps on a stretcher in Downing Street, until I receive a deputation of East End suffragists! I don't want, if I can help, to secure her the martyr's crown, but *que faire*?'

In England, families were now riven by the Home Rule question and friendships broken. Some of Asquith's own Cabinet were strongly against the Bill, and opposition in Ulster, headed by Sir Edward Carson, grew ever more bitter. As the time for the Bill's third reading approached, civil war seemed all too likely. The Conservative leader Balfour, speaking for 'a clean cut' between North and South, said of the situation: 'We are in the rapids now, and even to the dullest hearing the mutterings of the cataract must surely be audible.' The crisis was escalating daily; and in Government circles it often seemed as if people spoke of little else.

When moving the second reading of the Home Rule Bill, Asquith had put forward an Amending Bill providing for any county in Ireland to vote for exclusion for up to six years (i.e. until after the next general election). The Nationalists, determined on a united Ireland, give or take six years, thought that this concession would show them as reasonable and willing to negotiate, thus gaining public sympathy; the Ulster Unionists rejected the plan outright. Their leader, Carson, refused even to lay it before the Ulster Convention, saying: 'We do not want a sentence of death with a stay of execution for six years.'

Churchill, egged on by Lloyd George, with whom he had resumed his friendship, and with Asquith's reluctant approval, spoke at Bradford days later, saying that this offer 'represented the hardest sacrifice ever asked of Irish Nationalism', and concluding: '. . . let us go forward together and put these grave matters to the proof'. Implicit in his words was the suggestion of force – or so the public saw it.

'In afternoon Barb and two maids went to help protest at the great meeting in Hyde Park against British troops being used to quell Ulster,' wrote Lucy Broadwood (daughter of the piano manufacturer Henry Broadwood) in her diary on 4 April. For the idea of using Britons to quell Britons was one of horror. Could even the most dedicated soldier be asked to march on his own people? Asquith believed they could not. 'There is no doubt,' he wrote to Venetia, '. . . if we were to order a march upon Ulster that about half the officers in the Army – the Navy is more uncertain – would strike.'

'Strike' they did, in what came to be known as the Curragh Mutiny, when British cavalry officers stationed at the Curragh near Dublin informed their Brigadier-General that they would resign or accept dismissal when told that they must be prepared to serve against Ulster if necessary; and their commander approved the decision. Out of the seventy officers there, fifty-seven accepted the offer of Sir Arthur Paget, Commander-in-Chief in Ireland, to resign their commissions in the British Army, or to accept being dismissed from it, rather than enforce the Home Rule Bill in Ulster whenever it passed into law. Technically, the fifty-seven were not guilty of mutiny as they had resigned before refusing to carry out a direct order.

In London, the Government responded with dismay and limp indecision, finally backing down with the claim that there had been an 'honest misunderstanding'. 'Not since 1688, when James II lost his crown,' wrote George Dangerfield in *The Strange Death of Liberal England*, 'had the army refused to obey its orders, as it now refused to obey them; not since 1688 had it controlled the country; this was the first time since that violent year, that an Opposition had promoted a rebellion, and for the first time in all history that a Liberal Government had virtually ceased to govern.' The central fact was that any attempt by a Britain already divided on the subject to coerce Ulster by force would be met with armed resistance.

Immediately afterwards came another dramatic development in the Home Rule saga. Gun-running had been practised in a small way since the founding of the Ulster Volunteer Force in 1912, with guns brought over in fishing boats and hidden in boxes of herrings, or in the coal transported by colliers. But these were not nearly enough to arm the 100,000 men of the Ulster Volunteer Force, let alone the many more who had signed the Ulster Covenant.

In the spring of 1914 Major Frederick Crawford, a former officer in the British Army, managed to buy a large quantity of arms and ammunition from an arms dealer in Hamburg. These were successfully brought to Ulster through a combination of immaculate military organisation on the part of the Ulster Volunteers and a brilliant hoaxing of the authorities. Germany, interestedly watching the developments over the Home Rule Bill, was only too ready to turn a blind eye to anything that might aggravate the situation – such as the departure without impediment of a large cargo of arms to Ireland.

When a brief story in *The Times* alerted the authorities Major Crawford moved the arms to another small ship, renaming it the *Mountjoy II*. When a large truck drove to the Belfast dockside and parked there as if waiting for an incoming load, while a contingent of UVF men marched to the docks, it seemed that both were waiting for the arrival of a small tramp steamer, the SS

Balmerino. Its captain, in on the plot, made sure that its approach was as suspicious as possible. The authorities duly took notice and, when the captain stalled their questions, became ever more certain that they had got the arms ship. Finally, when the captain could hold them off no longer, they searched the ship – to find its papers blamelessly in order and its cargo merely coal. Meanwhile, twenty miles away at the port of Larne, the *Mountjoy* was being unloaded and bundles of rifles taken round the country, to be hidden under floorboards.

It was a political coup of a high order. 'Magnificent! Magnificent! Nothing could have been better done, it was a piece of organisation that any army in Europe might be proud of,' said Lord Roberts (Field Marshal Earl Roberts of Khartoum, VC), the popular Ulster-born General who had been in command in the Boer War and who had only refused Carson's offer to lead the UVF because of his age (he was then eighty-one).

In London a Nijinsky summer had already begun. 'London seemed to be having such a season as it had not known for years – what fun it all was,' thought Ottoline Morrell, who herself held a salon every Thursday in Bedford Square that became a centre for artists and writers like Diaghilev, Lytton Strachey and Duncan Grant. From the first burst of fine weather early in the spring that heralded the post-Christmas 'Little Season' to the last of the early Courts at the beginning of March, the weeks were packed with dances. That spring, the fashionable thronged Hyde Park, strolling beneath the trees, their fresh green leaves not yet soot-laden – for the muslin dresses of later summer, a sudden shower brought the hazard of sooty raindrops – or sat on little green chairs to watch riders go by.

After a brief break for Easter, parties began in real earnest at the beginning of May. In one week alone there were four balls on one night, for which dinner parties were given beforehand, especially by those hostesses who, like Margot, had a debutante daughter to launch – the seventeen-year-old Elizabeth, an extremely pretty girl, was to be presented in June. But to Margot's surprise and disappointment there were not the expected number of invitations to balls and parties for her. The reason was political: most of the families rich and grand enough to have given such invitations were Conservative – some with estates in Ireland – who strongly supported

Carson and were therefore against Asquith, a hostility that rubbed off socially on his family.

As Beatrice Webb wrote in her diary for 23 April, 'in the party papers and among little cliques of the fashionable and wealthy the talk was of civil war and revolution. For about three days, members of the governing class glared at each other and social entertainments were boycotted by one of the party clans or the other.'

Beatrice Webb's claim that these enmities lasted a mere three days was nonsense. The whole of political London, including wives, families, friends and connections, seemed to have taken sides. In George Dangerfield's memorable phrase, 'People dined against each other in the deadliest fashion, and drawing room met drawing room in mortal combat.' Margot herself, and Elizabeth, suffered a miserable and bitter snub because of this partisanship,* which finally destroyed her belief that the friendship between Souls could withstand even the strongest political disagreement.

In May 1914 George Curzon, one of Margot's oldest and most beloved friends, was to give a magnificent coming-out ball for his eldest daughter Irene, to which the King, Queen† and the whole of Society would be invited. No expense was to be spared: a seventy-foot-long supper room was built in the garden, hung with tapestries brought up from Hackwood, another of his palatial homes; three grand pianos were brought in, a twenty-strong band was hired, and a powdered footman stood behind each chair at the dinner for fifty-two beforehand. Margot looked forward to bringing Elizabeth, just back from Munich and a favourite of Curzon's (he had told Margot that she reminded him of a white rose, 'pure and full of fragrance'), and for whom it would be a chance to see what a grand ball in the old style was like.

But the time of the ball approached and no invitation came. Margot could not understand this, especially as several members of the Asquith family and political colleagues were going. Both she

---

* Even after the 1914–18 war the old Duchess of St Albans threatened to walk out of the church at a wedding if seated anywhere near the Asquiths. (Dame Peggy Wakehurst, *In a Lifetime Full*.)

† At the last minute the King and Queen could not come because of the death of the Duke of Argyll (husband of Princess Louise, Queen Victoria's fourth daughter), which meant Court mourning. Thus every woman guest there connected with the Court wore a black ball gown.

and Curzon were – or had been – Souls and, although always in opposing political parties, this had never cast a shadow before. Curzon himself had said, the previous year, when unveiling a portrait of Asquith at his old college, Balliol: 'We do not carry our political differences to the point of obliterating personal friendship, or public esteem. God forbid that such a day should ever come!'

Although Margot had no suspicion of it, that day had arrived. On the continued non-appearance of an invitation, she asked her old friend Mrs Keppel to find out what had happened. When she learned that Curzon was so angry at Asquith's determination to bring about Home Rule that he would not have Margot or Elizabeth in his house, she was both wretched and enraged. She remembered how often he had been to Glen, how she had consoled him in an unhappy love affair, their close friendship through the years ('Your love dearest George has even been among my most precious possessions'), expanded to include his wife ('goodbye dearest George & with love to both of you'), his visits to Downing Street since her husband became Prime Minister. Her stepdaughter-in-law Cynthia, who invariably denigrated Margot while continuing to accept clothes and money from her, said to friends she thought the ball would be all the better without Margot.

Apart from the distress of a rupture with such an old friend, this vitriolic piece of social ostracism hit all the harder because the chief sufferer was the innocent Elizabeth. For Elizabeth this privation was wretched. The months of her debutante season were supposed to be the ones that put her on the social map, that gave her the chance of making real friends among her contemporaries and shining at the balls and parties which she knew she would love. Now, because of the political enmity felt for her beloved parents, she was deprived of all this. It was, in a sense, like being sent to Coventry.

Violet, too, thanks to her open and vigorous espousal of Home Rule in support of her father, was similarly affected by this social ostracism. But for her it was less oppressive: she had her own circle of friends as well as the devoted adoration of Venetia, so that missing the parties and balls given in grand houses was not so meaningful. Others of the Asquith family were not so omitted, perhaps because their support was less vociferous, cogent, or outspoken.

Curzon wrote to reassure her that his 'personal attachment' to her would never waver but added: 'You must be living in a world of your own if you do not realise that at a time when political feelings are so highly strung it would be impolitic to invite, even to a social gathering, the wife and daughter of the head of a Government to whom the vast majority of my guests were inflexibly opposed, and that the meeting might have provoked a scene which would have been much more painful to me, and to you, than your absence could be to either or both of us. It is no good not to recognise these facts, or to be deeply hurt by them.'

Margot responded instantly, saying that she could not imagine a painful scene provoked by herself and Elizabeth entering a ball-room and that she was only hurt when 'unwavering old friends' deserted her. She concluded by saying that she looked forward to the day when she herself would again be received by these 'devoted old friends' and when 'darling Elizabeth won't be looked on as a bomb'. It would not come for some time.

In the last days of June 1914 Lichnowsky reported to the German Chancellor, Theobald von Bethmann-Hollweg, that 'I thought the foreign situation, as far as we were concerned, very satisfactory, especially as our relations with England now manifested a warmth and cordiality that had hitherto been conspicuously absent'.

THIRTEEN

Nothing except the death of a monarch could deflect the grinding wheels of the social season from their preordained track. Every night in those summer months there was dancing in rooms where columns were wreathed with roses and smilax, banks of syringa masked fireplaces and were heaped on marble console tables; when the weather was hot, blocks of ice, covered with banks of hydrangeas, freshened the air. 'Never had there been such displays of flowers . . . lolling roses and malmaisons, of gilded, musical-comedy baskets of carnations and sweet-peas . . . huge bunches of orchids, bowls of gardenias and flat trays of stephanotis,' wrote Osbert Sitwell.

Extravagance was the watchword: at some dances there was not one band but two; at cotillion dances there were presents for all the guests of brocade and gold hatpin stands, flower-shaped menu holders, wreaths of roses for hat trimming, artificial flower corsages, china matchboxes and, for the men, silk braces, silk socks and ties.

Clothes at the evening Courts were ever more lavish. In June Margot presented Elizabeth, wearing a dress of white satin with a white and silver train depending from her shoulders and trailing the regulation three feet; the last Court of the Season saw both Venetia and Margot – excitedly described as wearing 'a wonderful dress of Egyptian embroidered sphinxes on black, sashed with a rich petunia, with a train of sphinx tissue lined with petunia chiffon' – curtseying to the Sovereign. Margot, accompanied by Violet, fittingly dressed in mauve, was presenting the daughter of a friend.

There were grand first nights. The most spectacular were Diaghilev's June productions of Rimsky-Korsakov's *Le Coq d'Or* and *La Légende de Joseph*, with its music by Strauss, for which everyone dressed to the nines – Margot in black tulle and diamonds in Lady Cunard's box, Lady Irene Curzon in silver gauze with a tiara of

turquoises, Diana Manners in white and gold with a pearl bandeau*
round her beautiful head. Asquith, despite his dislike of opera, went
in a party that included Venetia, writing to her afterwards: '...
later on, at the Opera, amid all the indecency and glare & noise of
Strauss's worst moments, I felt more than happy ... I wish I were
going to be with you again this evening. I am sure I should like the
Coq more than *Joseph*.'

In July Alexandra Rose Day, instituted two years earlier, almost
swept Londoners off their feet. Selling these pink roses (made by the
disabled) was an idea conceived by the dowager Queen as a means
of raising money for hospitals and one of the attractions was her
own starring role. Peeresses sold pink wild roses to all passers-by,
servants came up the steps from their basements to buy one to pin
on their cotton summer uniforms and they were even attached to
the collars of dogs as the Queen made an unusually long ceremonial
drive, up St James's, along Piccadilly, through Hyde Park and along
Holborn to the City and back down Pall Mall, with a heap of pink
roses in her lap and her face enamelled to such perfection that her
almost seventy years hardly showed.

Extravagance and exoticism were everywhere: Hazel Lavery,
wife of the Society portrait painter John Lavery, brought back a
small black page from Tangier who attended her constantly; another woman walked in the park leading a small black pig with
gilded trotters and a big pink bow round its neck. On hot days, the
Coterie would swim in the Royal Automobile Club pool with its
mosaic columns, white Sicilian marble walls and bronze balconies
overlooking the green water.

Sometimes the continuing activities of the suffragettes hampered
people's movements that summer. 'After much red tape admitted
to the National Galleries', wrote Dora Leba Lourie, an American
girl from Roxbury, Massachusetts, touring Europe, on 16 July. 'The
suffragists have so scared London that it is almost impossible to
go through the Galleries.' Edward Cazalet, entertaining a friend in
Cambridge for the day, took her to the Fitzwilliam Museum, where
they were 'highly amused by the numerous attendants ready with
outstretched hands to seize Nora lest she be a militant suffragette!'

---

* Only married women (or widows) wore tiaras; young single girls wore bandeaux
  or circlets.

But these were pinpricks compared to a tragedy that hit the Coterie hard. At the beginning of July a young baronet, Sir Denys Anson, hired one of the Thames pleasure-boat steamers together with a six-strong band for a trip up and down the Thames. His friends, all in evening dress – among them Diana Manners, Raymond and Katharine Asquith, Duff Cooper and Iris Tree – came on from dinner parties, and the group, waved off by Venetia, who did not want to join them, set off from Westminster Pier at midnight.

Just as they were passing Battersea Church on the return journey Denys, a strong swimmer, dived into the water and headed for the bank (whether he did it as a prank or was, as the captain said later, 'chaffed into it' by some of the girls is not known, as the party said as little as possible afterwards). About seventy yards out he suddenly disappeared and one of the band, also a strong swimmer, plunged in to try and save him. But both were swept away and drowned although a third volunteer, Constantine Benckendorff – the son of great friends of the Asquiths, the Russian Ambassador Count Benckendorff and his wife – was saved. Dawn was breaking when the search finally had to be given up.

None of them could have guessed that the tragedy was a macabre foreshadowing of the deaths that would soon claim so many of that golden group. For as the writer Vera Brittain later commented: 'That unparalleled age of rich materialism and tranquil comfort, which we who grew up at its close will never see again, appeared to us to have gone on from time immemorial, and to be securely destined to continue for ever.'

For the young – and a good many of their elders in that privileged society – life may have seemed one long round of gaiety. Yet over all hung the threat of armed conflict in Ireland. It is difficult to convey the mounting sense of tension as the moment approached when the Home Rule Bill would finally become law.

From the start, the King had been certain that Ulster could not be included in the Bill as it stood, writing in his diary: 'Ulster will never agree to send representatives to an Irish parliament in Dublin', a warning ignored by Asquith, who wrote to Margot that although the King was a 'nice little man with a good heart', it was a pity he was not better educated.

First, what *was* Ulster, geographically speaking? Both Carson and

Bonar Law agreed that of the nine counties of which Ulster was composed, four were largely Protestant, three (Donegal, Cavan and Monaghan) mainly Catholic and two – Fermanagh and Tyrone – almost evenly balanced with communities of both faiths (but with a majority of Protestants) dotted at random over them. Both leaders held out for the exclusion of the six counties with substantial Protestant populations.

Their position was a strong one: it was now clear that an armed Ulster, backed by a British public hotly against the idea of using force against people they saw as fellow Britons, could not be coerced. All this was faithfully reported to Venetia, along with increasing protestations of devotion ('I dine at Grillions tonight – but I am always thinking my darling of you').

Former friends fell out, dinner parties were arranged along strictly party political lines, there were daggers looks in the Strangers' Gallery as Tory and Liberal ladies found themselves inadvertently seated side by side. There were endless meetings, secret and otherwise, between the leaders of the parties, letters flew back and forth; but as both sides stood rock-like in their entrenched positions, the crunch crunch crunch of approaching doom grew ever nearer.

If the average newspaper reader, walking down a busy street, had caught sight of a poster with the word 'War!' on it, he would have immediately assumed that Ireland was ablaze and that the bloody civil conflict everyone feared had begun. The idea that the greatest war history had ever seen was less than six weeks away would never have entered his head.

Watching from the wings was Imperial Germany, ever anxious to promote political discord in Great Britain and clearly a friend to Ireland. During the early summer Samuel Gurney, the youngest of Isabel Talbot de Malahide's eight children by her first husband John Gurney, was motoring in the west of Ireland and Isabel wrote in her journal: 'Even the donkey-boys would say: "It will be a different matter when the Germans come", if anything happened that they did not like, or anyone told them to be kind to their donkeys.'

Margot, of course, knew that the stakes were high, though as with most people it was the Irish Question that preoccupied her thoughts. 'This promises to be the greatest session in Henry's life. If he can't carry his Home Rule Bill his career will be over and the fate of his party sealed for many years to come,' she wrote in her diary, adding: 'The whole West End of London thinks Home Rule a crime. I've never thought this, I've only felt that it is a blunder.'

The arrival in London of President Woodrow Wilson's roving envoy 'Colonel' (a style he awarded himself) Edward Wendell House did little to divert attention from the Irish Question. In his diary House, who arrived on 9 June, wrote of his meeting with the Foreign Secretary, Sir Edward Grey: 'I told of the militant war spirit in Germany, of the tension of the people, and I feared some spark might be fanned into a blaze, and that she would move quickly when she moved. That there would be no parley or discussion. That when she felt a difficulty could not be overcome by peaceful negotiation she would take no chances but would strike.

'I thought the Kaiser himself and most of his immediate advisers did not want war because they wished Germany to expand and grow in wealth but the army was militant and aggressive and ready for war at any time. That there was a feeling in Germany, which I shared, that the time had come when England could be secure no longer merely because of her isolated position. That modern inventions had so changed the situation that the Germans believed she would be within striking distance before long . . . I gave my opinion of German aerial strength and what they might achieve . . .' It was a remarkably accurate summing-up.

Grey also recorded the meeting later. 'He had just come from Berlin, and he had spoken with grave feeling of the impression he had received there; how the air seemed full of the clash of arms, of readiness to strike. This might have been discounted as the impression which would naturally have been produced on an American seeing at close quarters a continental military system for the first time. It was as alien to our temperament as to his, but it was familiar to us. We had lived beside it for years; we had known and watched its growth ever since 1870. But House was a man of exceptional knowledge and cool judgment. What if this militarism had now taken control of policy?'

But with the question of Home Rule rapidly reaching crisis point, and every available minute of the various leaders' time devoted to finding a way to resolve the conflicting, intractable viewpoints, hardly any notice was taken of the assassination, on 28 June, of the Archduke Franz Ferdinand of Austria, the heir to the Austro-Hungarian empire. The Archduke and his morganatic wife Sophie, whom Margot had met at Windsor Castle the previous year, were shot at Sarajevo by a nineteen-year-old Serbian student, one of seven potential killers planted along their route. It was a tragedy, yes of course it was, said everyone, the Court Ball was postponed and several embassy dinner parties cancelled but no one thought that this single act of violence so far away could be the spark that lit the tinderbox.

When someone brought up the subject at one of the Downing Street dinner parties in the all-male circle over port after the ladies had left the room, Asquith asked one of the guests, the thirty-three-year-old Constantine Benckendorff of the tragic riverboat cruise, what he thought of it. 'Incontinently I started on an impassioned harangue – the arguments of which would certainly not have found my father's approval,' recorded Constantine later, expressing the view that in this question Mitropa (Middle Europe) would find Russia not only united but entirely intractable.

'Mr Asquith listened to me with some attention, ruminatively sniffing, as was his wont, through his rather prominent nose, but kept his counsel to the end. But there was no such restraint on the part of the rest of the table, nearly all of them of my generation and close friends. They vociferously jumped down my throat from several angles, the excellent port having made its way round the table several times. The interminable and acrimonious discussions raged for so long that the most attractive guests, dispatched by Mrs Asquith to persuade us to join the ladies, had every difficulty in fishing us out of the dining room.'

To Venetia, however, Asquith merely mentioned it briefly, simply as a news item before going on to the more pressing concern of Ulster ('Tomorrow we have a Cabinet . . . I will tell you of the queer things that are going on about Ulster') and ending, 'I wonder if you want to talk to me as much as I want to talk to you?' Even Colonel House's advent, fresh from his meeting with the Kaiser and full of tales of war fever in Berlin, did not ruffle his customary serenity.

For Russians, well aware of Imperial Germany's enmity towards them, these signs were taken seriously. On Wednesday during the first week of July, Constantine was suddenly sent for by his father, as usual incommunicado in his study that day as he wrote his weekly personal letter to his Foreign Minister. 'Cony, I think you had better pack up and go back,' he said. 'I think this time we are in for it.'

Others disagreed. *The Times*, expressing the views of many, declared on 16 July that any attempt to 'bully the Serbs would constitute a fresh peril to European peace, and that, we are confident, the [Austrian] Emperor and his most sagacious advisers very clearly perceive'. The following day, at the Mansion House, Lloyd George said that while there was never 'a perfectly blue sky in foreign affairs', he remained confident, despite the clouds, of overcoming the current difficulties.

As for Asquith, it took more than Grey's warnings to shake his assumption that the statesmen of Berlin and Vienna were as pacific, and as fully in control of their countries' armed forces, as he was himself. His letters to Venetia, full of references to Ulster, end with the first semi-avowals of his true feelings for her. 'You told me to tell you everything; there is one thing I can never tell you but you know it.'

And then, on 13 July 1914, came his outright declaration: 'I love you'.

The situation over the Home Rule Bill was now so tightly balanced that it seemed more and more unlikely that conflict could be avoided. The 'political cut' was in full swing: the Marchioness of Londonderry, as the wife of an Irish peer from Ulster, one of the leading anti-Home Rulers, would no longer have any of her old Liberal friends, including Margot, to her house and shouted constantly from the Gallery of the House of Commons when she disagreed with a speaker. Wives of Ulster sympathisers had even begun attending Red Cross classes and rolling bandages in preparation for the civil war they believed was coming; and throughout that July there were prayers in all the churches to save Ireland from internal conflict. To round things off, the Archbishop of Canterbury fulminated against a Premier 'who continued to play bridge with young women until the small hours of the morning' when civil war was round the corner.

On 15 July, according to Asquith's contemporary note, he pointed out to Bonar Law that a failure to settle would mean a general election, with great difficulties afterwards for whoever won it. The next day it was decided that Asquith should advise the King to intervene, with the object of negotiating agreement through a conference of the various party leaders. At Buckingham Palace he found the

King under a canvas awning in the garden. 'He was full of interest about the conference and made the really good suggestion that the Speaker should preside,' wrote Asquith.

The King, who had spent a great deal of time in Cork as a young naval officer, felt that if he got all the parties together at Buckingham Palace some sort of compromise could be reached without resorting to violence and accordingly summoned the Ulster representatives, the Home Rulers, Asquith and Lloyd George for a conference there on 21 July 1914.

The next day the diplomat Count Harry Kessler attended one of Margot's luncheon parties in Downing Street. It was a typical mixture. Besides Kessler there were the politician and author Count d'Haussonville, Lady Paget, writer and intimate friend of Queen Victoria, the influential French Ambassador Paul Cambon, the famous Russian opera singer Chaliapin and, noted Kessler, 'a little Indian lady in Indian costume'. Asquith had just come from the conference about Ulster at Buckingham Palace. Despite the serious situation in Ireland he seemed cheerful, as if, thought Kessler, 'he hadn't a care in the world. Only once, in response to a question from d'Haussonville, did he say the situation was "very serious" in the east as well.' During the party, Elizabeth confided to Harry Kessler her distress at the social boycott to which she was being subjected. 'She is trying to take it lightly, she never went out much, but one notices that it still hurts nonetheless.'

Nor was the meeting that could have settled all this, the Buckingham Palace Conference, going at all well. On only its second day, Asquith was writing to a friend: 'I have rarely felt more helpless in any particular affair, an impasse with unspeakable consequences, upon a matter which to English eyes seems inconceivably small and to Irish eyes immeasurably big. Isn't it a real tragedy?' Once again, the 'tragedy' was the intractability of both sides.

When Harry Kessler gave a luncheon party at the Savoy the next day Asquith, who had accepted Kessler's invitation, cancelled at the last minute. The reason was that he had to see the King – to report the failure of the Buckingham Palace Conference. Kessler, who did not know that the Conference had failed, was well aware of its importance. 'The situation in Ulster seems very serious. England stands before a civil war,' he wrote. When one thinks of the motionless, scarlet-tunicked sentries who today stand guard outside

Buckingham Palace, their faces impassive beneath their bearskins no matter what compliments, insults, sexual invitations or challenges are thrown at them, what he then added seems almost unbelievable: 'Yesterday the Irish Guard before the Palace gave the Irish nationalist leaders an ovation.'

That same afternoon the Asquiths gave a garden party for around 700, where Kessler heard the news of the Conference's failure from Lady Randolph Churchill, as they talked with her son Winston and the German Ambassador Prince Lichnowsky. 'She said the Ulster Conference had as good as failed. Lichnowsky asked how it would end. Churchill had only one, ominous, answer: "Blood, blood!"'

The same day, almost unnoticeably to the average Briton, fell the first of the fatal blows that were to strike down peace. Austria presented a Note to Serbia, to which a reply was demanded by 6 p.m. two days later. Among its requirements were reparation for the murder of the Archduke Franz Ferdinand, on the grounds that it was planned in Serbia, the punishment of those who had committed the crime, an apology read to the Serbian army – and the right of Austrian officials to root out anything in Serbia they regarded as anti-Austrian. It was, virtually, an ultimatum.

As the Cabinet sat gloomily, still trying to resolve the problem of Tyrone and Fermanagh, the Foreign Secretary entered. Then, in Winston Churchill's words: 'the quiet grave tones of Sir Edward Grey's voice were heard, reading a document which had just been brought to him from the Foreign Office. It was the Austrian ultimatum to Serbia.

'He had been reading or speaking for several minutes before I could separate my mind from the tedious and bewildering debate which had just closed . . . but gradually . . . the parishes of Tyrone and Fermanagh faded back into the mists and squalls of Ireland, and a strange light began immediately, but by perceptible gradations, to fall and grow upon the map of Europe.'

Few others saw much to worry about. 'Very little interest taken by the English public who thought it was the usual Balkan trouble that would settle down,' recorded one London woman – there had been strife and conflict in the Balkans for decades as the various countries struggled for identity and territory under the shadow of the fading Ottoman Empire. On 24 July, however, Germany officially announced her support for the Austrian position.

Ottoline Morrell, on a weekend visit to the Asquiths at The Wharf, found only a small party there: Montagu – to her the most interesting – Violet and three of the Asquith sons. 'Most of the talk was about the assassination of the Crown Prince,' she recorded later. Walking with Asquith along the river bank and into the fields, she asked him what would happen about Austria and Serbia. 'This will take the attention away from Ulster, which is a good thing,' he answered with a laugh.

When the conversation came up again at The Wharf Montagu, by contrast, feared it would lead to a European war. Pacing up and down the room, he said: 'Of course, I suppose we shall have to go to war sooner or later with Germany about the Navy, and this may be as good a time as any other – they are probably not so well prepared now as they would be later.' He was the only one there, she noted, who seemed disturbed.

The next day Sir Edward Grey left for a fishing holiday in Hampshire and most of the other ministers also left London. Only Churchill, who had ordered a test mobilisation of the First and Second Fleets, remained. He kept them mobilised.

FOURTEEN

The extraordinary thing about the outbreak of the Great War was the speed, suddenness and surprise of its arrival. So little did anyone expect it that the Prime Minister himself was perfectly agreeable when, a mere nine days before it began, Margot dispatched their daughter Elizabeth to stay with Mrs Keppel in Holland – Elizabeth had been complaining of boredom in London after the expected invitations of her first Season had failed to arrive.

It was the same for others. The novelist Elinor Glyn and the hostess of the château near Paris at which she was staying were surprised and offended when, on 23 July, the Austrian Ambassador, another guest, suddenly left – neither could think why. In England, people continued to make plans to holiday in Europe.

War had actually seemed more likely at the beginning of the century when Germany began its immense programme of naval expansion, clearly designed to challenge Britain's then unquestioned supremacy of the seas. A few years later, in 1908, the Foreign Secretary, Sir Edward Grey, after describing the Kaiser as 'like a battleship with steam up and screws going but with no rudder, who will run into something one day and cause a catastrophe', had gone on to say: 'I don't think there will be war at present but it will be difficult to keep the peace of Europe for another five years.'

Even more presciently, the First Sea Lord, Jackie Fisher, had declared in 1911 that war would break out in September or October 1914. He believed – as happened – that the Germans would inevitably build larger warships after the arrival of the British Dreadnought in 1906, which would in turn mean the widening of the Kiel Canal; this, he estimated, would take around eight years. He also believed that the Germans would like to get the harvest in first.[*]

---

[*] Subsequently Fisher amended this to 'a Bank Holiday in 1914'.

Few would have agreed with him. Until almost the last moment no one anticipated war; at the time there was, indeed, much that would seem to militate against it. Ties of blood and friendship linked many, from the Sovereign downwards, to Germany, fraternal visits by British ships to the High Seas Fleet's home ports had taken place that June, the Kaiser was on holiday, his Chief Minister was entertaining his usual shooting party on his estate in Silesia and the acting Head of the German Foreign Office was on honeymoon. Nothing shouted of emergency.

Germany had come late to the race for colonies but her anxiety to acquire an empire seemed to have quietened down with compromise settlements (though these still lacked her signature). Britain was, in fact, slightly more suspicious of France than of her eventual enemy, though she was still determined that Germany should not become the leading European power – a glance at the 1914 map of Europe shows Germany, like a great mailed fist, clutching most of northern Europe in her grasp – as British foreign policy had always aimed at maintaining the balance of power.

Not only the Liberals but many Conservatives felt that Germany had no warlike intentions: as late as June 1914 Sir Edward Grey thought that 'the German Government are in a peaceful mood and that they are very anxious to be on good terms with England'.

Once events had been set in train by the Austrian ultimatum, however, they moved with great swiftness.

During 24 July Germany and Russia made it clear that they would respectively support Austria and Serbia and Sir Edward Grey, speaking for the British Government, asked that Germany, France, Great Britain and Italy 'who had no direct interests in Serbia, should act together for the sake of peace simultaneously'.

The next day Serbian troops mobilised and by the evening Serbia had responded to the Austrian ultimatum, conceding most of the points but refusing to allow Austrian officials into Serbia to pursue their aims there, as this brought into question Serbia's survival as an independent nation; on this, they asked that the Hague Tribunal arbitrate. Immediately, Austro-Hungary broke off diplomatic relations with Serbia.

When Elinor Glyn arrived that day at Cowes, where Society gathered every year during the first week in August for Cowes Week for days packed with regattas, sailing, spectating and parties, she found the place abuzz with a rumour that the Regatta might be put off. Most people discounted this although Lord Ormonde, the Commodore of the Squadron, told Elinor he thought there must be something in it, for Prince Henry of Prussia, who never failed to come, had cancelled his visit.

To most eyes the situation did not seem particularly threatening to Britain – the Kaiser was still on his usual summer cruise in the North Sea on the Imperial yacht *Hohenzollern*, and if the Emperor of Germany was on holiday there was probably little to worry about. ('Cruise' was in fact rather a misnomer: the *Hohenzollern*, a ship known for her rolling, spent most of her time at anchor in a fjord, surrounded by the spectacular Norwegian scenery of tumbling waterfalls, sheer cliffs, pine forests, flowery meadows and deep blue water, while the Kaiser pursued his rigid timetable of exercises before breakfast, sailing or shore excursions, afternoon naps and punctual meals eaten off heavy silver.)

Although the Kaiser had encouraged Austria to come down heavily on Serbia he did not believe that this would, or should, result in a major war. When he saw the Serbian response to Austria's ultimatum, while still on his cruise, he wrote on it: 'A brilliant solution – and in barely 48 hours! This is more than could have been expected. A great moral victory for Vienna; but with it every pretext for war falls to the ground, and [the Ambassador] Giesl had better have stayed quietly at Belgrade. On this document, I should never have given orders for mobilisation.'

Asquith had written in a contemporary note that, although Serbia had capitulated on the main point, 'it is very doubtful if any reservation will be accepted by Austria, who is resolved upon a complete and final humiliation'. He had realised straight away that Russia would come to the aid of Serbia and that therefore Germany and France would be drawn in, but Britain, he hoped and believed, could remain merely 'a spectator'. It was, he thought, 'the most dangerous situation of the last forty years'.

In Berlin, strolling home after morning service that Sunday, 26 July, as Margot was sending Elizabeth to Holland, the Reverend Harold Williams heard one of the bands that often played. 'On this particular Sunday it was not the usual jaunty regimental march that was being played but "Deutschland, Deutschland über alles" and that could only have one meaning – things were definitely getting serious. War, of which we had so often heard rumours, but which had always seemed so utterly incredible, might be really coming at last.'

Then, Russia was seen as the chief enemy for her involvement in the Balkans. At The Wharf, Asquith was as usual writing to Venetia, this time enclosing the telegram he had received from the British Ambassador in St Petersburg, showing the Russian viewpoint, and their anxiety to bring Britain in – his practice of revealing Government secrets to her had begun. 'I contemplate with horror returning to London tomorrow without a chance of seeing & talking to you, most beloved, till the end of the week.'

In Cowes, Winifred Tower, from a keen sailing family, was looking forward to the various regatta races and the general jollity. She noted that the deep-water moorings of Cowes Roads were very gay that year, crowded with more than the usual weekend fleet, brought out by the glorious summer weather.

On 27 July, the first day of the Castle Yacht Club Regatta in which her family had an entry, she went into the town early to get the newspapers, and on the way met a friend who reported gloomily on that morning's news, of riots and shooting in the streets of Dublin, 'the first blood of the civil war, everyone said'. Three civilians had been killed by rifle shots from British soldiers, called in by the authorities after a successful gun-running venture.

This second gun-running was by the Nationalist Volunteers – formed the previous November as an answer to the UVF in Ulster and now numbering 100,000 – and also ready to fight. After Crawford's successful operation to Larne with German aid, the Nationalist Volunteers decided to do the same thing, again buying guns from a willing Germany.

This time, though, there was nothing clandestine about the enterprise, which took place in broad daylight, almost 1,000 guns being landed openly at Howth, near Dublin, on 26 July. Erskine Childers, who had brought them from Germany on his yacht *Asgard*, distributed them to the waiting Volunteers, at first without interference from the authorities, but then the Army was called in and some soldiers, heckled by a jeering crowd, loosed an unauthorised volley, with tragic consequences.

When Asquith heard the news that Sunday night, he hurriedly

left the bridge table at The Wharf at 11.00 p.m. and was motored up to London, arriving at 1.00 a.m. The next morning he wrote to Venetia: 'The malignancy of fortune could hardly have devised a more inopportune coup, and how the devil the soldiers came to be mixed up in it at all, still more to fire their volleys, at this moment passes my comprehension . . . the whole thing . . . must react most unfavourably on the chances of peace & settlement.'

He continued with a description of one of their guests at The Wharf, Lady Ottoline Morrell, a striking figure six feet tall with long red hair and a penchant for flamboyant clothes: 'You should have seen her in her evening war-paint, blackened eyes, green silk trousers, and a turban with a long protruding feather; as you say, a little above life-size in every way for a place like The Wharf.'

He did not say that four years after marrying Margot he had found himself deeply attracted by the youthful Ottoline. They had originally met at a dinner party in 1898, when Ottoline was twenty-five and Asquith forty-five. After telling her that he took an interest in her reading, he would lend her books and visit her in her sitting room high up in the family house in Grosvenor Place.

Here, in this book-lined sanctum, with its profusion of ferns and family photographs, they would sit on a deep sofa with white muslin cushions and talk of poetry and religion until one day this father-like figure made amatory advances. Asquith's 'pounce' so upset the inexperienced Ottoline that she fled, cancelling her third term at Somerville College, Oxford. This may sound a drastic reaction but in those days sex was a subject little discussed, so therefore often came as a shock, particularly to young girls who were frequently left in ignorance until marriage. Those who had managed to pick up a little information would probably have also absorbed the fairly general presumption that for a woman sex would be something to be undergone as a duty, if not actively unpleasant.* Thus, Ottoline's bolting is understandable. Later, however, a veteran of marriage and several affairs, she successfully renewed her friendship with Asquith.

---

* As late as 1910 Havelock Ellis, the physician and writer on human sexuality, was noting that 'by many, sexual anaesthesia is considered natural in women, some even declaring that any other opinion would be degrading for women'. Study after study had emphasised that it was normal for women to gain little or no pleasure from sex.

The débacle of the Dublin shootings so dominated the news that on 27 July Winifred wrote in her journal that 'it now seemed that bloodshed there was inevitable'. Even the report that the King was not coming to Goodwood or Cowes took second place, while the last sentence of Prince Henry's telegram cancelling his visit – 'Recalled to Berlin owing to European crisis. Au revoir, I hope' – seemed to hint at only a temporary absence.

In Berlin it was a different matter. 'From week to week I had watched the threatening storm approaching without believing that it could ever burst,' wrote the Reverend Harold Williams. 'As long as the Kaiser was away on his usual summer cruise in Norwegian waters, what need to worry?' But the Kaiser had suddenly broken off his cruise and returned to Kiel on his way to Potsdam. Excitement reached fever pitch when the following afternoon, 27 July, he entered Berlin.

'As his car passed slowly up the Unter den Linden towards the Palace, the crowd was so dense that it was forced to go slowly, and I found myself pushed so close to it as it passed that I could have touched its royal occupant. I noticed that he was wearing a brass cuirassier's helmet that covered the back of his neck as well as his forehead. His face looked bloodless and yellow, while his eyes stared fixedly ahead with a hard, almost fierce expression. Evidently this was a very different man from the imposing Siegfried-like figure I had seen some months before on his grey charger with his Field Marshal's baton in his hand as he led his finest troops up the Friedrichstrasse.'

Yet in Britain there was still no realisation among the public at large that the country was teetering on the edge of war; for many, the Irish Question was still at the forefront of their minds. In London, life appeared normal. On the Serpentine young men wearing straw hats took their lady friends for a row over the calm water. Dogs yelped playfully at the ducks and from a bandstand nearby the breeze wafted snatches of melodies from *The Merry Widow*. People strolled around in an unhurried manner, or stood quietly admiring the colourful flower beds. Little groups discussed the latest gossip. For those who wanted to sit, one penny bought the use of a deckchair anywhere in the park, at any time, for however long they wanted.

In the country, where a telephone was often a luxury, much

getting about was done on bicycles or horses and the arrival of a telegraph boy usually spelled bad news, little of what was going on in Europe had impinged.

Margot's regular luncheon parties continued; on most days the Downing Street dining table would be surrounded by the usual mixed collection of guests. Asquith often had no idea who would be there until he walked in from the Cabinet Room.

When Margot read a report in *The Times* that on Monday, 27 July Sir Edward Grey had told the House that he had proposed that Germany, France and Italy hold a conference with Great Britain and that while France and Italy had agreed, no reply had been received from Germany, she was intensely worried. She telegraphed Elizabeth to return at once and at the last minute managed to dissuade her astonished older sister, Lucy Graham-Smith, from embarking for a painting holiday in France.

On the next day, 28 July, Serbian reservists being transported on tramp steamers on the Danube apparently accidentally crossed onto the Austro-Hungarian side of the river at Temes-Kubin and Austro-Hungarian soldiers fired into the air to warn them off.

It was enough: unknown to the Kaiser, Austro-Hungary's ministers and generals convinced the eighty-four-year-old Emperor Franz Joseph to sign a declaration of war against Serbia. At once, Russia began general mobilisation. In Berlin, the Prussian War Minister, Erich von Falkenhayn, noted in his diary that he kindly pointed out to the Kaiser that 'he no longer has control of the situation'.

Some within the Government realised this. As Churchill wrote to Clementine on 28 July, 'Everything trends towards catastrophe & collapse. I am interested, geared-up & happy. Is it not horrible to be built like that? The preparations have a hideous fascination for me. I pray to God to forgive me for such fearful moods of levity – Yet I wd do my best for peace, & nothing wd induce me wrongfully to strike the blow.'

That same day Mary Gladstone, daughter of the great Liberal Prime Minister, lunching at Downing Street, sat between Asquith and his son Beb. Turning to the former, she said:

'If ever a war takes place in the world again, I hope it will be now.'

'Why?' asked Asquith.

'To settle Ireland,' she replied.

To which the Prime Minister responded: 'You're as bad as Winston who, last night, seeing there was more hopeful news, said: "I'm afraid we shall have a bloody peace".'

Even as late as 29 July, Margot recorded that both the Archbishop of Canterbury and Lord D'Abernon, lunching with her in Downing Street, 'were amazed when I told them I had stopped my sister Lucy going to paint in France and had telegraphed for Elizabeth to return from Holland'.

Asquith had realised the full implications. His diary entry for that day had faced what would happen. 'The Amending Bill and the whole Irish business are, of course, put into the shade by the coming war, for it now seems as if nothing but a miracle will avert it.' At one of their daily private meeting times, 7.30 in the evening, when both went up to change for dinner, he went to Margot's room, where she was taking her customary pre-dinner nap. Unable to sleep as she thought of the possibility of war, she sat up at once as he entered the room, seeing by his face that something momentous had happened. Unusually, he stood stock-still – customarily he walked backwards and forwards when telling her the gossip of the day. He told her that he had sent telegrams to all Government offices warning them that they must prepare for war.

The next day, the 30th, Bonar Law said to Asquith that he and Carson proposed that the second reading of the Amending Bill be postponed for the time being. 'He thought that to advertise our domestic dissensions at this moment would weaken our influence in the world for peace,' noted Asquith.

In the afternoon Margot went as usual to the Gallery in the House of Commons. The Gallery was packed, with Lady Londonderry and the diehard Tory ladies and Ulster supporters on one side and Margot and the Liberal ladies on the other. So preoccupied was she with what she knew would be in Asquith's forthcoming statement that she hardly noticed the frigid greeting of some of the aristocratic Ulster ladies nearby. Then, calmly and gravely, Asquith announced that the second reading of the Amendment Bill had been put off, to allow the House to concentrate on 'the issues of peace and war, which are hanging in the balance'.

They all turned to her. 'Good heavens, Margot, what does this mean? How frightfully dangerous!' Putting off the Amendment Bill would mean, they said, that by that night the Irish would be fighting.

'What it means is that your civil war is postponed,' replied Margot, 'and you will, I think, never get it.'

As she got up to leave she was immediately surrounded by a crowd of others watching from the Gallery, asking her what this meant.

'Looking at them without listening and answering as if in a dream, I said: "We are on the verge of a European war."'

That night at dinner in Downing Street the discussion was of how long the war would last; most there thought three weeks to three months. Violet thought four weeks and Margot a year. Asquith said nothing.

Yet the news had hardly penetrated the rest of the country. That day in Cowes Winifred Tower was alarmed to see two first-class cruisers, *Drake* and *Leviathan*, unexpectedly appearing early in the morning, 'but we were somewhat reassured by the appearance of *Germania*,* Harry Krupps' racing schooner, being towed to Southampton for the coming regatta'.

Feeling that this was a good sign, the Tower family set off for the Thames Yacht Club races that day. But, reading that morning's papers on the way, Winifred found herself getting more and more depressed by the news of the international situation. As they passed the battleship HMS *Venerable* she saw that it was loading up with stores and ammunition, and that there seemed to be a number of destroyer and torpedo boat patrols around. While they were at the regatta, a trainload of reservists arrived.

The Lady magazine was similarly oblivious. In its issue of 30 July – written, of course, several days earlier – it reported simply: 'London will soon be what is technically known as "empty" – that is, about ten per cent of its six million inhabitants will have distributed themselves within the next week or two over moor, field and seashore in search of a healthy and invigorating change of air and scene.' The main concern of the magazine's social editor that week was the risk to householders from burglars who might strike while they were away.

Winifred Tower's mother and sister, who had been to London that day, came back saying that all was calm and that people in

---

* She was afterwards seized by the Prize Court.

Cowes were unnecessarily excited by all the rumours flying around. But at ten o'clock in the evening the Provost Marshal of the Isle of Wight, a family friend, came over on his motorbike to tell them that the island's forts were being garrisoned and railway bridges and telegraph exchanges guarded.

Winifred went up to the roof of their house to look out for the late passenger steamer from Southampton. It was a scene quite different from the usual one. 'The searchlights were playing all round and the ships off Calshot* turned theirs full on every vessel entering or leaving Southampton Water. The *Cincinnati*, of the Hamburg-American Line, went down the Needles Channel brilliantly lighted up and with every light reflected in the water.' She proved to be the last German ship but one to leave British waters.

Even Beatrice Webb, acute social observer that she was, remained impervious to the realities of the situation. On 31 July 1914, the first day of a conference in Derwentwater, Cumbria, the main entry in her diary is a complaint that among a group of sixty people some Oxford undergraduates had refused to retire to bed at 11 p.m. as had been agreed beforehand. 'The eight Oxford boys ... sat at a separate table, drank copiously and defiantly of the beer they had ordered in, hoisted the Red Flag in front of the house and brought the police inspector to remonstrate with us for the uproarious singing of revolutionary songs at the station and in the market place, at the exact time when the great Keswick Evangelical Convention was arriving for the week of Religious Experiences.'

Later, in August 1918, she added a note: 'All through the last week of the Barrow conferences there had been the rumblings of the approaching earthquake without our awakening to the meaning of it. Sidney had refused to believe in the probability of war among the great European powers.'

On 31 July Russia ordered general mobilisation and Germany sent an ultimatum to Russia, demanding that they halt these military preparations within twelve hours. Russia took no notice and, amid scenes of wild enthusiasm in Berlin, a State of War was declared in Germany. Britain immediately asked both France and Germany to respect Belgium's neutrality; France agreed at once but Germany did not respond. 'Envious persons are everywhere

* At the open end of Southampton Water.

compelling us to defence,' said the Kaiser, 'the sword is being forced into our hand.'

Germany was placed under martial law, France began to issue banknotes owing to the scarcity of gold and silver, the Stock Exchange closed and the Bank Rate was raised from four to eight per cent.

In Berlin, Harry Kessler ordered or bought what he would need for a war: 'field equipment: boots, coat, revolver. Brownings [a make of revolver] can no longer be had.' All day huge crowds swayed back and forth on Unter den Linden, mainly composed, he noted, of groups of adolescent boys and girls. At 11.30 at night they were still there, marching and singing patriotic songs.

At 11 a.m. that morning of 31 July, Asquith went into Margot's bedroom on his way to Cabinet and Margot looked up from her writing desk, where she was as usual dealing with her correspondence and household matters, to hear her husband say that there was now no hope of peace.*

---

* According to the memoirs of Sir Almeric FitzRoy (Clerk to the Privy Council), 'no decision was reached in favour of any further precautionary steps' in that day's Cabinet.

FIFTEEN

'The city has simply broken into chaos,' wrote Churchill to his wife on Friday, 31 July. 'The world's credit system is virtually suspended. You cannot sell stocks & shares. You cannot borrow. Prices of goods are rising to panic levels.'

In Downing Street, the Governor of the Bank of England was waiting to get governmental consent to the suspension of gold payments – something that had not happened for nearly a hundred years. Asquith, who had had an interview with the King in the afternoon, wrote to Venetia that George V 'had just received the most depressing telegram from "William" deploring the perfidy of "Niky" [his cousins the Kaiser and Tsar respectively] in mobilising while the talking was still going on'.

Things, he told her, looked almost as bad as they could be. What seemed to concern him almost equally was the prospect of the cancellation of his proposed visit to the Sheffields' house at Penrhos, to which she had invited him. 'I fear much about tomorrow to which I have looked forward day by day as the one oasis in my desert pilgrimage. If I come, it will be by train wh. gets to Holyhead at 6.45 p.m. If I can't, do telegraph & write to me most beloved, and give me your love & tell me your plans. I *must* see you. *All my dearest love* . . .'

He did not go and next day was writing, 'I can honestly say I have never had a more bitter disappointment. All these days – ever since Thursday in last week – full of incident & for the most part anxious & worrying – I have been sustained by the thought that when today came I should once more see your darling face, & be with you, and share everything and get from you what I value most, & what is to me the best of all things in the world – your counsel & your understanding & your sympathy & your love.'

In Germany, war fever and preparations were well under way.

On the night of 31 July Harriet Jephson, staying in Altheim (in western Upper Austria), heard a herald going round the town, rousing everyone, with blasts on his trumpet and crying, '*Kommen Sie heraus! Kommen Sie alle fort!*' (Come out! All come away!). This was a call to the reservists, all of whom left Altheim.

'Today the crowd cheered madly,' wrote Lady Jephson, a Canadian writer travelling in Austria. 'They sang "Heil Dir im Sieger Kranz" [Hail to thee in victor's crown] and "Deutschland über alles", showing the utmost enthusiasm. To my horror, I find that the banks here now refuse foreign cheques, and will have nothing to do with letters of credit. I have very little ready money with me, and the situation is not a pleasant one!'

In Switzerland, anyone German who could leave had left, and all Swiss men were called to the border. Dora Leba Lourie found that her view of twelve lakes and the Austrian border seen from a peak 6,000 feet high did not compensate for the worrying rumours that Germany and Russia had declared war on each other. She and her friends would, they realised, have to cut out their planned German trip.

In London Lucy Broadwood, a keen newspaper reader, saw for herself that the likelihood of war was increasing, and took her jewel box and valuable miniatures to Lloyds Bank. 'Germany's ultimatum to France still a mystery,' she wrote. 'Very sultry day. Rain and thunder at night . . . signs of military activity in our streets.'

Additional trains were laid on to help Germans and Austrians to go back to their countries, but even the extra night trains were so packed that many could not get away. At Charing Cross Station there were tears as friends and relations saw off large groups of French leaving for their home country – three chefs from Buckingham Palace among them. To these, the King had sent a message by the Master of the Household: that he was proud to have had them in his service and that their places would be kept open for them. So many young waiters left to return to France, Germany and Switzerland – Italians still remained – that hotels found themselves short-staffed. The Savoy alone lost seventy men.

With Armageddon only three days away, some still believed it might not happen. The Foreign Office issued a statement (printed on Saturday, 1 August): 'The Foreign Office wishes it to be known that there is no reason to believe at present that British subjects travelling or residing on the continent are in any danger though they may be put to considerable inconvenience.'

On the same day the Liberal *Daily News*, under the headline 'Why We Must Not Fight', declared: 'For years . . . this country has been preached into an anti-German frame of mind that takes no account of the facts. Where in the wide world do our interests clash with Germany? Nowhere.' Another Liberal paper, *The Nation,* said it was 'safe to say that there had been no crisis in history in which the political opinion of the British people has been so definitely opposed to war as at this moment'. Various countries declared themselves neutral: Greece, Bulgaria, Turkey, Holland, Denmark, Norway, Sweden, Italy – and Belgium.

Intellectuals expressed their dissent from a different perspective: much English scholarship had grown from German roots and the idea of finding themselves at war with a country to which they owed so much was immeasurably distressing. 'We regard Germany as a nation leading the way in the Arts and Sciences, and we have all learnt and are learning from German scholars,' ran a letter in *The Times* signed by eminent academics from Oxford, Cambridge, Aberdeen and Harvard. 'We consider ourselves justified in protesting against being drawn into the struggle with a nation so near akin to our own, and with whom we have so much in common.'

This was, of course, part of the trouble: the links – of blood, culture, friendship – with Germany were so strong, especially for the ruling elites of both countries, that wrenching them apart was not only difficult to do but difficult to comprehend. As crowds gathered around the offices of the *Daily Mail* in Carmelite Street waiting for the latest edition with its up-to-date news, there was little excitement – let alone jubilation – only a deep and serious interest. In a country ruled by a Government whose whole ethos was anti-war, and in which there was no cult of military glorification, it could hardly have been otherwise.

Large parts of Britain were still unaware of the desperate situation. Yachts went on arriving at Cowes for Cowes Week and the major races continued as usual, although the German East African liner *Prinzregent*, arriving at Southampton at 9.00 a.m., turned round at once and made off with all speed after receiving a wireless message. 'We couldn't believe the long-awaited war was really coming, even then,' wrote Winifred Tower.

But the passenger steamers were all late – the Admiralty had taken over the best boats to act as Examination vessels – the crew of the royal yacht *Britannia** had all left to join the Naval Reserve, newspaper boys did a roaring trade and everyone clustered round the local post office where telegrams were constantly being pinned up. At seaside resorts, trippers even fought each other for a newspaper as these arrived at railway stations; in London, with the announcement of the mobilisation of the Naval Reserve, small groups gathered under lamp-posts or in front of lighted shop windows to read the news.

On that Saturday, France and Germany both gave orders for general mobilisation. In Berlin, where the order was issued, it became known at six o'clock in the evening to enthusiasm and excitement everywhere. 'You could [now] breathe,' wrote Harry Kessler. 'The sultry pressure gave way and a cool determination took its place.'

The Reverend Harold Williams had spent the afternoon in the pine-wooded Grünewald, wandering beside its lovely lakes. After supper he decided to find out what was happening in the city. 'I found Berlin gone mad with excitement. Somewhere near the corner of the Friedrichstrasse I saw a large placard bearing the fateful words Ultimatum an Russland. Now I knew what was urging the crowd to a frenzy – THE DAY had come at last!'

By now the crowd was so dense that no one could move. At ten o'clock there was a sudden roar. Williams could just make out that the Kaiser had appeared on the palace balcony. 'War, so long awaited, was now a practical certainty and the Berliners were beside themselves with excitement that could no longer be suppressed. "Lieb Vaterland, magst ruhig sein, Fest steht und treu", and *Die Wacht am Rhein*, they sang. *Deutschland* yelled the young men again and again. *Deutschland, Deutschland über alles* screamed the crowd. Then the dark thought came to me: How many of them will Death not have claimed before this war that they are hailing so jubilantly and vociferously is over!'

Just over an hour after the German ultimatum, Germany declared war on Russia. That night of 1 August Count and Countess

---

* The famous racing cutter built for the Prince of Wales in 1893. During her forty years of service she won 231 races.

Benckendorff dined with the Asquiths, their habit of dinner parties unaffected by the crisis.

It was not a sunny evening. Old friends though they were, Benckendorff and Margot had an altercation over the Count's categorical belief that it was not the Kaiser but his war party that was to blame for declaring war. 'I will never believe the Kaiser is not boss of his soldiers,' said Margot fiercely.

After the Benckendorffs had left, Asquith's notes at the time describe Sir William Tyrrell, Private Secretary to Sir Edward Grey, arriving with a long excusatory message from Berlin to the effect that the German Ambassador's efforts for peace had suddenly been arrested and frustrated by the Tsar's decree for complete Russian mobilisation.

Perhaps, thought Asquith, the Tsar could be brought to withdraw that order and peace could be re-established. It was a faint hope but even the faintest was now worth pursuing, and there was only one person who could do it.

Quickly Asquith, Tyrrell and two colleagues drafted a personal appeal from the King to the Tsar, Asquith called a taxi and he and Tyrrell then set off for Buckingham Palace at 1.30 a.m. The King, in Asquith's words, 'was hauled out of bed, and one of my strangest experiences was sitting with him, clad in a dressing-gown, while I read the message and the proposed answer'. The telegram was sent at 3 a.m. Later, the Tsar responded: 'I would gladly have accepted your proposals had not the German ambassador this afternoon presented a note to my Government declaring war.'

Asquith was not the only one who declared himself (to Venetia) 'not quite hopeless about peace', even three days before the start of the war. Many MPs did not believe that the German army would march through Belgium and that therefore intervention would not be necessary. In Cabinet, Lloyd George, all for peace, was, said Asquith, 'more sensible and statesmanlike for keeping the position open'. Churchill, by contrast, was 'very bellicose and demanding immediate mobilisation'. The pivot, on which everything depended, was the question of Belgium and its neutrality.

Ensuring this was a long-standing commitment. In 1839, the major European powers had agreed to guarantee the neutrality of Belgium, a country which had often been fought over and which, if neutral, would constitute a 'buffer' between France and Germany.

In 1870, as the Franco-Prussian War raged, Britain successfully requested the reaffirmation of this agreed neutrality towards Belgium from France and Germany. In response, Britain bound herself to intervene if either breached that neutrality.

The Cabinet broke up, having arranged to sit again the next day, Sunday, 2 August. Before the business of the day began, the German Ambassador Prince Lichnowsky went to 10 Downing Street to see the Prime Minister and, as he wrote later, 'to try and win him over to take a neutral attitude'. According to Lichnowsky, the Prime Minister was deeply moved and spoke of a war with Germany as 'quite unthinkable', adding that 'it would be very unpopular in this country'.

The Lichnowskys had become friends of the Asquiths almost from the moment they arrived in London in November 1912. The Anglophile Prince ordered his clothes from an English tailor, wore a monocle and, like Winston Churchill, hooked his walking stick from a pocket; his wife Mechtilde was a clever, unaffected woman who had published a number of books. They entertained grandly, with footmen in seventeenth-century livery – but the next day, according to Harold Nicolson, then at the start of his career in the Foreign Office, 'Princess Lichnowsky, laughing and hatless, could be seen running races with the dogs and children in the park'. Nothing could have been more calculated to appeal to the Asquiths.

What Lichnowsky had said was true. Writing that same day, one London woman* recorded that the popular feeling was that war would be dreadful and England would do better to keep out of it. 'Uneducated people cannot understand what is at stake, nor obligations of national honour,' she wrote. 'Nor can they grasp we must fight for Russia against Germany ... Many people still more interested in their Bank holiday than the war – general annoyance at their arrangements being upset.'

In Downing Street, the Prime Minister wrote immediately to Venetia about his visit from the Ambassador. 'I had a visit at breakfast time from Lichnowsky, who was very émotionné and implored me not to side with France. He said that Germany, with her army cut in two between France and Russia, was far more likely to be

---

* She preferred, even in her diary donated to the Imperial War Museum, to remain anonymous.

"crushed" than France. He was very agitated poor man and wept. I told him that we had no desire to intervene and that it rested largely with Germany to make intervention impossible, if she would (1) not invade Belgium, and (2) not send her fleet into the Channel to attack the unprotected North coast of France. He was bitter about Austria, & seemed quite heartbroken.'

Asquith went on to tell Venetia his view of the situation as it then stood: 'Happily I am quite clear in my own mind as to what is right & wrong. I put it down for you in a few sentences.

1. We have no obligation of any kind either to France or to Russia to give them military or naval help.
2. The despatch of the Expeditionary Force to help France at this moment is out of the question & wd. serve no object.
3. We mustn't forget the ties created by our long-standing and intimate friendship with France.
4. It is against British interests that France shd. be wiped out as a Great Power.
5. We cannot allow Germany to use the channel as a hostile base.
6. We have obligations to Belgium to prevent her being utilised & absorbed by Germany.

That is all I can say for the moment. If only you were here, my beloved! How I miss you – in this most critical of crises. Think of me & love me & *write*. Every day I bless & love you more.'

As he wrote, Margot was taking their daughter Elizabeth to Communion at St Paul's Cathedral. After the service she dropped Elizabeth back at No. 10 and then called on the Lichnowskys. She found the Ambassador's wife, the Princess, lying on a sofa, her dachshund beside her and her eyes red and swollen with weeping. The dachshund yapped at Margot and the Princess wept, pouring out her misery at events and concluding by expressing her dislike of the Kaiser. 'I have always hated and loathed our Kaiser. Have I not said so 1000 times, dear little Margot, he and his friends are brutes!' she sobbed. 'I will never cross his threshold again.'

Lichnowsky himself was walking up and down the room wringing his hands and raging against the Kaiser, calling him mad, ill-informed, impulsive, one who never listened to advice. 'Oh say there is surely not going to be war!' he cried to Margot. 'Dear Mrs

Asquith, can nothing be done to prevent it?' Both Lichnowskys, weeping, continued to castigate the Kaiser. Margot did her best to console them and then left.

London was crowded that Sunday, both with Bank Holiday trippers and travellers baulked from returning to the Continent because of the packed trains. All, said Beatrice Webb, in a state of suppressed uneasiness and excitement. Like good socialists, the Webbs were attending an anti-war demonstration in Trafalgar Square. 'It was an undignified and futile exhibition, this singing of the "Red Flag" and passing of well-worn radical resolutions in favour of universal peace,' thought Beatrice.

As the morning continued, churchgoers saw carts of provisions for the troops rumbling west through Piccadilly. In the morning post offices round Britain received messages telling them to stay open 'until instructed to close', and that mobilisation letters might be arriving.

Guards were put on arsenals, docks, bridges and signals and the German Hamburg-Amerika and Norddeutsche Lloyd lines stopped sailing. Anywhere around a port was a hive of activity. Robert Saunders, headmaster of the school in the small Sussex village of Fletching, in a letter of 2 August to his eldest son in Canada told him that 'the reservists are being called up, all the railways are guarded, wire entanglements, trench guns etc, have been hurriedly put round Portsmouth and even our post office has had orders to keep open day and night. Everything points to the Great War, so long expected, being upon us.'

Dora Leba Lourie saw many of her compatriots stuck because they had run out of silver or gold money – her party luckily still had some gold coins. All the porters and men-servants had left their hotel in Meiringen. 'Only two men in hotel besides proprietor and men in our party.' (They moved to nearby Grindelwald but could not get away until 18 August.)

In Berlin, where Russia was clearly perceived as the enemy, Harry Kessler reported to his regiment, where he was told that eleven spies had been shot in Kiel already and four in Spandau, and that people suspected of poisoning wells had been hung in Alsace. The peasants, terrified of the Russians, had set up road blocks with hay wagons and wire and everyone, even if in uniform, was made to stop and show their papers.

That day, 2 August, Germany invaded Luxembourg and Britain said that she would not allow Germany to make the Channel the base for hostile operations. At seven the same evening Germany sent an ultimatum to Belgium demanding 'with the greatest regret' free passage of its troops through Belgium, using the pretext of an imminent French attack on Germany and demanding an answer by seven the next morning. Such passage was essential to the successful carrying out of the Schlieffen Plan* (basically a plan to avoid a war on two fronts).

Refusal, Belgium was told, would mean that Belgium would be regarded as Germany's enemy.

On the other side of the Atlantic, Alan ('Tommy') Lascelles,† waiting in the port of Santos, Brazil, for a ship to take him back to England, noted drily, 'What luck the Liberals have! Few things except a European row could have cut the Ulster knot.'

In Cowes, Winifred Tower and her family soon got used to hearing gunfire. Although the King had sent a telegram cancelling the Regatta only the day before, and the Needles Channel was completely closed, so many yachts persisted in trying to go through it that the forts on the island had to fire warning shots across their bows to deter them.

In church that Sunday an appeal was made for gifts for the Rest Hospital that the War Office had asked their local Red Cross detachment to provide and, wrote Winifred, 'the following day we all went stark staring mad on the subject of nightshirts, cutting up bale after bale of flannel to make impossible garments until the entire stock of material in the town was exhausted'. Many Islanders thought the Germans would attempt a landing in Sandown Bay; prudently, the Tower family kept their boat *Puffin* out, so that in case of need they could slip into Beaulieu River.

That night a densely packed throng assembled in front of

* Germany had believed war with Russia likely and, if this happened, assumed that France, as Russia's ally (and keen to avenge her own defeat in the Franco-Prussian War) would also attack. To avoid a war on two fronts, Germany planned to defeat France rapidly and then turn to the Eastern Front for a major offensive against Russia, which she believed could not mobilise as quickly as France.

† As Sir Alan Lascelles he was later Private Secretary to both King George VI and the present Queen.

Buckingham Palace, with rows of cars parked by the Victoria Memorial – many of their occupants had come on from dinner at private houses, clubs or restaurants. From time to time, 'God Save the King', the 'Marseillaise' or 'Rule Britannia!' would break out, to be taken up by everyone, varied by shouts of 'We want King George!'

In Berlin, Harry Kessler wrote in his diary: 'One knows that the war will be frightful, that we will suffer perhaps occasional setbacks, but trusts that the qualities of the German character – dutifulness, seriousness and stubbornness – will in the end bring us victory. Everyone is clear that this war must result in Germany's world domination or its ruin.'

SIXTEEN

At midday on 3 August Britain's greatest military hero was boarding the Dover to Calais boat to return to his duties as Consul-General of Egypt – the Government had ordered all Heads of Missions to return to their posts at once.

Field Marshal Earl Kitchener was a legendary figure, a great General of Napoleonic stamp, an invincible warrior, brave as a lion and famously cool under fire. He was, in short, a national idol, in the days when successful generals were hero figures revered by all. He had won great victories, modernised the Indian army and in Egypt had enacted sweeping reforms for the benefit of the people. Margot had met him in Egypt when he was a mere Colonel although already well known, and thought him 'a man of energy and ambition, a little complacent over his defects. He has not got an interesting mind.'

Kitchener's impressive appearance helped to build his almost mythic reputation. Tall – at six foot two he overtopped most of his contemporaries – he was broad-shouldered and upright, with an impassive countenance and a slight cast in his right eye that made people feel he was looking right through them. His presence was so commanding that, as his daughter once put it: 'Every chair he sits in becomes a throne.' The splendour in which he managed to live – a 500-acre estate in Kent, an art collection, precious artefacts from Egypt, gold and silver tableware – added to his godlike stature, as did his impenetrable reserve. He was also notoriously secretive and disliked discussing his *modus operandi* with anyone, a trait that would in the future cause resentment and difficulty.

As the day progressed through mounting tensions and chaos it became clear that Asquith could not simultaneously perform the duties of Prime Minister and Minister for War (which he had taken over on a temporary basis in March). The popular press, voicing public opinion, was clamouring for Kitchener – now on board the Dover–Calais boat – and the Prime Minister wanted him recalled. The boat should already have sailed but had been held up owing to the lateness of the boat train from Victoria. Kitchener was urging the captain to depart, as he had a train connection in Paris to catch, when a telephoned message from the Prime Minister arrived.

Reluctantly, Kitchener disembarked and returned to London, where he made it clear to the Prime Minister that if he were needed he would not accept less than a Secretaryship of State – in other words, ministerial rank.

Asquith wanted Haldane, his close friend and the man who, when previously Minister of War, had introduced valuable reforms to the Army, to return to his old post; it was, too, customary that the War Minister should be a civilian rather than a soldier. But, a pragmatist ever, the Prime Minister wanted Britain's favourite soldier there 'in case'. And 'in case' looked by now almost inevitable: Germany was in full war mode, with river and motor traffic stopped. 'An order has come out that petroleum is to be reserved for the Government and when I made another attempt to cash a cheque to-day, again the bank refused,' wrote Harriet Jephson, stuck in Austria.

After the German ultimatum to Belgium, delivered the previous evening, the Belgian Council had sat until midnight, reconvening at 1 a.m. to discuss its reply. It finally broke up at 4 a.m. on the morning of 3 August, sending a reply stating that Belgium could not accept the German proposal. Germany, though, was already moving trainloads of troops and supplies to be ready in force for an advance through central Belgium. Early that morning the King of the Belgians telegraphed to King George, making a 'supreme appeal' to England for help and saying that Belgium would fight.

This moved the Cabinet deeply and the phrase 'plucky little Belgium' soon became well known. As Asquith told Venetia, the prospective German march through Belgium 'simplified matters'. Or as Lloyd George put it: 'The threatened invasion of Belgium [had] set the nation on fire from sea to sea.'

Everyone in the Cabinet that morning realised that this meant war. 'If, in a crisis like this,' said Sir Edward Grey, 'we ran away from our obligations of honour and interest with regard to the Belgian Treaty I doubt, whatever material force we might have at the end, whether it would be of very much value in the face of the re-spect we should have lost.' Even the staunch socialist Beatrice Webb recorded that 'the public mind was cleared and solidified by Grey's speech'.

At 8 a.m. that morning Germany invaded Belgium. At 2 p.m. Sir Edward Grey sent a telegram to the British Ambassador in Berlin, Sir Edward Goschen, instructing him to deliver the ultimatum, to expire at midnight German time, that unless Germany 'took all steps in their power to uphold the neutrality of Belgium' Britain would declare war on Germany.

Margot and Violet, who realised that this meant the recall of the German Ambassador and his wife, called on them to say goodbye. The Lichnowskys were a popular couple; he was distinguished-looking and kindly, she attractive but had allowed herself to put on too much weight. However, Margot was prepared to overlook her usual prejudice against fat women ('and . . . black socks, white boots and crazy tiaras') in Princess Lichnowsky's case because of her enterprising and affectionate nature. Leaving them, Margot was 'too sad to speak'.

In the afternoon, when Asquith and Lloyd George went to the House of Commons, they had to leave their motors behind because of the dense, cheering crowds, making their way on foot with the help of the police.

Margot, listening in a packed Gallery, looked down over the jour-nalists in the press gallery at the Members below, heads bowed as if in prayer, as they listened to her husband announce that an ulti-matum had been sent to Germany on the question of the neutrality of Belgium. He spoke with immense gravity. 'We have asked that a reply to that request, and a satisfactory answer to the telegram of this morning – which I have read to the House – should be given before midnight.'

He rose and walked down to the door of the House in a roar of cheers, then called on the Speaker and announced, 'a message from His Majesty signed with his own hand' to more cheers. Walking onto the floor of the House, Asquith handed the document to the Speaker.

The House responded with wave upon wave of cheering. After the session was over, Margot went down from the Gallery to the Prime Minister's room to find her husband; going in, she stood by the window gazing out. For some time both, wrapped in their thoughts, remained silent. Finally, Margot walked over to stand behind her husband's chair and ask: 'So it is all up?' Without looking at her Asquith answered: 'Yes, it's all up.' She saw that there were tears in his eyes as he spoke.

The Opposition was determined not to be outdone in loyal patriotism. 'The House was great today,' wrote Holcombe Ingleby, the popular Conservative MP for King's Lynn, to his son, 'and would have been greater had it been shorn of the dirty crowd of Little Englanders [those with an anti-Imperialist stance]. The Liberal Government did well – for them: up to Saturday they were intending to stand neutral, then the combination of Winston and circumstances was too strong for them and they decided to do their duty in a half-hearted sort of way. However the infringement of Belgium will drive them into definite action and we must then go the whole hog. In fact we are in for the biggest thing in wars that the world has ever seen. We may even get to know the respective value of the Battleship and the submarine.' The following month, they would dramatically learn the effect of the latter.

The first preparations had begun even in the smallest villages, where the post office was the hub of local life. Banknotes were being refused (in favour of coin), mobilisation posters were being distributed, various prize ships were seized from the Germans, Red Cross meetings were held, reservists were rejoining their regiments or ships and celebrating before they left with beer and song: 'Are we downhearted? No!' The main stations, too, resounded with cheers and patriotic songs as troops poured in from all over the country.

In the distant shires, war news vied with local preoccupations. In Derbyshire's Peakland, where men were mowing and haymaking in gloomy weather, farmer's wife Maria Gyte noted: 'Men working in the hay. Wm mowed Croft heads. Nothing can be talked about except the war. This has come on so suddenly. First Austria and Serbia. Then Russia mobilises. This does not please Germany and she invades France before war is declared. England has fought for peace but it is feared she will have to fight as Germany is proving very aggressive. Sir Edward Grey's speech in paper this morning. Wm also mowed Little Butts. Foxes are a real problem.'

That afternoon, in a small, secret room in the Foreign Office, a Second Secretary, Harold Nicolson, together with a colleague, was busily stamping the word 'Germany' on the thousand-odd documents, printed and complete except for the name of a country, that would inform every department of Britain and the Empire that Britain had declared war on (name to be filled in). Opposite the cupboard containing them – Cupboard A – was a similar cupboard – Cupboard B – with documents identically printed except that they said (country's name to be filled in) has declared war on Britain. The stamp Nicolson was using was one of a great many, each printed with the name of a different country.

As the hours leading to the expiry of the ultimatum were slowly ticking away, the Prime Minister was writing one of his almost daily letters to Venetia who was, he thought, leaving the Stanley house in Anglesey for Mells Park, the Somerset house of Sir John Horner, the father of his son Raymond's wife Katharine. Mells was an Elizabethan house set in a park full of wonderful trees; it was reputedly acquired by an earlier Jack Horner who found its title deed hidden in a pie given to him to carry to London by the last Abbot of Glastonbury, filched it out and kept it, a theft commemorated in the nursery rhyme 'Little Jack Horner' (it is only fair to note that other accounts say the house was legitimately bought in 1543).

Asquith had met Frances Horner, Katharine's mother, even before he met Margot, and the Asquiths and Horners soon became firm family friends. Raymond, on his first visit, mentioned that Mells was full of priceless pictures, going on to describe another family friend, Lord Haldane, bathing in a large pool below the house. 'To see his immense but stately figure clad in a very scanty bathing dress recklessly precipitating from dizzy altitudes into this green and flowery pond . . . proved to me more conclusively than anything else could have done the real bigness of the man.'

The ancient, grey stone manor of Mells, with its mullioned windows, its secluded gardens and its forty bedrooms, had been the home of the Horner family since the sixteenth century. It was a house where people constantly came to stay. As a bachelor, Asquith would come down to Mells on a Saturday afternoon, leave at 10 p.m. on Sunday night, drive to Bath and catch the night train to London, ready to be in court the next morning; and he and Margot had spent the first few days of their honeymoon there.

Venetia, as one of the Coterie, often visited Mells. Asquith was so desperate to see her ('the longing to see & hear you & be near & be with you is so keen and ever growing') that he planned if possible to visit Mells, over a hundred miles from London and involving a journey of several hours, in the next few days. 'We are on the eve of horrible things,' he wrote. 'I wish you were nearer my darling; wouldn't it be a joy if we could spend Sunday together? I love you more than I can say.'

By the evening it was clear that Germany had broken her treaties: she had taken over neutral Luxembourg and was invading France before even declaring war. At 6 p.m. the King held a Privy Council meeting to sign Britain's order for general mobilisation and the Cabinet met for the second time at 6.30 and sat for an hour and a half. While they sat, crowds waited in Whitehall.

There was little hope of German compliance with the ultimatum. War fever was in full spate. Trapped in the small Austrian town of Altheim, Harriet Jephson wrote: 'Troops are marching through the streets and leaving for the Front all day long. The ladies of Altheim go to the station as the trains pass through, and give the soldiers coffee, chocolate, cigars, and zwiebacks. They get much gratitude, and the men say (poor deluded mortals): "Wir kriegen für Sie" (We fight for you). I saw my doctor's wife today. She was quite calm, but looked miserable. Her eldest son left for the Front this morning. I sympathised, and she said, choking back a sob: "Man gibt das beste für das Vaterland" [One gives one's best for the Fatherland]. No letters come, nor papers; and we are only allowed to send postcards written in German.'

Edward Cazalet, visiting Berlin with a fellow undergraduate, realised they must leave at once – but the paper money for which they had earlier exchanged their gold sovereigns would buy nothing. Fortunately the *Times* correspondent came to their rescue, getting them each a passport and providing five marks in coin, with which they were able to board a train on the morning of 4 August.

'I shall never forget the intense excitement of that journey,' wrote Edward in his diary. 'Each time we stopped various people were arrested and to our horror we heard some of them were shot. The train was packed like nothing else on earth. Even the corridor was crowded. People were simply lying on top of one another ... we were forbidden to open a window as it was feared someone might throw a bomb out.' At Flushing they caught a paddle boat to England, passing the Fleet at anchor, and arrived to find none of their letters had reached home; 'they must have been torn up at the German frontier'.

The Reverend Harold Williams, out for dinner in Berlin that evening, heard such a noise in the street that he looked out and saw special editions of newspapers being sold giving the news of the ultimatum. He took a taxi to the British Consulate; as he rode in it he was shouted at and a flaming torch thrust against the window. On his arrival, the British Consul refused to ring up the Embassy to find out if the ultimatum news was true, so he left.

At home he received an order from the Kaiser that the English church was to remain open – his mother, Queen Victoria's daughter Vicky, on her deathbed had made him promise that he would always protect her beloved church. At the same time a brown paper parcel arrived at the British Embassy containing all the Kaiser's British insignia and medals, with a message that he had hitherto felt honoured to possess them but now had no further use for them.

In London, the windows of the Admiralty were thrown wide open in the warm night air. 'Under the roof from which Nelson had received his orders were gathered a small group of admirals and captains and a cluster of clerks, pencils in hand, waiting,' wrote Winston Churchill. 'Along the Mall from the direction of the Palace the sound of an immense concourse singing "God save the King" floated in.'

People had gathered outside Buckingham Palace since the shadow of war began to overhang the country. Now the crowds thickened and intensified, filling Parliament Square and surrounding the Victoria Memorial until there were some 10,000 people densely packed. The knowledge that war was now imminent had brought them together in a demonstration that was part patriotism, part a spirit of national bravado and part loyalty to the Crown. Calls for the King began until, at 8.15, he, the Queen, the Prince of Wales and Princess Mary came out onto the balcony, to an outburst of cheering.

In the Foreign Office, Nicolson and his colleague had nearly finished stamping 'Germany' on their piles of documents when at 9.40 p.m. a Private Secretary, hatless – a real sign of emergency then – came running over from No. 10 and shouted: 'Stop! The Admiralty have intercepted a message that Germany has declared war on us.' Resignedly, they opened Cupboard B and began stamping endless papers with the message that Germany had declared war on Britain. At the same time, a formal letter announcing this was sent to the German Ambassador, together with his passport.

After the Royal Family had gone in, many of the crowd followed a body of Frenchmen and Englishmen who were marching up Victoria Street with the Tricoleur and the Union Jack side by side, singing the 'Marseillaise' and 'God Save the King'. In front of the Palace the crowd was swelling all the time and at 10 p.m. the King and Queen came out on the balcony again, to cries for a speech and recurring chants of the national anthem. This time, Princess Mary could be seen peeping out from under the raised blind of her bedroom window.

'It is enough to drive one mad, being an ocean's width away from it all,' wrote Alan Lascelles, expressing the popular fervour as he waited in Santos for a ship to take him home. 'On 30 July everyone was talking of Ireland. The cry [was] of "Civil War!" "Civil War!" The cry *The Times* and the Tories treated us to every day has been stilled in five days.'

Margot, in Downing Street, was so stunned by the speed with which Britain stood only a few hours from war that when she got home to No. 10 she went to bed. Her thoughts must have been echoed in many minds – 'How did it ... how could it have happened? What were we all like five days ago? We were talking about Ireland and civil war ...' She got up for dinner, then after dinner she went to look at her sleeping children before joining Asquith, Sir Edward Grey and Lord Crewe* in the Cabinet Room.

At 10.25 the Foreign Office received a telegram from Sir Edward Goschen saying that Germany was not going to reply to the British ultimatum, which meant, of course, that Britain would now be the one declaring war: the intercepted message was mistaken. It was back to the original documents – but what about the letter sent in error to the German Ambassador?

To the Foreign Office, where diplomatic protocol was regarded as Holy Writ, this was a near-calamity. Something immediate had to be done, even if it meant that the drama of the day descended into near farce. The unpleasant task of retrieving the letter and substituting it

---

* Leader of the Liberals in the House of Lords as well as Secretary of State for the Colonies.

with the correct wording fell to Nicolson as the most junior there. He rushed to the Embassy – Britain's ultimatum would expire in half an hour – and rang persistently until a sleepy footman, struggling into his uniform jacket, answered. Sticking his foot in the door, Nicolson demanded to see the Ambassador, to be told he had gone to bed. After insisting, he was taken up to Lichnowsky's bedroom. There, by the light of a pink-shaded lamp on the bedside table, he saw the Ambassador lying in his pyjamas on a brass bedstead behind a screen. On the blotter of a Chippendale writing table in the window lay a half-opened envelope. Nicolson guessed that the Ambassador, realising its contents from the feel of the passports, had flung it down despairingly.

Nicolson exchanged the letters as discreetly as he could. As he left the room the Ambassador raised himself up. 'Please remember to give my regards to your father,' he said sadly. 'I shall not see him again.'

At 10.30 Asquith sent a message to Lloyd George next door in No. 11 to join them. Outside, crowds were cheering and singing; inside everyone was waiting tensely, eyes wandering from the door through which any message would come to the clock on the white marble mantelpiece as the time for the expiry of the ultimatum drew ever nearer – midnight in Germany was 11 p.m. in England.

Those gathered in the Cabinet Room sat smoking cigarettes in silence as the minutes slid past. Occasionally, without a word, someone would come in or go out. When the voice of Big Ben boomed out eleven times no one in that room could speak.

Unable to bear any more, Margot left to go to bed. As she was passing the foot of the staircase she saw Winston Churchill 'with a happy face', striding towards the double doors of the Cabinet Room. He had walked over from the Admiralty to tell the Cabinet that telegrams had been sent to every British warship to tell them that war had been declared and 'they were to act accordingly'.

Churchill hastened into the Cabinet Room, breaking the silence in which the others had been sitting since the last 'Boom!' of Big Ben had died away ten minutes earlier. 'His face [was] bright, his manner keen and he told us – one word pouring out on the other – how he was going to send telegrams to the Mediterranean, the North Sea and God knows where!' wrote Lloyd George later. 'You could see he was a really happy man. I wondered if this was the state of mind to be in at the opening of such a fearful war as this.'

The Foreign Office announcement, made immediately, set off a wave of wild excitement. People stormed the plinth of the Nelson monument, bestrode the lions, a procession was led down the Mall by a car flying a huge tricoleur, taxicabs circled the memorial in front of Buckingham Palace, their passengers shouting, cheering and singing, there was more cheering for the King, the national anthem and patriotic songs were sung. Lord Lonsdale, a great sporting figure known as the Yellow Earl, climbed onto the roof of a taxi waving his hat and declaring: 'England has declared war on Germany. England expects that every man will do his duty.' The tumultuous cheering that followed rang out through the early hours.

So began the bloodiest war in our history. As the Foreign Secretary, gazing out of his office window at the setting sun as the first lights of the Mall twinkled through the growing dusk, had remarked to the editor of the *Westminster Gazette* the evening before: 'The lamps are going out all over Europe we shall not see them lit again in our lifetime.'

SEVENTEEN

The day after war was declared there was an atmosphere almost of carnival in the streets. Flag-sellers did a roaring business with Union Jacks and Tricoleurs, young men drove round in taxis shouting and singing, at large stations women handed cigarettes and chocolates to reservists reporting to their regiments, other men rushed to enlist.

Even the very young were affected. A young Irish boy wrote:

Dear Lord Kitchener,

I am ... 9 yrs of age and I want to go to the front. I can ride jolley quick on my bycycle and would go as despatch ridder. I wouldnt let the germans get it. I am a godd shot with a revolver and would kill a good vue of the germans. I am very strong and often win a fight with lads as big as mysels. I want a uneform and a revolver and will give a good account of myself.

Please send anencer.

Yours affectionately

Alfie Knight*

Kitchener was now in charge and the nation felt little could go wrong. On 5 August Asquith appointed him to the post of Secretary of State for War, with a seat in the Cabinet, an annual salary of £5,000 and a special allowance of £1,140 (in addition to his Field Marshal's pay). Against Cabinet opinion, he correctly predicted a long war that would last at least three years, require huge new armies to defeat Germany and suffer enormous casualties before the end would come. It would, he said, plumb the depths of manpower 'to the last million'. He himself had the onerous task of raising this

---

* Lord Kitchener responded politely that Alfie was a little too young.

great army and seeing that it was ready and trained to maximum efficiency.

The immediate rush to the colours was such that *The Times* reported that it took the recruiting officer at Great Scotland Yard twenty minutes to get through the waiting crowds; by 7 August mounted police were necessary to keep control of those racing to join up. 'It'll all be over by Christmas so hurry up, or you'll miss the fun!' was heard on all sides. It was the same in Germany, where the Kaiser told his troops as they marched jubilantly off: 'You will be home before the leaves have fallen from the trees.'

Observing the cheering crowds in Trafalgar Square, the philosopher and pacifist Bertrand Russell noted unhappily that the 'average men and women were delighted at the prospect of war'.

Everyone learned of the outbreak of war in a different way. In the absence of radio or television, newspapers were a prime source of information, often superseded by word of mouth. 'It is now 8.00 a.m. and the footman who called me has just announced that England has declared war on Germany. Is it really true?' wrote Edward Cazalet's younger brother Victor, an eighteen-year-old Eton schoolboy, son of the millionaire William Cazalet, in his diary on 5 August. John Fowler, hearing rumours of a coming war while with his wife in Newquay on their usual summer holiday, had returned to his home in Wareham at the beginning of August. 'I met a man in the road who had just heard from his brother in London that war had actually been declared. I sat down at 9.00 a.m. and applied for a commission in the 3rd Battalion 24th South Wales Borderers.' The reply was a curt order to get ready to sail for India.

Holiday trippers wrestled with one another for the *Daily Mail*; in country towns people fought over the batches of newspapers as they arrived by train from depots; telephone messages reached large houses (the only ones with telephones); and post offices pinned up notices outside. Reservists were called up immediately, leaving from the nearest station amid gifts and cheering.

Why was there such enthusiasm? This was the sort of atmosphere normally to be found at jubilees or other great national days of celebration. On 2 August, Keir Hardie had addressed the anti-war rally in Trafalgar Square to applause; on 6 August he was shouted off the stage by his own constituents in Aberdare by clanging bells, boos, hisses and singing of patriotic songs.

The answer probably lies in the fact that few had any idea of what war would be like. Britain had not been involved in a European war for over half a century; the South African War thirteen years earlier had been a conflict in a distant land that barely affected the majority of the population. For most people, the war would be undertaken with a certain sense of safety: air warfare had not really been considered and, unlike European countries, Britain had no borders over which she could be invaded and her Navy – acknowledged to be the best and strongest in the world – would prevent any incursions over the Channel.

Then, too, most of those who had cheered, shouted and waved their straw hats in the air outside Buckingham Palace the previous night and the following day were – as photographs of the time show – young men, in any nation always the most likely to view the prospect of battle favourably.

Over and above this was a high level of emotion: a mixture of generalised excitement, the release of tension that had built up to almost intolerable levels in the previous two or three days, with the rivalry caused by the naval arms race adding a piquant edge to patriotism, a feeling of adventure and a chivalric sense of honouring obligations and coming to the rescue of a small but gallant country. Germany's violation of Belgian neutrality could be said to have brought the whole country together.

Outside the capital and the Bank Holiday crowds, many were more thoughtful. 'After a breathless suspense of some days, during which we all wondered what England was going to do, the bomb has finally exploded – and only just in time to save our honour,' wrote Beatrice Trefusis, a young woman who had been to finishing school in Germany and much admired German music and culture. 'How barbarous the world still is! ... the thought of two such highly developed nations as England and Germany being at war with one another is AWFUL.' At the same time, Beatrice sensed an inevitability about it. 'One can't help feeling that Germany has been waiting and watching for this for years and must now rejoice that the opportunity to get at us has come at last. The last winter I was in Germany in 1908/9 I was acutely sensible in one way and another of their hatred of us, and somehow felt that they were only awaiting a favourable moment to spring. And now it has come.'

Some saw it as a kind of 'detoxing' of the national body. 'War

... is the sovereign disinfectant, and its red stream of blood is the Condy's Fluid* that cleans out the stagnant pools and clotted channels of the intellect,' ran a famous essay by Edmund Gosse, the critic and *littérateur* who had been until recently the Librarian of the House of Lords. 'I suppose that hardly any Englishman who is capable of a renovation of the mind has failed to feel during the last few weeks a certain solemn refreshment of the spirit ... we have awakened from an opium-dream of comfort, of ease ...'

For Winifred Tower, the announcement of war came almost as a relief. Before it, she wrote, 'every day seemed like weeks, everything was unsettled, and we were wishing one minute for peace at any price, and the next were furious at the idea that we might back out of our Treaty obligations. But it was impossible to believe that "the Day" had really come. We had talked about it, argued about its possibilities, volumes had been written about it. It had been a sort of nightmare always hanging over us, and yet I don't suppose many of us ever thought that it would become a reality in our time ... but now it is upon us, and so suddenly that it seemed like a bad dream that we should soon wake from to find our world unchanged.'

Edwin Lutyens, who heard the announcement of war in his club, the Athenaeum, went out onto its top balcony to see the reaction of the crowds in the Mall, and heard 'Rule Britannia' ('very badly sung'), the 'Marseillaise' and 'God Save the King'. He could also see the German Embassy, 'but there was no demonstration – a few boys booed and perhaps 12 policemen moved them on gently and without effort. There was no stone throwing.'

In Britain on that morning of 5 August huge headlines in every newspaper proclaimed 'England declares War'. Territorials leaving for training were cheered by crowds, notices of the newly passed Alien Act were posted everywhere. This declared that all Germans in the country must at once report themselves to the police on penalty of a £100 fine or six months in prison, nor were they allowed to have in their possession any arms, petrol or inflammable spirit, car or bicycle and their telephones were to be cut off. Some Germans† were even arrested as spies.

In Berlin the windows of the British Embassy were broken the day

* A disinfectant solution that could be taken internally or externally.
† One source gives the number living in London as about 50,000.

after war was declared and mobs surged round it. When the British Ambassador sent a complaint to the Kaiser, the officer bringing the Kaiser's reply sat down at once before delivering the message as a deliberate insult; and the German footman tore off his livery, threw it on the ground and spat in the Ambassador's face. The French Ambassador also was treated with a scant lack of courtesy: sent on a twenty-four-hour train journey to Denmark with no food provided and, near the frontier, obliged to pay 5,000 francs – in gold.

It was a sharp contrast to the way in which Margot's friends, the German Ambassador and Princess Lichnowsky, left their Embassy in Carlton House Terrace on 6 August. Just before seven, Mechtilde Lichnowsky, in a white silk blouse, check skirt and neat black hat, emerged to take her dachshund for a last, ten-minute walk before climbing with the Prince into their car. With them went all the hundred-odd Embassy staff, in a fleet of five buses, with ten luggage trolleys that had been loaded by a small army of porters. In the rushed departure the Prince left behind a copy of Marcus Aurelius, given to him by Margot when she said goodbye and inscribed: 'To the most true and honourable of men' which as she wrote later, 'I believe he is.'

As they were driven away, the policemen on guard saluting, both Lichnowskys turned for a last look at the house where they had been so happy. A small crowd waited at Liverpool Street Station to see them go. As the train steamed out just before 9 a.m. Government officials raised their hats and a few women waved handkerchiefs. At Harwich the Ambassador was received by a detachment of the Rifle Brigade, who presented arms.

On 6 August Asquith, at his most powerful, made a compelling speech in Parliament explaining why Britain had gone to war and the measures now needed. Its force was such that no politician voted against the Government, though a few abstained. 'The House has read, and the country has read, of course, in the last few hours, the most pathetic appeal addressed by the King of Belgium, and I do not envy the man who can read that appeal with an unmoved heart,' he said.

'We are fighting to vindicate the principle that small nations are not to be crushed in defiance of international good faith', he declared, 'by the arbitrary will of a strong and overmastering power.'

It was a twentieth-century restatement of Britain's abiding principle in relations with her Continental neighbours: the maintenance of the balance of power, with the added force of an honourable moral stance.

War preparations began at once. Searchlights and guns were set up in Hyde Park and on Admiralty Arch. Green Park was turned into a camping ground for cavalry and artillery, their horses tethered to the railings. Huts went up all round London and in the garden of No. 10. There was a widespread fear of invasion and rumours about spies abounded. Income tax was doubled to 2s 8d in the pound and super-tax and the duty on beer were also doubled.

The greatest fear was of food running out. 'The shops are besieged by crowds trying to lay in provisions for the duration of the war. Everyone seems to think there will be a famine in a few weeks time,' wrote Gabrielle West, a young woman living in Stroud. 'The shops won't sell more than 6lb sugar, or 3lb of rice and that at 6d and 4d per lb. We virtuously abstained from running up prices by buying an immense store. Our hoard consisted of 8lb cheese, 6lb sugar, a tiny ham and two tins of cocoa. Some people filled their carriages and motors with sacks of flour, boxes of prunes and raisins and whole cheeses and sides of bacon.'

In London, as a well-off Kensington resident reported: 'Well to do people are buying enormous quantities of food. One woman rang up Barker's of Kensington at 4 a.m. and ordered from the night watchman £65 worth of provisions, coal, groceries etc. Taxis are laden with provisions people are taking home. Some of the big stores have run out of fish. Smaller shops refuse to quote prices for meat and will not undertake to deliver goods at regular customers' houses on account. They are selling provisions over the counter at fancy prices. Our grocer could not undertake to deliver our standing small order but finally did so.'

Gold and silver coinage became increasingly hard to come by and most of it was drawn in or retained by the Government, with paper money issued in lieu. Lloyd George made a strong speech urging people not to hoard gold and to use notes or crossed cheques. Not everyone trusted these: when Margot's friend Alice Keppel and her daughter Sonia got back from Holland just as war started, to find the banks closed and the house shuttered, Mrs Keppel had to borrow a gold sovereign so that they could have boiled eggs and toast and coffee at the Ritz.

A powder magazine and cases of ammunition were stored in Hyde Park. The Defence of the Realm Act (DORA) was passed, allowing the Government to requisition what it wanted (later implementations included a ban on flying kites, starting bonfires, buying binoculars, feeding bread to wild animals, discussing naval and military matters or buying alcohol on public transport). On the first Sunday of war St Paul's Cathedral was so crammed that 'Church full' notices had to be put outside; postal services were disrupted; 'sleeping valises' (an officer's roll-up sleeping bag, waterproof on the outside, blankets within) sold out; and the popular and efficient manager of the Ritz was forced to resign because of his German origins.

Those abroad were heading home as fast as they could. The last boat, crammed with 8,000 passengers, left Dieppe on 10 August, arriving safely. Alan Lascelles, on his way home from South America, had a more unnerving voyage. A fast German liner now converted into an auxiliary cruiser, the *Kaiser Wilhelm der Grosse*, of the Norddeutscher Lloyd line, fitted with two guns at her stern and two forward and steaming at twenty-two knots, caught up with their passenger liner, the *Arlanza,* and signalled, 'Heave to, or I fire', followed by 'Have you women and children on board?' Several women, reported Lascelles, sat down and sobbed, otherwise there was little emotion shown. 'Suddenly two large poles crashed into the sea, close by my head; it was our Marconi installation going overboard, by German orders.' What the German ship fortunately did not know was that the *Arlanza* was also carrying a large cargo of frozen meat – and three-quarters of a million sterling.

In August Miss Agnes Baden-Powell, President and founder of the recently established Girl Guides, wrote a moving letter giving the first wartime instructions to everyone in the Guide movement. Guides were encouraged to think of the skills in badges which would be useful, especially First Aid, cooking, nursing, knitting and gardening.

Those who are at home can help by:
1. Go and cheer up families who have had to part with a father or son.

2. Take care of children and babies, wash up and do some mending.
3. Prompt obedience to orders with a cheerful face.
4. If troops are nearby they will need assistance in cookery, washing, sewing and rolling up bandages.
5. The Territorials will have many cold nights in camp and would appreciate woollen helmets and scarves.
6. Collect magazines, books and papers.
7. Sew seeds and plant vegetables.

Many of us will not be called into the fighting line but let us put forth all our strength to help others to be resolute and hopeful, confident that good will come.

In one sense, this sentiment was rather how the British public saw the war on which their country had just embarked. Conscription would have been an abhorrent thought then; so that if only volunteers fought, many would indeed not be called 'into the fighting line'. But everyone knew that fighting troops must be helped and supported, to win whatever battles they were rightfully engaged in – the sense of national honour, of pride in their country and belief in its invincibility made the British people certain both of the moral justification for the war which nobody had expected or wanted and its eventual outcome.

In Germany, where 'At last!' was a more common reaction, Count Harry Kessler welcomed the beginning of the war with rapture. As his regiment moved out to the Belgian border he wrote to a friend: 'These first weeks of war have brought forth something from unknown depths in our German people, which I can only compare with an earnest and cheerful spirituality. The whole population is as transformed and cast into a new form.

'This already is the priceless gain of this war, and to have witnessed it will certainly be the greatest experience of our lives.'

EIGHTEEN

From the first day of war Asquith wrote to Venetia constantly, some-times as many as three letters a day, saw her whenever he could and complained bitterly or miserably if this was impossible. The day after war began he was grumbling that 'it is difficult . . . to be away from London for even an hour in these anxious times,' telling her of the number of people who needed to see him and the decisions that needed to be taken. 'Still there may be a lull and I picture to myself the delight of a few hours by your side.'

The only really happy times of his day, he told her, were when he was reading her letters or writing to her. Then, in the age-old cry of lovers everywhere, he concluded: 'Isn't it a wonderful thing that we – you & I – should be like that? . . . My darling – I shall see you Saturday – and am always & everywhere *Yours*.'

Asquith was now a man of sixty-two; far behind him were the days of his early struggles at the Bar, the travelling from Hampstead to Chambers on an omnibus, the 4d lunches at cheap eating houses. Fifteen years earlier his lean, almost ascetic looks, indicative of firm purpose and moral vigour, had deeply impressed Margot; although he had cut down greatly on his drinking his face, fatter and more florid, bore the marks of good living; his manner had less of serious-ness and more of frivolity. But his skill as a politician and his clarity of thought had never been more evident than over the past month, culminating in his great speech on 6 August, which drew the House together – and united the whole country.

This unison meant that there was no need for propaganda – in the sense of an edited version of events or presenting the public with ideas and facts that showed Britain in a favourable light or which justified her actions. For Asquith, this was fortunate: he had little idea of the power – the rapidly growing power – of the press, a press that was the sole channel of information for most people. Much of this conduit was in the hands of Lord Northcliffe, as owner of both *The Times* and the *Daily Mail* the most powerful man in Fleet Street, a fact of which both Lloyd George and Winston Churchill were acutely aware.

Even if Asquith had realised the extent of newspaper influence, he would have scorned to make use of it; he should, he felt, be judged by his actions, and the idea that he might stoop to manipulating public opinion was so beneath his view of what was right as to be abhorrent, a conviction underlined by the austerity and earnestness of his upbringing. It was, he knew, one of the reasons for Lloyd George's success as a politician, but something to be viewed with tolerant disdain while respecting Lloyd George's genuine zeal for social reform and persuasive ability in achieving it; '. . . there was no one in Parliament who took less pains to secure popularity,' wrote Harold Begbie, writer, political journalist and author of several re-cruiting poems, of the Premier. 'Above all things, he never plotted behind closed doors; never descended to treason against a rival.'

The British Army, though now in better shape thanks to the Haldane Reforms, was small in comparison to the large conscript armies on the Continent but conscription – or 'compulsion' as it was some-times called – would have been hotly resisted in Britain, not only by the Liberal Government but by the trade unions.

The new War Minister wasted no time. His first step, on the second day after taking office, was to call for 100,000 single men between the ages of nineteen and thirty to volunteer, in an appeal disseminated through the press and pinned up as posters through-out the land, usually in local post offices.

Then, almost every village, however small, had a post office, which did far more than handle mail. Post offices were telephone exchanges, sent out telegrams, were the local fount of all knowledge, put up notices for the authorities, dispensed gossip – often picked up by 'overhearing' one of the telephone calls that went through them – and received, through Head Office, governmental decrees. Only three days after the declaration of war, one of these was sent out: all gold coinage to be remitted to Head Office and notes or postal orders to be used instead.

The call to arms was a message taken up all over the country. Parsons preached it as a duty from pulpits, special hymns were sung in church with services often concluded by the national anthem, committees were formed to encourage men to join up, bands paraded down the streets attracting them to the recruiting stations, employers encouraged and sometimes even ordered their male staff to do so.

Probably the most effective recruiting agent was the iconic poster of the great warlord himself, pointing his finger at the viewer over the slogan 'Your Country Needs **You**'. Few could resist that searchlight gaze, that semi-accusatory pointing finger. Certainly, no one else could have raised and organised an army so swiftly and efficiently.

Reservists went straight away. Major Edwin Bedford Steel, for example, received his orders for mobilisation at 5.30 p.m. on the day war was declared. He left for Aldershot the following morning, slept in the mess billiard room that night and was in camp – which he was commanding – the following day. Within two days the necessary draught horses had arrived and were immediately put into training to get them used to the heavy army ambulances and wagons – some of them had never pulled anything heavier than a trap. By 11 August the riding horses too had come.

By the end of the month Violet, her first thought as always for her father, was writing to his Private Secretary, Bongie: 'I do really think that <u>some</u> of the boys should enlist. Father will be asked why he doesn't begin his recruiting at home . . .' Only to the closest of friends would Violet have mentioned anything that sounded even faintly critical of her father; over the years Bongie, whom she knew was devoted to Asquith, had become one of these intimates, and to him she poured out her thoughts and emotions. He for his part had been in love with this brilliant, witty girl almost since first meeting her ten years earlier.

One of them, the thirty-one-year-old Oc, was, in fact, already trying to enlist, though at first hindered by his contract with his employers, the trading firm Franklin and Herrera, who did not want to lose him. Oc, the least intellectual of Asquith's first five children, had initially thought of a career in the City, for which an ability to speak French was then deemed essential and, after Winchester and New College, Oxford, had spent six months with the then seventeen-year-old Violet and her nineteen-year-old maid in Paris (the only proviso being that Violet should not go out alone).

Wanting a more adventurous life, he joined the Sudan Political Service – where Violet visited him during the winter of 1910–11 – then left to work for Franklin and Herrera, often in South America.

The declaration of war brought an immediate response from him. 'It is obviously fitting that one of my father's four sons ought to be prepared to fight,' he said. 'I cannot sit quietly by reading the papers . . .' His two older brothers were, he told his employers, married (initially, recruiting was aimed at young single men between eighteen and thirty, with only those of nineteen and over allowed to fight overseas) and his younger brother Cys was still not fully recovered from his debilitating illness in Egypt.

With Beb and Cys, though, Oc went almost straight away to a training course at the public schools camp near Salisbury, weeks that made them all fit and brown. His contract ran until September 1915 but he persuaded his employers to release him a year earlier and on 23 September 1914 he was commissioned into the Royal Naval Division. As there were not enough jobs at sea for all those who wanted to join the Royal Navy, the Division was to all intents a land-based force (although they still used naval terms such as port and starboard, and 'going ashore' for leaving camp).

Beb, whose military training had continued at the Crystal Palace, managed to secure a commission in the Royal Naval Artillery. One result of this was 'cuckooing', a phrase Cynthia used to describe their habit of flitting between friends and family rather than occupying a permanent home. When Beb joined the Army his small income from the Bar disappeared and, to save money, Cynthia gave up a permanent home for herself and their two little boys* (this also saved the cost of servants), living largely between Downing Street and Stanway, her family's large Jacobean manor house in Gloucestershire.

One of Oc's fellow officers was the poet Rupert Brooke, whom several of the young Asquiths had met through Robbie Ross the previous year. Violet was very taken with Brooke, a glamorous figure for whom women fell easily, and quickly invited him to her twenty-sixth birthday party a few weeks later.

Margot, though she refused to join any of the many committees set up, believing that they never got anything done, nevertheless did

* A third son was born after the war.

what she could in private, chiefly by regularly visiting the wounded in hospital and bringing them small presents of cigarettes, chocolate or tobacco. Later she extended this to taking parties of them to the theatre, and blinded ones at St Dunstan's for drives in her car.

At Stanway the men-servants – carpenters, gamekeepers, domestic servants – were threatened with dismissal by Cynthia's father Lord Elcho if they did not volunteer. 'I know my footman doesn't want to go – he has an old father who begged him not to,' wailed Mary Elcho. 'I shall have no chauffeur, no stableman, no odd man to carry the coals! I may have a 100 parlour maids but someone must carry the coals!' Violet, staying with the Elchos, described the scene in a letter to Venetia. 'He [Lord Elcho] has gone off to London leaving poor Lady Elcho to cope with the situation – which he created without consulting her in any sort of way. It is too cruel as the people here have hardly heard of the war.'

Others did their best to keep not only their husbands and sons but also their servants out of trouble. Lady Sackville, the chatelaine of Knole and a great friend of Kitchener, wrote to him to ask him to give her husband a safe staff job, and when he replied that he could make no exception for an individual officer she wrote back saying she quite understood, but that perhaps the carpenters at Knole might be excepted. Although she did not actually ask for the same exception for the footmen, she implied it, saying she knew that Lord Kitchener would feel as she did that parlour maids (in the dining room) were middle-class. 'I must say that I never thought that I would see parlour maids at Knole . . . instead of liveries and even powdered hair.' Kitchener's reply was polite but non-committal.

Almost as essential to the Army as men were horses. They were a vital cog in the war machine, needed by every part of it – even an infantry brigade of four battalions (about 4,000 men) had to have around 250 horses and mules to function properly in the field while cavalry, artillery regiments and the comet tail of back-up services an army carried in its wake needed far more. Mechanisation had only just begun and horses were much better at pulling guns or other heavy loads through mud or over difficult terrain than motorised vehicles, which frequently got stuck or broke down.

When war was announced the Remount Department of the British Army had to raise the supply of Army horses from 20,000 to 140,000 before the First Expeditionary Force could move out of the country. The only solution was to commandeer them from their private owners, of whom there were plenty: horses were a part of the fabric of life, especially in the country, to an extent hardly imaginable today – private cars, owned only by the well-off, were so few and far between that one could be heard a mile away across the fields. Farms relied entirely on horse power, tradesmen delivered goods in horse-drawn carts, the milkman's van was drawn by a pony, coal was loaded onto wagons pulled by horses and delivered from house to house, parsons visited on horseback, doctors often rode their rounds on a cob and hunting was one of the most popular winter sports.

To find them, the Government drew on the most efficient form of decentralisation: local knowledge. This took the shape of using men expert in horseflesh – well-known breeders, trainers, judges at horse shows, masters of foxhounds, owners of large stables – who could appraise a horse and assess its price. Each was given a 'district' to scour and took with him a copy of the latest horse census for that area, a Government cheque book, and written authority empowering him to commandeer any horse he thought fit. 'Poor Mr Fenner was awfully cut up yesterday as they came round and commandeered his black horse Kitty,' wrote Robert Saunders to his son in Canada. 'They have been round taking everybody's horses that were suitable and at Uckfield they took horses out of the carriages and carts.'

In a mere few days enough horses for mobilisation were got together.[*] As Asquith wrote to Margot on 18 August, '. . . the curtain is lifted today and people begin to realise what an extraordinary thing has been done during the last ten days. The poor old War Office, which has always been a byword for inefficiency, has proved itself more than up to date, for which the credit is largely due to Haldane and the Committee for Imperial Defence. The Navy too has been admirable; not a single torpedo has slipped through either end of the Channel.'

None of this was allowed to leak into the papers. 'There has never been anything more wonderful than the persistent & impenetrable secrecy in which everything both on sea & land continues to be enveloped,' wrote Asquith to Venetia. 'Imagine the Channel between

---

[*] Around nine million were requisitioned in the first few weeks.

Southampton & Havre & between Newhaven & Dieppe swarming now for nearly 3 days with transports carrying troops: the troops arriving on French soil with no doubt a lot of acclamation: whole regiments of khaki-clad guards & Highlanders, marching as they have been today, thro' the streets of London, with bands playing the Marseillaise, & apparently disappearing into space: and not a word in any newspaper to indicate what is going on.'*

He told her of the many Cabinet meetings, of the farewell visit of Field Marshal Sir John French, off to command the BEF in France. 'He starts (this is *secret*) on Friday morning in a torpedo destroyer for Boulogne.' He described the golf he was playing, the daily rubbers of bridge after dinner, the luncheon parties, and his constant longing for her presence. 'I miss you so much: if only you were nearer, & I could see you, even for a quarter of an hour, each day, it wd. make such a difference. Frances Horner has been here for lunch, & I told her I hoped for Mells on Sat (not mentioning you) . . . I pine for you . . . Am I a fool? What do you *really* think? Anyhow I *love* you.'

---

* Only on 18 August did an authorised statement that the British were across the Channel appear in the London press; and even at that time the German High Command did not know the whereabouts of the BEF (British Expeditionary Force).

NINETEEN

In Britain, the onset of war was still a cause for excitement and patriotic fervour into which everyone seemed to fling themselves. 'You can't live in London at the present without feeling an atmosphere of restless excitement that tells on the nerves and leaves you tired and more or less irritable and used up. Everywhere you go you see flags flying, appeals to enlist, men in khaki, special constables with their badges, photographs and war telegrams in shop windows and recruiting stations,' ran one of Robert Saunders' letters. (One casualty of this perfervid patriotism was Violet Asquith's growing friendship with Ottoline Morrell, like her husband a committed pacifist from day one. In May Violet had written to Ottoline that 'I long to be with you above all people'; at the end of August she was explaining her absence from Bedford Square, 'because I heard you didn't want to see anyone who was in favour of the war'.)

Women organised sewing parties or attended Red Cross first aid classes; many offered large houses as convalescent homes or hospitals. The Army & Navy Stores, Britain's best-known source of supply for all military or naval wants, was flooded with orders for greatcoats, warm underwear, thick socks, leather belts, torches and 'Boy Scout'-type knives fitted with corkscrews, tin openers and gadgets to remove stones from horses' hooves. Knitting – of socks, scarves, body belts – became the rage; women took knitting with them everywhere, to meals at home, to restaurants when dining out, even to theatres – theatre managers took advertisements telling women to 'Bring Your Knitting!'.

No longer did ministers have to watch for attacks by stylishly dressed women or pillar boxes burn with their contents; Mrs Pankhurst had told her army of suffragettes to disband. 'Our battles are practically over, we confidently believe,' she declared during the first week of war. 'For the present at least our arms are grounded, for directly the threat of foreign war descended on our nation we declared a complete truce from militancy.'

In towns, everyone turned out to watch local regiments set off for the depot, cheering them on their way. Some of these were the famous 'Pals' Battalions', so called when whole villages, communities or even professions enlisted together, such as the Glasgow Tramways Battalion. Liverpool was first, with four battalions of local men; London formed a footballers' battalion. '[We all] . . . fed the men with plums and apples which they were very grateful for, as it was a burning hot day,' recorded Winifred Tower. 'They were all very cheery and went off shouting and cheering and singing "Tipperary".'

Transport ships gathered in the main ports and large harbours such as Southampton Water, ready to take the BEF to France; the Downs were mined in case of invasion by German troops – then considered a real threat; large yachts were furbished as hospital ships (often at the owner's expense). One such was the *Liberty*, a steam yacht belonging to Lord Tredegar, who fitted her up with sixty beds and an operating theatre. It was staffed by six doctors and ten orderlies from the nearby hospital who gave up their jobs and offered their services free.

All the time this unending activity was going on Asquith – as busy as anyone with meetings of the Cabinet, with Kitchener, with Army commanders, with Churchill and Navy commanders, with officials from the Treasury – was writing to Venetia in tones of love and longing. 'There is no one else in the world who even suspects where my thoughts and aspirations (hopes I may not & cannot say) are always centred.' This letter of 20 August ran to several pages and concluded with a giveaway sentence: 'I wd give more than I can put down on paper to be able to – some sentences are best left unfinished . . .'

In Germany the beginning of the war was welcomed with rapture. Kessler had noted: 'The desire to go on the attack is great here.' Much of this was due to outrage at how Belgium had frustrated the Schlieffen Plan.

Essential to the Schlieffen Plan was a total disregard for the neutrality of Luxembourg, the Netherlands and Belgium. The natural Belgian desire to maintain this neutrality and defend themselves was regarded as hostile in the extreme – and as provoking the atrocities that followed (the German army killed between 5,500 and 6,500 French and Belgian civilians between August and November 1914, usually in near-random large-scale shootings of civilians ordered by junior German officers).

Of Paris, undoubtedly nervous of its likely fate, Dora Leba Lourie, now hastily en route for her home in America, wrote: 'Paris reminds one of a corpse – so still, so mournful, so inanimate. London does not seem to be affected by war so much as Paris.' Away from the capital and large towns, it was actually sometimes difficult to realise that the country was at war. 'It is extraordinary . . . how little people in the country districts seem to know or think about what is going on,' wrote one of Violet's correspondents.

In rural parts of Britain the war's main effect was the disappearance in large part of horses, gold coinage and young single men. 'Rather a shock!' wrote Gabrielle West on 20 August. 'Ernest [their garden boy] went this morning for his medical and didn't return. Later in the day we got a message from the postman that he has gone straight off to Bristol. So we have had to set to work to clean the stable, lift the onions, dig potatoes and clean the boots not to mention half a hundred other horrid unexpected little jobs.'

John Heath watched his father set off to enlist with three other men in their employer's Ford car from the Scottish estate where they worked. They looked, he thought, as if they might only be going on a spree rather than to battle, 'clad in tweedy suits, knickerbockers and stockings, or lounge suits being worn for the last time for many a long year. My feelings were a strange mixture of fear, patriotic pride, and a sense of loss as I followed them out into the drive to see them disappear round the corner and out of sight.'

The harvest continued, as did the recruiting meetings, with men still flocking to the colours. Rifleman Frederick James ('Bon') Dillingham, stationed at Sheerness, told his sweetheart of the life there. 'One poor chap this morning got 28 days cells for leaving his point on outpost duty. I were escort to him then another territorial I believe got 5 years for being found asleep on his post. I don't suppose the chap realized the serious nature of his work. They are very strict and punishment is very heavy they've no pity for anybody in trouble. While we are at this station they are breaking us in again to our old form by long route marches, outpost duties and continually on parade and trench digging.' Soon he was telling her: 'the quicker we get to France the better is the general idea here for they're nearly driving us "up the pole" [mad]'.

For others, the war made little difference. Small girls from well-off families still took afternoon walks with nurse and nursery maid in grey uniform coats and drank their morning milk from silver mugs given them at their christenings by godparents; older families continued to go on seaside holidays. 'We enjoyed the bathing immensely,' wrote Violet Bradby, spending August with her family at Cley-on-Sea in Norfolk, where they rented a house for four guineas a week. 'The blackberries were marvellous, the finest I have ever seen.'

As the weeks passed, the disappearance of young men became more marked. Often, villages or estates lost everyone eligible for military service except for the parson, the schoolmaster, farmers and a few farm labourers. At great houses a new feminine society came into being. The footman and butler left, their places taken by a head parlour maid and the under parlour maid while the land agent or estate factor's work was done by a female secretary. A general air of austerity descended and there was little in the way of dinner parties or entertaining. For a while, life took on a slower tempo as adjustments to these changes were made.

London was buzzing with activity. Raymond Asquith, up from Mells where he had been staying with his wife Katharine's family ('they have cornered all the petrol, sold all Charles Kinski's hunters, knocked off two courses at dinner and turned Perdita's pony cart into an ambulance'), found the capital 'seething with futility' and full of what he described as misdirected effort.

For his father, one aspect of this was the continuance of the Irish Question – the unyielding differences between North and South over Home Rule. As he wrote on 31 August: 'I sometimes wish we could submerge the whole lot of them and their island for, say, ten years, under the waves of the Atlantic.'

Harriet Jephson was still stuck in Altheim.* 'A fresh *Bekanntmachung* [notice] has been posted up forbidding us to leave the town,

---

* Harriet was not able to leave Altheim until finally, on 25 September, she was allowed to go, passing through Frankfurt and then France and landing at Folkestone after a nightmare journey. She wrote: 'No doubt we shall remember this journey to the end of our lives, but what can you expect from a people whose Prophet Nietzsche says: "What is more harmful than any vice? Pity for the weak and helpless – Christianity!"'

and ordering us to be indoors by nine o'clock. No papers! no letters! no news! no chance of escape! Two men were put in prison yesterday for laughing at Germany. Two Russians were stopped in a motor car, and when arms were found upon them they were put up against a wall and shot.' None of this deterred Harriet, when she heard of a successful British engagement in the North Sea, from rigging up an impromptu Union Jack, 'a red silk dressing jacket, lined with white, and draped over a blue silk parasol, which I tied knob out, to look like a pole'.

In early September the Asquith family suffered a collective blow. Sir Edward Grey, realising the effect on the public of a German at the heart of the prime ministerial household, came to tell them that they should no longer allow Elizabeth's beloved governess, Anna Heinsius, to continue living with them. Frau, as she was known, was newly married to a compatriot, Rolf Meyer. For many years she had been an intimate part of their family, they had visited her home in Munich and Elizabeth especially regarded her as a confidante.

Grey explained that having Frau in the house was much commented on, that everyone knew that the Asquiths spoke freely among themselves about what was going on and that it was Frau's duty as a patriotic German to report every scrap of information she could pick up. Asquith accepted this ('I don't see how I could do otherwise – do you?' he asked Venetia plaintively when he told her about it).

Frau was a German citizen, said Grey, and she might either deliberately or accidentally impart information she had picked up in the course of daily life in No. 10 to one of the spies with whom London was rumoured to be awash; and in any case it did not do for the Prime Minister of Britain to be harbouring a national of the country with which his own was at war. Passage was found for her to neutral Holland.

That it took Grey to point out not so much the possible dangers but the damage that Frau's continued sojourn at No. 10 would do to the public perception of Asquith as a dedicated wartime Prime Minister was one of the first signs of the Premier's inability to gauge the currents of national mood.

Asquith was, of course, extraordinarily busy. On 10 September he was able to report to Parliament: 'We have been recruiting during the last ten days every day substantially the same number of recruits as in past years have been recruited every year.' The total figure he quoted in his speech was 439,900; eventually a further two and a half million would follow.

He went to Aldershot to see them, noting that it was 'overflowing with K's new recruits – a very motley rabble in all kinds of old clothes'. He saw the first (aircraft) bombs, describing them as 'three hellish-looking cylinders like thermos bottles suspended by wires from the front of the plane and let free from time to time from heights of 3,000 or 10,000 feet'. He visited the barbed-wire cage where German prisoners of war were confined, living twelve to a tent. 'They ... wander about sometimes playing football, and have prayers twice a day,' he wrote to Margot. 'There are about 2,000, many of them sailors from the navy, but some Uhlans, and all sorts of spies, terrorists and odd soldiers. We talked to them as best we could; the only thing they complained of was the cold at night. It was a sad spectacle.'

On the same day, 14 September, at midnight, he poured out his thoughts to Venetia, lamenting that he could not get away and telling her that he had been putting together some disjointed notes 'about what I am to say on the Irish Bill. I do not think it will be very serious, for the Tories, at their party meeting, resolved to have only a single speech, a snarl from Bonar Law; and the Cecils, who wanted to roam and range at large, seem to have been silenced. It will be a really big thing if before the end of the week we get Home Rule on the Statute Book after three years of ceaseless conflict and worry. If this comes off I might almost begin to intone the *Nunc Dimittis*.' Two more letters followed next day. Two days later, he was writing to Margot: 'We had some strange scenes in the House yesterday as you will see. Bonar Law surpassed his own record in caddishness and silly malignity [over the Home Rule Bill].'*

Montagu, now Financial Secretary to the Treasury, was also writing to Venetia more frequently, as her attitude to him appeared to have softened. He told her that seeing her was 'heavenly' and he longed to be able to do things for her. He was in a state of great depression, feeling (quite wrongly) that his work was incompetent and that his colleagues looked down on him.

---

* All the same, after being put on the Statute Book, it was suspended for the duration of the war.

He was spending more and more time with the Asquith family; and his devotion to both Margot and Asquith was mirrored in the closeness evident in their letters to him, Margot confiding in him her wretchedness over Asquith's unacknowledged passion for Venetia.

It was a situation almost bizarre in its ramifications. Here were two men in love with the same woman – a woman who was the best friend of the daughter of one of them. A young woman who must have realised her friend's father was in love with her but who nevertheless played along with the relationship while keeping a hold on her other suitor – a suitor who could not conceive of the older man as any way a serious rival. A daughter who loved her father so all-consumingly that she was not only jealous of her stepmother but would never find another man to live up to him. A wife who loved her husband deeply, conscious of her fading attractions and miserably aware of his feelings for the younger woman.

Truly, Downing Street could have been called a cauldron of the emotions.

Already the difference in attitude between the various ministers was noticeable to sharp observers. At the end of August Beatrice Webb was talking of how Sir Edward Grey, Lloyd George, Haldane, Isaacs and Montagu were all working as hard as possible – 'no dinners or weekends'. There was no mention of Asquith, whose daily timetable still included nightly bridge and, usually, luncheon or dinner parties, although his formidable capacity for work meant that little slipped by him.

Next door, the Chancellor, formerly such an advocate of peace, had swung his immense energy behind the growing war machine. On 19 September, in a stirring address at Queen's Hall, London, he focused on the underlying moral issues. 'The stern hand of fate has scourged us to an elevation where we can see the great everlasting things that matter for a nation,' he declaimed. 'The great peaks we had forgotten, of Honour, Duty, Patriotism and clad in glittering white, the great pinnacle of Sacrifice pointing like a rugged finger to heaven.'

At the same time, wild rumours were flying round the capital. The well-educated, intelligent Beatrice Trefusis heard from someone she knew that one of the reasons for Kitchener's frequent visits to Paris 'was to have a French general shot. He was suspected of having

German sympathies, and they finally found three unopened telegrams from General French in his pocket. He had failed to bring up a force to relieve our Army Corps at a critical moment in the awful retreat from Mons,* when we were practically surrounded by the Germans. He had a German wife. Kitchener is not caught napping!' A few weeks later she was writing: 'We can't find out if the rumour is true that Prince Louis of Battenberg, our First Sea Lord, is shut up in the Tower. Awful thought!'

In the Isle of Wight, Winifred Tower heard the story that had swept most of England: that thousands of Russians had been landed in various parts of England and Scotland, preparatory to being poured into France to tackle the German armies advancing on Paris from the rear. When Euston Station closed for the day on Sunday, 30 August and train after train passed through Midlands stations with drawn blinds there was no stopping this belief, despite denials in the press. 'Everybody had a friend whose aunt's butler had seen them. The most popular [story] was the one of the old lady who was sure they had passed through her station because she had heard them stamping the snow off their boots.'

What was true was that the atrocities in Belgium noted by Count Harry Kessler, from the shooting of civilians as suspected partisans to the wholesale burning of houses and killing of their inhabitants, were having their effect in the growing number of refugees from that unhappy country. On Saturday, 5 September the Asquiths motored down to Hackwood Park, Lord Curzon's grand house in Hampshire – Asquith wistfully remembering drives with Venetia along that route ('those heavenly journeys; when shall we have another?') – to meet some royal ones, the Queen of the Belgians and her three children.

It was the first time Margot had met Curzon to speak to since he had written her what she called his 'ridiculous letter' after his ball in May. 'Poor old boy,' she wrote in her diary. 'But I never turn a hair if I'm really fond of someone. So I was quite at ease walking into the garden at Hackwood to join him and Lady Lansdowne.' They had been asked to dine and sleep, and after dinner a soprano gave a song recital with piano accompaniment.

---

* The Battle of and Retreat from Mons, in which the British were outnumbered by about three to one, lasted roughly from 22 to 24 August 1914.

It was not a well-chosen entertainment. Bonar Law, one of the house party, immediately got up and seated himself as far from the piano as possible, Curzon sank into a huge and comfortable red velvet and gilt Venetian chair, and listened with an interested but pained expression, until Margot asked for something more lively, when the soprano, hands on hips, launched into what she called a 'nigger song', 'Kissing at the Gate'. Luckily it was short, as its effect on the audience was unhappy. 'Bonar Law looked like a Scotch grieve who had heard that the effect of the war had held back the bidding for blackfaced rams at Lanark sale,' wrote Margot. 'The Queen with immobile profile appeared like a shocked nursery governess, Lord Lansdowne erect with a rather chilly smile, [and] Lady Lansdowne yawning.' Asquith, wisely, had taken up a position where no one could see his face.

The Queen and her children were not the only ones fleeing Belgium. The British Government had offered victims of war 'the hospitality of the British nation' and so the largest refugee movement to date in British history began – in total more than 250,000, including a workforce of around 60,000 men, many of whom worked in factories contributing to the war effort. Most, however, took shelter where they could, often arriving with only baskets and bundles of such possessions as they had been able to carry with them. Committees were formed to collect second-hand clothing and offers of food and lodging poured in – as for those Gabrielle West's family took in. 'We . . . put them up in the rooms above the stables. Today we heard that 50 refugees were arriving . . . they stepped out in a forlorn and apathetic manner, clutching bundles and baskets and numberless babies. All seemed to be huge families, the smallest lot being 6. These we commandeered . . . Their name is Feughel. They lived just under the church tower at Malines. When the bombardment began, fearing that it would fall on them, they lived for 3 days in the cellars and then fled. They got to Antwerp and came over in a refugee boat.'

All through the month of September Asquith's letters to Venetia gushed out – pages and pages of talk about what he had been doing, whom he had been seeing, war news (often, as he pointed out, secret) – 'The Japs rather jib at sending their troops to Europe. Our aeroplanes have done *excellently*' – and always ending with a declaration of love. 'I *love* you more than I can tell you.' 'Think of me beloved all the week and every day of the week. I wish I could make you feel how much I love you.' 'You know how much I love you – perhaps you are weary of being told.' Meanwhile, Margot suffered.

TWENTY

The Asquiths spent most of the first wartime Christmas season at Walmer Castle (later, as it was within such easy reach of France, Asquith met war leaders there). The new Warden, Lord Beauchamp, installed a few months earlier, had continued the custom of lending it to them. Asquith found its sea air 'very beneficial', but in winter neither the castellated stone walls of the original tower nor the red-brick walls of the extra dwelling added later, with its rooms that led one into another and little in the way of insulation, kept out the icy cold and the draughts of which Margot constantly complained. 'I must say I had looked forward enormously to going there,' she wrote, 'but the cold, discomfort, endless noisy corridors and small rooms have made me disappointed in the place . . .'

It was a depressing Christmastide. Raymond, Oc, Beb, Cys and Margot were all suffering from sore throats and 'flu symptoms. Frau was much missed ('Elizabeth and I cried a little over Frau'), and Beb had many arguments with his father, who noted a touch sourly: 'Another rather curious figure in our party was Beb, clad in khaki and growing an orange-coloured moustache, against wh. all but Cynthia protested.'

Just before New Year they drove to Godalming to spend Sunday with friends and look at a German prisoner of war camp. The captive soldiers appeared cheerful, singing and joking (only too happy to be out of the war, thought Margot). They wore uniforms of different shades, blue-grey, grey and a green-grey for fighting in woods. When she was told this, one of the prisoners said to her: 'Your army is not very invisible – your khaki is too yellow. It does well enough in hard veldt ground but in green countries it is not as good as ours.'

The gulf between 'the Front' and those at home was in general vast, underlined by the attitude that going to fight in the war or helping those who were fighting was something voluntary. Beb, who had seen active service, realised that a total effort was needed; he now believed in 'compulsion' and thought that the country was not sufficiently geared up for war, especially with regard to munitions. He also realised that the idea, now gradually taking hold, that it would be a long and bloody conflict had not been sufficiently disseminated. His views were a foretaste, all too accurate, of what the country itself would come to feel about its Prime Minister.

Margot herself was suffering deeply from unhappiness at her husband's obsession with Venetia and the gossip that she knew was circulating about them – by now, the whole of 'their' world knew about it. Again she confided in Montagu, the only outsider in that close network of family and friends, this time voicing her fears, couched as accusations that Montagu was somehow conspiring with younger members of their close circle to forward the intimacy between her husband and Venetia. 'Please don't bracket me with . . . Bongy or Venetia or Violet,' he wrote back. 'I don't understand them, I detest their relationship, and I do not share their confidences. I have I repeat never tried to prevent and certainly never tried to bring about meetings between Venetia and the P.M. . . . All the P.M.'s love it is important to remind you belongs to you now and for ever. He meets Venetia in very little different spirit than he meets Winston or myself – this is of course exaggerated but fundamentally true.'

Admittedly Asquith had never talked about his feelings for Venetia to Montagu, but it was a statement that showed how little Montagu understood of the true nature of the relationship between the Prime Minister and the girl he loved – and of how successfully she had downplayed her involvement with each to the other.

Margot did her best to celebrate Christmas with her usual generosity. Her present list, covering every member of the household and a number of friends, ran to two pages – in all, she gave presents to forty-three friends as well as family members. Violet got a red silk bag and a tea gown, Elizabeth a boa, muff, pearls and a bag, Puffin gramophone records, model aeroplanes and books, Cys pyjamas and a china cigar box, Oc a revolver and a dressing gown, Cynthia a blue Indian shawl, Asquith studs and an Empire jug and Beb a travelling cup set to use in the trenches. The maids got dress lengths or suitcases, the men-servants shirts or money, the messengers cigarettes. Venetia was given a china bowl.

*

That autumn had seen one of the most dramatic early events of the war. On 22 September *Aboukir*, *Hogue* and *Cressy*, three obsolescent cruisers sardonically known as the 'Live Bait Squadron', were patrolling the North Sea about forty miles from Ijmuiden in Holland. Their speed had been reduced to eight knots in order to open out to patrolling distance for the day. There was a slight swell and a chilly wind but a bright sun and the only vessel in sight was a small fishing smack, flying the Dutch flag.

On board *Aboukir* was fifteen-year-old Kit Wykeham-Musgrave, a smallish, fair-haired naval cadet who had just completed his first term at Dartmouth College ('I simply love Dartmouth so far. Chemistry is awfully nice – we have explosions'), writing enthusiastically of its swimming baths and how he had passed his swimming test. Both explosions and swimming would shortly figure dramatically in his young life.

As Kit lay asleep that morning there was a sudden detonation at 6.55 a.m. – *Aboukir* had been struck on her starboard bow, it was thought by a mine. Her captain signalled to this effect to the next ship in line, the *Hogue*. But it was not a mine but a torpedo, fired by the German submarine U-9, which had crept up behind the 'Dutch' fishing smack so that its periscope was hidden.

No one thought of submarines then as few believed they could do much damage. In 1914 a U-boat's chief advantage was that when submerged no surface ship could detect it; against this, under the water it was virtually blind and at around seven knots much slower than any warship. Only with a periscope – visible to an alert lookout – could it spot prey. This meant that either a submarine had to be in position before the attack or any target had to be moving extremely slowly – as the cruisers then were (the fishing boat, having done its concealing job, raced off at top speed).

'We were steaming line ahead with a distance of three miles between the ships,' wrote Kit to his grandmother three days later, after first thanking her for the sovereign she had sent him. 'I was sleeping down below at the time. We were woken up by a terrific crash and the whole ship shook and all the crockery in the pantry fell. Of course we thought it was a mine, and rushed up on deck; we had all the skuttles [*sic*] and watertight doors closed at once and everything that would float brought up and thrown overboard in as much time as we had.'

In those days there were no lifebelts, so the first order given by any captain whose ship was in danger of sinking was to throw overboard everything made of wood – mess stools, tables, sea chests – so that the crew would have something to cling to in the water. Also overboard went any hammocks that were already tightly lashed as these too were buoyant enough to serve as temporary, makeshift lifebelts. The men were told to strip, as clothes and boots could weigh them down in the water.

'The *Aboukir* at last went down suddenly,' wrote Kit, 'and we slid down her side into the water. Fortunately there was not a great deal of suction on the side we jumped off so with difficulty I got clear.' Her captain went down with the *Aboukir*. He was seen standing on deck until the last, and the men, struggling in the cold sea, gave three cheers for him.

Kit swam to the *Hogue* and was just going on board when she too was struck and sank in three minutes. He then swam on to the *Cressy*, where he was hauled up the side with a rope. It was fortunate that the average September temperature of the North Sea was a reasonable 20°C or few would have survived. As it was, the cup of cocoa Kit was given in *Cressy*'s sick bay was welcome – but he had hardly drained it when *Cressy* too was hit and everyone dashed up on deck. It was still only 7.15 – a mere twenty minutes after the first torpedo.

When *Cressy* began to list heavily Kit jumped for the third time off a sinking ship as she rolled right over, remaining keel upwards for twenty minutes before finally sinking at 7.55. The naked small boy, survivor of three sinkings within an hour, was picked up two hours later, unconscious and clinging to a piece of wood. In all, 1,459 British sailors died, many because, as Commander Hereward Hook, then a midshipman on the *Hogue*, wrote afterwards, 'the real old-time seamen just simply scorned to learn how to swim'.

U-9's feat meant that no one thereafter thought of submarines as mere toys, or discounted them as weapons. Instead, it brought a new dimension to naval warfare.

As men volunteered, so the pressure grew. Women or older men who had seen their husbands, sons, brothers or sweethearts go off to fight felt bitter against those fit young men who did not volunteer. Young men not in uniform, or not wearing the khaki armbands that showed they had already enlisted and were waiting for orders – up to 30,000 men a day had responded to Kitchener's first appeal so that finding enough uniform cloth and arms was becoming a problem – would be referred to as shirkers or 'White Lilies'. In the White Feather Campaign (founded as early as 30 August) young women went up to such men in the street and presented them with a white feather – which, it was hoped, would shame them into enlisting (the pacifist Fenner Brockway claimed that he received so many white feathers he had enough to make a fan).

One of those who had received his orders for mobilisation on the day war was declared was Major Edwin Bedford Steel, sent off as medical officer in charge with the first wave of British troops.

As casualties came in – mostly British but some Germans – his diary records that annexes were taken over or improvised for instruments, dressings, blankets and medical comforts. 'The wounded arrived from nearby battlefields and the doctors were kept busy, stopping haemorrhages, doing minor operations and putting on dressings. Some very nasty cases, chiefly shrapnel. Extended hospital into two barns, near church.' Some wounded were evacuated, including three serious cases to the American Ambulance in Paris by car.

By mid-September casualties were flooding in, the rain was pouring down and the hospital and annexes were overflowing. 'Our soldiers are wonderfully plucky and cheerful when wounded, the officers as a rule giving much more trouble than the men.' He was soon appointed Assistant Director of Medical Services of the 1st Cavalry Division, noting that a certain amount of expenditure was inevitable 'as we pay for what we get, unlike the Germans'. Another addition to the timetable was the need to keep the horses exercised – they got a daily one and a half hours' exercise.

Steel, like most people that autumn, believed the war would be short. 'I think that having spent the last two months in propping up the French, saving Paris, and practically clearing the Germans out of France, we are now going to take up our originally allotted position and see if we can drive them out of Belgium,' he wrote to his wife in October. 'So Part I is finished, we are starting Part II and

Part II I hope takes place in Germany and the sooner the better and may I be there to see it.'*

Those who had enlisted or been called up were largely still in Britain. 'This is the scene around me as I write this letter Ciss,' wrote Rifleman 'Bon' Dillingham to his sweetheart. 'I am seated on a waggon, two "Long Tom" 4.7 guns are on the hill and a stack of rifles with guppy guard over them while the others are digging trenches all around on Sunday morning mind whilst to the left is the cook preparing the "Oh mercy" dinner!!! They call it a stew cooked with lumps of wood in kettles called "Dixies" it's what we term a "Lightning Stew" we may as well go without it for what good it is. Out in front of us are picquets to warn us in case of attack and when I look across the water at Southend it makes me more fed up than ever, the scenery around us is very pretty but we've no eyes for that sort of thing at present anyway.'

Enterprising women joined the Women's Emergency Corps, started by the Hon. Mrs Evelina Haverfield, formerly a noted suffragette, described as looking 'every inch a soldier in her khaki uniform, in spite of the short skirt which she had to wear over her well-cut riding breeches' (no woman could appear in trousers or breeches without scandalising onlookers). Its headquarters, according to one description, buzzed with 'suffragettes, fashionable actresses, a couple of duchesses and a marchioness, and a handful of lady novelists'.

Here two young women who were passionate about the new and dashing sport of motorcycling were hired as dispatch riders, then asked to join the Flying Ambulance Corps, a voluntary organisation founded to help wounded Belgian soldiers. When the girls arrived at Victoria Station ready for departure in their motorcycling outfits, their leather breeches worn without a covering skirt were what shocked, not the fact that they might be risking their lives at the Front.

For during those first months the conventions, and social protocol, were as rigidly enforced as they had been in pre-war days. When Sonia Keppel, daughter of Alice Keppel, wrote to the butler she had known since babyhood because she was lonely in the big house to which she had been sent in the country, her letter beginning 'Darling

* Tragically, he was killed at La Clytte on 23 November 1914.

Mr Rolfe,' and ending 'Your loving Sonia' drew a rebuff from him. 'Dear Miss Sonia, You are getting a big girl now and you must call me Rolfe. And you must stop signing yourself "Your loving Sonia". It does not do. Yours respectfully, W. Rolfe.'

Other men and women did what they could, often by lending property – large houses for hospitals, cottages as homes for the influx of Belgian refugees, cars to ferry returned convalescent wounded to their homes, even yachts to defend the coast. These, in a very professional form of naval Home Guard, were armed with three- or six-pounder guns (according to size) and manned by a mixed crew of RNR men and the yachts' own hands. Some were commanded by retired naval officers, others by their owners who were given temporary naval commissions. Thus fitted out, they patrolled the coast, releasing the previous naval torpedo boats for other duties.

In London, women visiting their dressmakers for fittings for their autumn wardrobes had got used to the constant sight of marching men, some fully equipped, some so newly enlisted they only had a uniform cap above civilian clothing or with just a pair of puttees or a bandolier. Recruiting posters were everywhere – on the sides of every van, on every taxi, on every blank wall.

Already there was fear of Zeppelin attacks;* people were beginning to furnish their cellars as makeshift bedrooms, and to sleep with overcoats and a packed bag by their beds. Illuminated shop signs were forbidden, skylights had to be covered and blinds pulled down as soon as lamps were lit – it was not a complete blackout since street lamps, although reduced in number, were left on.

In a letter to Venetia of 24 October, under the heading of 'Most Secret', Asquith told her of a planned naval and seaplane raid on the Zeppelin sheds in the Kiel Canal: '*Nobody* knows of this except W [Winston] & myself.' Often he asked her if she had read a speech he had made and begged her to write; always he ended with a passionate affirmation of his love. 'My own darling, *I love you*.' 'My darling I love you always.' 'I don't think you know at all how much I love you! Do you?'

The frequent reference to his speeches was because he and Lloyd George, with other prominent Liberals, were making a series of

* The first Zeppelin raid on London did not take place until 31 May 1915.

them up and down the country that could be summarised as justification for the war – that Germany was responsible for its outbreak and for the dreadful things reported from Belgium and that it was incumbent on Britain not only to stand by her treaty obligations but also to defend the values of European civilisation that Germany would otherwise demolish.

These speeches, though not primarily intended as propaganda but rather as engendering support for the Government and its actions, had a powerful effect, although, as Raymond Asquith – one of such speakers at recruiting meetings – told his wife, 'It is becoming clearer daily that everyone perfectly understands the situation, that recruits are enlisting far quicker than the W.O. [War Office] can deal with them, and that there is nothing left for public speakers to do except abuse the Kaiser in stronger & stronger language.'

Anti-German sentiments had begun to find public expression, but so far mostly in attitudes and modes of speech rather than violence. Beatrice Trefusis, describing a visit to one of the largest p.o.w. camps, seemed to regard it only as an enjoyable outing. 'We have a large detention camp of German prisoners near here on Frith Hill [Surrey]. People go in hundreds to gaze at them as if they were animals in the zoo! They look quite peaceable and happy in their greyish-green service uniforms. I saw one of them solemnly doing the goose-step by himself!'

Others were less tolerant. Dachshunds were frowned on (and later kicked); the German Shepherd breed was renamed Alsatian;* in some districts shops with German names had their windows broken; anyone with a German name was suspected of being a spy.† Worst of all, there were such venomous attacks on Prince Louis of Battenberg, the First Sea Lord, that, although he had since the age of fourteen been both a naturalised British subject and served in the Royal Navy, because of his German ancestry he was forced to resign (two months later Fisher, who had retired in 1910, was brought back), sparking a letter in *The Times* from the Labour Party politician and trade union leader J.H. Thomas: 'I desire to express my extreme regret at the announcement that Prince Louis of Battenberg

* The Kennel Club did not reauthorise the use of the name 'German Shepherd' until 1977.
† During the war there were 9,000 cases of suspected spying, yet by the end only twenty-nine spies had been convicted.

has, by his resignation, pandered to the most mean and contempt-ible slander I have ever known.'

Spy fever, largely a product of the imagination, was everywhere. 'Joan has brought home a Polish girl who was a music and German mistress at Bentley Priory. Her name is Remizewska,' wrote Gabrielle West. 'At the outbreak of war the headmistress meanly gave her notice, fearing she would be mistaken for a German . . . The Jollys and Marlings are convinced that she is a spy and won't have her inside their house, so that Joan and I had to stay behind on Christmas Day and entertain her. No one wants them to invite her if they don't want, but they needn't go out of their way to refer to her as "your German spy friend".'

Even artists suffered, those who drew or painted the country-side being mistaken for spies anxious to pass information to the Germans. One was the Scottish architect and artist Charles Rennie Mackintosh, living and sketching in the Suffolk village of Walberswick: the local people, who had never heard a Glasgow accent before, mistook it for a German one. He was reported to the authorities – and banned from going within a mile of the coastline.

All through that autumn Asquith wrote an unending stream of let-ters to Venetia, irrespective of whether she was in London or at Stanway, or whether he was or was not going to see her the same day. Of the 243 letters he wrote to her in 1914, more than half were sent between the outbreak of war and the year's end – often several in one day. Each one commented happily on whether he had received a letter from her ('Beloved – you sent me the most deli-cious letter this morning') or sadly if the expected note had failed to arrive ('it was a great blow to get no letter this morning' 'I feel sad & impoverished, but I am sure it is not your fault').

He described Cabinet meetings and the foibles of his colleagues; military secrets were betrayed; he told her of high-level disagree-ments – 'We had a royal row in the Cabinet today between K & Ll. George, about Welsh recruiting and the Welsh Army Corps. They came to very high words; and it looked as if either or both of them would resign.' In other moods, they exuded love and longing. 'I wish with all my heart – all day, every day, & most of the night – that Penrhos was 200 miles nearer London.' 'No one will ever love you more – or so much. *Never.*'

He reminisced, as all lovers, or would-be lovers, do. 'I was think-ing all this morning, in the back of my mind – in the midst of almost countless & rather exacting interviews – what a distance you & I have travelled in the course of a *calendar* year. There are some things, wh. as I look back upon them, seem quite incredible now: missed opportunities, half-spoken words; still worse, words that only told half – or a hundredth part of – the truth.'

Fortunately Venetia was discreet. Even so, the potential danger of this correspondence was considerable. All the letters went by ordi-nary post – a risk in itself. If Venetia had left a letter lying about, it might have been seen by a servant and possibly sold to a newspaper – or even used to blackmail the Prime Minister, especially if it con-tained something covered by the Official Secrets Act (passed only three years earlier by his own Government).

Were they lovers? Now twenty-seven, Venetia was no ingénue and the fact that she wrote, or replied, to Asquith's letters every day implies not only encouragement but also intimacy. At the same time, it was then written in stone that no decent man had an affair with an unmarried girl – the fear of pregnancy alone was enough to deter anyone, let alone the Prime Minister of England. Although Venetia belonged to 'the Corrupt Coterie', who thought of them-selves as liberated, their excesses were mainly with alcohol and a certain amount of drug-taking (morphine could be bought over the counter at chemists).

It is true that contraception was available but really only for those who knew where to look, and a girl of Venetia's background would have found this difficult and unpleasant. A newly published pamphlet by one of the pioneers of birth control, Margaret Sanger, after mentioning quinine and laxatives, gives these unappetising in-structions (aimed, of course, at married women): 'After the sexual act, go as quickly as possible to the bathroom and prepare a douche. Lie down upon the back in the bath tub. Hang the filled douche bag high over the tub, and let the water flow freely into the vagina, to wash out the male sperm which was deposited during the act.' She recommended the use of Lysol, 'a brown oily liquid which added to water forms a clear soapy solution'. In the Venetia–Asquith rela-tionship it is extraordinarily difficult to imagine a situation where this kind of distasteful precaution might be taken unobserved or unnoticed.

Historians and family members have argued endlessly as to whether the affair was ever consummated. Asquith was a man to whom the physical was intensely important and his sexual relationship with Margot was now a thing of the past. On the other hand, he was morally upright, nor did he come from the aristocratic stratum of society where affairs (but only with married women) were almost *de rigueur*.

In sum, without any concrete evidence except a few of Asquith's sentences to Venetia, the most likely scenario is that it was a relationship charged with intense erotic obsession on Asquith's side and the willing acceptance of greater or lesser physical intimacies on Venetia's as the price to be paid for close friendship with someone of such intellectual calibre – with a man like Asquith, it is impossible to imagine that there was no physical approach at all.

One interesting possibility is that Violet's speculation on the relationship between her father and her friend, whether conscious or unconscious (she always denied knowing anything about it until many years later), may have accounted for her intense interest in whether affairs between couples of her children's generation were consummated or not. Leaning forward and looking closely at whoever had brought the subject up, she would demand: 'Is it *thorough-going?*'

The first inkling that this would not be a brief, glorious, almost painless (if one can use such a word) war had begun to seep into the public consciousness. There were frequent casualty lists, Belgian refugees told horror stories and wounded men and prisoners were beginning to arrive. Edward Cazalet, gazetted to the 5th Battalion Buffs ('I go next Thursday to Tent 3 to try my uniform on'), wrote how sorry he was to hear of the death in action of one close friend. 'He had only rejoined his regiment three weeks [ago].'

Yet there was still a powerfully enthusiastic feeling of patriotism, a belief that the war was a just cause that would inevitably bring victory in such short order that anyone who missed the chance to fight in this noble cause would reproach himself endlessly afterwards. It was 'gentlemen in England, now abed', cast in twentieth-century terms, and the presumed brevity of the conflict was still an article of faith with most. Even Raymond Asquith, one of the cleverest men in England and certainly, as the Prime Minister's son, privy to much inside knowledge, told his wife that if the Allies won 'this battle' (the first Battle of the Marne) in France the war would be over by Christmas.

Christmas, indeed, saw the famous 'Christmas truce', in which around 100,000 British and German troops stopped fighting. It began on Christmas Eve when German troops placed candles on their trenches and on Christmas trees and sang Christmas carols, to be answered by the British singing their own carols. Then came shouted Christmas greetings from each side. Soon there were sorties across No Man's Land and exchanges of presents of food, cigarettes, chocolate and beer or schnapps, and the swapping of uniform buttons and hats. The guns and the whine of shells stopped, men brought back their dead to be buried behind their own lines and some even played football together. In some places the truce lasted until Boxing Day, in others to New Year's Day.

Quickly, the generals on both sides issued orders that this must never happen again.

PART FOUR

1915

TWENTY-ONE

At the beginning of the war the German and French armies numbered well over a million men each, all largely conscripts, while the BEF stood at around 80,000. These were, however, professional soldiers who viewed the Army as their career and were thus much better motivated and trained, especially in fast and accurate marksmanship. It was estimated that the average British regular soldier was able to hit a man-sized target fifteen times a minute at a range of 300 yards with his rifle, a skill that would help to counterbalance the inequality in numbers in the early battles.

Although Britain had been determined not to be outdone in the naval arms race, she had not, unlike Germany, been preparing for war. Despite the speed with which the Government reacted, some of its preparations had what we would call a faintly Heath-Robinson air. Here is Mary Fancourt, a girl who lived in the east-coast port of Felixstowe, describing a rudimentary aircraft carrier. '[It was] an ordinary steamer with a flat-roofed garden shed sitting on its quarter deck. This housed a small seaplane which could be hooked out by crane to fly off the deck. It could only return to the ship in good enough weather for it to land alongside on the water and be hoisted aboard.' But as strategists knew, the greatest imbalance, which would inevitably soon tell, was in numbers of men.

For many recruits, however inspired they were with patriotic fervour, one of the attractions of the Army was a release from the desperate grinding poverty of everyday life. It offered decent food, clothing and shelter – far better than many knew at home – as well as regular pay (one shilling a day for privates). Unsurprisingly, areas dominated by mining and heavy industry were eager to volunteer – though not all, after generations of poor diet and housing, were considered medically fit enough to do so.

Food – and the need for tobacco – was mentioned by many of

them in their letters home. Private John Charles Hold, writing from Bovington Camp to his mother, the wife of the head gamekeeper at Medmenham in Buckinghamshire, fills his letter with details of what he ate. 'There is a lot of recruits comes in every day. Tell Janet to send me some of that tobacco when I write again. We are all as happy as sandboys now we have got used to it. We had roast beef for dinner today and potatoes and cauliflower. We had tinned salmon for Breakfast one tin between three of us, and for Tea we had bread and butter and cake. Your loving son J.C. Hold.' They got their envelopes and writing paper for nothing, he added. It was headed, in capitals: 'For God, For King, and For Country'.

For Rifleman Bon Dillingham, tobacco was the priority. 'Well dear you ask me if there is anything I'd like well "*S'il vous plait*" that is if you please in French would you make me up a parcel (I trust I'm not asking too much) of some Nosegay shag, half a dozen books of cigarette papers, as many cakes as you like to make, some acid drops, in fact anything that you can think of and some envelopes and writing paper at your earliest possible convenience put them in a strong parcel and address the same as your letter of today. And now dear Au revoir your loving sweetheart Bon.'

Bon also commented on the transport arrangements in France. 'It is rather funny to see the soldiers being moved about in London buses,* their friends on foot laughing at them as they go by – but it was funnier to see the first lot of Indian troops go through here on them the other day.' He also saw dogs harnessed like ponies in carts: 'one goes round with a milk cart and today I saw three abreast trotting along in a cart'.

By January 1915, 159 Unionist MPs had volunteered and forty-one Liberals, and the last of the Prime Minister's sons to join up, Raymond Asquith, was with his regiment. Recruitment was as essential as ever. More and more men were needed and the drive to find them was relentless and, often, pitiless. Girls were told to shame their sweethearts into enlisting or warned what might happen if they did not ('If your young man neglects his duty to his King and country, the time may come when he will neglect you. Think it over

---

* Five hundred London double-decker buses had been sent to France, to move troops quickly to the Front.

. . .'). Employers were urged to sack their staff for the same reason. The immensely wealthy – and patriotic – Duke of Rutland told all his tenants and workers that 'All who serve the Colours will have their situations kept open for them', while their families would live rent-free and continue to receive their men's wages (less their Army pay).

In similar vein, a letter in the *Daily Mail* ran: 'Doctor's wife, middle-aged, will undertake to perform the work of any tramway conductor, coachman, shop assistant, or other married worker with children, provided that the worker will undertake to enlist and fight for his country in its hour of need. The wages earned will be paid to the wife and family.' *Country Life* magazine, well aware of its constituency, asked its readers:

> Have you a Butler, Groom, Chauffeur, Gardener or Gamekeeper serving you who, at this moment, should be serving your King and Country?
>
> Have you a man serving at your table who should be serving a gun?
>
> Have you a man digging your garden who should be digging trenches?
>
> Have you a man driving your car who should be driving a transport wagon?
>
> Have you a man preserving your game who should be helping to preserve your country?
>
> A great responsibility rests on you. Will you sacrifice your personal convenience for your Country's need? Ask your men to enlist TODAY.

By now the early enthusiasm was not exactly replaced, but certainly augmented, by social and peer pressure. The families of those who had joined up and perhaps already gone to fight felt more and more resentful if they saw the strapping son of a neighbour remaining at home while others, as they saw it, died for him. Many men, therefore, felt pushed into enlisting, sometimes even by their parents. 'Jack left us this evening after 3 days' leave,' wrote William Brand, the Pampisford postmaster. 'We were much upset when it came to parting – perhaps I may never see him again. And the same old question troubles me "Was I right in letting him enlist?" I hope the time may never come when I shall have to say, as David said of old: "O, Absalom, my son".'

It was a question that would become increasingly acrimonious as the months wore on and the bloodshed increased. As it was, within a few months of the outbreak of war the Cabinet itself was split over conscription, which the Liberals vehemently opposed, while the Conservatives insisted it should be adopted. They were supported by two of the most influential members, Lloyd George and Churchill – the only two who had realised that not only a new kind of approach, but also a new kind of politician, would be needed in the future.

That January, Britain suffered her first air raid. Man's newly discovered ability to invent machines that could stay aloft in the air had taken different directions: England concentrated on aeroplanes, while Germany was known for airships. The German navy had been using those developed by Count Zeppelin for reconnaissance patrols over the North Sea since the beginning of the war and the German Admiralty wanted to use them also for attacks against England.

Somewhat reluctantly, the Kaiser agreed and on 19 January the first Zeppelin raid against Britain took place, when two Zeppelins dropped bombs on Great Yarmouth and King's Lynn on the coast of East Anglia. Only two people were killed, and sixteen injured, but the psychological damage was immense. For Britain, a country that long believed itself secure from invasion, the idea that an enemy could wreak destruction from above was terrifying, especially as these great silver airships seemed able to hover with impunity for as long as they liked above the frightened citizens below. The two above Great Yarmouth stayed almost three hours, their engines reverberating for miles in the night air.

It was a war run to a large extent on volunteers, from the recruits so numerous that the War Office had to open a second 'branch' in Trafalgar Square to cope with them, to countless sewing parties and relief funds. Class differences were still taken into account even in life-and-death matters. As the floodlit hospital ships sailed to England with the wounded aboard, great houses were turned into hospitals – the Duke of Portland's house in Cavendish Square, half of Arlington House, the Duke of Rutland's home, while the

Devonshire town house in Piccadilly became the headquarters of the Red Cross – or turned into convalescent homes for officers. Mrs Freddie Guest, wife of the ADC to Sir John French, ran a convalescent hospital for officers in Park Lane where it was blue silk pyjamas for junior officers on the ground floor and pink silk for senior ones above, while the Duchess of Leinster would send her butler to see what an officer would like for dinner.

Others organised comforts for the troops, sending warm clothing, cigarettes, chocolate, hams, or grooming kits for horses, and books and magazines to the War Library for (Army) Hospitals, as well as games like chess and gramophones. Musical instruments – the most popular were concertinas, mouth organs and mandolins – were sent to the Front, and for more strenuous leisure hours, footballs and cricket bats, stumps and balls.

Nor were all the volunteers adults. Boy Scouts took on duties as messengers and guides in the War Office and helped with mail delivery as more and more men went into the Army. Girl Guides did a variety of jobs, from filling sandbags, helping with laundry and padding splints in hospitals to running errands, working in soup kitchens and day nurseries and making ration bags for soldiers to ensure that tea, salt, sugar and tobacco were kept separate.

While their brothers volunteered for the Army, young women often joined the Voluntary Aid Detachment. 'I nagged and nagged and finally went off to be a VAD nurse at St Thomas's along with an Oxford friend whom I did not know very well,' recorded the writer Naomi Mitchison. 'Of course I made awful mistakes. I had never done real manual household work; I had never used mops and polishes and disinfectants. I was told to make tea but hadn't realised that tea must be made with boiling water. All that had been left to the servants.'

For even the kind of war work a well-born young woman did was still heavily circumscribed by the boundaries of class, and its ethos. Nursing, especially in wartime, was considered 'respectable' – had not the FANYs (First Aid Nursing Yeomanry), a group of well-to-do volunteer nurses, ridden out on their own horses to help the wounded in the Boer War of 1899, and then been officially founded as a service in 1907?

As with the FANYs, the great thing about VAD work was that it was unpaid, unlike, for instance, equally valuable work in a munitions factory. In those days few girls of reasonable means took paid jobs, in part because marriage and children was thought to be sufficient, in part because it contravened the rule that paid jobs were for those who needed them, and to take one if you could afford not to would be to deprive some poorer girl of a living.

No such reproach could be levelled at VAD work. The Voluntary Aid Detachment had been formed in 1909 and by the summer of 1914 there were 2,500 of these detachments spread across the country, staffed by 74,000 volunteers (who quickly became known as VADs). For although no girl of the middle classes ever did domestic work, thanks to the family's servants, as a wife and mother she did have to know how to cope with illness or accidents in the home.

So VAD work, and by extension the first aid classes run by the Red Cross and nursing organisations like the Queen Alexandra's Royal Army Nursing Corps, was viewed with approval by parents and enjoyed by their daughters, so much so that in the summer of 1914 VADs accompanied Territorials into camp for the first time – though well segregated apart from their duties of tending the 'wounded' in mock battles.

Once the war started they were often thrown in at the deep end and given the dirtiest and most difficult jobs by Matrons suspicious of girls seen as rich and non-professional, but most, like Lady Diana Manners, proved themselves.

Many longed to go to the Front and some, like twenty-six-year-old Cicely Acland, granddaughter of the original W.H. Smith, serving as a VAD at the London Hospital, managed it. At first the military authorities refused to allow VADs anywhere near the Front, but soon the shortage of trained nurses forced them to reconsider this decision; and female volunteers over the age of twenty-three and with more than three months' hospital experience were accepted. Cicely, who had decided she did not want to spend the rest of the war emptying bedpans, resolved to join her father, a Colonel, commanding his regiment at the French Front. She therefore applied for a week's leave from the hospital and booked a one-way ticket to France saying, 'No London hospital matron can bring me back!'

Once in France she enlisted at the local hospital at the Front, where she spent the rest of the war giving anaesthetics with a chloroform mask, sometimes up to eighteen hours a day. Over the years she learned *poilu* French with the vocabulary to match, which caused something of a stir when she joined her father at diplomatic dinner parties.

'Day after day we cut down stinking bandages and exposed wounds that destroyed the whole original plan of the body,' wrote another girl serving in a hospital near the Front. 'One man had both buttocks blown off, one arm had been amputated at the elbow ... Another lay propped on sphagnum moss to absorb the discharge from two large holes in each thigh.' It was tough, heart-rending work and, for a woman, the nearest she could get to actual fighting.

That January, Venetia Stanley decided that she, too, wanted to serve as a VAD in France. Early in the month she joined the London Hospital for a nurse's training that would be completed in April. She worked hard, and purposefully – no doubt appreciating the strange and novel sensation of doing something useful for the first time in her life. Her decision may also have been in part an escape route: she had confided to her sister Sylvia Henley that her relationship with Asquith was becoming too difficult to control. But Asquith – continuing to give her gossip, his everyday doings, news and war secrets in his near-daily letters – was not to be deterred. 'I long to hear every detail of your new life,' he wrote on 5 January. 'I think of you every hour and your love is the <u>best</u> thing in my life.' And on the same day at midnight he said of the new conditions in her life, 'I am quite determined that this shall not impair our daily love and confidence.'

Life as a VAD was hard work and Venetia's days were now much more fully occupied, yet Asquith's demands on her time were just as insistent. If she did not write at least one letter a day he was upset and did not hesitate to say so, as on 23 January: 'My darling – I confess I was very depressed when I looked this morning at my letters by the bedside and saw no sign of your handwriting. Thursday and Friday both blank days (except for a little jejune telegram) and Saturday to be the same!' His letters were lengthy, detailed and highly indiscreet – on 26 January, for instance, he described the future 'rearrangement' of French and British troops at the Front – hers, all starting 'Darling Mr Asquith', much briefer.*

---

* The speed of postal delivery, even in wartime, is surprising. In a letter dated 6 January 1915, Asquith writes: 'I was glad to find that (from the postmark), [your letter] posted at 6 p.m. got here the same evening.'

The following day, in a letter written at midnight, he told her that he had offered Montagu a Cabinet post as Chancellor of the Duchy of Lancaster. 'He was very *émotionné* and began to say all sorts of nice things about my friendship for him, & &, wh. I cut short.'

What Asquith did not know was that Venetia's attitude towards her would-be suitor, Edwin Montagu, was gradually changing. In a way that curiously mirrored Margot's early doubts about Asquith, she found him physically unappealing but intellectually attractive. There was no doubt that he was entertaining company; as Sir Lawrence Jones, author of *A Victorian Boyhood*, recalled, he had a 'long, ugly bony face, marked like a photograph of the moon. His eyes held me, sombre, patient, unhappy eyes of extraordinary intelligence. He held the talk; he was sophisticated and mocking, more amusing I thought than anyone I had met.' Or as Duff Cooper put it: 'He was a man whose ugliness was obliterated by his charm.'

So at the end of January she wrote to him: 'Next time I have my day off I'm determined, if you can, to dine with you, get a "late pass" and try and win or lose a little money. Will you arrange this?' Montagu, sensing that the barriers were slowly coming down, put not only a car but also his house, 24 Queen's Gate, at her disposal. Here she began to entertain her friends. By now she was no longer 'Dear Miss Stanley' but 'Dearest Venetia', and when he wrote to her on 1 February, 'You have been an angel friend to me, why not a wife?', she did not respond, as she had before, with immediate rejection.

Most of London's inner circle was now aware that the Prime Minister was in love with a girl less than half his age. His colleagues in the Cabinet, seated round the oval wood table in the Downing Street Council Room, would watch dismayed as a messenger would come in with a letter from Venetia which Asquith would open and, lost in concentration, read carefully before settling down to reply at great length, while around him were discussed vital questions affecting the lives of thousands bleeding and dying in the trenches. Sealing up the letter, he would then ring for the messenger who took it out for the post, and only then return his attention to the matter in hand.

Extreme emotion is impossible to hide and Margot was wretchedly aware of her husband's increasing passion. For her it was both miserably painful and deeply humiliating. She took some of these feelings out on Venetia's mother, Lady Sheffield, castigating her for not stopping her daughter's affair with Asquith. Once or twice she tackled her so forcefully that the browbeaten Lady Sheffield appealed for advice to her daughter-in-law Margaret, wife of Venetia's brother Arthur, then Governor of Victoria, Australia.

The letter that came back on the weekly mail ship was clear-sighted in the extreme despite the thousands of miles that separated them. 'It is difficult to know how to take such violent outbursts which I fear *are* caused by jealousy of the P.M. and also by wounded vanity and humiliation at not being able to retain the position and influence she once had,' wrote Margaret Stanley. It was all perfectly true.

She went on to say that she did not think it possible for Lady Sheffield to 'do' anything over Venetia's friendship with the Prime Minister. 'The only thing which could do any good would be that V should realise that her friendship for the P.M. was the source of annoyance and unhappiness to Margot – when I believe her generosity and large nature would induce her to avoid giving Margot pain and distress by being less intimate and seeing less of the P.M. – though it would no doubt be very difficult now to break off what is, after all, a very delightful friendship . . . As for the dear old P.M., you will never get him to see things from your point of view, I am certain.' In other words, the recommendation was to leave things alone.

Venetia, extraordinary as it may seem with hindsight, clearly either did not imagine or did not care that the constant professions of love and adoration, the assurances that she was at the centre of his life, could in any way distress the wife of the man who was so manifestly in love with her – a woman who had treated her with great kindness and entertained her so often. Then, too, if she kept up the pretence that nothing was going on, there would have been the deception, the constant need for a guard on her tongue during her frequent luncheons or dinners at No. 10.

As for Asquith, he neither attempted to justify his behaviour nor to explain it, only reassuring Margot of her place in his heart when she questioned his love for her. The demands of the premiership, and the all-embracing nature of his obsession, seem to have left little room for feelings of guilt (not, in any case, an emotion to which Asquith was often prey).

Perhaps for a long time Venetia may have convinced herself

that she was simply the PM's chosen confidante, that he needed someone on whom to unburden himself of the strains and stresses inherent in leading a country at war; and that his advances were no more than his well-known penchant for tactile contact with pretty young women, especially as Margot, with the passing years, had become shriller and more critical and, worse, the refreshing candour of her youth had become a habit of blurting out inopportune and uncomfortable home truths (often redeemed by a disarming letter of apology). But in the face of Asquith's increasing dependency, demands and avowals, Venetia's earlier attitude was no longer possible. Sometimes the hunger in his letters seemed almost to mask an intuitive knowledge that Venetia was no longer keeping Montagu at a safe distance.

For Margot the situation was a constant misery. It must have brought back memories of those earlier days when she had been the beloved object pursued with such passion, when Asquith had written so beseechingly, 'O Margot, love of my life', when he was begging her to marry him. 'It is sad getting old,' she wrote in her diary, just before her fifty-first birthday on 2 February. 'I should not feel it so much – or indeed at all – if I was quite sure I would keep my place in the hearts of those I love best, but I am not vain enough to feel sure of this!' A few days later she was recording: 'I went to Henry's dressing room and hugged him – I said "you have got everything – Fame, Power, Success, Love, Friends, Health, children – everything but a young wife!". He said with that wonderful emotion which I miss so much in his children – "I have got the youngest wife in the world!"'

Yet all the time Asquith's letters to Venetia continued, with their same burden of war secrets ('I always want you to know everything'), descriptions of the inner machinery of government and protestations of passion. In one he summed up his feelings: 'Whatever happens, I want you to know, once & for all (if this were my last testament) that I bless you as the pole star of my life.'

TWENTY-TWO

'This is the first month in which some people conjectured the war might end,' wrote Victor Cazalet in his diary on 1 February 1915. 'Oh God if it would.' For doubts were beginning to creep in that the war would be as short as had earlier been envisaged, although there were still those hopeful of it ending in months rather than years. Mrs Belloc Lowndes, novelist and wife of the editor of *The Times,* wrote in her diary of how she had heard – through his sister-in-law – of the Home Secretary's belief that the war would end that July; three days later Sir Philip Sassoon told her that his French relations thought that it would be over by May. She herself, much more presciently, wrote that 'England and English life would be deeply affected if not completely changed [by the war]'.

The war was going badly in France and on 19 February the first unrestricted U-boat campaign against Allied trade was started, with the U-8 torpedoing the neutral tanker *Belridge* as she travelled between two neutral ports. Both the German Empire and Great Britain relied heavily on imports and both sides now tried to blockade each other. To use the U-boat's chief weapon, the torpedo attack without warning, meant abandoning the previously agreed stop-and-search required to avoid harming neutrals. This inevitably resulted in a number of politically damaging (for Germany) incidents.

The Royal Navy might have been the largest and most efficient in the world, able to operate almost anywhere thanks to Empire ports, but it was also highly visible. U-boats had the advantage of invisibility and surprise. The sinkings of the *Aboukir, Hogue* and *Cressy* had greatly alarmed the Admiralty – by the end of 1914, U-boats had sunk eight smaller warships and ten merchant ships, with the loss of five U-boats – which became increasingly nervous about the security of the Navy's home anchorage, Scapa Flow. While defences were being installed, the Grand Fleet was dispersed to ports in Ireland and the west coast of Scotland. One U-boat, U-18, did manage to enter Scapa Flow but her periscope was spotted and rammed and she had to surface and surrender.

The twenty-one U-boats available in February 1915 were simply not enough to execute a successful campaign against the numerous merchant ships that sailed around the British coast, especially when some of these submarines were in port for repairs. But as the months passed their success rate increased and after 18 February, when unrestricted submarine warfare was declared, they sank almost two ships a day.

With the growing casualty lists and the erosion of that first unthinking confidence in victory, public opinion was shifting. There was an increasing intolerance of all things German. People with German names found life dangerous, no matter how long they had lived in England, slogans were painted on walls, children bullied at school. Anything that did not shout of patriotism, of doing all one could for the war effort, or of condoning in any way aspects of German life began to fall under suspicion.

One of these was the household at No. 10.

Margot came in for most of the censure. She had always been outspoken and frank and she refused to deny her love of German culture and music, and her affection for those Germans she had known and liked. The fact that her name, as Prime Minister's wife, was not prominent on any of the committees to raise relief or clothing also caused criticism; the amount of hospital visiting and private help and comforting she did was not generally known – as well as visiting London hospitals and talking to troops she would regularly drive to Folkestone and Dover on Sunday mornings to meet and assist the hordes of refugees still arriving.

And so the rumours began, that she played tennis with German officers at their prison camp at Donington Hall, that she sent food parcels to German prisoners containing secret Government plans, that her daughter Elizabeth was engaged to a German. She did her best to ignore such falsehoods but worried in case they affected her husband's reputation.

Asquith himself was imperturbable. His great gift as a Prime Minister was his single-minded clarity of thought, allied to an exceptionally quick mind, so that he operated with an apparent lack of effort, a quality he himself took pride in. His conclusions were presented with – in Roy Jenkins' phrase – 'urbane gravitas'. Churchill was to liken him to a great judge. 'He listened to the pleadings. He absorbed the arguments. He gave his verdict. And then he closed the court and gave his mind and his emotions to the pleasures of the day, literary or social.' It was the latter that had begun to concern not only his intimates but also the wider public.

When he married Margot he took at once to the enjoyable life her wealth and generosity brought. He had steadily begun to drink more and more, so much so that his Commons nickname was 'Squiffy' or 'Squiff' Asquith. 'Asquith by the way has become a public scandal,' wrote the author and businessman Frederick Oliver to his friend Leo Amery,* in 1907. 'Senile oscillation is going to be his undoing.' At the National Liberal Club Asquith would drink champagne – he had been warned about his intake of this as early as 1902 by his friend Haldane – followed by port and liqueurs, as well as smoking several cigars. Margot would beg him to cut down but he would only laugh. At home she tried to ration him by watering the brandy bottle but there was too much other alcohol around for this to be effective.

He seldom took exercise, preferring a gentle drive in his car every afternoon; his chosen evening involved a good dinner followed by bridge. Even conversation was tailored to the idea of leisure: after a day of hard work and immense and sustained intellectual exertion, what he wanted was light-hearted chat. Not for him the usual mulling-over of the day's events or even a serious discussion of literature (he was formidably well read and most nights read for an hour or two after dinner guests had left, often not going to bed until 2 or 3 a.m.).

As Harold Begbie wrote of him, 'chatter rather than conversation has been as it were prescribed for him, and when he should have been thinking or sleeping he has been playing cards'. It was not a persona to appeal in a wartime Prime Minister.

For Elizabeth, just turned eighteen, it was no longer a question of not being invited to parties because of her father's political measures; instead, she was enjoying herself as she had never done before, with exactly the pleasures she had been denied during her debutante year, dancing night after night or at the new *thés dansants* with the

---

* Journalist, linguist and later a distinguished politician.

young men home on leave and anxious to fill the hours before returning to the mud of the trenches.

Violet, another member of the family still at home, had also had vague notions of becoming a VAD like her friend Venetia, but the moment her father intimated that he would miss her she dropped the idea in favour of staying at home and supporting him, which she regarded as of primary importance.

As for Venetia, she was almost twenty-eight and thoughts of marriage had become more pressing. Most of her friends were now married – and some widowed – few eligible men were left in her circle and the daily casualty lists provided grim evidence that the number was shrinking daily; her best friend Violet had for years had an adoring suitor in the shape of Asquith's Private Secretary, Bongie Bonham Carter. Thus it was not surprising that Venetia had begun to view Montagu with more favour. His poor health made it certain that he would not have to fight, so there would not be the increasing risk of becoming a war widow, and although she had never found him physically attractive otherwise he had plenty to recommend him. He was clever, amusing, entertaining, as Chancellor of the Duchy of Lancaster (as well as Financial Secretary to the Treasury) he was a Cabinet minister, and he was exceedingly rich.

He also had a reasonable hope of becoming Viceroy of India, though when he asked Margot what she thought of his chances he told him she did not think it possible because he was Jewish (she added in her diary: 'I love Mr Montagu – he is the only person in the world I have mentioned certain aspects of my life to'). He had been Parliamentary Under-Secretary of State for India, his work was well thought of, his visit there had been a success and he was on excellent terms with many of the princes. It was a position he had had his eye on since his visit there in 1912, and he had already discreetly lobbied Lloyd George as the tenure of the present Viceroy, Lord Hardinge, would be ending the following year. It was time, perhaps, for Venetia not to open the door but to leave it ajar.

Asquith, naturally, was ignorant of Venetia's changing attitude. On 5 February he made his need of her clearer than ever: 'It may not be wise to be so dependent: to have put everything that one has or hopes for into one investment: to stand or fall entirely by one person: but it is too late now to make these calculations, and to attempt to draw up a balance sheet. *J'y suis – j'y reste.*'

For Venetia, beginning to think of marriage, this was a letter to cause mingled feelings of guilt and distress, emotions that must have been exacerbated when she received another three days later that declared: 'My love for you has grown day by day and month by month and (now) year by year, till it absorbs and inspires all my life. I could not if I would, and I would not if I could, arrest its flow, or limit its extent, or lower by a single degree its intensity, or make it a less sovereign and dominating factor in my thoughts and purposes and hopes.'

Yet she was doing little to discourage Asquith. For on 9 February – eight days after Montagu's most recent proposal – she assured the Prime Minister that she did not want him '*ever*' to stop loving her and wanting her. His reply, by return post, expressed the happiness she had given him with this single sentence: 'I am carrying about with me in my pocket the most delicious letter you have ever sent me.'

In the same letter, in an appalling act of indiscretion, he even forecast for her one of the most important, though disastrous, actions of the war: the Dardanelles Campaign. 'The only exciting thing in prospect (after seeing you on Friday) is what will happen in the Dardanelles next week. This as I said is supposed to be a secret, and indeed it isn't known to some members of the Cabinet.'

The Dardanelles Campaign had been triggered when the Ottoman Empire, neutral when the war broke out, closed the Dardanelles Straits, thirty-eight miles long and only just over a mile wide at the narrowest point (the Narrows) to Allied shipping, supposedly at the behest of German military advice.

Churchill had already conceived the idea of another Front that would cause the Germans to split their forces even further in order to support the Turkish army, then believed to be weak and incompetent. This, thought Churchill, would have the effect of reducing and therefore weakening German forces on the Western and Eastern Fronts. It was a brilliant, imaginative idea that would go disastrously wrong.

Thus, when on 28 October 1914 the Turks began attacking Russian shipping in the Black Sea and on 2 November Russia declared war on Turkey, Churchill ordered a British attack on the Dardanelles the following day (though Britain did not actually declare war on Turkey until 6 November), largely to test the strength of the opposing forces and fortifications.

The results were deceptively encouraging, so that it was believed that British naval strength, after destroying the forts that defended the Straits, could succeed in reaching Constantinople (now Istanbul). It was also agreed that, once begun, the operation must be completed – withdrawal would involve too much humiliation for the Allies. The final decision to go ahead was taken by the War Council on 26 January 1915. Before the campaign even got started, Lloyd George wrote prophetically: 'Expeditions which are decided upon and organised with insufficient care generally end disastrously.'

In the first attack the outer forts were reduced to rubble and the entrance cleared of mines, and it was decided to launch an invasion of the Gallipoli peninsula. The Royal Naval Division was among those taking part.

Violet heard of these plans through a friend in late February 1915 and seized the opportunity to write to Rupert Brooke. For the romantic Brooke, the idea of seeing the lands of the classics, where Troy once stood, was thrilling. 'Oh God! I've never been so happy in my life,' he wrote to her before they sailed in March. For Violet, his looks, his passion, his vivid, imaginative idealism, his magnetic personality were irresistible, and she made this as clear as she could without actually using the words 'I love you', writing instead: 'After-you're-gone is a bleak thought. The green fades from the grass whenever I think of it, & the sky comes down and turns into a ceiling.'

Brooke was fond of her and enjoyed her company. 'It has been very good being with you. I would rather be with you than with anyone in the world. And you've been very kind to me.' At the same time, he delicately warned her against falling in love with him. 'When I give thought to it at all, I <u>hate</u> people – people I like – to care for me. I'm selfish.'

Violet was not prepared to notice this. She went to see her brother Oc and Brooke off, but it was Brooke who held her attention. 'I longed so terribly just to <u>see</u> you once again, as the ship moved away,' she wrote to him, '& I mistily gazed & gazed searching all the Khaki bodies for your face & not finding it. They were <u>all</u> other people – they were none of them you . . .'

She told him of the disappearance of her friends. 'Gradually every man with the rough number of limbs and faculties is being sucked out to the war – & I feel as if I were sitting on a beach at low tide amongst old boots & wreckage. Those who have remained have acquired an artificially inflated value – Montagu & Duff Cooper the only two men left in London – from whom in peace women with aesthetic sensibilities shuddered and shrank – now swoon on divans surrounded by troops of odalisques . . .'

She told him of her vague thoughts of nursing ('a prospect I regard with genuine abhorrence'); and she told him of the 'delicious warmth' it gave her when he said he liked being with her. But nothing she said provoked a romantic response.

In his sermon on Easter Sunday, 4 April, the Dean of St Paul's read Brooke's sonnet 'The Soldier'. Already well known, Brooke now became nationally famous. Its lines 'If I should die, think only this of me' must have been unbearably poignant for many.

Just under three weeks later Brooke himself was dead. 'These laid the world away; poured out the red/Sweet wine of youth', he had written in his sonnet 'The Dead'. His youth, his beauty, his romantic imagination made him an iconic image of the young men dying daily, and his death a national tragedy. Violet, so enthralled by him, was shattered; the following year she confided to Virginia Woolf that she had loved Brooke 'as she had never loved any other man'.

On the Western Front, the initial manoeuvrings over, the two opposing armies dug themselves into trenches. 'We've been in the trenches again, this time for seven days,' wrote Trooper Ben Smeeton from Clipston, who had enlisted at eighteen in the Clipston Troop (a 'Pals' Troop') of the Northamptonshire Yeomanry. 'To tell you the truth, it was like living in a brook, it wasn't a clean sand-bag trench like the last, but just an earthen bank in front and not bullet-proof at the top. You had to stoop down whilst walking unless you cared to risk a German bullet by standing up! Their trenches were three hundred yards away this time.'

As more and more of Kitchener's volunteer army arrived, the need for hospitals, ambulances and nurses increased. One of the worst problems was that of wounds becoming septic. In France, unlike the Boer War, fought in the dry plains of South Africa, septicaemia was an ever-present threat, transmitted from the dead bodies of men and horses, lying bloated on their backs with their legs in the air, and the heavily manured soil itself.

Without antibiotics, gas gangrene, as it was called, was a real killer. 'You could smell gas gangrene in a wound as soon as you opened the door of the room,' recalled one nurse. 'The only treatment was constant dressings soaked in a solution of hypochlorous acid.' Those likely to die of it would be put near the door so that they could be taken out without fuss. If a man died during the day he was carried out on a stretcher covered with a flag, while those who could rose to their feet.

Some rich women founded or ran their own units. The Duchess of Sutherland raised and paid for an ambulance unit of eight trained nurses and a surgeon, together with dressings, disinfectants and medical supplies. Sister Millicent – as she told her team to call her – confided to her diary that 'What I thought would be an impossible task became absolutely natural; to wash wounds, to drag off rags and clothing soaked in blood, to hold basins equally full of blood, to soothe a soldier's groans, and to raise a wounded man while he was receiving extreme unction. These actions seemed suddenly to become an insistent duty, easy to carry out.'

The beautiful Duchess of Westminster, who was untrained, founded a hospital at Le Touquet, where she owned a villa, and staffed it with trained nurses. She and some friends made themselves useful in other ways, writing letters for the men or reading to them, doing clerical work, ordering the food, and taking down the particulars of all new arrivals. These they greeted in full evening dress, complete with tiaras ('to raise their spirits') recorded nurse Lynette Powell. Some of the richer among the VADs, while quite prepared to do the muckiest of jobs, brought their own lady's maids with them. For the less privileged, the initial training in England often entailed avoidable difficulties that undermined health and morale alike.

Vera Brittain (though writing a year later) described some of these – notably one frequent problem: the lack of hot water and the distance between the VADs' hostel and the hospital where they worked. Like the professional nurses, the VADs had to be there at 7.00 a.m., first to breakfast, then to go on duty at 7.30. 'Theoretically we travelled by the workmen's trams but in practice these trams were so full that we were seldom able to use them, and were obliged to walk, frequently in pouring rain and carrying suitcases containing clean aprons and changes of shoes and stockings, the mile and a half from the hostel to the hospital.'

As they had to allow a quarter of an hour for changing – the VADs' cloakroom was at the top of four flights of stone stairs – this meant getting up at 5.45, washing in icy water (there was only one bathroom between twenty girls, powered by an ancient and unreliable geyser) and leaving the hostel at 6.15 for the half-hour walk to the hospital. At night the tram situation was usually the same, which meant another walk back, plus suitcase, after a hard day's work at the hospital. As for the tepid water, which made the daily wash and weekly bath a shivering ordeal, as Vera Brittain pointed out: 'Any gas company could probably have installed an up-to-date gas heater in half a day, but it had not occurred to anybody to order this to be done.'

After immediate treatment in a field hospital, many of the wounded were shipped back to England. Those convalescing became a familiar sight in their blue hospital suits, white shirts and red ties, often with bandages round head or arm or leaning on a crutch. They would be offered free transport, free drinks, money was often pressed into their hands and they were given free seats at cinemas and theatres. At the Chiswick Empire, with several wounded in the front row, the music-hall star Hetty King sang the hit song of the year:

We don't want to lose you but we think you ought to go
For your King and your country both need you so.
We shall want you and miss you,
But with all our might and main,
We shall cheer you, thank you, kiss you,
When you come back again.

Margot, who often visited the wounded, bringing them comforts and writing to the wives and girlfriends of the severely injured and those who died of these wounds, was frequently criticised for doing no obvious war work. She knew her limitations: she could neither cook, nurse, handle a committee nor sew. When Queen Mary tried organise some of the wives of public figures into sewing for soldiers, Margot – after a long period of silence as everyone tried to think what to sew – stood up to say that competing with shops that were already having a difficult time might be a bad idea. Instead, she suggested making surgical shirts, which no stores sold, and immediately ordered a large number from a sewing-woman she knew.

But her main war work was what she felt she could do best: having all the serving men of the Asquith and Tennant families to stay when they came on leave, with their wives, and 'lending' (her euphemism for giving) them money if they were short to go out and enjoy themselves.

Venetia, training at the London Hospital with one of her friends, Monica Grenfell (the daughter of Ettie Desborough), was now working long hours, in a routine that involved cleaning the ward, turning patients over and bed-making, tasks that appalled Asquith, who could not bear the thought of his beloved doing manual work. '[Your conditions] fill me with *loathing*. That you should be turned out at 7 a.m. to sweep rooms & empty slops & do sluts' work is a thought wh. I can hardly endure.'

Nevertheless, he continued to bombard her with letters, expecting her to do the same, and claimed as much of her time as he could. When he found she had agreed to meet Violet at a time when he thought they could have had an hour together – even putting off his visit to the King to do so – he was gently reproachful. He worried that she had got too thin, that her hands were suffering from the work she was doing, that she was not getting enough fresh air; he disliked her wearing what he called the 'disgusting' VAD uniform (VADs wore stiff white cuffs, collar and belt into which they stuck the scissors needed for bandages, dressings and sewing, and a blue ankle-length skirt with a long white apron over it). It was not difficult to see that what he would really have liked was to have her as idle and unoccupied as in pre-war days, able to see him whenever he was free.

On St Valentine's Day he reminded her of the day he had fallen in love with her. 'It is 3 years (do you remember?) since you became the pole-star. My allegiance has never wavered; and never will . . .' And on the 17th he wrote her a sonnet ('My Love importunate goes out to the / Pulse of my Being, pivot of my days, / My life-ship's Compass on the uncharted Sea . . .').

Often, on her evenings off, Venetia would go to Montagu's house, which he was delighted to allow her to use both as a refuge and as a place to meet her friends, for whom he would give dinners.

Right The dancer Maud Allan, dressed for her show-stopping 'Salome' dance. She was banned from the stage in Manchester but smart Londoners flocked to her sensuous performances. Within months of Asquith becoming Prime Minister, Margot invited Maud to give a private performance in the Downing Street drawing room *(below right)*. The two women remained close friends.

Left, below left and below right
When Asquith became Prime Minister No. 10 was an inconspicuous-looking house on a little-known street down which anyone could walk; only when the suffragettes stepped up their activity was a policeman stationed outside. Little had been done in the way of refurbishing the rooms, but Margot brought many of her own pictures, rugs and ornaments. The grand dining room *(below left)* could be used for either large or small parties.

Right The Declaration of War on 5 August was greeted with cheers and singing – most of the men in this crowd in Trafalgar Squre are young, and therefore the most excited at the prospect of a fight.

Left Asquith was known as the chief opponent of the franchise for women and physical attacks on him, from assaults with whips to the hurling of stones and even an axe, grew more and more frequent as the years passed. Here, two suffragettes accost him as part of their 1908 'Pestering the Politicians' policy.

Above left Duff Cooper and his wife, the former Lady Diana Manners. Both were members of the Coterie, the group of young people of whom Raymond Asquith was the acknowledged leader. Diana was also one of the circle of young women who made much of the Premier.

Above right The Chancellor David Lloyd George *(right)* and Edwin Montagu, Asquith's Private Secretary, en route to the House of Commons to present the 1914 Budget.

Above left Winston Churchill, adored by Violet Asquith, was made First Lord of the Admiralty by Asquith in 1911 and flung himself into making the Navy as super-efficient as possible. Here, he and his wife Clementine are arriving for the launch of the dreadnought HMS *Iron Duke*, which went on to serve as the flagship of the Grand Fleet during the war.

Above right Sir John French *(left)* with Asquith, when he visited the Front in 1915. On his return from Dover, Margot met him late at night at Charing Cross – she was the only person allowed into the station.

The uneasy relationship between Margot and Violet (*right*), the only one of Margot's stepchildren living at No. 10 in 1914, is illustrated by their strained expressions – both were jealous of each other's closeness to the Prime Minister, who wrote: 'It is a grief to me that the two women I care about most should be on terms of almost chronic misunderstanding'.

Margot was given the money to buy The Wharf, in Sutton Courtenay, by her devoted admirer J.P. Morgan, the millionaire American financier. It was within such easy reach of London that it became a much-needed retreat during the war – Margot entertained there almost every weekend.

Asquith and Lloyd George at The Wharf in May 1915. Although Margot had already become highly suspicious of him, Asquith did not believe that Lloyd George had any designs on his position and was still on good terms with him.

The wedding of Violet Asquith and Maurice ('Bongie') Bonham Carter, Asquith's senior Private Secretary, in November 1915. The Asquiths were criticised for its lavishness.

Above left Venetia Stanley was tall, dark and handsome: a masculine description that many of her contemporaries felt suited her. She was highly intelligent, indifferent to convention and an excellent listener – all qualities guaranteed to appeal to Asquith.

Above right Elizabeth Asquith, aged eighteen, described here in *The Tatler* as 'an indefatigable worker in the cause of our wounded heroes'. The inset photograph shows her at one of the tea dances she frequented with officer friends home on leave.

THE LATE LIEUTENANT RAYMOND ASQUITH

Eldest son of the Prime Minister, was killed in action in France on September 15. He was a most brilliant scholar, a barrister with a large practice, and a soldier who never failed to do what was expected of him. He gave up his work in November 1914, receiving a commission in the Queen's Westminsters, and was gazetted Lieutenant in the Grenadier Guards early in 1915

Photographs   *Arbuthnot*

MRS. RAYMOND ASQUITH

Who was married to Lieut. Asquith in 1907, is the daughter of Sir John Horner, of Mells Park, Somerset. She is left a widow with one son and two daughters

Above Raymond Asquith's death in the Battle of Flers-Courcelette on 15 September 1916 was reported in this article in *The Bystander*. Often spoken of as the most brilliant man of his generation, his death created shockwaves round his circle.

Asquith *(centre)* and Sir Edward Grey *(right)* in Paris for the Inter-Allied Conference at Chantilly in March 1916 to discuss the offensive on the Somme, which would take place in July. By now Asquith's former trust in his Foreign Secretary had, according to Margot, all but evaporated.

Margot and Puffin, pictured here leaving court after Margot's successful libel action against the *Globe* newspaper, which had falsely accused her of consorting with German officer prisoners and printed letters accusing her of being a traitor.

Margot with Lytton Strachey who always wrote of her with slight but lofty disparagement: 'as one looks at her small, weather-beaten (perhaps one should say life-beaten) countenance one wonders . . . there does seem a suggestion of something going on underneath.' But he never could resist her invitations.

By 1923, Margot was better known than ever. The second volume of her autobiography had been published the previous year – like the first, it was a best-seller. Here, as Queen Elizabeth in a pageant at Worcester College, she indulges in her love of dressing up.

Left After the war, Margot's attitude to Violet relaxed and her genuine affection for her stepdaughter shone through. Another bond was formed by the campaigning they did together when Asquith was seeking re-election.

Below Margot and Asquith at The Wharf in 1924 – Margot still as erect as a soldier at sixty. It was around this time she wrote: 'If for no other reason, my life has been happier than that of any other woman I have known, because I married a man whose mind was anchored when most men are at sea, and whose love for me never usurped his interest in our conversation.'

'Sometimes – in my worst moods – I am jealous of everybody who likes you & whom you like,' wrote Asquith. 'But that does not last. If only I could even make you know . . . what the loss of you wd. mean to me of desolation & despair!'

For Venetia, already worried by the intensity of the Prime Minister's feelings, this phrase must have brought home to her the impossibility of the situation in which she now found herself.

TWENTY-THREE

Victoria Station had become the hub of wartime London. In the early morning, after the ambulance train had arrived and just before the leave train steamed out at half past eight, it was a seething mass of khaki, with soldiers ('Tommies', as they were called), packs on their backs and carrying rifles, puffing on their favourite brand of cigarettes, Woodbines. Close by platform seven, a former bookstall was now a bureau de change, for uniformed troops only, changing French money into English and vice versa. There were soldiers in the canteens – served by volunteers – and wives, mothers and sisters saying goodbye. The station was the only place in London where kissing in public by respectable people would not have been thought improper. In the evening, as the home-coming leave train arrived, there were more embraces and, this time, joyous faces instead of sad ones.

'Everywhere in London there seemed to be soldiers,' thought Elsa Freeman, a young woman working at a hospital, who expressed the general need not only to be actively involved but also to be seen to be so. 'We feel if we are playing tennis or carrying golf clubs or something, and we meet a man in khaki, we want to call out: "Please, we were at the hospital till 1 o'clock", or "This is my first day off for weeks".'

Scouts and Guides were more active than ever. Scouts acted as messengers for the Army and helped guard coastal areas and stations; one was killed when the Germans shelled Scarborough and his coffin, draped with the Union Jack, passed into the church through lines of fellow Scouts. Guides made tea, washed up at hospitals, sewed and mended. The Fortrose Guides knitted scarves and socks for the Seaforth Highlanders at the Front; Edinburgh Guides held a Belgian fruit and flower day that raised £2,500 for the Belgian relief fund. Other children knitted scarves and socks – those who had had

German governesses had to unlearn the German style of knitting.

In mid-March the Pampisford postmaster recorded that 2,000 pairs of socks were sent to the Cambridgeshires. 'The money for them was raised from the wealthier Class,' he wrote. 'This was in response to an appeal from the Front – it appears the men were unable to wash anything. When clothing was dirty and worn it had to be thrown away.' Some better-off children 'adopted' lonely soldiers, writing them letters and sending presents of cigarettes and chocolate.

Murmurs about a Coalition government had begun some time earlier. In March Lloyd George, whom Margot alternately mistrusted and was beguiled by, told her that the Opposition 'was longing for a Coalition'. Kitchener, the most popular man in the country, was gradually alienating the Cabinet by his secrecy, refusal to delegate and general lack of organisation.

On 15 March, after Germany's declaration of unrestricted submarine warfare began to cause serious merchant shipping losses, the British Navy imposed a total sea blockade on Germany, prohibiting all shipping imports including food. The signs of a long conflict were now apparent, although many, like French Corporal Ernest Mansat and his wife Marthe, still clung to the hope that the war would be over soon.

'My darling little love,' he wrote to her in April 1915. 'I . . . am very sad that you were without news for three days, but be reassured, my little treasure, that I am well. My little Marthe, I am upset that you are upset, however it isn't my fault, as I seize even the smallest opportunity to press my heart to yours, those two hearts that love each other so much . . . You tell me that the war should be over in three weeks, if what you say is true, my treasure, how happy I will be to think that at the end of this time I shall take my beloved in my arms.' A few days after writing this moving letter Ernest was killed in a German bombing attack on the Belgian town of Elverdinghe. He was awarded the Croix de Guerre.

The Dardanelles Campaign proved to be a naval disaster. The British fleet of battleships, cruisers and destroyers, targeting the Narrows, ran into a new line of mines placed there secretly by the defenders ten days before. Three British battleships were sunk and three crippled – amounting to two-thirds of the naval force there. With mine-sweeping ineffective and the Turks on the higher, strategically important ground there was little the Navy could do. The only alternative was to land troops on the beaches – but this took much-needed time to organise.

The very day after the attack Asquith was pouring out his fears at the prospect of ever losing Venetia in a letter written late at night that implied he had a half-suspicion of coming change. 'So you can realise the unspeakable blankness – the tragic pall of black un-relieved midnight darkness – wh wd overspread me if I had to go on living and working and worrying, I won't say without you (for you won't doom me to that, I know) but with all the avenues closed or only open in dim distant far off vistas.'

The continuous torrent of letters, loaded with the gossip and se-crets of the Cabinet, full of war news and requests for her opinion, were all interwoven with hope, passion, concern, love and depend-ency. As Lloyd George and Winston and Balfour were arguing about the munitions shortage, he was telling her, 'I love you more than life'. Letters were streaming out daily, desperate, imploring, demanding. 'I wonder if you can realise how, at every hour of the day, I am thinking of you, picturing your supposed environments, envying the people (even the spotted patient) who are within range of your eyes and hands, wondering what is passing in your mind and thoughts, fearing and hoping for the future and loving beyond measure.'

Through all this Margot suffered deeply, a mixture of emotions that ranged from simple jealousy to resentment of Venetia's behav-iour and the knowledge that for herself the allure of youthfulness was no more, with an inevitable lowering of self-confidence when she compared herself to her young and vibrant rival. What made it worse was the humiliation of knowing – Margot's antennae were nothing if not sharp – that all her friends knew and discussed the affair, whereas for her it was still a yawning, unadmitted gulf be-tween herself and the being she loved most in the world.

On 12 and 13 April the Asquiths stayed at Windsor Castle. Here, for the first time, they met the recently enforced alcohol ban, pushed through with his usual vigour by Lloyd George.

Alcohol had become such a problem that it had, believed the Government, begun to interfere with shipbuilding and munitions-

making. Lloyd George, one of the first to see the intimate relationship between 'the Front' and those at home, declared: 'We are
fighting Germany, Austria and drink, and as far as I am concerned,
the greatest of these foes is drink', and started a campaign that
asked national figures to pledge that they would not drink alcohol
during the war.

His greatest coup came at the end of March, when he had managed to persuade King George V to promise that no alcohol would
be drunk in the royal household until the war was over. The next day
the King instructed his Private Secretary to write to Lloyd George
that 'if it be deemed advisable, the King will be prepared to set an
example by giving up all alcoholic liquor himself and issuing orders
against its consumption in the Royal Household so that no difference shall be made, as far as His Majesty is concerned, between
the treatment of rich and poor in this question'. Accordingly, from
6 April a mandate was issued that no alcohol would be consumed
by the Royal Family or household. 'We have all become teetotallers
until the end of the war,' wrote the King sadly in his diary. 'I hate
doing it, but hope it will do good.'

The King became used to barley water but his courtiers were not
so happy. Ettie Desborough, at Windsor that month, described Lord
Rosebery, unaccustomed to ginger beer, getting such hiccups that he
could not continue talking to the Queen, whereas, said Ettie, 'the
only cheerful person was Margot, who took copious swigs from a
"medicine bottle" and talked a great deal. According to Raymond
Asquith, this flask must have contained brandy (often considered
medicinal); writing to his brother-in-law Edward Horner the same
month, he remarked that Lloyd George himself, 'hitherto a lifelong
teetotaller, now calls loudly for brandy after every meal, and Margot
can touch nothing else'.

From Port Said, Oc sent a telegram to his father at The Wharf on
behalf of the whole Naval Division: 'All of us amazed and alarmed
at reported spread of temperance. Stand fast.' This, commented
Raymond drily, 'appeared to affect the P.M.'s mind much more
powerfully than the King's letter in *The Times*'.

However, Lloyd George continued his campaign, though privately
few took any notice. By the autumn he had managed to get drink
forbidden in restaurants, pubs and clubs unless served with a meal;
soon after that the hours during which spirits could be bought were

greatly reduced (by May 1916 brandy was unobtainable without a doctor's prescription); and clubs were ordered to close by 10.30 (this ban, known as 'the beauty sleep order', resulted in the proliferation of 'underground' nightclubs).

Few MPs took much interest in debates as to how to combat the perils of alcohol – least of all Asquith – and any suggestion that Parliament should become an alcohol-free zone was rejected with sturdy indignation. Churchill's reaction was typical. When Lloyd George began to discuss 'the Drink question' with him, he announced grandly that he was not going to be influenced by the King and, said Frances Stevenson, 'refused to give up his liquor – he thought the whole thing absurd'. (A similar campaign in Russia failed: when vodka was banned, families all over the country simply made their own.)

At Windsor, which Margot regarded as 'a little too big for the King and Queen' ('King Edward and beautiful Queen Alexandra were much better suited to castles and palaces'), the guests waited in the drawing room, the men on one side and the women on the other, while the Queen walked up the line of men chatting to them and the King talked to the women. His questions, 'Do you like travelling?' 'Are you seasick?' 'Did you enjoy yourself today?' 'What is your favourite flower?' may have seemed banal to Margot but, once seated next to her at dinner, he launched into the more interesting subject of the alcohol ban, and his feeling that he had been talked into spearheading the campaign on false premises.

He told her that he felt he had been 'sold' as he had never intended to give up drink unless the Government passed drastic legislation on the subject. But, having done it, he was ready to share the sacrifices of the poorest of his subjects. 'He is a dear little fellow,' thought Margot, 'fundamentally humble in spite of his manner noisy and crude.'

He went on to tell her that when his cellar man had locked up the cellars his servants had arranged a large wreath of empty bottles outside the door and put a crêpe bow on them with a placard and the word 'Dead' written on it. Both of them laughed and the King, looking at Margot as if she disbelieved him, said that no German workman had stopped work from strikes or drink. 'I loathe drink more than anyone,' she noted in her diary. 'I've suffered from it with grooms and butlers and seen its fatal effects on the temperament and intellect of young men but I feel the British workman should have his stimulants just the same as all the soldiers have theirs.' What she did not mention was her own husband's drinking habits.

While at Windsor, Asquith had to go to London for a Cabinet meeting. Margot, from whom thoughts about the unspoken Venetia 'situation' were never far, gave a letter to her husband's valet to put in his car. In it, as she wrote in her diary, 'I told him how <u>much</u> I loved him and how well I knew that I was getting older – that I was irritable – that there were other females in the world etc, that I had no common jealousy that would deprive him of unshared leisure or pleasure ... my love was constantly re-equipping him for Happiness, but that in moments of discouragement I also wanted re-equipment and a little stimulus.'

It was an extraordinarily generous letter and it drew forth a generous, reasoned response from Asquith.

My own darling,

Your letter made me sad, and I hasten to tell you that you have <u>no</u> cause for the doubts and fears which it expresses, or suggests.

You have and always will have (as no one knows so well as I) far too large a nature – the largest I have known – to harbour anything in the nature of petty jealousies. But you would have just reason for complaint, and more, if it were true that I was transferring my confidence from you to anyone else. My fondness for Venetia has never interfered and never will with our relationship ...

... I <u>never consciously</u> keep things back from you and tell them to others. These last 3 years I have lived under a perpetual strain, the like of which has I suppose been experienced by very few men living or dead. It is no exaggeration to say that I have on hand more often half-a-dozen problems than a single one – personal, political, Parliamentary & – most days of the week. I am reputed to be of a serene, 'imperturbable' temperament, and I do my best in the way of self-control. But I admit that I am often irritated and impatient, and then I become curt and perhaps taciturn. I fear you have suffered from this more than anyone, and I am deeply sorry, but believe me darling it has not been due to want of confidence and love. Those remain and will always be unchanged.

Ever your own <u>husband</u>.

What neither of them knew at the time was that Venetia was drawing Montagu closer. 'My darling (I begin like this not because I find you expect it but because I want to),' she wrote to him on 13 April, 'Don't fail me on Friday. I want you very much, and write me one line to say you still love me . . .'

At the same time, she was reassuring Asquith that their relationship was unchanged. 'I cherish what you said on our last drive to the Hospital (a divine drive) on Sat week,' he wrote to her. 'That between you & me things are absolutely unchanged. I could not bear to think what wd be my case if it were otherwise.'

Margot was not entirely reassured by Asquith's loving letter. An unmarried Venetia would continue to be the stumbling block on Margot's path back to her former closeness with her husband. Unknowing of Montagu's love for Venetia – and of his renewed hopes – she regarded him as the only person she could speak to about this problem that overwhelmed her life. He was an intimate of them both, he was understanding and kind, he knew Venetia well and, she hoped, might be able to influence her. Yet at the same time she did not wish to imply that her husband was in any way to blame. On 16 April she wrote him a pathetic letter, enclosing the one Asquith had sent her and asking for its safe return.

Dearest Mr Montagu . . .

I have as you know often wondered if Venetia hadn't ousted me faintly – not very much – but enough to wound, bewilder and humiliate me – (I have been chaffed about her more than once). Venetia as I said to Henry has many fine points: she is unselfish and kind but she leads (not in Hospital) the kind of life I hate* (after being out 10 years!) and she is not <u>candid</u> with me. She has not much atmosphere of moral or intellectual sensibility and in the old days she always made mischief between Violet and me just when Violet was <u>most</u> devoted to me but in spite of all this I really have no sort of personal dislike and <u>always</u> suggest Venetia for everything – Meetings Newcastle [where Asquith made an important speech that April], Walmer, Wharf, Debates, dinners etc.

My jealousy is <u>not</u> small as from wounded vanity it is <u>Love</u> for Henry (and the <u>knowledge</u> alas! that I am no longer young and

* Margot meant: almost entirely frivolous.

I dare say – in fact I always observe – as men get older they like different kinds of women) and the passionate longing that nothing and no one should even hang a chiffon or tissue paper veil between him and me even once a month – our relationship is absolutely unique. Every night however late I go and sit on his knee in my nightgown and we tell each other everything – he shows me <u>all</u> his letters and all Venetia's and tells me every secret . . .

When H arrived Tues night at the Castle and came into my room where I was lying in the dark he took me in his arms and tears were on his cheek, he said my letter had touched him so terribly he had thought of nothing else (he told me Venetia had lunched and he spoke of her with great sweetness). Tear all this up and don't think me wanting in Reverence or diffidence in writing it to you.

<u>Your</u> part to play is to persuade both Violet and Venetia that if they don't marry they will be miserable formidable egoists and amateurs. Your loving

Margot

On the same day Asquith concluded a letter of several pages to Venetia with the words: 'You are dearer to me than the whole world, and I never loved you as I do today.'

The Venetia problem was much nearer to a solution than Margot realised. The day after Margot had written her letter to Montagu, Montagu went to stay with Venetia at Alderley for the weekend of 17–18 April. She must have taught herself to stifle her feelings of physical repugnance – although he asked her why she always turned away from him when he embraced her – for those two days saw them on the point of an engagement. The moment after he had left on Sunday she wrote to him, a tangled and confused letter that illustrates the corner into which she had painted herself.

'What can I say after this short time you've been gone. That I want you back fearfully. Yes I do. I also know that Sunday has made it very difficult for me to go on writing to the P.M. as tho' nothing had happened. Darling what am I to do? obviously what I ought to do would be to try and carry on as I've been doing, you've both been fairly happy under that regime and as there can be no hard and fast rule of right and wrong and as I feel none of that that people call duty towards themselves that would be the simplest plan. But are you both happy and can I make you so if I'm not and should I be now? Then again when to tell him. Just before Newcastle, oh no not there . . . Why can't I marry you and yet go on making him happy, but you'd neither of you think that fun and I suppose my suggesting it or thinking it possible shows you how peculiar I am emotionally. I wish to God I'd got a really well defined idea of right and wrong but nothing that one does to oneself seems wrong, and that's how one gets into so infernal a tangle . . . My very dearest, I want so much to see you, I'm rather frightened about what I feel, first lest it shouldn't last and secondly lest yours shouldn't. Write to me and say you are coming next Sunday, I want you fearfully. I am so perplexed and wretched, I want so much to be happy and yet not to make anyone else unhappy. You made everything seem so simple, but now you are gone it is as tangled as ever. Go on loving me and above all make me love you . . .'

She concluded with 'Darling, I <u>think</u> I love you.'

The same afternoon she wrote to Asquith to tell him she was thinking of getting married – but did not say to whom, or when. To Asquith it must have appeared that she was speaking hypothetically – after all, she was twenty-eight, marriage was every woman's de-sired goal then, and if she left it too long her chances would narrow, so that it was, indeed, time she thought about it.

Asquith replied at midnight, before going to Newcastle, to tell her how much he would mind '<u>quite enormously</u>, <u>who and what</u> was the man. But whoever it was – through no fault of yours, my be-loved and best, but entirely thro' mine, for you have never deceived or deluded me for a single moment – life would have lost for me its fountain, its inspiration, its outlook.' But it is difficult to believe that he took her letter as anything more than an expression of intent.

Next day Venetia talked of their dilemma to Montagu. 'I feel so ungrateful to him and yet at times I resent very bitterly that he should stand in the way. And yet I know that you are right and that it wd be almost impossible for me to go to him and say "In spite of the fact that you've again and again told me that if I were to marry life would have nothing left to offer you, I am going to marry Edwin". How could he have been so cruel as to say that to me.'

Montagu, devoted to Asquith and very conscious that he owed him his career, was equally perplexed. 'As regards the Prime,' he wrote, 'I can't see the way out – but best beloved, we must find one.'

Both men were now pushing Venetia to a decision. The next day, Asquith told her: 'I would rather know the worst – without disguise or delay . . . The only thing I mind is suspense and uncertainty. Deliver me from that. Your own lover.'

By the same post came an agonised letter from Montagu saying that they could not go on as they were. 'Your plan of being happy as we are won't do. I think your proposal is not half worthy of you. I fear I must assume after your last letter that you love the P.M. If so then the sole question is whether you propose to let that love fill your life as long as it will last. If so don't let me go on in a concealed and unrequited love of you but tell me so . . .'

TWENTY-FOUR

It was five o'clock in the afternoon, the shelling that signalled the start of a major German offensive had died down and the Allied soldiers were waiting tensely for the first wave of German troops to attack. Then, as they waited, every nerve alert, the sentries of the French and Moroccan troops fighting for control of the little town of Ypres in western Belgium saw a misty, yellow-green cloud rolling across the ground towards them.

At first the mysterious cloud was thought to be a smokescreen to conceal the advance of the Germans hidden behind it. To counter the expected attack, all Allied troops in the area were ordered into the firing line of their trench to be ready to repel them. But the cloud itself proved to be the deadly enemy.

On that day, 22 April, in defiance of the Hague Convention, which outlawed chemical warfare, the German army had released 168 tons of chlorine gas over a four-mile front.[*]

Within ten minutes it had killed about 6,000 of the men facing it – a two-minute exposure to chlorine, breathed in as little as one part in 10,000, caused pulmonary lesions. Men gasped for breath, with blue faces and livid skins, their terror unbearable as the fluid rose higher in their lungs until they died, primarily from asphyxiation and afterwards from lung damage. Many more were left blinded and stumbling helplessly about – when combined with water, chlorine gas forms hydrochloric acid, destroying moist, soft tissues such as eyes and lungs.

There was no respite. Being denser than air, the gas quickly sank into the trenches so the only way men could save themselves was by climbing out of these trenches – and into heavy enemy fire. As

---

[*] It had previously been used against the Russians but as it had quickly frozen had made little impact.

quickly as they could, those who survived ran, abandoning their positions and leaving a four-mile gap in the front line. But the German High Command had not foreseen the staggering effect of the gas so that, with the coming of darkness and lack of follow-up troops, the German forces could not exploit this advantage.

It was known that liquid could protect against this gas, so Canadian troops made rough-and-ready masks by urinating onto bits of cloth and clapping them over their faces. By this means they managed to hold that part of the line against further attacks until 3 May. Soon, Allied troops were supplied with makeshift masks: cotton pads enclosed in butter muslin and tied behind the head with tapes. Within three months the British had developed 'gas helmets' and gas ceased to be a major threat.*

The news of the gas attack fuelled the simmering hostility against all things German that was taking hold of the country. 'In the paper was written the horrible, slow death the soldiers have to die after the poisonous gases the Germans use – it makes one feel ill and boil with rage,' wrote Elsa Freeman. 'I never had any personal hatred against the Germans but on reading this they fill me with loathing . . . they die in slow agony, black glaze on the face of suffocation – I really had to go into my room and sob after reading about it.'

Almost simultaneously the Gallipoli Campaign began. After the failure of the naval attacks on the Dardanelles, it had been decided that ground forces were necessary to eliminate the Turkish mobile artillery. This would allow minesweepers to clear the waters for the larger vessels and a joint British Empire and French operation was mounted to capture the Ottoman capital of Constantinople and secure a sea route to Russia.

Disquieting news from both Fronts about the shortage of munitions began, first in a trickle, then a flood. The casualty lists were terrible,† so great that a lowering of the physical standards for join-

* The British Army (including troops from the British Empire) had 188,000 gas casualties but only 8,100 fatalities among them. Russia lost over 50,000 men to gas while France had 8,000 fatalities. In total there were about 1,250,000 gas casualties in the war but only 91,000 fatalities, over half of which were Russian. However, these figures do not take into account the number of men who died from poison gas-related injuries years after the end of the war; nor those who survived but were so badly incapacitated by poison gas that they could hold down no job once they had been released by the Army.

† By Easter 1915 the death toll was 140,000.

ing the Army was necessary: men no longer had to be at least five foot six inches tall but could join up at five foot three inches (in July the Army agreed to the formation of 'Bantam' battalions, of men between five foot and five foot three in height), and the age limit was raised from thirty-five to forty.

At this point Venetia, whose nursing training was almost complete, decided to go with Monica Grenfell and work in the British Hospital at Wimereux, near Boulogne. This had been set up by Lady Norman, the wife of an MP, in the Hotel Bellevue, which was 300 yards from the sea but unfortunately close to a railway station. Being so accessible from England, it was the destination of choice of many an upper-class young woman – Asquith, cross at Venetia's decision, called it 'an annexe of London Society' (there was much in what he said: although Monica was about to see horrendously wounded men with faces or limbs blown off as well as the naked bodies of those she had to wash, Ettie would not let her make the journey there unchaperoned).

Venetia was due to report to the Wimereux hospital on 10 May. Her decision to go may have been a simple feeling that she should do her best for those who, in effect, were fighting for her intermingled, perhaps, with the desire for a new experience outside her more or less frivolous life or the wish for a space away from both the men pursuing her to clear her mind about the future. In any event, she made the decision before telling either Asquith or Montagu – to whom she had now virtually committed herself. 'You decide to spend your life with me if it can be done, then without a word to me fix up 3 months at least in France,' he complained.

But two days later he was declaring, 'Yesterday was the greatest day of my life . . . the most wonderful woman in the world delivered herself into my safekeeping, into my hands, for better or worse.' Venetia had finally made up her mind. She would marry Montagu but on one condition: she would have sex with him only when she chose, and she would also have the right to extramarital affairs.* 'We can have such fun & I'm sure could be so really happy & if that can't be made a good basis for marriage I don't know that I shall ever find a better,' she said.

With this agreed, she was accommodating when he asked her to

---

* As stated by Naomi Levine, who was allowed to see the original letter.

convert to Judaism – exchanging one religion for another meant little to her. The Jewish religion made no demands of him, he told her, except a rare visit to the synagogue and, for them both, Passover at his mother's house.

But still neither of them knew how to tell Asquith. Venetia had hoped to do it during a weekend that the three of them spent at Walmer Castle but simply could not bring herself to – instead, overwhelmed by the strain and worry of the situation, she developed an appalling headache, retired to bed and the opportunity passed.

Asquith was due to travel to Newcastle to give a major speech to munitions workers there and, on the basis of an assurance from Kitchener, told the munitions workers that he did not believe that any army 'has ever entered upon a campaign or been maintained during a campaign with better or more adequate equipment. I saw a statement the other day that . . . our army . . . was being crippled or at any rate hampered, by our failure to provide the necessary ammunition. There is not a word of truth in that statement.'

They were words that would shortly be held against him with devastating effect.

After the start of the Gallipoli Campaign, it was six weeks before the first troops were landed, giving the Turkish commanders time to plan their defensive measures, a factor that would make the following month, May, one of the worst of the war.

These measures were extraordinarily efficient, from the siting of trenches and guns to the taking of the Turkish troops on long marches to avoid lethargy. By the end of May British casualties were enormous, the medical facilities overwhelmed and dysentery was rife. One British soldier wrote that the beach on which he had landed, Helles, 'looked like a midden and smelt like an open cemetery'. Australian and New Zealand troops suffered even more.

The campaign failed, with heavy casualties on both sides. If the breakthrough Churchill had believed in had been achieved the Turks, allies of Austria and Germany, would have been unable to prevent Britain and France from joining the Russians in the war against Austria-Hungary and Turkey.

Soon after the Anzac landings came the sinking of one of the world's most famous passenger ships, the large and luxurious *Lusitania*, holder of the Blue Riband for the fastest Atlantic crossing.

She sank in eighteen minutes; of the 1,959 passengers and crew aboard her – including 128 Americans – 1,198 lost their lives.

The effect on public opinion was instant and explosive. The novelist D.H. Lawrence summed up the feelings of many when he wrote: 'When I read of the *Lusitania* I am mad with rage . . . I would like to kill a million Germans.' Top-hatted stockbrokers led a protest to the House of Commons demanding the immediate internment of all aliens, whether naturalised or not; parents threatened to remove their children from schools attended by the children of resident Germans.

'The mob in London . . . are rioting and looting and setting fire to German shops,' wrote Beatrice Trefusis. 'Germans have been turned out of the Stock Exchange and markets are having a thoroughly bad time. Many Germans are voluntarily surrendering to the police to escape the mob. Those above military age will probably be repatriated.' Many were: 10,000, mostly women – some merely Englishwomen married to Germans – and children were taken from their homes and sent to Germany via Holland.

The riots were worst in Liverpool, where workers in the dock area had been on the ill-fated ship – 200 shops were destroyed – and spread through the poorer neighbourhoods of large English cities. The sinking of the *Lusitania* also turned public opinion in other countries against Germany, and was a major factor in the eventual decision of the USA to join the war in 1917.* In England, it made recruiting rise.

---

* At the time, and after a series of stiff Notes from America, to placate the US the Germans called off their sink-on-sight policy on 18 September 1915 but resumed it on 1 February 1917.

TWENTY-FIVE

In May 1915 the war was going badly for the Allies. The Battle of Aubers (on the 9th) was an unmitigated disaster for the British Army – more than 11,000 British casualties were sustained on that day alone, the vast majority within yards of their own front-line trenches, one of the highest rates of loss during the entire war. The Gallipoli Campaign, again with huge losses, and appalling conditions, had stalled and within the Cabinet Churchill and Fisher were at loggerheads about it, Churchill as the campaign's chief advocate while Fisher, as First Sea Lord, had always expressed doubts about it. Submarines were successfully sinking merchant ships that brought food – and fuel – to the British Isles, and the Zeppelin raids were increasing.

To a world used to land or sea battles these huge silver monsters appearing out of the darkness caused disproportionate fear as they glided – seemingly impervious to anti-aircraft fire – over land and sea. The first two had attacked in January, causing Churchill to tell a friend[*] that he expected 100 of them would leave for England on 26 January, the eve of the Kaiser's birthday, though Cynthia Asquith recorded an opposing rumour that 'the Kaiser refused to countenance Zeppelin bombing raids on London because so many of his relations lived there'.[†] Many people took no precautions against them; others, like Alice Keppel, had the baths filled with water every night as a measure against incendiary bombs.

The Government, and in particular Asquith, came in for much of the blame. William Brand, the Pampisford postmaster, wrote

---

[*] According to Mrs Belloc Lowndes' diary of 18 January 1915.
[†] There was an eventual total of fifty-two raids on coastal towns and London, with around 500 fatalities. The raids went on until May 1916, when incendiary bullets were invented: these caused the hydrogen-filled fuel tanks to explode and the airship to burn and crash.

joyfully that 'the country is humming – the sinking of the *Lusitania* did it! It has made this weak-kneed, wobbling government of ours stir – and they want it.' Anti-German feeling* was in full flow; *John Bull*, the ferociously patriotic and extreme right-wing magazine owned by Horatio Bottomley, called for a vendetta against every German in Britain, whether naturalised or not. 'You cannot naturalise an unnatural beast, a human abortion, a hellish freak. But you can exterminate it . . .' The Asquiths were rumoured to be in debt to their German friends. '(1) People think you have sold England to the Germans to pay your debts. (2) That is why you daren't intern the big Germans,' said one anonymous letter received by Margot – it referred to naturalised Germans like Sir Ernest Cassel, friend and financial adviser to the late King Edward VII.

(Interestingly, even in the midst of the most frenzied anti-German outbursts, there does not seem to have been so much as a murmur against the Royal Family, although the King himself was half-German. The likelihood is that of the two Sovereigns within living memory, Queen Victoria was so closely identified with the Empire and Edward VII was both popular and admired for his strengthening of Britain's position on the Continent that no one thought of them as anything but English, while the Danish Alexandra was widely loved. All the same, George V prudently changed the family name from Saxe-Coburg-Gotha to Windsor in 1917.)

As Asquith's colleagues saw him, bland, well fed, calm, scribbling letter after letter to Venetia in the Cabinet Room as vital questions of the war were debated and men were dying in hundreds of thousands, all but the most loyal felt that enough was enough. Even his style, measured, rational, dispassionate, was against him, while the speed at which his mind worked and his total and effective concentration when working alone in his study were of course hidden; by contrast, his sybaritic lifestyle was well known.

Active was what Lloyd George undoubtedly, and visibly, was. His vigour, fiery oratory and obvious and heartfelt determination to prosecute the war to the utmost began to seem more and more attractive. Certainly, the press baron Lord Northcliffe thought so.

* So virulent was it that soon afterwards Asquith had to announce a policy of internment for all aliens of military age. Eventually, 30,000 were sent to the Isle of Man.

Both Lloyd George and Churchill had realised the influential part the press, with its rapidly increasing circulation, could play in the formation of public opinion – and the powerful weapon that public opinion had become – and both, especially Lloyd George, cultivated Northcliffe. Asquith, unfortunately, had a *de haut en bas* attitude to the press generally and the popular press in particular.

Northcliffe carried great influence, ruling his newspaper empire from an office that was more like a library, where visiting ministers could relax and feel at home or where, walking up and down among its comfortable armchairs, green velvet curtains, shelves of leather-bound books and profusion of flowers, he would dictate a leading article for one of his papers with speed and fluency. In an era when there was no television or radio he dominated the dissemination of information as no other man has before or since. His position was strengthened in wartime because as early as 1907 he had been warning that Germany, left behind the previous century in the race for colonies, was bent on conquest – 'I believe that Germany is deliberately preparing to destroy the British Empire', he had said in the *Daily Mail* – and he had warned that Britain needed to spend more money on defence by her armed forces.

When war broke out, he determined to make the *Daily Mail the* newspaper read by the British Army – every day 10,000 copies were delivered to the Western Front by military vehicles – and he also encouraged soldiers to write in with their own experiences, while for the better-educated another of his papers, *The Times*, was essential reading. Such was Northcliffe's influence on anti-German propaganda that a German warship was sent to shell his country home in Elmwood, Kent, in an attempt to kill him; his gardener's wife was the only fatality. The result was that any position he took up carried great weight. Asquith would soon learn how much.

It was a time of acute difficulty both for the Government and for Asquith personally, yet on Wednesday, 5 May he had managed to take Venetia for a drive between 5.30 and 6.50. In his letter, written at midnight, he spoke of that 'hour of perfect delight & happiness' and of how there was 'in your divine eyes a soft & beatific radiance I shall remember to my dying day' before concluding 'for life, till death, you are the love of my heart, the joy & glory of my life'. Two days later – and three days before Venetia was due to leave for Wimereux – after another such drive, he told her, 'I think this week has taught us to know one another better than ever before – if that were possible.' He was sadly mistaken. The woman to whom he had made these avowals had still not summoned up the courage to tell him of her engagement to another man.

Venetia left London, she told Violet, with real joy: she had had a miserable fortnight and, although convinced that once everything about her future was settled she would be very happy, each day things seemed to get more difficult. 'Edwin was a real angel, most patient and un-moody and not in the least resenting my horror and misery at all the things that seemed to come in the way.'

Once at Wimereux, plunged into the hospital routine and the conditions that beside her home appeared squalid, her previous life with all its difficulties seemed remote. It gave her the courage to do what she had signally failed to do before she left: tell Asquith of her engagement. She wrote to him from Wimereux that she was to be married to Edwin Montagu.

When Asquith received her letter he was devastated. All he could manage to write back, on 12 May, were a few lines:

Most Loved – as you know well, <u>this</u> breaks my heart.
I couldn't bear to come and see you.
I can only pray God to bless you – and help me.
Yours.

For him it was a brutal, blunt blow that had come without any warning. Although he had, probably always, known that one day she would marry if the right man presented himself, he had had no idea that she had a prospective husband in mind – nor had he received any such hint. And if she had been thinking of someone, then Montagu, so often gently mocked by them both, was the last man he would have suspected. 'I don't believe there are two living people who, each in their separate ways, are more devoted to me than she and Montagu and it is the way of fortune that they two should combine to deal a death-blow to me.'

He could not believe that Venetia had fallen in love with Montagu ('He is not a <u>man</u>: a shambles of words and nerves and symptoms, intensely self-absorbed and – but I won't go on with the dismal catalogue'); and he was right, as evinced by Venetia's diktat on the sexual side of the marriage. In his misery, he turned to Venetia's married sister Sylvia Henley for comfort and as a confidante; in the next few years he wrote her numerous letters, often discussing Venetia in them.

Reaction to Venetia's engagement varied widely. Violet first had confirmation of it from Montagu himself, when he came round to say goodbye to her – she was going out to visit Oc, who had been wounded. Leaning against the mantelpiece, he told her calmly that he and Venetia were going to marry. When Violet, who knew of Lord Swaythling's financial veto on marrying 'out', asked him about the religious difficulty, he replied: 'We can get round that.'

Violet was horrified at the thought of the engagement. 'The reasons against it are too obvious to require definition . . . M's physical repulsiveness to me is such that I wld. lightly leap from the top storey of Queen Anne's Mansions or the Eiffel Tower itself to avoid the lightest contact – the thought of any erotic amenities with him is enough to freeze one's blood.' She certainly shared the commonly held attitude towards those of Jewish blood – at eighteen she was describing a dance as 'flat' because of 'meeting no one I was particularly fond of & seeing so many jews'.

When she learned that by 'getting round' the question of religion Montagu meant conversion, her reaction was even stronger: she was, as she put it, 'shocked to the marrow'. Like almost everyone else, she believed that Venetia was doing this solely for the money – the strong social undercurrent of anti-Semitism meant that the idea that anyone would voluntarily become Jewish provoked emotions ranging from astonishment to abhorrence. While Asquith, heartbroken and despairing, struggled to maintain his usual serene façade in the face of ever-worse news from the war, her family censured Venetia for her ruthlessness and for turning Jewish for the sake of Montagu's £10,000 a year.

Her sister-in-law Margaret Stanley wrote: 'he is such a repugging creature, and how she brought herself to accept him I cannot think . . . I cannot help feeling very sorry and regretting that she had acted unworthily – as according to my idea she has. I don't mind her rejecting Christianity as she never professed to be a Christian, but I do regret her having assumed the profession of a faith that she equally doesn't believe in, and this for the sake of money. *That* is the ugly thing. Arthur [Venetia's brother] is also very sorry about it but has not taken the line that ferocious old P-in-law has, who will neither see her at present (tho' he says he will by-and-by) nor give her a present or any money for a trousseau. Venetia's future has always been rather a problem. And if she is going to be really happy and settled one must shut one's eyes and swallow the ugliness of her marriage – (and the bridegroom!).'

Venetia's sister Sylvia, the Prime Minister's new confidante, told her husband that her only fear was that Venetia might in the future fall in love with someone – 'as she certainly isn't at present with Edwin'. She also believed that Venetia hated seeing Asquith drawing closer to herself. 'I am certain it cuts her . . . she is very anxious to see him. He does not want to . . . he said he felt he wd say things which wd be so bitter . . .' Sylvia, though dazzled by Asquith's mind, and friendship, was also slightly wary on her own account – he had a habit of holding her hand when he sat beside her on a sofa – telling her husband that Asquith 'has a hot nature and I fancy platonic friendship is not usual to him'.

Asquith had already tried his luck elsewhere. That July, Duff Cooper wrote in his diary: 'Went to see Diana. She was very intrigued by a letter she had had from the Prime Minister. He had been to see her the other day and they had discussed at length Venetia's marriage. Diana is quite certain that Venetia was his mistress, which rather surprises me. This letter, which was rather obscurely expressed, seemed practically to be an offer to Diana to fill the vacated situation.

'She was in great difficulty as to how she was to answer it, partly from being uncertain as to its meaning, partly from the nature of the proposal it seemed to contain. She was anxious not to lose him but did not aspire to the position of his Egeria [i.e. counsellor] which she felt sure would entail physical duties that she couldn't or wouldn't fulfil. I advised her to concoct an answer which should be as obscure as his proposal and leave him puzzled – the old lecher.'

There was one letter Venetia must have found almost as difficult to write as that to the Prime Minister: the one explaining both her marriage and her religious change to his daughter. For although Violet always claimed that at the time she knew nothing of the intimacy of the relationship between her father and her friend, the two young women were the closest possible friends and Venetia, in and out of No. 10, had never been secretive about the Friday drives. Violet, for whom her father was the pivot of her life, for whom she would have sacrificed anything and anybody, must have seen his misery and known the cause, even if only subconsciously. If so, angered with Venetia for hurting him, any stick would do to berate her friend with.

'As to my ultimate plans,' began Venetia, 'I think I have quite made up my mind to be married to E. in such a way as not to separate him for ever from his family. I know it will cause a good deal of very adverse comment amongst a good many people but that will pass away in time and I don't believe many of the people who are really fond of one will mind much. They will all say they couldn't possibly have done it themselves but then one always says that whenever anyone marries. It won't change me; I shan't live religiously or spiritually a different life than if I'd married a complete free-thinker.'

She went on to say that by doing this, a personal act of compliance, she made two people whom her future husband loved – his mother and brother – reconciled to his marriage and that she would herself live in greater comfort than if she had refused to convert. 'Of course there would be absolutely no difficulty about doing it if this bloody money wasn't involved but I do admit that I mind the fact that nearly everyone will think it has been done for that alone,' she continued.

Then came the main thrust of her letter, a heartfelt plea for her best friend to understand her motive, to accept it, and not to let it make a difference to their friendship. 'Darlingest I couldn't bear it if you thought it very terrible. But you won't, beloved, you have meant so much to me over the last eight years. You have given me everything that I have enjoyed. I couldn't bear to think that anything would come between us, so don't feel strongly about it because I feel it's absolutely clinched and nothing can alter it.'

Her loving words evoked no understanding response. Outrage simmers through Violet's reply. 'You call it "a mere act of compliance" (one might apply that term to any false word or action that had a sedative value). It is an "act of compliance" that through the ages people have been tortured and burnt rather than perform. If people had so "complied" how could any faith, or any nation, or anything worth living for have survived? You will say that it is all a matter of the purely abstract and as such does not trouble you. It does trouble me, intensely, so that I shall be the only one of us two to suffer from any estrangement or difference between us in these regions.

'As to Mr Montagu, I'm afraid I <u>do</u> feel differently. I can't imagine ever feeling the same towards him. I feel he has abused your altruism, taken advantage of one of the very biggest and finest and most glorious things in your nature to make you – or let you, it's all one – do a thing not glorious.'

She went on to make an excuse of sorts for Venetia – 'everyone who has known you and loved you as he and I have done for years, is aware of your amazing, spendthrift, helpless generosity to others . . . tho' I don't know why under the heading of others you shouldn't give us a thought and only consider Lady Swaythling!' before castigating Montagu again ('I am amazed at Edwin').

To Montagu she wrote a letter so furious and hostile that he must have reeled when reading it. She put the blame for Venetia's conversion entirely on him; she told him that his behaviour in asking her to become Jewish – she brushed aside his reply that Venetia had 'offered' to convert – was 'contemptible' and almost amounted to moral blackmail. Venetia, however, to whom he showed this diatribe, took it fairly calmly, saying that while Violet's 'high moral principles' allowed her to condemn the actions of her friends, they somehow could always be employed to justify the same actions by herself. 'So don't let us resent anything she may say.'

The rest of the Asquith family viewed the engagement with their habitual detachment. Oc wrote to Violet from Egypt that he hated the whole business, 'but my social self-indulgence is such that the crimes of my friends rarely make me wish to forgo their society'. Raymond, writing to his sister-in-law Cynthia, summed it up in his usual witty, laconic and *épater les bourgeois* style.

'I am entirely in favour of the Stanley–Montagu match. (1) Because for a woman, any marriage is better than perpetual virginity, which after a certain age (not very far distant in Venetia's case) becomes insufferably absurd. (2) Because, as you say yourself, she has had a fair chance of conceiving a romantic passion for someone or other during the last 12 years and has not done so and is probably incapable of doing so. This being so I think she is well advised to make a marriage of convenience. (3) Because, in my opinion, this *is* a marriage of convenience. If a man has private means and private parts (specially if both are large) it is a convenience to a woman.

(4) Because it annoys Lord and Lady Sheffield. (5) Because it profoundly shocks the entire Christian community.

'Of course I see your point when you say you wouldn't like to go to bed with Edwin. I don't mind admitting that I shouldn't myself. But you must remember that women are not refined, sensitive, delicate-minded creatures like you and me: none of them have much physical squeamishness and Venetia far less than most. You say she must have weighed the consequences and so she did, quite carefully: but what frightened her most was not the prospect of the bed being too full but of the board being too empty. She was afraid that her friends might give her up in disgust but after sounding a few of them – Katharine [his wife] e.g. and Diana [Manners] – she concluded that it would be all right and decided to flout the interested disapproval of Mr H.H. and the idiotic indignation of Miss V. Asquith.

'. . . I do not think he will be either a dull or a tyrannical husband, and I understand that the terms of the alliance permit a wide licence to both parties to indulge in such extra-conjugal caprices as either may be lucky enough to conceive.'

Margot, naturally, was delighted that at last Venetia was no longer a threat – she felt so exuberant that she even suggested to Jackie Fisher, when she ran into him in the hall of Downing Street waiting to see her husband, that they waltz (Fisher was a noted and enthusiastic dancer). Fisher promptly seized her by the waist and they twirled round the room together.

For Violet, Asquith's misery was both heart-wrenching and a chance to serve her idol. As they drove down to The Wharf one Sunday in May their talk was of the subject that preoccupied them both: Montagu and Venetia. That night Violet wrote in her diary: 'It is so wonderful to feel he really needs me & that I make a difference to him (I was deeply moved by meeting him coming away from my bedroom last week in London one night late – having left a little note on my pillow saying "don't go away from me now – I need you").'

The next day, at midnight, Asquith scribbled a few words to Venetia: 'This is too terrible. No hell can be so bad . . .'

TWENTY-SIX

More blows for the Government were to come. On 14 May 1915 *The Times* printed its famous 'Shell Dispatch', sent from the Front by its military correspondent Colonel Repington in defiance of the censor.

Charles à Court Repington had been a serving soldier before he joined *The Times*, and gained his information on military matters through his contacts in the Army and the War Office. Particularly valuable to him was his close friendship with the Commander-in-Chief of the BEF, Field Marshal Sir John French. Through Sir John he had been able to visit the Western Front in November 1914, at a time when most rival war correspondents were banned from France.

Colonel Repington, at the Front to see the end of the heavy fighting which followed the first German gas attack in April, saw that whereas the French maintained a heavy bombardment for four hours a day, British guns could only afford forty minutes. 'We obtained insignificant results at the cost of heavy loss.' A shortage of artillery ammunition had also been a reason for the failure of the previous British attack at Neuve Chapelle in March 1915, Sir John told him. Repington then witnessed the failed attack at Aubers Ridge (on 9 May), and was particularly moved by the losses of the Rifle Brigade.

'I therefore determined to expose the truth to the public, no matter at what cost,' he wrote in his autobiography. 'I sent off to *The Times*, on May 12, without consulting anyone, a telegram which became famous, and stated among other things "that the want of an unlimited supply of high explosive shells was a fatal bar to our success".' References to the lack of heavy guns, howitzers, trench mortars and rifle grenades were cut out but it was still enough to blow the Government sky-high.

His article concluded: 'to break this hard crust [the German defences] we need more high explosive, more heavy howitzers, and more men . . . It is certain that we can smash the German crust if we have the means. So the means we must have, and as quickly as possible.' The impact of this on the House of Commons was enormous and when a debate on the subject was postponed, the impression of a governing party swinging in the wind was reinforced.

All round the country there was now the realisation that this bitter struggle might continue for years, with who knows what outcome; long gone were the days when young men had urged each other cheerfully 'not to miss the fun'. 'This is such a different coming of age than I would have expected a year ago,' wrote Edward Cazalet on his twenty-first birthday, 15 May. 'The people on the estate offered to give me a present but I refused to accept one although very grateful at the thought. I felt it would be impossible to receive anything when such awful misery appears on every side. I said that perhaps after the war one might think of festivities.'

When, the very day after the 'Shell Dispatch', Jackie Fisher resigned, after months of conflict with Churchill over the Dardanelles Campaign, now lurching from bad to worse, the crisis deepened. Fisher had demanded that the operation be discontinued and resigned when overruled. Nothing was going right for the Government; and there were calls for a more forceful direction of the war.

Fisher had been threatening resignation for several weeks. When Margot ran across from the barn she slept in at The Wharf to say goodnight to Asquith in his bedroom – after the inevitable game of bridge was finished – he told her of the First Sea Lord's resignation (the previous week Margot herself had met Fisher in an ante-room and taken the opportunity to scold him for neither resigning nor holding his tongue about the Dardanelles expedition). But the fact that he had done the former still amazed her. Asquith said that when Fisher had first resigned he had sent for him, only to be told that he was neither at the Admiralty nor at his house. 'I sat down and wrote "By order of the King I command you to return to your post,"' Asquith informed his wife, telling the messenger to use detectives if necessary to find the missing Admiral.

When Fisher arrived, Asquith told him: 'You will cover yourself with infamy and ridicule if you resign <u>now</u> – at the moment that we are in difficulties. Infamy for deserting the ship and ridicule for not having resigned on the spot the day it was discussed in the War Council. If you want to resign you must write all your reasons in black and white for me to show the King before either of us will accept your resignation.' To Margot, Asquith added: 'He can't make his objection to the Dardanelles expedition a reason as he has initialled every single order for ships etc.'

The next evening Asquith came as usual into Margot's bedroom at 7.30 – if held up by Commons business he would join her in the bathroom later.

'Well, darling,' said Margot. 'Is Fisher resolved to go?'

'Yes,' said Asquith, 'and I made him write his reasons. His reason is simple – he merely wrote: "I cannot get on with Winston Churchill".'

To the public, losing the man who had fathered the modern Navy was yet another blunder to be laid at the Government's door. (Fisher's resignation was good news for one household: the Cazalets. As Edward wrote in his diary at the end of the month, 'Spent the day at home. It was the last day for a long time that we are to be waited on by menservants, as all ours are going to leave this week to enlist, and so mother has engaged all Lord Fisher's staff of parlour-maids, he having to give up Admiralty House!')

Unlike Lloyd George and Churchill, who well knew the value of the 'right' public image, Asquith's natural attitude to the press could best be expressed as 'rising above it'. 'Henry is as indifferent to the Press as St Paul's is to midges,' said Margot; and it was true. As long as he was satisfied he was doing his job properly, he felt that he could continue to ignore the swirling currents of plot, counter-plot, whispers and rumours as he had always done.

Margot was not so sanguine. Always quicker and more intuitive than Asquith, and fanatically loyal to him, she would lie awake at night torturing herself with fears for him or wondering how to dispel the wilder tales that encircled both them and their family – among them that Asquith held shares in Krupps, and that their daughter Elizabeth was engaged variously to the son of Admiral Tirpitz or a German general. When an especially dreadful casualty list was printed, or a ship sunk, she would sob bitterly for the widows and children left behind.

With the terrible news of Gallipoli, the casualties at Ypres, chemical warfare and the shell shortage bursting on a horrified public, Lloyd George seized his moment. He blamed Kitchener for the shortage of munitions and Asquith for the conduct of the war.

Northcliffe had followed up the article from his correspondent Colonel Repington with a blast of his own in the *Daily Mail* of 21 May 1915, advocating conscription and criticising Kitchener in a blistering attack on his competence: 'Lord Kitchener has starved the army in France of high-explosive shells. The admitted fact is that Lord Kitchener ordered the wrong kind of shell – the same kind of shell which he used largely against the Boers in 1900. He persisted in sending shrapnel – a useless weapon in trench warfare. He was warned repeatedly that the kind of shell required was a violently explosive bomb which would dynamite its way through the German trenches and entanglements and enable our brave men to advance in safety. This kind of shell our poor soldiers have had has caused the death of thousands of them.'

Criticism of the country's most popular figure backfired, however. On reading the *Daily Mail*'s leading article, 'The tragedy of the shells: Lord Kitchener's grave error', many papers hastily dissented from these views, overnight the circulation of the *Daily Mail* dropped from 1,386,000 to 238,000, a placard was hung across the newspaper nameplate with the words 'The Allies of the Huns', while almost 2,000 furious members of the Stock Exchange collected a pile of *Daily Mails* and, after giving three cheers for Kitchener, ceremonially burnt them. Northcliffe, however, was not deterred, and continued his attacks on Kitchener.

With the Northcliffe press fuelling a public outcry on these issues, it was clear something had to be done; and it was equally clear that Lloyd George, the darling of Northcliffe's two most influential papers, was in a position to demand this. What he wanted was power to run the war and the first step towards this was to reshape the leadership. He joined forces with Bonar Law to demand a Coalition from Asquith.

Still distraught at the loss of Venetia, the Prime Minister listlessly agreed, asked for the resignations of the Cabinet and went to the Palace to offer them to the King, who asked him to form a new Government. Margot, who had never entirely trusted Lloyd George and now believed him a demon incarnate, tried to enlist the help of friends to foil what she saw as his plot to seize power. As Elizabeth told Cynthia, Margot 'thought with her heart'.

On personal matters, Margot's heart was more buoyant than it had been for a long time. She had been longing for years for both Venetia and Violet to marry – only then would they cease to be her rivals for Asquith's love. Now it appeared that, with Venetia gone, Violet too might take the plunge into matrimony. One evening in May Asquith told Margot that Violet had practically made up her mind to marry Bongie Bonham Carter, his Principal Private Secretary.

'It is what he [Asquith] and I most desire,' Margot carolled in her diary. 'He longs for her to marry.' She went on to excuse her own late marriage. 'Girls who don't marry before they are 30 make a cardinal error in life. I didn't marry before I was 30 but it was not because I could not love enough but because I loved too much and was in love for nine years with one man (with several side affairs). I suffered from just the opposite defect. The present girls have no temperament. I had too much.'

Her delight at the loss of one rival for her husband's affection and the potential disappearance of another was quickly tempered by pity for his misery and unhappiness at what was, in effect, a vote of no confidence in his leadership. He in his turn knew how distressed she would be at the dilution of his authority. Walking into the bathroom on the evening of 17 May, he told her what had happened with an unusual abruptness.

'I've had to take very drastic measures. I wrote to all my colleagues to resign. I shall form a Coalition Government.' Immediately Margot climbed out of the bath, flung a towel round herself and exclaimed in horror: 'Oh darling – so it's come to that! How terrible – our wonderful Government and our wonderful Cabinet!' She could say nothing more for fear of weeping.

The next day, 18 May, she wrote to their friend Haldane: 'I confess I have had a sleepless night of misery over H's decision of yesterday. Our wonderful Cabinet gone!! Smashed!'

Asquith's daughter-in-law Cynthia, who saw him constantly, believed that Venetia's defection had much to do with his immediate acceptance of the idea of a Coalition. Like many women able to pick up faint nuances of expression or behaviour, Cynthia was keenly observant as well as being familiar with her father-in-law's customary mien. In addition, as she recorded in her diary, a friend had told her that the news of Venetia's engagement to Montagu and conversion to Judaism meant that 'the poor PM is absolutely broken-hearted, that it is stimying all public troubles'. Perhaps, she added, 'if truth were known, it is really the cause of the Coalition!'

It was certainly a sizeable factor. Asquith had always been able to compartmentalise his life: hence his ability not only to 'consume' the vast quantities of work he was able to deal with apparently effortlessly with speed and efficiency but also to switch off completely during the leisure time he so enjoyed. But with Venetia it was different: for almost three years she had so dominated his entire mental landscape that she invaded his thoughts when his whole focus should have been on the vital decisions being taken in Cabinet, while much of his leisure was spent either seeing her or planning how he could see her. And, fond as he was of Montagu, he did not think him in any way worthy of Venetia; nor was her conversion to Judaism for what appeared to be mercenary reasons in any way worthy of *her* – although he relished the good life, the moral ethos of his Congregationalist upbringing was never far below the surface.

Above all, she was his obsession; so dependent on her had he become that it is not difficult to see how her loss, together with the discovery that his divinity seemingly had feet of clay, almost destroyed him.

As Asquith's star sank, so that of Lloyd George rose. On 20 May, as the Prime Minister was re-forming his Government, the *Manchester Guardian* declared: 'No Ministry now formed can hope to render its full service to the nation which does not give full and free scope to the contriving genius and powerful initiative of Mr Lloyd George . . . For the particular work which now above all needs to be done – the organisation of the whole industrial resources of the nation for the purposes of war – there is no one in or out of office who can approach him in capacity.'

Cynthia, lunching at Downing Street the next day, noted the great difference from Asquith's normal demeanour after Venetia's thunderbolt. The atmosphere in No. 10 was, she thought, tense and miserable. 'Mr Asquith generally presents the most extraordinarily mellow serenity to the world, and is an imperturbable buffer between himself and all crises private and public.

'I have never before seen him look either tired, worried, busy or preoccupied, and I have seen him weathering a good many storms now, but this time he looked really rather shattered with a sort of bruised look in his eyes, and I felt very sorry for him. It must be a fearful situation for him – the necessity of carting colleagues and the difficulty of yoking a heterogeneous team.

'Margot was wildly strung up, very sad about poor old Haldane who is to be ousted and wild with Harmsworth [Lord Northcliffe] for his attack on Kitchener in the *Daily Mail* headed "Kitchener's tragic blunder".'

That night Asquith went to Violet's bedroom, where they talked until almost 3.00 a.m. about politics, Venetia and Margot, whose distress at what was happening to her husband was making her behaviour almost unbearable. 'I have sometimes walked up and down,' said Asquith, 'till I felt as though I was going mad. When one needed rest, to have a thing like the *Morning Post* leader flung at one – all the obvious reasons for and against things more con-troversially put even than by one's colleagues . . .' Then they talked about Violet's affairs. 'He was infinitely wonderful,' wrote Violet in her diary. 'No two people have ever so completely & perfectly un-derstood one another – been so inside one another as he & I.'

Lloyd George and Bonar Law had insisted on certain conditions in the forming of the Coalition. Both Churchill and Lord Haldane, the Lord Chancellor, had to go. Haldane had been attacked in the press since the beginning of the war for his supposedly pro-German sym-pathies, largely because of his well-known admiration for German culture, evinced by a remark that he had made at a dinner party one evening in 1912, later made public by his host, that Germany was his spiritual home (he had merely been referring to his philosophy studies there forty years earlier). His far-sighted work on stream-lining and strengthening the Army conveniently forgotten, he was vilified almost daily; once, he received more than 2,500 abusive let-ters in a single day.

Behind the scenes Asquith had fought, though without success, to keep Haldane, his oldest friend. But if he had remained, the impres-sion that the Government was not wholehearted in its prosecution of the war would have been strengthened, and for the hundreds of thousands of those who had lost beloved sons or husbands this would have been desperately hard. The King, who realised his worth, promptly awarded him the Order of Merit, but the country rejoiced. 'I see they have cleared out that Germanised old rotter Haldane – Lord how that man is hated!' wrote William Brand in Pampisford.

Margot was miserable at Haldane's fate. Cynthia, describing him as 'the best Lord Chancellor we ever had', wrote in her diary that night that when Margot heard that he had gone 'she lay on her bed and sobbed and appeared at dinner that night looking a wreck'. After the dinner Margot wrote to Haldane's mother that thenceforth she would loathe Bonar Law, adding, 'and never care for Arthur Balfour as much again' (Balfour, another of Haldane's oldest friends, had also failed to support him).

Churchill's departure was a condition insisted on by three of the new Cabinet ministers – Bonar Law, Curzon and Carson (but not Lloyd George) – primarily because the entire responsibility for the Gallipoli disaster was laid at his door by the press, he had said and written some unwise things, and he had been unable to work with Fisher. At this difficult moment Lloyd George found time to castigate former members of the Government for their inefficiency, in a speech that was widely praised in the press but that further convinced Margot that this was all part of a plot he was engineering to topple her husband.

In the long run, she was right.

TWENTY-SEVEN

'Rumours as to the meaning of this sudden and unexpected change fly hither and thither,' wrote Beatrice Webb of the new Coalition. 'Some say that it has been engineered by Lloyd George and Balfour: others declare that it is the only way round the administrative incompetence of Kitchener; others again hint that the government is expecting a big disaster at the Dardanelles and the breakdown of the Russian defence and want to silence criticism; whilst the knowing ones whisper that it means compulsory military service ... Lloyd George is the one Minister who has scored a popular success (with emphasis on popular). He is "the man of the hour" with the Tories; he is still trusted by large sections of the Radicals and the Labour men.'

She was quite clear as to how the Coalition had come about, talking of Haldane's lack of initiative from 'his free use of alcohol, tobacco and all delectable food', and pointing out that the same complaint lay at the root of Asquith's 'slackness'. 'He has become senile from self-indulgence.' As did many people, she believed that Asquith was apathetic and disinclined to trouble about anything 'until it becomes a public scandal'.

Among those who knew – that is, the inner circle of Society – Asquith's private life had long been cause for concern. Margot had known it was a subject of gossip but even she might not have suspected how far this had gone. 'Miss Venetia Stanley who has only just stopped a very very serious flirtation with the Prime Minister – some say they loved each other so much he was meditating eloping!!! (hence no care for his high office and High Explosives!),' wrote the Duchess of Rutland, friend of Margot and former Soul. 'Well, she is going to marry Mr Edwin Montagu. To do it she has to change her religion and be a Jewess!'

Though the fact of the Coalition was public knowledge, all the names of those to fill the important Cabinet posts had not yet been announced (they were to appear in the press on 26 May) and there was considerable jostling to obtain a coveted position personally or for one's party. Asquith was not too wretched to secure most of the important governmental posts for those of his own party. Carson, Asquith's great opponent over Home Rule, became Attorney-General and Curzon was offered, and immediately accepted, the office of Lord Privy Seal.

'H says he feels as if he is dealing with children,' wrote Margot in her diary. 'The intelligence is of a low level . . . B. Law has brains that would fill a wine glass! (he did not know where the Dardanelles were) but he is very nice and plays bridge well. Lansdowne is old and has no war temperament. Walter Long an angel, as loyal as possible and adoring Henry . . . Curzon is loathed by the whole lot. Poor Curzon (whose suggestion that we should fight Greece to make it our ally has covered him with ridicule) left too soon and is in consequence bitter but he has great charm – I see him often and laugh with him. He hates Arthur Balfour and Ld K. Austin [Chamberlain, Secretary of State for India] and Bonar are jealous of each other and Selborne* is a 1st class bounder. Ld Bob Cecil is delightful and a really clever man . . . K a hero in the country but hell in the war office as he is a muddler.'

She did not mention Lloyd George but his leading role in the new Coalition was accepted on all sides, even by Balfour, despite his rather sour remark (on 21 May): 'Lloyd George appears to have a kind of licensed irresponsibility and people forgive what they, at the time, considered the most heinous crimes.'

A new post, that of Minister of Munitions, was created for Lloyd George, work into which he plunged with dispatch, enthusiasm and success (although he had had to hand over the Exchequer to Reginald McKenna, he was allowed to go on living at 11 Downing Street). The creation of this post also saw a major reduction in the power of the War Minister, Lord Kitchener.

What no one had any doubt of was Lloyd George's ability to get things done. As Minister of Munitions he took immediate action; and no one was more persuasive than Lloyd George when he was moved by genuine emotion. When he held a meeting of all the

* The Earl of Selborne was the President of the Board of Agriculture and Fisheries.

principal arms manufacturers with the aim of getting them to pool trade secrets and thus increase efficiency, they demurred, talking of their duty to their shareholders and workforce.

Suddenly Lloyd George leaned forward. 'Gentlemen,' he said, 'Have you forgotten that your sons, at this very moment, are being killed in hundreds and thousands . . . by German guns, for want of British guns? Boys at the dawn of manhood, they are being wiped out of life.' His voice broke and his eyes filled with tears as he said: 'Don't think of your trade secrets – think of your children. Help them! Give me those guns.' He got them.

Fuelled by his immense energy, factories sprang up round the country, staffed not only by men but by women glad to be able to earn money. Many of these were former suffragettes. When war had been declared Mrs Pankhurst had immediately called off all forms of suffragette activity, offering her followers for war work. Apart from simple patriotism, she realised that if women proved indispensable to the war effort, it would be difficult to deny them further opportunities after the war had ended. When Lloyd George offered work in munitions factories with (so far unheard-of) equal pay for men and women,* women flocked to work in them. Formidably energetic and powered by the single-minded aim of winning the war, he co-opted businessmen to produce military equipment, he made vigorous, compelling speeches – and his reputation with the public as the sort of man needed at the top grew proportionately.

Much of this Margot realised, but it did not alter her belief that her Henry was the right man in the right place. It would have to be up to her to defend him as best she could. In her mind the Welshman had become a sinister figure, no longer colleague but enemy, and as she heard his praises sung everywhere she became more and more unhappy and despairing. Asquith, she knew, would not lift a finger to defend himself. He never had and he continued to believe it was beneath his dignity; his actions, he thought, would speak for him and he believed that if he did his duty, how he spent his leisure time was up to him. There was no one, she thought, to touch him. 'There never has been anyone like Henry,' she wrote in her diary on the night (15 June) he spoke on the Coalition in the House.

---

* For piecework; for full-time jobs women, as less experienced and therefore slower, got less.

'Everyone near him and opposite him like so much waste paper.'

The speech itself, she thought, was 'quite perfect, touched with just that passion and emotion that is rare and distinguished. Frances Balfour and I trembled with excitement.' She ran down from the Ladies' Gallery to his room and wrote him a short letter telling him of her feelings.

The following night, when she went as usual into his bedroom, next to hers, she found him rereading her letter, clearly in the grip of deep emotion. She put her arms round him and he wept. It was, Margot understood, a mixture of emotions that caused this brief crack in his calm and genial façade and for once she allowed herself to mention in her diary the effect of his loss of Venetia. 'He is fearfully tired, hates the coalition (though the others are not giving any trouble and our men are) and is low about Venetia's marriage and Violet's indecision. He was quite wonderful and said my letter was noble and infinitely precious to him. We sat a long time together.'

Margot was not the only wife who wrote letters to ministers. Churchill had been replaced by her old friend and former Premier Arthur Balfour (two more opposite personalities could hardly be envisaged). For the Navy, Balfour's silken nonchalance was a poor exchange for Churchill's thrust and brilliance. When Churchill realised that the fiasco of the Dardanelles was to be laid entirely at his door – although the Prime Minister had supported and encouraged the plan – his grief was profound. Clementine Churchill, unable to contain her feelings, wrote to Asquith on 20 May 1915 to beg him to keep her husband on:

My dear Mr Asquith,

For nearly four years Winston has worked to master every detail of naval science. There is no man in this country who possesses equal knowledge, capacity & vigour. If he goes, the injury to Admiralty business will not be reparable for many months – if indeed it is ever made good during the war.

Why do you part with Winston? Unless indeed you have lost confidence in his work and ability?

But I know that cannot be the reason. Is not the reason expediency – 'to restore public confidence'. I suggest to you that public confidence will be restored in Germany by Winston's downfall . . . he has the supreme quality which I venture to say very few of your present or future Cabinet possess – the power, the imagination and the deadliness to fight Germany.

Margot was furious at Clemmie's letter but Asquith did not answer it – probably the wisest course as there was little he could have said in mitigation. Clementine was told that he read it out loud at the luncheon table, with amusement; and in a letter to a friend he described it as 'the letter of a maniac'.

Violet, who adored Winston, told him her view of a Coalition. 'It is the sacrifice of one's friends to the blind prejudice of their enemies – what is called the principle of give and take irrespective of quality or justice or even expediency.' Churchill himself was so upset he decided that if he could not be in the Government, he preferred to fight. From the trenches, he wrote to Clemmie a letter to be opened in the event of his death. 'You have taught me how noble a woman's heart can be,' he wrote on 17 July, concluding with a reference to his view that one day his belief in the Gallipoli Campaign would be vindicated: 'some day I shd like the truth to be known. Randolph [his son] will carry the lamp.'

Four days later the sympathetic Montagu, calling at Admiralty House, saw Clementine. 'She was so sweet but so miserable and crying all the time,' he wrote to Venetia (his engagement to whom had now been announced). 'I was very inarticulate but how I feel for her and him.' Later he wrote a charming and encouraging note to Clementine: 'My dear Mrs Winston, My heart bled to see you so unhappy . . . it is true that Winston has suffered a blow to prestige, reputation and happiness, which counts above all . . . But [he] is far too great to be more than pulled up for a period. His courage is enormous, his genius understood even by his enemies and I am as confident that he will rise again as I am that the sun will rise tomorrow . . .'

Margot too relented, and asked Clemmie to tea, during which they argued furiously. Clemmie 'got up held on to the tea table and harangued me in fish-wife style on Henry's defects till I got up and sat at my writing table calmly while she screamed on a long ro-domontade till I stopped her and said: "Go Clemmie – leave the room – you are off your head – I had hoped to have a very different kind of talk."' Margot then began to abuse Clemmie for her letter to Asquith, telling her that she was 'very very foolish as you will do Winston harm in his career'. At dinner that evening – to which the Churchills had been invited – Asquith was able to have a word alone with Clemmie, reporting afterwards that 'we parted on good and even affectionate terms, and I trust I have dispelled her rather hysterical mutiny against the Coalition and all its works'.

By December Churchill was commanding a battalion* at the Front. His bravery in action was noted by his brother officers, especially the fact that he never flinched under fire. 'It's no damn use ducking – the bullet has gone a long way past you by now,' was a favourite expression. Violet, who knew how courageous he was, told her father she was frightened Winston might die at the Front, to which Asquith answered crisply: 'Well! It would at any rate be an honourable death – far better that he should die like that than live to do what he contemplates.' Margot's view was even simpler: 'No one has given more trouble to their Prime Minister than Winston and LlG'.

Nor was Asquith in any state to withstand the constant pressures. Venetia's loss was still affecting him deeply. There has often been argument over how much – or how little – her defection affected his judgement and actions. What is certain is that misery makes for apathy, fatigue and a 'Why on earth bother?' attitude that is not only visible to others but which cannot help affecting one's own behaviour, as it did with Asquith. Gone was his usual imperturbable geniality; instead there was a creature silent, bowed and listless. The month after Venetia told him of her engagement Margot's diary is filled with remarks like 'I never saw H so silent and taciturn', 'H never uttered', 'a mixture of over-fatigue and real depression'.

Her letter to Violet of 7 June showed not only her acceptance of her husband's obsession but also her belief that Violet knew about it. It also revealed her dispassionate view of Venetia and Montagu's engagement. 'Father is happier over V's marriage tho' not converted – he thinks he wd mind less were it anyone else but I tell him whoever she married he would mind deeply as he has been very much in love . . . [Montagu] is wonderful over it all – courageous, convinced and very humble. They were both old enough to know their own minds and no one must tease them now.' Then, aware of Violet's

---

* The 6th Battalion, Royal Scots Fusiliers, soon afterwards merged with another because of high casualties, when Churchill was told to return to Britain.

almost hysterical reaction to Venetia's conversion to Judaism, she adds: 'There's a good deal of bosh in the religious campaign *au fond*, tho' superficially it takes one in . . . It is Montagu's physique that I could <u>never</u> get over not his religion.'

With the Coalition, the idea of conscription drew much nearer. It already had supporters in the Cabinet and throughout the nation there was the knowledge of a long, bitter struggle ahead that needed all-out effort. At a meeting in the village school in the small Derbyshire farming village of Sheldon, in the midst of sheep-shearing, muck-spreading and cabbage-planting, all the men between seventeen and forty had their names marked down for future military service. Not all were taken: Maria Gyte's diary talks of a number of farm workers, men whom one would suppose were made fit by hard work on the land, being turned down for medical reasons.

More and more, there was resentment that the brave and patriotic should go, quite probably to die, while others remained comfortably at home; 'another family has two sons of military age,' wrote William Brand of Pampisford. '"Don't mean to go," they say, "until they fetch me" . . . It is left for those few who have sons and husbands at the front to realise and sorrow.'

As Raymond Asquith, who that January had joined the Queen's Westminster Rifles, wrote to his wife at the end of May: 'Today I had luncheon with Lady Sybil* at Primrose House . . . She seems to want conscription. It is very odd how many people do now-a-days. The idea they have at the back of their minds seems to be that if their lovers are being killed, it is only fair that their footmen should be killed too. I don't feel that myself.'

What helped to make these feelings so bitter was the simulacrum of normality that overlay much of life. Holidays were still taken, families often renting a house – to which those who could afford them frequently took their own servants so that the smoothness of the household routine was uninterrupted. Often these were at the seaside, where both sexes wore almost identical one-piece bathing dresses, as no man would have dared expose his torso (the beach, incidentally, was about the only place where men and women felt

---

* Lady Sybil Grant was the writer daughter of a former Prime Minister, Lord Rosebery.

comfortable going bareheaded out of doors). The poor, with the extra wages earned in Lloyd George's factories, enjoyed themselves freely in pubs and on racecourses, the rich continued to drink champagne, shoot grouse and party.

'The menu was composed of far-fetched American delicacies – avocados, terrapin and soft-shell crabs,' wrote Lady Diana Manners of the Coterie dances given for her by a rich admirer. 'The table was purple with orchids . . . the dancing, sometimes to two bands, negro and white . . . started immediately after dinner . . . We kept whirling to the music till the orchids were swept away in favour of wild flowers, for breakfast bacon and eggs which appeared with the morning light.' These 'dances of death', as they became known, were in part a treat for those home on leave, in part a reaction against the hideousness of the long, ever-growing casualty lists. It was behaviour that many thought was inappropriate.

They would have thought the same if they could have looked in on the Asquiths. On summer Sundays Violet and Asquith would often visit Garsington, the grey stone Tudor manor house five miles from Oxford into which the Morrells had recently moved. Sometimes they would bring friends with them to see for themselves this esoteric ménage of pacifists, important literary figures and semi-perpetual house party of leftward-leaning intellectuals disporting themselves on lawns flanked by yew hedges or engaging in argument in the drawing room, its panelling painted Venetian red, its air scented with the bowls of pot-pourri and orris root that stood on every mantelpiece and window sill. Through her brilliant, silk-curtained rooms the red-haired Ottoline moved surrounded by her pack of pug dogs.

To Ottoline, observing him closely, Asquith never seemed depressed, or worried by the war. He remained 'the same genial self-indulgent old man, interested in everything he found to hand . . . Already at this time he seemed to have lost the austerity that had held his rather lazy easy-going pleasure-loving temperament in shape.' If she had known* that Asquith's reaction when, on a visit to Calais on 6 July for an Anglo-French conference on the conduct of the war, being told that the meeting was arranged for 8.00 a.m.,

* In a letter from Rothesay Stuart-Wortley, ADC to his father General Wortley, to Lord John Manners, quoted by Catherine Bailey in *The Secret Rooms*.

was to say, 'Oh, but I don't get up till 8.30!', she might have put it even more strongly.

Yet at the same time as many of the rich were enjoying themselves, volunteers all over the country were aiding the war effort. A new body, the Women's Institute, was set up to encourage women to produce more food and counter waste, and give impetus and a sense of community to those living in villages, hamlets and small towns. Queen Alexandra* sponsored a Work for Women Fund to help women thrown out of work by the war; one popular suggestion – taken up eagerly by Scottish Guides – was raising 'A Hundred Miles of Pennies'. Novels, magazines and illustrated papers were collected for servicemen; other Guides collected waste paper for wood pulp and learned how to sew sandbags for the trenches.

Women volunteers worked cutting up string to the right length for those making up parcels of wool that had been sent from America, to be dispatched for knitting up to the Belgians now settled round the country; all day long other women wheeled trolleys holding tea, biscuits or cakes up and down the lines of munition workers making shells and rifles in factories.

Yet the idea of social change – the social change that was gradually, almost imperceptibly, taking place – was far from the minds of those who, eventually, would be most affected by it. So odd did it seem to Cynthia Asquith that when her family car arrived in London it would be driven by an 'unliveried man' that she thought it worthy of remark in her diary. A little later she recorded how, when staying in the house of an absent friend, it was impossible to lunch or dine there because 'there are only two housemaids, so we can only have breakfast and tea in'.

Venetia had refused to give up the Wimereux hospital on becoming engaged and had stayed in France as long as she could – Montagu had had to cross the Channel twice to plead with her to return and marry him, the clincher being the fact that the two rabbis performing her conversion were leaving for the Front on 12 July. She was quite open about her attitude to this – 'I go through the formula required because you want it for your mother's sake and because I think one is happier rich than poor' – and she ignored

* Although the Queen Mother, or Dowager Queen, she was usually known simply as Her Majesty Queen Alexandra.

the speculation and jokes about it ('Didn't she even have to propose Judas Iscariot's health?')

Not everyone disapproved; Cynthia Asquith, who liked her creature comforts, relished Montagu's beautiful and lavishly comfortable house, found him delightful to talk to and thought that he would give Venetia exactly the life she wanted.

Venetia had asked Asquith to meet her in Boulogne on his return from his first visit to the Western Front at the beginning of June. He had been taken to see a bathing station, set up in an old jute factory with its great vats, where troops came for a much-needed hot bath, were given fresh underwear and had their clothes disinfected; and he was greeted with loud cheers by a line of them in vests and pants and holding their boots as they waited their turn to plunge into the steaming vats.

The emotional crises the Prime Minister had been through had left him looking so tired and careworn that this was noticed by Roland Leighton, the fiancé of Vera Brittain. '[The Prime Minister] was brought along to have an informal look at us, and it was arranged that he should see the men while they were having a bath in the vat. We only had about half an hour's notice and had to rush off and make arrangements for the "accidental" visit. I and two other subalterns being at the moment in a mischievous mood decided to have a bath at the same time and successfully timed it so that we all three welcomed Asquith dressed only in an identity disc.

'I still don't quite know what he was doing over here when he is wanted so much in England; but perhaps the shell question had something to do with it. He looked old and rather haggard, I thought.'

It was the first time Asquith and Venetia had met since she had dropped her bombshell. Bongie, who had accompanied him, was disapproving, fearing that she might try and lure Asquith back. 'I was rather beastly to her, I am afraid,' he wrote to Violet: 'I cannot help feeling that having cut herself adrift I do not want anything to be done which may re-open relations, save on a permanent and satisfactory basis.'

He need not have worried. Asquith had been cut too deep, and was too clear-sighted, not to realise that the old intimacy was no longer possible. Instead, he told her how for two years she had been the centre and mainspring of his life; how everything in it hung upon her; of the 'terrible and heart-rending hours' that had made his life 'a veritable hell'. He assured her that he never had or would reproach her; that he would always love and worship her; but that he needed some time to 'stand aloof'. It was the most loving and chivalrous of goodbyes – and marvellously flattering.

Soon after Asquith's visit to France, Beb, at the Front, was wounded in the face by shrapnel when a shell burst near him during the constant bombardment. Several of his teeth were broken and his face badly cut, but what was most noticeable about his return – he was sent home on leave – was his bitterness over what his comrades and the soldiers under his command had suffered over the shell crisis and the shortage of ammunition.

He was soon back in the trenches again. The next time he returned on leave he was withdrawn and silent, avoiding his family, thinking only of his fallen comrades and shutting himself up in his room to write poetry. Hardly anyone was then aware of shell-shock (by the end of the war it was well recognised although little understood). It was clear, though, that Beb's mental condition rendered him unfit for any Army duties and he was diagnosed with 'nerves'; he did not return to military service until June 1916.

The marriage between Venetia and Montagu finally took place on 26 July 1915, on the estate of Montagu's elder brother, the second Lord Swaythling, Venetia in a wedding dress from Paris with diamond aigrettes in her hair. After it, the newlyweds went straight to visit their friend Diana Manners, in hospital with a broken ankle – she had broken it three weeks earlier on a visit to Brighton with Raymond, Katharine, Duff Cooper and Montagu, going down some steps to bathe. Asquith did not go to the wedding but sent her two silver boxes as a present.

On 30 July the Germans put their new weapon, the *Flammenwerfer*, or flamethrower, to shattering use against the Allies at the Battle of Hooge.

It was one of the most feared weapons of the war. Eleven days before the battle, British infantry had captured the German-occupied village of Hooge, in Flanders. Using flamethrowers for the first time, the Germans recaptured it. Though few men were lost to actual burns, it had a demoralising effect. After the earlier poison gas attacks, and the stories of Belgian atrocities, feeling against the Germans had so hardened that the Christmas truce was but a memory and many saw them as no more than brutes.

Second Lieutenant Edward Henn, of the 9th Battalion King's Royal Rifle Corps, who had been through the advance at Hooge, felt this strongly. Of a friend who, married to a German, had gone to live in Sweden, he wrote: 'I have no doubt that, whatever the reason, she is doing the right thing by going to Sweden. Living here, close to the firing line, one realises that it is wrong to love one's country's enemies. If you want to take up a neutral attitude, go and live in a neutral country, that is quite licit, but I don't think any other form of neutrality is.'

So long had the casualty lists become, and so full of her friends, that when she heard twenty-five-year-old Billy Grenfell, Ettie Desborough's second son and a member of the Coterie, had been killed in action on 30 July, a mere six weeks after his older brother Julian's death of war wounds, Cynthia Asquith wrote despairingly in her diary: 'It is the end of one's youth all this. Soon one will hardly remember who is alive and who is dead. In a sense Death is being annihilated – the division grows narrower and narrower.'

TWENTY-EIGHT

Downing Street that June was not a happy place. The atmosphere inside No. 10 was one of strain, tension and distress. Asquith, still miserable from the loss of Venetia, was beset on all sides – the dreadful news from the Front, the infighting in the new Cabinet, the growing demands from the Tories and members of his own party for conscription and the conflicts over it, the difficulties with Kitchener, who by now had driven his colleagues to despair with his secretiveness and lack of organisation, the long hours and diplomatic exertions needed to gain agreement on every decision. Violet, his constant support, was away in Egypt, visiting Oc, who on 6 May had been shot through the left knee during the Gallipoli Campaign and evacuated to a hospital in Alexandria. His wound, reported Violet, seemed healed ('he is still very lame but extremely agile', she wrote to the faithful Bongie). Margot, whose perceptions were often penetrating, had realised that the man supposedly her husband's staunchest ally would soon become his declared rival. 'Northcliffe will try and run Ll.G against father now. I see tiny signs of it,' she told the distant Violet.

Everything seemed to be going wrong for the Asquiths. Now there came a vicious attack from an unexpected quarter: Lord Alfred Douglas, son of the Marquess of Queensberry and the young man to whom his lover Oscar Wilde had written, 'it is a marvel that those red-roseleaf lips of yours should be made no less for the madness of music and song than for the madness of kissing. Your slim gilt soul walks between passion and poetry.'

However, since those days the litigious Douglas had not only converted to Catholicism but had also married, and become outspoken in his condemnation of homosexuality. The Asquiths now found themselves involved in his vendetta against the popular Robbie Ross, the close friend and executor of Oscar Wilde and a distinguished art critic and gallery owner, whom Douglas had been persecuting for a considerable time. (The underlying reason for this was that both men had been in love with Wilde and Douglas saw Ross as a rival.)

Lord Alfred also had a long-standing grudge against Asquith. In September 1908, just after Asquith had become Prime Minister, he had had to ban a Catholic procession in which the Host was to be carried through the streets round Westminster Cathedral, attended by dignitaries of the Roman Catholic Church in their vestments, when it was found that such a procession would actually be breaking the law (it was contrary to the Catholic Emancipation Act; and it was also feared that it might cause Protestant riots). Asquith had had no option but to ask the Archbishop of Westminster to omit the illegal elements – the public display of the Host – from the procession in order to bring it into conformity with the law. Douglas did not view it like this and wrote a strongly worded article attacking Asquith.

The next stage was a letter to Asquith in February 1914, accusing Ross of being 'the filthiest and most notorious Bugger in London. For whom the Prime Minister had created a job carrying with it a large salary',* and threatening to make the whole affair public.

Asquith took no notice of Douglas' threats and neither he nor Margot allowed them to affect their friendship with Ross – Margot, for whom loyalty was paramount and for whom a congenial guest came a close second, constantly asking him to dinner at Downing Street. Douglas continued making so many accusations of homosexuality and blackmail that eventually Ross filed a suit for criminal libel on 24 March 1914. It was finally settled, with Ross putting up such a poor show in the witness box that the judge came down heavily in favour of Douglas.

This was not enough for Douglas, who wrote again to Asquith. 'If I can establish it as a fact that you still continue to receive this horrible man in your house and to allow him to associate with your wife, I shall in the public interest and in view of your official position feel it my duty to call public attention to the matter.'

Asquith promptly passed Douglas' threatening letter to the Director of Public Prosecutions, who sent it to the Home Secretary

---

* Ross held the position of Adviser to the Inland Revenue on picture valuations for estate duty, for which he was paid £1,000 a year.

(then Sir John Simon). 'I return this horrible letter,' said Simon, giving the impression that he would have preferred to handle it with a pair of tongs. 'You are quite right to leave it unacknowledged.' Asquith must have thought that was the end of the matter. It was not.

In another letter (to Ross) Douglas had declared: 'It is my intention to give you a very severe thrashing with a horse-whip. I am bound to come across you one day or another when occasion serves and you shall be whipped within an inch of your dirty life.' He tried to make good his threat when they met unexpectedly at the London house of Margot's brother Eddy, now Lord Glenconner, striding up to Ross and shouting: 'You have got to clear out of this. You are nothing but a bugger and a blackmailer.' Some of the men present pushed Ross into another room, behind a large table, but Douglas came after him until he was pulled back. Margot, typically brave and ready to support a friend, came to Ross's rescue and left the party with him, driving him to Downing Street to recover while Douglas was left shouting with rage until finally persuaded to leave.

Soon afterwards, Ross's friends got up a testimonial to him, referring to his 'services to art and literature' accompanied by a gift of £700 from the 700 signatories – among them Bernard Shaw, H.G. Wells, William Rothenstein, Lady Ottoline Morrell and her husband Philip, the Earl of Plymouth, the Bishop of Birmingham and the Asquiths. The account of this, together with the list of those who had signed, was printed in the *Morning Post* of 29 March.

Douglas was outraged by this show of public support for Ross and tried, unavailingly, to bring Churchill to his side, writing to him and enclosing a copy of the letter he had sent Asquith in February with the suggestion that Churchill put himself forward as the next leader of the Liberal Party. But Churchill, like Asquith, wisely ignored the letter.

Now Douglas launched his worst and most stinging attack against both Ross and the Asquiths, publishing a satirical sonnet entitled: 'All's Well with England'. After referring to Ross as being 'officially condoned', he continued:

Out there in Flanders all the trampled ground
Is red with English blood, our children pass
Through fire to Moloch. Who will count the cost?

Since here at home sits merry Margot, crowned
With Lesbian fillets, while with front of brass,
'Old Squiffy' hands the purse to Robert Ross.

There was nothing the Asquiths could do except endure it.

London was beginning to look more like a wartime city; in its streets wounded soldiers were a familiar sight, many bandaged around the head or on crutches, nurses dashing by, cap ribbons fluttering in the breeze, to get back to their wards on time. Small boys still swapped cigarette cards but – rather in the same way that the Allied High Command often shuffled generals – they would exchange an Allenby for a Foch, or a Kitchener for a Haig in their efforts to complete a set of 'Allied Army Leaders'. There were more women in black and bands playing popular tunes ahead of marching columns. 'Raw recruits led by band still make one cry,' wrote Cynthia Asquith, 'and everywhere the rather undignified, bullying posters – very, very dark at nights.'

Lloyd George was still pursuing his anti-alcohol campaign, largely disregarded by the majority. Kitchener was one of the few who had 'taken the pledge'; not so most of Parliament, save for a handful of ardent teetotallers such as Lloyd George's fellow Welshman Leif Jones, who felt that reduced opening hours alone were not enough and that duty on beer and spirits should be raised higher still (as a result he was nicknamed 'Tea-Leif Jones').

By contrast, Lloyd George's success as Minister of Munitions was great. His energy was immense, his single-minded determination to get things done unstoppable and his gift of persuasion coupled with forceful argument irresistible. By the end of the year his department had built sixty new munitions factories and commandeered over 700 depots, workshops and laboratories, quickly raising the production of shells from 70,000 per month in May to 120,000 by September.

The casualty lists, displayed on the front of *The Times* under the heading 'Killed in Action', were growing longer – as Margot had written earlier to Violet, 'everyone we meet almost has lost someone dear . . . one can only pray that those we love may lose a limb as I almost feel no one will return to us'. Yet for those whose menfolk were the 'wrong' age for volunteering, life went on much as normal, as evinced by the pages of advertisements clamouring for those in-dispensables, servants (even Cynthia Asquith, who cried poverty most of the time, felt she could not do without at least three ser-vants if she rented a flat for Beb's leave – a housemaid, a Belgian refugee who acted as butler, and a cook).

What was noticeable about these pleas for help from those who felt they could hardly survive without a few extra pairs of hands to assist them was that virtually all were for women servants. For although in general the life of the country was curiously untouched – the trains ran on time, restaurants and theatres were full, dinner parties were given constantly, seaside boarding houses were filled throughout the summer by working people taking holidays – in one sense it had changed dramatically and would continue to do so: it had become much more female. Women had begun to fill more and more of the jobs formerly held by men.

In domestic service – still the largest employer – male servants were becoming a rarity; outside the four walls of home, women were increasingly working in offices and, as Government posters exhorted, 'Do your Bit, Replace a Man for the Front', taking over jobs formerly done by men. They worked on the land, in the recov-ering textile factories making khaki cloth, on the railways despite the opposition of some of the unions – in May 1915 the Manchester Tramway Workers had passed a resolution against the employment of women – and, with Lloyd George's encouragement, filled muni-tions factories.

There were still those who thought the war would shortly be over. 'After dinner . . . I talked to Colonel Fitzgerald for the first time,' wrote Cynthia Asquith. 'He said the most difficult thing Kitchener had to contend with was the optimism of people as to the duration of the war.'

Anti-German feeling was stronger than ever. 'One might as well try to dam Niagara with a toothbrush as stop an anti-Haldane talk just now,' wrote Colonel Repington in his diary after returning from a dinner party. And that June Sir Edgar Speyer, a British citizen, Privy Councillor and baronet, financier, patron of the arts, friend of the Asquiths and with a fair claim to be called the 'father' of the London Underground, had been driven into exile because he had been born German and lived in Germany until twenty-five. After countless attacks on him he wrote an open letter to the Prime

Minister in *The Times* of 17 May: 'Dear Mr Asquith . . . I am not a man who can be driven or drummed by threats of abuse into an attitude of justification. But I consider it due to my honour as a loyal British subject and my personal dignity as a man to retire from all my public positions. I therefore ask you to accept my resignation as a Privy Councillor and to revoke my baronetcy. I am sending this letter to the Press.'

Asquith replied, referring to the 'baseless and malignant' attacks on Sir Edward and stating that: 'the King is not prepared to take any action such as you suggest in regard to the marks of distinction which you have received in recognition of public services and philanthropic munificence'. But the persecution and mutterings were such that he left England for the US and never returned. As for the Asquiths, this perceived 'friendship with a German' was another stick to beat them with.

When war broke out, flying machines were still a comparative novelty and the number of aircraft on all sides was very small: France, for example, had less than 140 aircraft, Britain around 180. It was, after all, only four years since factories had shut down for the afternoon on the day of the great *Daily Mail* Air Race of 1911 so that workers could gaze up wonderingly at the flimsy contraption of wood and canvas with a man in it passing overhead. The race had been won (by a French pilot) at an average speed of forty-five miles an hour, with one local newspaper reporting that on level ground a train went faster than an aeroplane but going up hills the aeroplane had the advantage. Of the thirty entrants, only four managed to complete the 1,000-mile course, with crash landings the commonest hazard.* Even as late as January 1915 Virginia Woolf thought it worthy of a diary note that 'an aeroplane passed overhead'.

At first aeroplanes were used only for observation, with some of the more diehard Army officers disbelieving even of that; tethered balloons, they felt, were perfectly good enough. But as both sides dug themselves into the trenches, aircraft, able to go wherever they wanted, became ever more important.

Around July 1915 the first true fighter aircraft took to the air, armed with automatic weaponry – until then, observation pilots

* The only pilot casualty was a broken leg.

had either been unarmed or had a pistol or rifle thrust into their hand before take-off. Some planes were able to fire successfully because they were 'pushers', their propellers and engines at the back instead of the front, leaving a clear frontal view for the pilot/gunner.

It was the beginning of the era of the 'air ace', like Germany's famous Red Baron, Manfred von Richthofen, who shot down eighty planes in air-to-air combat. The element of single combat meant that flying was invested with an aura of chivalry and airmen were thought of as 'knights of the air', to use a common phrase – an attitude emphasised by the high casualty rate. When fighting (as opposed to observational) aircraft became operational during the war, 52,000 out of France's total of 68,000 aircraft were lost in battle.

At the beginning of September there was a week of Zeppelin raids on London, with bombs dropped on the City, on the Strand and at New Cross. When they fell in the silent countryside the noise was so deafening that pheasants rose up and screeched and in nearby villages people covered their lights. Most of the time, however, Zeppelins stayed well out to sea where, on a clear day, they had a view of seventy-five miles and could report back on the doings of all shipping in that area.

People regarded these 400-feet-long airships half with terror, half as a spectacle. 'The window rattled behind me: then all the windows rattled and we became conscious of the booming of guns getting nearer,' wrote Beatrice Webb, as always a dispassionate observer. '"At last the Zeppelin", Sidney said, with almost boyish glee. From the balcony we could see shrapnel bursting over the river and behind, somewhat aimlessly. In another few minutes a long sinuous airship appeared high up in the blue black sky, lit up faintly by searchlights ... It moved slowly ... the shells bursting far below it – then there were two bursts that seemed nearly to hit it and it disappeared ...* It was a gruesome reflection that while we were being pleasantly excited, men, women and children were being killed and maimed ... There was apparently no panic, even in the crowded Strand. The Londoner persists in taking Zeppelin raids as an entertainment ... "Did you see the Zeppelins?" was the first question, in the most cheerful voice, which every man, woman

---

* The total number of casualties was small: the twenty raids in 1915 killed 181 people and injured 415.

and child asked each other for at least twenty hours afterwards.'

D.H. Lawrence, in a letter to Ottoline Morrell, took a more romantic view. 'Then we saw the Zeppelin above us, just ahead, amid a gleaming of clouds: high up, like a bright golden finger, quite small . . . I cannot get over it, that the moon is not Queen of the sky by night, and the stars the lesser lights. It seems the Zeppelin is in the zenith of the night, golden like a moon, having taken control of the sky; and the bursting shells are the lesser lights.' For a pleasanter side effect of the dim shop lighting and street lamps half blotted out with blue or green paint was the reappearance of the stars in London's night sky. Buses too were almost blacked out, with only small blue or green glow-lights showing through their windows. In Park Lane, with the black of Hyde Park on one side and the great dark masses of the buses ahead, 'in the far distance all you see is a continual kaleidoscopic change of glow-worm red, yellow or green lights', wrote one woman. Even the lake in St James's Park had been drained, so that no tell-tale silvery glimmer should serve as a guide to the death-dealers above.

With the huge demand for manpower the question of conscription was becoming ever more urgent, and on 21 September Margot was writing to her stepmother* Marguerite: 'I need hardly say we are bribing every country down there [the Balkans] and indeed everywhere as H says if France, Russia, Italy, Belgium etc will sign a paper "we want no more help from you (in way of money and equipment)" then and only then could we afford conscription as conscription is a real stopper, not only to all trade but even to necessary trade as it spells strikes and rows in every trade in England. But if we didn't help our allies every hour they could not fight another ten days. It seems cruel when at the end of it all we shall get nothing at all. Northcliffe has done incalculable harm . . . he has made every ally think "England does not do its bit". It is obvious every human being must be told off to do something and it may be we shall be forced to conscription but to put everyone's back up just now when we hunger for Labour not soldiers is insane. Just now three men count and three only, K. Henry and Lloyd George.'

* Eighteen months after the death of Sir Charles in 1906, Marguerite remarried. Her new husband, Geoffrey Lubbock, was a good-looking man several years younger, who worked in the City. They had two sons together.

By October even Kitchener was ready to consider conscription and the move towards it was steadily becoming stronger. The war was costing £3 million a day and rising, and more fighting men than ever were needed, but the pace of recruiting had slowed down. Some men were earning very high wages in the new wartime industries and did not want to leave; there was confusion over whether the Government wanted men in essential industries like mining or shipbuilding to join up; some simply did not want to go to war, often because they had wives, children and perhaps parents to support. When the trade unionist shop steward George Wyver enlisted in 1915 his wife burnt his letter of confirmation. 'She told me I was more important to her and my family than to King and Country. We had 3 boys at the time and I must admit my wife's point of view was the correct one.'

Socially, the absence of men was noticeable. Colonel Repington, forced to walk so slowly through a pea-souper fog that he arrived half an hour late for dinner, 'found a large party at two tables; majority men for the first time since the war began'. A few days later he met at lunch the American Ambassador, Walter Hines Page, who told him of Americans who wrote to the Embassy, 'men wanting to find pretty widows, women wanting to adopt soldiers' children'.

In other dining rooms death was the detested presence. The toll on the younger generation of men was terrible with, proportionately, more of those in the upper classes killed – subalterns, who led their men 'over the top', were the first to be hit.* Among them were many of the Coterie: as well as Billy and Julian Grenfell, Cynthia Asquith's brother Ivo Charteris, Margot's nephew Charles Lister, whom she adored, and seven young male Tennant cousins, Diana Manners' admirer Patrick Shaw-Stewart and John Manners, son of Margot's great hunting friends Hoppy and Con Manners, were among those who fell.

'Oh why was I born for this time?' lamented Cynthia. 'Before one is thirty to know more dead than living people . . . all the settings of one's life – given up to ghosts.'

---

* One study revealed that one in five Etonians who fought in the 1914–18 war was killed. The national average was one in every thirteen men.

TWENTY-NINE

Divisions in the Government were now almost inevitable. On 19 October 1915 Carson, the Attorney-General, resigned in protest at the conduct of the war in the Balkans, which had become another theatre of war.

Finally it had become impossible to avoid conscription, anathema to the Liberals. Reluctantly, Asquith allowed a Bill for limited conscription, to affect only unmarried men or widowers without children between the ages of nineteen and forty-one, to be put forward (it was passed three months later as the Military Service Act of 27 January 1916); and the last of the Asquith sons, Raymond, left for the Front. The Montagus gave a small dinner party for him to celebrate his last night at home. 'Raymond was at his best, very cheerful and brilliantly witty,' wrote Duff Cooper in his diary of 19 October. 'It would really be the end of everything if he were killed.'

Many of those who had volunteered had revised their ages upwards in order to join up, so that some of the servicemen Margot saw looked ridiculously young. Her heart was also touched at the sight of the wounded, swathed in bandages, with missing limbs or in wheelchairs. What could she do for them? She decided to take groups of them to the theatre or the cinema and afterwards bring them back to tea at Downing Street. It was a great success and Margot got on with them extremely well. She had always talked to the shepherds at Glen or the girls in the East End exactly as to her own friends, as she had never been hampered by the idea that one should adopt a different tone to those considered 'beneath' one socially.

Asquith now suffered a second 'loss', albeit one of which he thoroughly approved. Just before Venetia's wedding on 26 July his daughter Violet had become engaged to her long-time suitor and his own Principal Private Secretary, Bongie Bonham Carter. Violet, who had known for years that Bongie loved her deeply, now finally turned to him, perhaps partly because of the gulf that had suddenly opened up between her and Venetia, the adored friend to whom she had talked of 'these years of being in so many ways almost inside one another's skin', partly for the reasons that had impelled Venetia: she was twenty-eight and marriage, once like a distant city on the horizon which one will eventually reach, was now a looming imperative.

Violet and Bongie were married on 30 November 1915 at St Margaret's, Westminster, with a guard of honour of wounded soldiers, mounted police to keep back the crowds, Elizabeth Asquith and Margot's niece Kathleen Tennant as bridesmaids and little Randolph Churchill, dressed à la Russe in a velvet suit with fur, one of the three pages. The sizeable sum of £200 was collected by MPs as a wedding present for the couple. Inside the church, as Cynthia Asquith put it, there was 'everyone one has ever heard of'. Although Asquith had refused to have a reception as an unseemly expense in wartime, with a congregation of the rich, famous, glamorous and eminent these nuptials could not escape the tag 'Society wedding', thus attracting the hostile attention of various left-wing newspapers and a section of the public. Asquith, as usual, took no notice of such comment.

Margot was genuinely pleased that her stepdaughter was marrying an admirable man, writing her a letter on her wedding day that expressed her own warm feelings and also hinted at her own emotions over Venetia, so recently resolved. 'My darling,' it began, 'You have been with me . . . since you were six & I have often been clumsy & tactless & un-understanding but darling you will forgive all this now & remember & believe that I have never failed you nor will I ever fail you . . . if ever I see an unimaginative female daring to cast even a shadow between you & Bongie I will kill her with my own hand. You shan't have a moment's depression or neglect if I can prevent it – the pain is too great.'

Well aware of the strength of the bond between her husband and his daughter, Margot was also hopeful that Violet's marriage would draw her away from Asquith. If she had seen the exchange of letters between them, with their strong, lover-like undertone, she would not have been reassured. All her life Violet had worshipped – this is not too strong a word – her father; all her life he would continue to be the most important man in it.

'For twenty years (ever since you were eight years old) you have been to me the most perfect of companions, & I have tried to be to you not a Father, but an intimate and understanding friend,' began Asquith's wedding-day letter to his daughter. 'During all that time we have never failed one another, thank God! I can't remember even one moment when we have ever been apart . . . It has been a perfect relationship. Do not let us break or even suspend the chain which has always bound us together. Let us maintain the close intimacy – as it always was and always ought to be. I beg and pray of you to keep our divine companionship as it has always been.'

Violet's response, written on her honeymoon, cannot be described as other than a fervent protestation of total worship. 'Most beloved – I read your precious letter in the train with many tears – but also with a great and deep pride that I shld have meant anything to you – who have always meant everything to me – since I can remember and are still the closest – the most passionately loved of all human beings to me. You lie at the very bottom of my heart – nothing can ever get beneath you – or that deep & absorbing love of you which has always been the first principle of my existence . . . nothing has ever compared with it.

'"Being alone" with you has always been my wildest – most thrilling joy – from old Maresfield Garden* days – when we slept together – and our little lunches tête à tête in yr Mount St rooms . . . to nowadays when we motor off together to The Wharf – or one of our Nests – or you come and say goodnight to me in my room . . . It has been the romance of my life . . . And Beloved what I want you to know and realise is that I need you now, not only as much but more than ever before . . . ' It was, she concluded, a great comfort that her new husband understood her love for her father.

As marriage did not alter Violet's closeness – or her physical need to be close – to her father, Margot continued to be made miserable by it. 'I'm a fool to mind and wicked too but she gets on my nerves to such a pitch that when she is away on her holidays I feel a different

* The Asquiths' home in Hampstead until 1894.

being!' she wrote in her diary in January 1916, two months after Violet's wedding.

Perhaps it was this tension that caused her to appeal to Cys for reassurance. He gave it to her gladly, writing on 11 January, 'Darling Margot, to suppose that I don't love you intensely or could ever be "bored" by you is bosh. It's rather unfair to lump together all "Asquiths". And condemn them as frigid!'

PART FIVE

1916

THIRTY

As 1916 opened, the effects of the war were felt everywhere. Conscription meant that more men than ever disappeared from civilian life – most museums closed because of lack of keepers (though the Reading Room at the British Museum remained open). Territorials were drilling in Hyde Park, the new Lloyd George restrictions (brought in in November 1915) on the sale of spirits and beer dictated that none could be bought on Saturdays and all alcohol sales were to be strictly cash – a clear effort to do away with the weekend binge, often on credit, that affected work on Mondays. Blackouts were everywhere around the east coast, in large cities and in places that could be seen from the sea. Tobacco, fruit, furs and paper were either prohibited or so highly taxed that they were uneconomic, so that newspapers became thinner and books fewer.

'Diana and I spent a few days at Parkstone in Dorset at the beginning of Jan,' wrote Winifred Tower. 'It was very dark when we arrived but two days later the lighting restrictions were withdrawn as it is well up Poole Harbour and not visible from the sea. It was extraordinary to see a town with all its lamps lit again.' It was a part of the coastline where German submarines had been active – one was sunk when the night patrol spotted her signalling (for which, without radio, she had to rise to the surface).

Most building had stopped. 'On my return to London trade was very bad, and no jobs could be had at the trade so I took a job at Woolwich Arsenal on munitions,' wrote George Wyver. 'Oh, what a job, most of the time we were hanging about and still had to work overtime to 8 & 9 pm.' Fed up with this, Wyver enlisted later. By now all troops wore respirators slung around their necks when in the trenches, and there was a system of sounding gongs down the lines if a gas attack was expected. 'Compulsion has come in,' wrote Victor Cazalet. 'At last we have really begun the war.'

By February Margot was convinced, with justification, that Lloyd George and Northcliffe were working together to remove Asquith from the premiership. Most Liberals, too, distrusted Lloyd George but realised how great was his contribution to the war effort. As Margot never made any secret of her opinions they also realised her dislike and distrust of Lloyd George, so it soon became the general view that she was responsible for causing a breach between the Prime Minister and his Minister of Munitions.

It was a time when whatever Asquith did seemed to be wrong. In March, when he was in bed with a bad chill, he was accused of using this as an excuse to avoid making a statement on recruitment. Northcliffe seized the opportunity to strike again. 'The Times would be pathetic if it were not <u>contemptible</u>,' wrote Margot furiously in her diary. 'When he is ill he is shamming, when he is Kodaked smiling he is taking things lightly, when he is serious he is overstrained, when he is silent he is asleep, when he speaks he is oratorical – "we do not want oratory we want deeds".'

The continuing problem was Asquith's total disregard of the press and therefore of the public opinion-formers, and dislike of anything that smacked of propaganda for himself or the Government. His sense of collective responsibility meant that he often accepted blame or criticism where it was not strictly his fault, while his way of life laid him open to the charge of idleness. 'In war it is necessary not only to be active but to seem active,' Bonar Law had written to him warningly in February, but whereas Lloyd George understood this all too well, Asquith did not appear to have an inkling.

His peacetime routine continued almost unchanged – in the weekdays luncheon and dinner parties, always with post-prandial bridge. 'Henry came in after midnight,' wrote Margot of one December evening. 'He shut my bedroom door with the usual little bang I know so well and walked up and down quite happy. He had enjoyed wonderful bridge, Henry and Geoffrey Howard* (a very bad player) against Montagu and Edward Grey. They had smashed E. Grey and Montagu.' Their hands had been wonderful, he told her, adding that he had called five diamonds, been doubled and made them. 'I could see he was happy as a boy for the moment,' wrote Margot, 'tho' his face looked tired and I was sorry it was so late and

---

* Liberal MP and Vice Chamberlain of the Household.

wished <u>for once</u> he would go to bed and not read as he always does every night for two hours.'

Weekends, usually with house parties, were spent at The Wharf or Walmer Castle. Victor Cazalet, asked by Violet to the Castle for the weekend of 5 February 1916, recorded it in his diary, travelling down on the 1.54 train with fellow guests. 'We arrived at Walmer Station at about five and walked to the Castle . . . where we had great difficulty in finding our way in – eventually we came to a passage leading on to a nice round tea table & Margot Asquith appeared. The conversation bordered on the scandal about her poor self [the constant accusations of pro-German activities] and the way she was persecuted. I did not talk at all. The chocolate cake was delicious.

'After tea in came Elizabeth Asquith & the P.M., a dear fatherly old man to look at . . . I had uniform on and did not dress for dinner. I talked nonsense with Violet most of dinner, everyone was very occupied with their neighbours. I tried to listen to Asquith but heard only a little. He quoted the whole of some obscure poem by Fitzgerald from the Persian (not O.K.)* to Violet. Then the ladies went out and I sat by Asquith.'

They talked of the recent Zeppelin raid, of the Ypres Cloth Hall which Asquith said was the most beautiful ruin in the world, recounting how a staff officer had said to him: 'Those wonderful little minarets have been shelled for some months or so and yet have never been in such great danger as they are now.' With a visit by Kitchener pending, they should expect, said Asquith drily, to see the choicest at Broome (Kitchener's country estate, Broome, was adorned with antiquities he had simply taken).

'Then we joined the ladies and the table of bridge was at once started. Bridge and golf are all they like. The genius of this great man is that he can work for some hours on the most stupendous question in the world's history and then throw it all off and think only of his interests.'

Or as Cynthia Asquith, less overawed and equally exposed to bridge and golf on a visit to Walmer a month later, put it, 'P.M. sniffs and looks bored at any mention of shrapnel or anything to do with the war.' It was not a good image to filter out from the heart of Government.

* *The Rubaiyat of Omar Khayyam.*

*

March began with the joyful news that Oc would be coming home on leave. Oc and Cys had always been Margot's favourites; she loved them deeply and had always wished they had been her own children. Three days later, on 4 March, Margot was at Walmer Castle with Elizabeth when she heard Oc was expected to lunch at Downing Street and that Asquith would bring him to see them that evening. They arrived at 7.30. 'I heard his jolly voice shout "Margot!" as he tore his coat off in the Walmer passage and we were in each other's arms. He took me on his knee in Elizabeth's bedroom as if I were a little girl and put his arms round me and thoroughly coozled me. Henry and I could not speak for joy – I spent 2 hours in his bedroom on Sunday and told him all my sorrows and all the news and he was thrilled.'

Apart from Oc's leave, almost the only bright spot for Margot at that time was her victory in a libel action against the *Globe* newspaper, the worst offender in a series of allegations about her pro-German sympathies, mainly in anonymous letters – some were signed 'Patriot' – from 'readers'. 'Surely we do not need traitors, or the husbands of traitors, in our midst?' asked one.

Today it is hardly believable that the British wife of a British Prime Minister should be accused, without a shred of evidence, of treachery to her country and described, as Margot was, as 'a traitor and a disgrace to her sex' – then, as now, extraordinary epithets to attach to the wife of the Prime Minister.

It was stated as fact that Margot played tennis with German officer prisoners at Donington Hall (which housed many of them) and sent hampers to them from 'a well-known firm in Piccadilly', statements that roused other 'readers' to a froth of indignation and cries of treachery.

Earlier in the year, another publication that had made the same sort of allegations had had to apologise publicly and at Margot's wish had paid £100 to the Red Cross. 'I would not have minded had this paper not been read by our Tommies at the Front but when our poor devils are being poisoned by gas . . . For me to be believed to be playing tennis with brother officers of the very men who are out shooting and torturing them is more than I can stand.' The slanders in the *Globe* were more forceful, repeated over a longer period and, as it was a more widely read paper, more damaging.

Margot was determined to put a stop to these falsities. She swore an affidavit to the fact that she had never even seen Donington Hall, let alone been there, the Adjutant of Donington Hall confirmed her statement and the head of Fortnum and Mason declared that the only hampers she had ordered there were those sent to the Asquith boys at the Front.

The case was so serious and so defamatory that the judge hearing it had no hesitation in granting an injunction against further publication of such libels within a fortnight of its being brought (on 18 December 1915) and when it came to trial Margot was awarded £1,000 damages. Although she had expected to win, it was deeply unpleasant for her to think that there were those of her countrymen prepared to believe that she might be a traitor.

After Margot had won her case against the *Globe* there was no more libel in the press but she still received 'hideous letters of abuse' almost daily. She had never made a secret of her admiration of German music and culture and she believed – as did many others in Government, though not so openly – that the Kaiser rather than the German people was responsible for the war. Like Haldane, she had been part educated in Germany (though only for a year, when being 'finished' in Dresden). But the mood in the country was so fanatically anti-German that Margot's more reasonable approach, coupled with her outspokenness, did not play well.

When Churchill came home on leave from the trenches in March 1916 he insisted, against all advice – including that of the Asquiths, with whom he had dined the previous night – on attacking the Naval Estimates in the House. The effect was damaging in the extreme, as at the last minute he spoilt his case by arguing for the return of Fisher, with whom he had quarrelled so irrevocably as First Sea Lord. Balfour seized on this last point and, with all the dialectical swordplay of which he was master, routed Churchill. Violet, who had always adored Churchill, went with Margot to the Ladies' Gallery to listen to him. Afterwards, when they went down to join a small, unhappy group, Margot, whom they had expected to savage Churchill with one of her caustic remarks, was sympathetic. 'He is young, and if he goes back and fights like a hero all will be forgotten.'

But Churchill did not wish to do that. Tackling Asquith in his room in the House, he told him he wanted to leave the Army.

Asquith did his best to dissuade him ('it would be surrender') but on the way back to the Front Churchill wrote asking to be released from his command. As he was known to be as brave as a lion there was no question of him seeking a cushy job; what he wanted was to be made the best possible use of – and he felt that would be in Parliament. (Churchill also took advantage of his time at home to support the introduction of British Summer Time in May 1916, brought in to aid production, chiefly of war materials.)

The furious Asquith wrote to Sylvia Henley: 'That unstable little cur Winston has evidently again fallen under evil influences since our interview . . . Well, I have done my best to save him from a colossal blunder which will ruin his own future, henceforth he must stew in his own juice.' Again, Margot felt a softer approach would have been better, and told Asquith so – a view that was met by surprise, tempered by disagreement, from Asquith.

The Asquiths, cushioned by money and power, were sheltered from the privations beginning to affect most British families. Except for the magazine articles she was constantly being asked to write, as late as May 1916 Margot's day still exudes a strongly pre-war flavour. She woke early, was brought morning tea at 6.00, then 'I pull a pile of letters, and all 3 blocks and lists (dinner, lunch, weekends) near me; and after tea is taken away, put a pile of stylo-pens, envelopes, paper, address book, red Book Diary, album, gum, towel, scissors and MS paper on tea bed table; and start off making list for telephone of names to invite for dinner, lunch or week-ends and filling gaps; writing letters of personal thanks for flowers, fruit, books, 'letters from the front' forwarded by friends as well as written by them from Egypt, S. Africa, India, France, Salonika, etc, Charity letters, and, what I find <u>most</u> trying, answering letters asking for things – war work which entails my writing to Boards of Trade, Works, Munitions, War Office, Foreign Office and Admiralty. My sec. Miss Way does a heap of things but it is not the same as if I write myself.'

After this, her housekeeper arrived and 'we discuss rooms for week-end or middle-of-week guests in London (<u>always someone</u> sprung on me who wants to stay, or dine, or lunch, or go to play, or go to public meeting, church or city ceremony), My housekeeper makes a note of the meals and hours and beds and days that are wanted, also all flowers for day by day, and Wharf or Walmer Saturdays to Mondays. After my housekeeper, my cook comes, my nurse who is nursing [my sister] Lucy, Elizabeth's maid who makes her summer dresses, then my own maid [to help me dress]; my butler outside my door, and at 10 my secretary Miss Way . . . Henry comes to my room between seeing people at 10.30. We talk over the news and plans, and he tells me if he wants the motor to see the King, or who he wants asked to lunch or dinner . . . ' It was a routine that suited both the Asquiths.

'If I were Margot I would whitewash the Prime Minister's face,' said Cynthia Asquith. 'He is so much attacked for callousness because he looks rosy and well.' In April 1916 Britain only had six weeks of wheat left and bread was a staple part of most diets. Food prices rose and by October 1916 coal was in such short supply that it was rationed by the number of rooms a family had in its house.

Even the Game Laws (which governed when it was legal to shoot) went into abeyance and anybody who owned any land, from garden to estate, could shoot any partridge or pheasant he found on it, at any time – this was partly to produce extra food, partly to stop the birds eating farmers' crops.

Those with privileged lifestyles no longer flaunted their wealth but saw friends or dined out in more muted fashion. Household staffs were shrinking. 'Katharine [Asquith] rather pathetic trying to find a parlour maid. They are almost as extinct as the dodo,' wrote Cynthia Asquith. Although Margot had written that August: 'I Margot Asquith do pledge myself this day not to <u>buy</u> for my own body one single garment till Aug. 4th next year (1916). No clothes: coated, skirts, shirts, underclothes, hats, golfing clothes, shoes, boots, stockings, ribbons, veils or flowers. (I may have to buy 6 pairs of golfing washing gloves, but I will see if I have got any.) <u>Nothing of any kind of fur flowers or clothes</u> will I buy,' she was, unsurprisingly, criticised for continuing to entertain in her usual extravagant style. Cynthia complained in March that over twenty people had been asked to dinner, 'when with few exceptions their only status was as bridge players. If you must have bridge, why not have one or two tables? Why shock London by feeding twenty bores in order that you may have your bridge?'

THIRTY-ONE

Asquith was still unaware of the strength of the feeling steadily growing against him and believed that he had vanquished the disaffected. At an April 1916 weekend at Garsington he was in good spirits: calls for his resignation had been beaten off and the King had warmly congratulated him on this, so when Ottoline beckoned him up to her study to give him a piece of her mind about the way conscientious objectors were treated, he followed 'with an amiable grin'. He did little more than smile, however; more than a third of the 16,000 registered as 'conchies' went to prison at least once, although the majority were happy to accept non-combatant work such as stretcher-bearing.

The next crisis was close at hand: where Ireland was concerned, nothing could be taken for granted. Although the battle for autonomy was almost won – the Government had signalled its intention to grant it by passing the Home Rule Act in September 1914 – a number of extremists decided this was not good enough.

On 24 April a proclamation was posted in Dublin announcing that an 'Irish Republic' had been formed under a 'provisional government' of the seven men whose names were attached to the document. Attacks were launched on key buildings, the Republican flag hoisted above the General Post Office – the heart of what became known as the Easter Rising – and it was hoped that a rebellion would be triggered throughout Ireland. In Dublin the fighting lasted for six days before the authorities managed to restore control. Three hundred and eighteen rebels died and well over 2,000 were wounded. Fifteen people were executed including all seven signatories.

That spring, Margot looked back to her wedding over twenty years earlier, adding a note to a diary entry written at the beginning of her marriage, in which she had complained of Asquith's reserve. 'I can truly say no words of mine today can at all describe how differently things have turned out for me!!!! My <u>in-loveness</u> (for 9 years) with Peter Flower – my love for Evan, my hundred and one loves and friendships are like so much waste paper!'

So perfect did she think Asquith that she even found in him those qualities of romance and emotional intuition that she had once believed lacking. 'There are many and various languages of the heart. <u>Henry knows them all.</u> I know even the slang and the patois! . . . Henry is probably the most emotional big man that ever lived and no one can say he has not got himself in perfect control.'

Not everyone saw him this way. On the last day of May the Asquiths were invited to Garsington again, this time for the day. There, amid the screams of the peacocks, the writer Lytton Strachey, nucleus of the embryo Bloomsbury Group, observed the Prime Minister. 'I studied the Old Man with extreme vigour,' he wrote to a friend, 'and really he is a corker . . . he seemed much larger than when I last saw him (just two years ago) – a fleshy, sanguine, wine-bibbing medieval Abbot of a personage, a glutinous lecherous cynical old fellow – oogh! – You should have seen him making towards Carrington* – cutting her off at an angle as she crossed the lawn. I've rarely seen anyone so obviously enjoying life; so obviously, I thought, *out* to enjoy it; almost, really, as if he'd deliberately decided that he *would* and let all the rest go hang . . . On the whole, one wants to stick a dagger in his ribs.'

Later, Strachey recorded that 'there was a look of a Roman emperor about him (one could imagine a wreath on his head). It was disgusting and yet, such was the extraordinary satisfaction of the man that in spite of everything one could not help feeling a kind of sympathetic geniality of one's own.'

That same night of 31 May, while the Asquiths were sleeping at The Wharf after the excitements of Garsington, the largest – and only major – naval battle of the war took place: the Battle of Jutland. As dawn broke, wreckage could be seen floating in what seemed a sea of molten silver – every fish within miles, killed or stunned by mines and explosions, had risen to the surface, their scales glinting in the misty light. Although more British ships were sunk and more men lost than German, the engagement could still be accounted a

---

* Dora Carrington – always known by her surname – was one of the artists of the Bloomsbury Group. She was deeply in love with the homosexual Lytton Strachey.

victory, since it achieved its object of sweeping the German High Seas Fleet off the seas and into port, never again to put to sea to challenge the British Navy. The Grand Fleet, by contrast, was still a fighting entity and able to continue its blockade of Germany, one of the greatest factors in the eventual Allied victory.

However, the communiqué presented the following day by Balfour made it appear a defeat, since he gave only the greater British losses* without mentioning the forced retirement of the German fleet. Typical of his *dégagé* attitude was Curzon's story, told at a dinner party attended by Cynthia Asquith, who recorded that just before the Cabinet had risen the day after the great battle, he had said: 'Surely the First Lord will say a few words to us about the battle?' Asquith seconded this but Balfour only replied coldly, 'There is nothing to say to you – only a few anecdotes and I don't suppose you would care to hear them.' Balfour was also criticised for not having attended the Naval Memorial Service.

Altogether, the comment of William Brand, the Pampisford post-master, seems justified. 'Ah, Arthur Balfour, you'd better chuck it! No good were you as Leader of the House of Commons – no good are you at the Admiralty. Go back to your philosophy and golf! Or better, as the Government have a marvellous knack of putting square men in round holes, it would be fitting as you are a bachelor to make you a professor of Eugenics.'

Only days later came news that broke over Britain like a thunderclap. On 7 June 1916 Margot's diary notes that 'at 10.30 a.m. Henry came into my bedroom with a look of tragedy on a new and worn face. I thought Raymond or Oc had been killed.' But it was the death of Lord Kitchener he had come to tell her about.

With the Russian Front crumbling, Kitchener had been invited to Russia to advise on military matters. He sailed from Scrabster to Scapa Flow on 5 June aboard HMS *Oak* before transferring to the armoured cruiser HMS *Hampshire* – a survivor of Jutland – to head for the Russian port of Archangel. That evening, just before half past seven, in a force 9 gale, *Hampshire* struck a mine laid by the newly launched German submarine U-75 and sank west of the Orkney Islands. Kitchener, his staff, and

---

* The British lost fourteen ships and over 6,000 lives and the Germans eleven ships with over 2,500 casualties.

643 of the crew of 655 were drowned or died of exposure.

Margot had been dressing for church when Asquith told her the news; Raymond's son was to be christened that day. Two of his godparents were to be Duff Cooper and Lady Diana Manners. In *Old Men Forget*, Duff Cooper gave a lively account of Margot's arrival at St Paul's Cathedral.

'Dean Inge conducted the ceremony and Mrs Asquith, who arrived a little late, felt bound to impart to him the news, which she brought hot from Downing Street, that Lord Kitchener with all his staff had been drowned in the North Sea. The Dean, accustomed to expect the worst, betrayed no emotion, slightly raising his eyebrows. She, disappointed at not having produced the effect she expected, and aware of his deafness, repeated her information louder, to be rewarded only by a slight inclination of the head. Finally she raised her voice to a pitch that took the whole congregation into her confidence, and the journalists present hastily left for the nearest telephone.'

After the service, Diana Manners went straight to a charity function in the Caledonian Market 'praying that I should be first with the news', only to find she had been preceded not only by the story of Kitchener's death but also by the rumour that he was safe and sound, shouted out by a man on stilts. As they heard this, the crowd broke spontaneously into the hymn 'Now Thank We All Our God'.

Kitchener's body was never found, giving rise to numerous conspiracy theories. His death was seen as a huge blow to the war effort, though not everyone mourned his loss. C.P. Scott, editor of the *Manchester Guardian*, is said to have remarked that 'as for the old man, he could not have done better than to have gone down, as he was a great impediment lately'.

The 'Kitchener effect' was summed up by Colonel Repington: 'His old manner of working alone did not consort with the needs of this huge syndicalism, modern war. The thing was too big. He made many mistakes. He was not a good Cabinet man. His methods did not suit a democracy. But there he was, towering above the others in character as in inches, by far the most popular man in the country to the end, and a firm rock which stood out amidst the raging tempest.'

Asquith now had to fill the post of War Minister. At first he wondered whether Bonar Law, as leader of the Unionists, should be the man. But then he decided that Lloyd George, as the highly successful Minister of Munitions, whose zeal and energy were in no doubt

– and whom many wished to see more intimately involved in the war's direction – could not be passed over. Warnings that he was putting his most dangerous critic and rival in the place where he could do him, Asquith, the most harm were disregarded in the belief that he was doing the right thing for the country.

For Margot there was a new spurt of hate mail, as rumour had gone out that she caused Kitchener's death by signalling to the Germans which ship he was on and when it left port. When she asked Asquith who would take over the War Office he told her he thought Lloyd George had the best claim. It was the proverbial red rag to a bull: Margot, believing as she did that Lloyd George was conniving against her husband, reacted too forcefully. 'Like a perfect fool I was violent which spoilt all our talk – I said to have a sly dishonourable brilliant man at the War Office and a Northcliffe [supporter] was unthinkable!! – the whole army would rebel and War Office resign etc, that I would rather leave Downing Street forever than see such a hideous blunder.' It was a reaction that could have been designed to make Asquith dig his feet in more firmly.

Asquith was often his own worst enemy. When, with the war at this desperate stage, Bonar Law came down to The Wharf to see Asquith, he was shocked to find him in the middle of a rubber of bridge with three of his young women friends. It was Whit Monday, and theoretically there was no reason why the Premier should not relax; but most other men would at least have received the leader of the Opposition (as Law still considered himself) in the more work-manlike surroundings of study or library.

Lloyd George's appointment was confirmed on 7 July. When Asquith told Margot, her intuitive mind immediately envisaged what would happen. 'It is too late now,' she wrote mournfully in her diary. 'I played my cards badly with Henry: I said I would rather see him dead before he should make such an appointment, that I would go to Scotland and cease to take the faintest interest in the Cabinet or politics and was far too vehement and out of proportion. I have cried bitter tears over it and foresee great trouble.' She thought that whatever happened Asquith's reputation would be destroyed: if Lloyd George did badly Asquith would take the blame, if he did well 'he will take care to cut Henry out'.

'We are out,' she wrote presciently in her diary. 'It is only a question of time when we shall have to leave Downing Street.'

THIRTY-TWO

In the eyes of the public the appointment of Lloyd George, this man of fervour, determination and energy, could not have been more timely. Conscription had been extended with the Military Service Act, thus greatly strengthening the Army. 'All sorts and conditions are being raked in by the military here,' noted William Brand. 'All but the twisting, wriggling single shirker . . .'

The fate of many of them was to be cannon fodder. The Battle of the Somme, fought to break through the German lines north and south of the River Somme in northern France, had just begun.

The attack was launched on 1 July on a fifteen-mile front, from north of the River Somme between Arras and Albert, on a day of brilliant sunshine under a cloudless blue sky, and preceded by an eight-day preliminary bombardment of the German lines; 'whole reaches of the enemy's trenches have been battered out of existence,' wrote the *Times* correspondent. 'As we stood in the shadow of some trees, twenty yards from a road which led directly down to the trenches, detachments of our troops could be seen swinging across country in half-companies, companies and battalions. Long before they came close one heard the steady roar of their feet – tramp-tramp! Tramp-tramp! And always as they passed they whistled softly in unison. Some whistled "Tipperary", some "Come back, my Bonny, to me" and some, best of all in the place and surroundings, "la Marseillaise".'

Four days after it had started Raymond, who had joined the Grenadiers in order to fight at the Front, wrote to 'Dearest Margot' describing how his regiment had been rushed there in buses to re-lieve the Canadians. He concluded his description of a week spent in the mined trenches, blackened tree stubs, broken and dismembered bodies and stink of death and corruption by saying, 'we have ten more days before we can change our linen or take our boots off'.

The Somme was the main Allied attack on the Western Front during 1916. What makes it stand out from the other terrible Great War battles was the scale and immediacy of its casualties: 58,000 British troops (one third of them killed) on the first day alone of the battle – the bloodiest day in the history of the British Army.

'I do not know what the country will be brought to over this cruel war,' wrote Maria Gyte in Sheldon, Derbyshire, where some of the farm lads had left already. That autumn the first tanks had gone into service and at home another tracked vehicle, meant to make life easier for farmers becoming short of labour, was emerging. In Scotland John Heath witnessed the debut of one of the earliest tractors. 'Puffing its way over the unsuspecting grass, the ploughshares left a trail of six new furrows at each circuit of the field. On the first day, many local farmers and farm labourers came along to see for themselves just how this newfangled machine would cope with the art of ploughing. Mr Macintosh was not impressed and expressed his views in no uncertain terms. "Ye ken what I think? Yon contraption will never dae the work o' a guid pair o' horses."'

So many horses had been lost that alternatives were now being found. John Heath's older cousin had joined the yeomanry in the early days of the war, but now the horses had gone and the men had been issued with bicycles. 'The regiment had obviously been shocked by this unheard of act and when the last of the horses had gone they had a memorial stone erected to their memory,' wrote Heath. 'He had a photograph in his wallet which he showed me. It was of a simple stone slab bearing a verse, of which I can only remember the closing lines, summing up the men's awful feelings of loss: "Our hearts were warm, theirs cold as icicles, They took away our horses and gave us bloody bicycles."' Even moving house had become difficult as there were no horses to pull the wagons. If lorries did arrive, they were usually driven by a young woman.

Children too did their bit. In Aberdeenshire the Alford Girl Guides gathered sphagnum moss, cleaned it and then laid it out in the sun to dry – it had natural antiseptic properties and was used as dressing for wounds. All over the country Guides knitted socks, raised money to sponsor hospital beds, collected waste paper for pulp, bones and fat from kitchens to make nitroglycerin (now difficult to import) and tufts of sheep's wool from hedges to make blankets and learned how to make barley bread to save on the import of wheat. By June 1916 the medicinal herbs that had previously been imported from Germany were no longer available, so Guides were asked to collect – among others – foxgloves, hemlock, henbane, aconites, broom, valerian, rue and feverfew from hedgerows.

Boy Scouts helped by watching the coastline – for signs of distress as well as for enemy vessels – guarded railway bridges, acted as messengers and hospital orderlies, raised money for ambulances and for 'rest huts' – small buildings behind the front line where men could rest, read or chat when briefly off duty in the trenches. One of their most important contributions was helping farmers with planting and harvests.

In the counties where potatoes were a main crop, country children helped lift them at harvest time. In Fifeshire John Heath recalled that a special school holiday called the 'Tattie Holiday' was arranged in mid-October to help with potato-picking. The children had to be over thirteen, and at the field ready to start at 7.30 a.m. 'Each was allotted a "bit". This consisted of a stretch of land about thirty feet long and the width of about five furrows. The horse-drawn digger kept circling the field, levelling the furrows and exposing the potatoes. The pickers had to clear their 'bit' before the digger came round again. For this, working till it was quite dusk, the pickers were paid one shilling and sixpence.'

That summer and autumn of 1916 the war could hardly have been going worse. Although the munitions situation had improved, the slaughter of the nation's young men was causing horror and revulsion. The country was turning against the Government's conduct of the war; and the Government itself was riven by interdepartmental quarrels, with the papers of the Northcliffe press mercilessly and constantly attacking it. Asquith, as Prime Minister, was the main target.

There was more bad news with the renewal of the U-boat campaign. In August 1915, bowing to American pressure, the Germans had largely called off these sea wolves, but in the autumn of 1916 they renewed their assaults. Balfour at the Admiralty had no answer. Lloyd George summed up the position when he wrote: 'Even the woeful tale of increased sinkings of our ships by German submarines and the apparent impotence of the Admiralty to stop the disastrous process did not daunt him [Balfour]. His one comment after hearing the Admirals read out the list of sinkings for the previous day was: "It is very tiresome. Those Germans are intolerable."'

To Lloyd George and his supporters, lethargy and nonchalance seemed to be the order of the day.

On 7 September Asquith left London to visit the Front and talk to Sir Douglas Haig, the General who had been appointed Commander-in-Chief in place of Sir John French in December 1915, and who had ordered the Somme offensive in an attempt to break the stalemate on the Western Front and relieve the pressure on the French at Verdun. In France, Asquith was able to see his son Raymond – to whom, according to Raymond himself, he had never written once during his time at the Front. 'If Margot talks any more bosh to you about the inhumanity of her stepchildren you can stop her mouth by telling her that during my 10 months exile here the P.M. has never written me a line of any description,' wrote Raymond to his wife on 22 August 1916. 'I don't see why he should. He has plenty of other things to do and so do I . . .' Or, as Beb once put it, his father 'had at times excessive belief in the power of the unspoken word.'

Asquith described his meeting with Raymond in a letter to Margot: 'He was very well and in good spirits. Our guns were firing all round and just as we were walking to the top of the little hill to visit the wonderful dug-out, a German shell came whizzing over our heads and fell a little way beyond . . . We went in all haste to the dug-out – 3 storeys underground with ventilating pipes electric light and all sorts of conveniences, made by the Germans . . . One or two more shells came but no harm was done.'

Asquith's relationship with his eldest son was an uneasy one. As far as the glittering prizes of early life went, Raymond had swept all before him, outdoing even his father's illustrious record. Yet he seemed to lack purpose or direction, something inexplicable to Asquith; he admired his son intensely, loved him deeply, yet found it difficult to be uncomplicatedly proud of someone so brilliant yet whose attitude was one of sophisticated disdain to most of what life had to offer and who did not seem to have evolved a clear path ahead. 'Raymond had all the gifts but didn't know what he wanted to do, and this made him unhappy,' was the comment of one member of the Asquith family [to the author].

A few days later Raymond went into action, in an attack that was certain to receive devastating fire. As he climbed out of his trench to lead his men forward into a hail of machine-gun fire and bullets he was hit in the chest. He knew immediately that his wound was fatal but, to reassure his men, lit a cigarette as he was carried off on a stretcher to the dressing station. He gave his flask to the medical orderly with him, asking him to pass it on to his father. He died shortly afterwards – only five of the twenty-two officers in his battalion were untouched.

Two days later, Margot was enjoying the large weekend house party at The Wharf that she had organised. Asquith, who had returned from France, had joined them there, well and happy and talking a lot about Raymond. According to her diary, he told Margot: 'Our offensive was going amazingly well, munitions satisfactory, the French fighting magnificently.'

That Sunday evening, while the men lingered over their port after dinner, Margot, in the drawing room with the other women, played bridge with her thirteen-year-old son Puffin, allowed to stay up as a special treat as he was going for his first term at his public school, Winchester, the next day. At about a quarter to ten she was called to the telephone. As soon as she heard the voice of Asquith's new Private Secretary, she guessed the reason for his call. 'Terrible, terrible news,' he said. 'Raymond was shot dead on the 15th.'

Margot sat down. She heard Elizabeth laugh in the sitting room and was conscious of the hum of conversation and smell of cigars floating down the passage from the dining room. She pulled herself together, went back into the sitting room, and said: 'Raymond is dead. He was shot leading his men over the top on Friday.'

Elizabeth, who adored Raymond, burst into tears; Puffin, who could not remember Raymond ever even speaking to him (Raymond paid little attention to his younger half-siblings), got up from the bridge table and, head bowed, took his mother's hand. Margot walked out of the room with her two children, rang the nearest bell and told the servant to fetch the Prime Minister. She left the children and walked to the end of the passage to meet Asquith as he came through the dining-room door. They stood facing each other. When he saw her tear-wet face he put his arm round her as she said: 'Terrible, terrible news.'

'I know,' he said, before she could continue. 'I've known it . . . Raymond is dead.' He put his hands over his face and they walked back into the empty bridge room. Asquith sat down in a red armchair, put his head in his arms on the table and began to sob violently. Margot sat on his knee, put her arms around him, and held him silently.

For Asquith, Raymond's death was an overwhelming blow. 'I am a broken man,' he wrote to one friend. 'But I try to go on day by day.' As Violet Asquith told Robbie Ross: 'It is very hard to see Father suffering so – though he has been wonderfully brave. Raymond's life was a romance to him – which he watched unfolding with a thrilled expectancy he never felt about his own.'*

All Raymond's friends felt that someone irreplaceable had gone. Duff Cooper, learning of it en route to a holiday in Scotland, wrote in his diary: 'It was the worst shock I have ever had. I shall never forget that awful moment . . .'

At Raymond's memorial service at the Guards Chapel on 13 October, Asquith and Margot wept throughout. She had loved Raymond deeply, feelings complicated by their differences. As it was, she believed his emotional reticence sprang from the loss of his mother. 'If I had been his mother – If!' she wrote miserably. 'We were such friends till he went to the Bar. After that I used to sit in my Cavendish Square boudoir with my door open to hear him come in, and watch him walk upstairs past my open door nearly every night – (not to go and see Violet who was ill, or Elizabeth, who was the baby – but to smoke alone). If I had been his mother I would have brought him in to smoke his pipe with me . . .'

Letters flooded in: Raymond's life had touched everyone he knew. Margot alone received over 200 and Asquith many more. As Oc wrote to Violet on 20 September: '"After the war" becomes daily a more parched and flowerless prospect for our generation and the killing of Bosches less unpalatable.'

For Margot there were added sorrows. In the same week there were similar memorial services for two of her nephews, also killed on the Somme. It had become a ghastly stalemate, with huge casualties daily and increasingly dreadful conditions. Torrential rains in October turned the battlegrounds into a muddy quagmire and the death lists seemed never-ending.

In London alone, almost all the material sold for coats and dresses now was black.

* Letter from Robbie Ross to Gryer.

THIRTY-THREE

A movement against the Prime Minister had been growing for some time. The effortless style he had cultivated so successfully that it had become part of his persona, his belief that taking a decision too quickly often meant taking the wrong one and therefore one should come to a conclusion slowly, and his deliberate adherence to a lifestyle still involving golf, bridge, pretty women and drink all militated against him. Then came a new, and potentially fatal, factor to add to those already adversely stacked up.

On 13 November 1916, Lord Lansdowne wrote a private Memorandum questioning the continuation of the war. Lansdowne was a man of great influence. As Foreign Secretary in the Conservative Balfour Government he had negotiated the Anglo-French Entente Cordiale in 1904; following the Liberal victory in 1906 he had become Conservative leader in the Lords; in August 1914 he had convened a vital meeting at Lansdowne House that committed the Unionist Party to war and helped stiffen the resolve of Asquith's Cabinet. Such was his knowledge and experience that Asquith had invited him to join his Coalition Government as Minister without Portfolio, and he also sat on the inner Cabinet committee responsible for the conduct of the war. Now, sickened by the terrible daily slaughter on the Somme with no apparent gain, he felt he should commit his doubts to paper. Continuing the war would, he believed, bring social and economic disaster all round.

'What does prolongation of the war mean?' he wrote in what became known as the Lansdowne Memorandum. 'Our own casualties already amount to over 1,100,000. We have had 15,000 officers killed . . . We are slowly but surely killing off the best of the male population of these islands . . . The financial burden which we have already accumulated is almost incalculable. We are adding to it at the rate of £5,000,000 a day. Generations will have to come and go before the country recovers from the loss . . . Can we afford to go on paying the same price for the same sort of gain?' It was a question a number of people were already asking themselves.

His Memorandum further set out terms for a negotiated peace on the basis of returning to the status quo ante-bellum, a position that found supporters within the Cabinet. At the end of November the Memorandum was leaked. Although *The Times* refused to print it, the *Telegraph* did. But the peace initiative was doomed, like Asquith's Cabinet itself; and the only result was an increase in the clamour for more aggressive action and attacks on the Prime Minister's dilatoriness.

Two days later, Cynthia Asquith was writing in her diary: 'London appears to be seething with intrigue and politicians behaving like "politicians". Lloyd George is hand in glove with Carson and Winston, and they are doing their best to unseat the P.M. and throw out the Government. The other night . . . there was a very narrow squeak and the Whips were frantically summoning the supposed supporters of the Government. They rang up Lloyd George's house and his wife naively said: "He is out but I know where he is – he is dining with Carson." This created great scandal – Carson being prime instigator of the vote of censure, and Carson turned up for the division and Lloyd George did not.

'Their plot is to unseat the P.M. and Lloyd George is to be Prime Minister and Winston is to go to the War Office. They are credited with having "got at" Bonar Law, and their boast is that they will be in office in a month . . . I asked [Bluetooth]* if he diagnosed Lloyd George as pure knave. But he gives him credit for sincerity in as much that he really thinks himself a Chatham with a divine mission to save the country, therefore holding any means which will put him in power justifiable . . . he is loathed by all the Liberals now – in fact, he is only popular with the dukes, an amusing whirligig of time.'

Cynthia's grasp of the situation was in essence correct. What nobody knew, although her diary hints at it, was that during the last fortnight of November an elaborate plot to take the direction

---

* Harold 'Bluetooth' Baker was a Liberal MP who had been Financial Secretary to the War Office from 1912 to 1915 and admitted to the Privy Council in 1915. He was a contemporary and great friend of Raymond Asquith. He was nicknamed Bluetooth or Bluey after an early king of Denmark, though according to Cynthia Asquith's *Diaries* nobody could remember why.

of the war out of the Prime Minister's hands had been worked out by a secret group, known as the Monday Night Cabal. This was headed by Alfred Milner, former suitor of Margot and old Balliol friend of Asquith but now his implacable enemy, with Sir Edward Carson – always on the other side of the political divide – and, of course, Lloyd George.

Backed up by Northcliffe, whose newspapers had for months derided the Prime Minister, they had been meeting for the past four weeks. Their aim, which would inevitably have the effect of removing the Prime Minister from office, had to be achieved subtly: with his colleagues in the Government Asquith's position was still a strong one, and the majority of both Liberals and Unionists were mistrustful of Lloyd George and his schemes. Bonar Law, indeed, believed Lloyd George to be 'a self-seeker and a man who considered no interest but his own', as his friend Lord Beaverbrook noted in *Politicians and the War, 1914–1916*.

On 18 November, after heavy snow had fallen into the rat-infested, stinking, muddy trenches, the Battle of the Somme was called off. The shock was tremendous: all those young lives lost, and to what purpose? The Allies had advanced only five miles. The British suffered around 420,000 casualties, the French 195,000 and the Germans around 650,000. Only in the sense of relieving the French at Verdun could the British claim any measure of success.

The establishment of the Dardanelles Commission, to examine what had gone so wrong in that campaign, only exacerbated the situation and further destroyed public confidence in the conduct of the war. By November, nearly all Belgium and some of the richest provinces of northern France were in German hands, with Russia's armies broken; and German submarines were accounting for around 100,000 tons of British shipping every month – in October 1916 their U-boats had stepped up their campaign, sinking well over 800,000 tons of British merchant shipping that month alone.

All these disastrous setbacks rebounded on the Government and it seemed only a question of time before Asquith fell. Rumours of plots and counter-plots swirled round London as during that last fortnight of November Lloyd George and his friends the press lords, together with Sir Edward Carson, planned how to take the conduct of the war out of Asquith's hands, at one point discussing the possibility of replacing him.

The first step was the proposed formation of a small War Council (there was already a largish War Committee) of four, with Lloyd George as Chairman in charge of the day-to-day running of the war. Other members were to be Bonar Law and Sir Edward Carson, with Asquith as nominal President.

It was clear that the Prime Minister was suffering from strain, much of it brought on by grief. Margot told the editor of the Liberal *Daily Chronicle* that Asquith wept every day in his bedroom over his dead son, news which reached the plotters. 'Poor Henry, he never forgets for one moment that Raymond is dead – gone,' she recorded in her diary. 'His courage is touching and his wonderful simplicity. No self-pity, no pose none of the things I have so often seen by which people draw attention to themselves when they are suffering – but he will never get over it.'

Asquith was still drinking heavily, a cause of intense worry to Margot. That November, Cynthia recorded, with a rather unfair use of the word 'obsession', that Margot had 'an obsession about drink; her grandfather and Lucy's husband both died of it, and she has had anonymous letters about the PM'. Years later, alcohol would also contribute to the death of her daughter.

At the end of November Asquith was persuaded to give partial support to Lloyd George's idea of a War Council, with himself at the head of it. Later that day Bonar Law went on to meet Lloyd George and Carson at the Hyde Park Hotel but came away still hostile to Lloyd George, believing that his plans boiled down to the simple goal of removing Asquith and taking his place. That evening, Margot insisted upon Lloyd George accompanying her to hear Mendelssohn's *Elijah* oratorio in Westminster Abbey. '[She is] using all her arts to prevent a smash,' wrote Frances Stevenson in her diary; 'when Mrs A. pays attention to D. it means that she knows that the position of the P.M. is wobbling & that it lies in D.'s power to save or smash him.'

Next day, Bonar Law went to see Asquith and told him of the plot, to the annoyance of Beaverbrook. Asquith made an appeal to his loyalty, and two days later wrote him a long letter from The Wharf. 'I take a less disparaging view than you do over the War Committee,' he wrote, summing up the new proposal calling for the dissolution of the then large and somewhat unwieldy Committee, to be replaced by a body of only four –'myself, yourself, Carson and Lloyd George'.

Asquith went on to show that he saw through the plot clearly. First, he pointed out that he did not see how Carson could be included in the proposed Committee, as there were others with far greater and more intimate knowledge of 'the secret history' of the previous twelve months. 'That he should be admitted over their heads at this stage to the inner circle of the Government is a step which, I believe, would be deeply resented, not only by them and my political friends, but by almost all your Unionist colleagues. It would be universally believed to be the price paid for shutting the mouth of our most formidable parliamentary critic – a manifest sign of weakness and cowardice.'

Then he tackled the nub of the matter. 'As for Mr Lloyd George, you know as well as I do both his qualities and his defects. He has many qualities that would fit him for the first place, but he lacks the one thing needful – he does not inspire trust . . . Here again, there is one construction, and one only, that could be put on the new arrangement – that it has been engineered by him with the purpose, not perhaps at the moment, but as soon as a fitting pretext could be found, of his displacing me.'

The press campaign continued, with Carson managing to influence the *Morning Post* to declare Lloyd George the necessary man, upon which Bonar Law told his fellow Unionists, until then completely in the dark, of the scheme. All of them were against it, seeing in the whole plan merely a plot to install Lloyd George as 'dictator'. As Lord Lansdowne wrote to Bonar Law the next day: 'The meeting in your room yesterday left a nasty taste in my mouth . . . I think we owe it to Asquith to avoid any action which might be regarded by him as a concerted attempt to oust him from his position as leader.'

At this crucial moment an argument was brought forward that tipped the balance. It was put to Bonar Law that Lord Lansdowne's Memorandum, now in the hands of the Cabinet, and his letter in support of Asquith, meant that the two were working together for a negotiated peace, an unsatisfactory conclusion to the war that might leave Germany strong enough to strike again at a later date; whereas with Lloyd George at the helm, the sacrifices to date would not be thrown away and the war would be pressed on to victory – and peace with honour.

Lloyd George, master of the stirring phrase, wrote to Bonar Law: 'The life of the country depends on resolute action by you now.' For Bonar Law this was decisive reasoning. He would stand by Lloyd George.

On 1 December Lloyd George formally proposed a War Council of three, with himself as Chairman. This was reported in the press the following day – naturally, via a Lloyd George leak.

It was the first Margot had heard of it. When she asked Asquith about it he told her there was a deadlock: he had replied that he could not serve under someone else but that Lloyd George was determined on running it and would resign if he did not. With that he proposed that they set off for Walmer Castle, where they were due to entertain a house party.

Margot, horrified, could not believe that he was contemplating leaving London with so much at stake. But the exhausted Prime Minister was adamant, insisting that he needed 'sea air and rest from his colleagues'; and on Saturday, 2 December they set off, with Margot, tired and miserable, shutting herself away in a separate carriage in the train, saying that she wanted to sleep. 'I felt it was all up,' she wrote in her diary, 'that I was living among the blind, that Henry was going to be betrayed.' She was right – but mistaken to think that her husband did not know of his perilous position. 'I am in the centre of an aerial tornado, from which I cannot escape,' he had written to a friend a few days earlier.

That afternoon Edwin Montagu saw Lloyd George, and immediately afterwards dispatched a letter to Asquith. 'The situation is probably irretrievably serious,' he wrote. 'I have just come from LlG, with whom I have spent an hour of hard fighting but it seems to me to be of no avail, and I fear he has committed himself . . .

'He regards it as essential that the small War Committee should sit so frequently, and act with such rapidity, that the P.M., whoever he were, ought not to have a place upon it, but he is loud in his assertions that you are the right Prime Minister in the right place. He will not budge from this position.'

Montagu continued with one of the most serious aspects of the possible resignation of Lloyd George, a man with all the press behind him and much of the country, and the gift of oratory. 'The speeches that he will make will, in my opinion, not only make it impossible for the Government to carry on, but will plunge this country into recrimination and public debate in the face of the enemy which will hearten them up, and shake to its foundations the Alliance. Added to this, I think it will be quite impossible if Lloyd George and Derby* go – and they are going together – for Bonar Law to remain . . .'

On Sunday, 3 December, although the newspapers were full of Lloyd George's threat to resign if he did not succeed in chairing the proposed new War Council, Asquith remained calm. 'I could see he shared none of my fears,' wrote Margot. Later that morning, Violet's husband Bongie was sent to Walmer in a War Office car to bring the Prime Minister back to London, accompanied by Margot in another car. Both reached Downing Street at 2.30 p.m., where they lunched. Margot retired to Asquith's study, while Asquith saw Lloyd George; later they were joined by Bonar Law.

The agreement that emerged looked at first like a compromise but was in fact a stitch-up: the Prime Minister would not sit on the War Council but would have the right to veto any of its decisions and would retain 'supreme and effective control of War policy'. As Curzon wrote that day to Lord Lansdowne: 'Practically, Lloyd George issued an ultimatum to the Prime Minister, putting the latter in the complete background . . .' He concluded: 'Had one felt that reconstitution under the present Prime Minister was possible, we should all have preferred to try it. But we know that with him as Chairman, either of the Cabinet or War Committee, it is absolutely impossible to win the war . . .' The omens for a palace coup were clear; only the victim was unaware.

When Asquith joined Margot at 7.45 to dress for dinner with the Montagus in Queen's Gate he told her that he thought 'the crisis looked like being over'. But he was still uneasy. Lloyd George had protested 'his perpetual <u>devotion</u> and <u>loyalty</u>', reported Asquith (perhaps that alone should have made the Prime Minister suspicious). 'He almost put his arm around my neck and begged me not to believe all the stories . . . that he wanted to take my place.'

Margot was not deceived. 'No one will ever forgive you or him or believe in you ever again if you sit in the next room while the War is conducted without you,' she told him. Later she wrote of her disbelief in her diary: 'I felt sure that Henry had not made it clear to

---

* Asquith had appointed the Conservative Lord Derby Director-General of Recruitment in the Coalition Government in 1915.

Lloyd George that as President of the War Council he – <u>Henry</u> – <u>was</u> controlling the war and that <u>nothing</u> would induce him to abandon this position tho' he was quite willing . . . [over] unimportant things to let Lloyd George take the chair in his absence.' But Asquith told her that she was quite wrong and that Lloyd George did not want to oust him.

Others were less inclined to believe in Lloyd George's straight-forwardness. 'A fact with him is nothing static,' said Sir Almeric Fitzroy, 'no matter of definite shape or precise limits, but something fluid, like Quicksilver, which under pressure of circumstance may take any form you like to give it.'

By the time the Asquiths reached the Montagus, one piece of information that would have alerted Asquith that all was not as he thought was known to Montagu – who did not mention it to Asquith, probably because he was unaware of the message it carried. As Montagu had left the War Ministry for home, he had spotted Northcliffe waiting there, obviously for Lloyd George. What Asquith – and certainly Margot – would have realised instantly was that this was so that Lloyd George could brief the press lord on the meeting with Asquith that afternoon.

That evening, the only one who appeared conscious of the crisis was Margot. When Duff Cooper, who recorded the scene in his diary, went up to the drawing room after dinner he found some of the party – his hostess Venetia, Lady Wimborne, Lady Jekyll and Lady Gwendoline ('Goonie') Churchill – sitting on cushions round the fire. 'They were all looking very pretty and were beautifully dressed. I liked the scene – lovely women warming themselves at the fire this bitter night while under their feet the fate of Empire was being decided.

'In the next room Margot with a face as long as a book was playing bridge. At last Edwin, Reading and the Prime Minister came up – the two first rather white and careworn but the PM happier, less concerned and I must say more drunk than I have ever seen him. We played bridge – Venetia and I against the PM and Lady Goonie. He was so drunk one felt uncomfortable. He talked continually and foolishly – made false declarations which we pretended not to notice.'

Margot was still so unconvinced that the agreement, as described by Asquith, was satisfactory that she brought the subject up again after they had returned home, this time sitting on his knee and asking him whether he had made it quite clear to Lloyd George that he [Asquith] would never give up his direction of the war. 'He was quite surprised and almost irritable: he asked me if I took him for a fool – I said "No, but I took Lloyd George for a knave".'

The results of the Lloyd George–Northcliffe rendezvous appeared in next day's *Times*, where the crisis was reported reasonably impartially in the leading article. It was left to the paper's New York correspondent to slip in the stiletto. 'The figure of Mr Lloyd George stands alone,' he declared. 'He represents the people in their own democratic sense. He has been publicly right almost as often as his associates have been publicly wrong. It is unmistakable that the succession of Mr Lloyd George to Mr Asquith would be hailed in this country and among many of the best friends of the Allies as a step forward.

'If Mr Lloyd George holds the centre of the stage at this hour, it is because he seems to have done more than any other public man to help win the war, and to be ready to do still more.'

Asquith either had to let these comments pass – and be accepted as truth – or call Lloyd George's bluff, in which case he would probably resign and concentrate on denouncing the Government. He chose the latter course, writing to Lloyd George to say that he, Asquith, must chair the new Council.

The next day, Tuesday, 5 December, Lloyd George duly resigned, a resignation that was followed by that of Balfour, who was advocating a trial of the proposed new War Council. Asquith called the other Liberal ministers to the Cabinet Room to secure their backing for a reshuffle of the Government minus Lloyd George. All of them agreed, many because they believed Lloyd George was an untrustworthy troublemaker.

It was a different story with the Conservatives and Unionists. Bonar Law had always feared Carson, who now threatened him with losing the leadership of his own party if he did not give in and join Carson and the Tory backbenchers in backing Lloyd George. Lloyd George's agreement with the Conservatives in the Cabinet to remove Asquith from power was the first step that would eventually, and fatally, split the Liberal Party

Later, Margot described Bonar Law as 'with the intrepidity of a rabbit and the slyness of a fox, determined to break the Coalition, rather than let them [Carson and Lloyd George] <u>break</u> him'.

Asquith, faced by revolt from Bonar Law and Carson, refused to reinstate Lloyd George as Chairman, and broke the *impasse* by sending his resignation to the King, confident that when it came to the crunch most of his Tory colleagues would prefer him to Lloyd George; and he would be able to re-form a government.

Cynthia Asquith was at No. 10 for dinner that night. 'It was great luck for me to dine at Downing Street on so historic a night,' she wrote. 'The atmosphere was most electric. The P.M. had sent in his resignation at 7.30 – a fact I was unaware of when I arrived and only gradually twigged . . . I sat next to the P.M. – he was too darling – rubicund, serene, puffing a guinea cigar (a gift from Maud Cunard), and talking of going to Honolulu. His conversation was as irrelevant to his life as ever . . . I had a great *accès* of tenderness for the P.M. He was so serene and dignified. Poor Margot on the other hand looked ghastly ill.' After dinner Asquith, as always refusing to allow politics to invade dinner-table conversation, played bridge as if nothing had happened.

'The King had sent for Bonar,' continued Cynthia, 'but, of course, it would be very difficult for him to accept the office on the terms which had made Asquith resign it. The King is alleged to be very terribly distressed and to have said: "I shall have to resign if Asquith does".'

The company discussed the prospective attitude of the various Liberal ministers and came to the conclusion that not one of them would take office under Lloyd George, with the possible exception of Montagu, an idea flatly repudiated by all the Asquiths. 'Was it my last dinner in Downing Street?' wondered Cynthia. 'I can't help feeling very sanguine and thinking the P.M. will be back with a firmer seat in the saddle in a fortnight. I only hope to God he is – disinterestedly because I really think him the only eligible man. Incidentally, what could happen to all our finances I daren't think!'

Margot did not have her husband's passivity in the face of the coming storm. 'Strange tales are about regarding Margot,' wrote Marie Belloc Lowndes. 'I am told on good authority that she actually wrote to Lord Stamfordham telling him to ask the King to take no notice of Asquith's letter of resignation as "he was not himself when he wrote it". She sent this along by hand and was surprised that it had no result.'

The next day, 6 December, Lloyd George, Bonar Law and Carson visited Balfour, who was ill in bed and agreed that the best thing would be to form a government in which Lloyd George would be Chairman of the War Committee and in which Asquith should be included. That afternoon Asquith, Bonar Law, Lloyd George, Arthur Henderson (the Labour leader) and Balfour attended a conference at Buckingham Palace, called by the King to try to resolve the crisis.

Significantly, the King had asked Balfour to arrive half an hour early to seek his advice; Balfour, seizing his opportunity, spoke of the need for a division between the direction of the war on the one hand and the office of Prime Minister and Leader of the House of Commons on the other.

Asquith adamantly refused to serve under either Lloyd George or Bonar Law and, returning to Downing Street, called another meeting of his Liberal colleagues in the Cabinet Room, where he asked them if he should serve in a Lloyd George government. They replied that they would sooner see him dead. With Asquith's resignation still in place, the King had no option but to send, in traditional fashion, for the leader of the Opposition, Bonar Law. But Law realised that any government headed by him and including Lloyd George would inevitably be dominated by the latter – and advised the King to send for Lloyd George. At seven o'clock on the evening of 6 December he did so and Lloyd George accepted the task of trying to form a government. 'I'm not at all sure that I can do it,' he told Frances Stevenson immediately afterwards. 'It is a very big task.'

Asquith still believed this would be impossible as he knew that his Liberal colleagues in the Cabinet had refused to serve under Lloyd George and that the Unionists too were against the War Minister: Curzon, with some of his colleagues, had called on Asquith in Downing Street where he told him that they did not believe that Lloyd George could form a government as none of the Tory ministers would serve under him or Bonar Law.

Lloyd George, however, was equal to this. Knowing that the only man approaching Asquith's status and prestige was Balfour, he realised that with Balfour 'on board' others would follow. He must also have known that Balfour's loyalty to Asquith was, at the least, suspect and that he was, therefore, the chink in the Liberal armour.

The approach to Balfour was made through his fellow Tory, Bonar Law, who called on him at 9.30 that same evening. He found

Balfour sitting in his bedroom in a dressing gown and, after telling Balfour that his acceptance 'would greatly help with the rest of our Unionist colleagues', offered him the irresistible bait of the Foreign Office – the post Balfour had always wanted.

With no thought of what he owed Asquith, Balfour sprang up and said: 'Well, you hold a pistol to my head – I must accept.' His agreement marked the final break-up of the cross-party camaraderie unique to the Souls.

With Balfour's acceptance in his pocket as the most powerful of weapons, for Lloyd George it was thereafter a question of picking off in separate interviews those who had said they would stand out against serving under him. He first tackled Curzon, again through an intermediary and, on the offer not only of a seat in the Cabinet but also in the War Cabinet, obtained his agreement too. After that the others fell into line, although with one stipulation: Churchill should not be included. Montagu remained as Minister of Munitions (a post he had accepted in June 1916).

The next morning, 7 December, Lloyd George had a meeting with the Labour Members, whom he charmed into giving their support. 'I think I shall be Prime Minister before seven o'clock,' he told Frances. And he was; that evening, his Government in place, he kissed hands as Prime Minister.

Asquith was out – he had been Prime Minister for eight years and 241 days. So, too, was Lansdowne, and his Memorandum was shelved.* Lloyd George had taken the precaution of visiting Haig when the Commander-in-Chief had come to London in November, telling him that 'Lord Lansdowne had written a terrible paper urging that we should make peace now', yet when Haig heard of Asquith's fall he was sympathetic, while recognising his faults. As he commented in a letter to Lady Haig of 6 December, 'I am personally sorry for poor old Squiff. He has had a hard time and even when "exhilarated" seems to have had more capacity and brain power than any of the others. However, I expect more action and less talk is needed now.'

That day, Cynthia and Beb Asquith lunched at Downing Street.

---

* The main points, proposing a negotiated peace, were published in the *Daily Telegraph* in November 1917. It became known as the 'Lansdowne Letter' and Lord Lansdowne himself as the 'Marquis of Hands Up' and 'Lord Lands-Us-Down'. Another piece of mockery was the taunt 'Are We Lansdowne-hearted?' 'No!'

Cynthia found Margot packing, talking of plots and intrigues, and anxious for everyone to know that Asquith had been toppled by dirty work. She noted in her diary: 'Found Margot at the top of the stairs, looking ghastly ill and in a great state of mind, saying she had only just remembered the Connaughts were coming to luncheon and that they were thirteen.* She had asked Cys to have his in bed, as he has for the last week owing to influenza, but he refused to be complaisant. Went to see Venetia at 4.30. She said Montagu had had dozens of frenzied letters from Margot, full of insults. "I hear you are going in with them – where is friendship? Where is loyalty?"'

Asquith was much calmer. The economist Maynard Keynes, dining with them two nights after Asquith's downfall, reported (to Virginia Woolf) that though Asquith seemed quite unmoved and almost magnanimous, Margot was distraught. '[She] started to cry with the soup, sent for cigarettes, and dropped tears and ashes together into her plate – utterly overcome.'

Both Asquiths, however, were furious at what they saw as Balfour's treachery; as he wrote to a friend, Asquith was particularly angry that, after retaining Balfour in the Admiralty, he should have been 'rewarded by his being, two days later, the first of the Tories to go over to Ll.G. for whom he has jackalled ever since'.

Margot did not mince her words when Balfour threw in his lot with 'the scoundrels'. She wrote to his sister-in-law Betty Balfour: 'I know chivalry is not his strong point, but this no one would have believed', although she did add later, 'as you know, I shall always love Arthur'. To a friend, years later, talking of her husband's feelings, her verdict was more damning. 'That Ll.G. (a Welshman!) should betray him, he . . . could understand but that Arthur should join his enemy and help to ruin him he never understood.'

Churchill's summing-up, in *Great Contemporaries*, of Balfour's part was more poetic: 'a powerful, graceful cat walking delicately and unsoiled across a rather muddy street'.

Asquith himself wrote to Sylvia Henley on 10 December: 'You cannot imagine what a relief it is not to have the daily stream of boxes and telegrams: not to mention Cabinets and Committees and

---

* The superstition that thirteen was an unlucky number, especially at table, was then widespread.

colleagues, etc. We are spending Sunday here by the sea [at Walmer]: unluckily it is a gloomy day, but the vast crowd of shipping in the Downs is a wonderful sight. I am writing in the little room where two years ago one Sunday Kitchener and French visited me and had a battle royal which I had to compose. The King offered me the Garter, but of course I refused.' And a little later: 'It is a novel sensation for me to be master of my own time all day long.'

He had served for a longer continuous period than any prime minister since Lord Liverpool, with greater responsibilities and strains than anyone previously. He had suffered the death of his eldest son as well as fearful anxieties for the other two who were fighting. He had introduced better conditions for the poor; had made the House of Commons all-powerful; under his Government the Royal Navy had been rebuilt and key Army reforms introduced; and had held together disparate parties and personalities. But the war had to be won and he was not the man to do it – as everyone except himself realised.

Only to Margot did he say what must have been his true feelings. 'I feel as if I have been stabbed.' When he kissed her, she felt that his face was wet with tears.

AFTERMATH

Margot was alone in Downing Street on the Asquiths' last day there, 9 December – Asquith was at Walmer Castle with Violet and Bongie, Elizabeth in Dublin. Summing up her own feelings about the coup, she wrote: 'I have been through deep deep water since Sat Dec 2. When a Government falls in one week or I should say four days you may be quite sure its overthrow has been planned long long before. I have seen the causes of this staring me in the face for months. Directly LLG was put in the War office I knew it was our Doom. It has been. It was the first time that Henry gave way to blackmail ... the same night Rufus [Isaacs] and Winston and others went to Henry and told him what LLG would do if he did not get what he wanted. One or two others and Bongie and Violet all thought it would be an excellent appointment. I cried and sobbed over it. I could not <u>believe</u> it. H and I were on bad political terms for three or four weeks. He said when I asked him why that Rufus, Bongie, particularly Montagu, said that if LlG was denied his way he would stump the country against H <u>and force a General Election!!</u>

'It was enough to make an angel weep. To stump the country with the backing of Northcliffe and the Press against his own P.M.!! who had not only saved him body and soul but who was 1000 times more respected and loved and trusted by the people than LLG ever was.'

When he moved into No. 10 Lloyd George, who worked harder, had far more correspondence and a finger in many more pies than his predecessor, immediately made changes. During the first few days of his Government he created the Cabinet Secretariat, a new office of experts and specialists that supported the War Cabinet, and the Prime Minister's Secretariat. The job of this latter – hated by the civil servants – was largely as a two-way channel of communication between the Prime Minister and the various Government departments, on which it kept a relentless eye. So many were the extra staff needed that they could not all fit into the limited office space in No. 10, so huts were built in the garden for them, a collection of buildings that quickly became known as the 'garden suburb'.

One of the new inmates of No. 10 was Frances Stevenson, now one of Lloyd George's two Private Secretaries (and the first woman to hold that post), who organised his office and worked, if possible, even more closely with him.

Astoundingly, the Prime Minister managed to install both his wife and his mistress under the same roof, a ménage that endured for several years without confrontations, explosive rows or the departure of one of them. The secret perhaps was that this silver-tongued Welshman managed to make each feel that she was the most important woman in his life, so that each could tolerate the other from what she assumed was the superior position, while male contemporaries – many of whom had mistresses themselves – were not going to give him away. It was a situation that curiously mirrored that of the man he had displaced.

Immediately following Asquith's replacement, some 130 Liberal MPs – roughly half the number elected in 1910, the last pre-war election – declared their readiness to follow Lloyd George. Asquith, still the official leader of the Liberal Party, refused to serve in Lloyd George's Cabinet; instead he became leader of the parliamentary Opposition.

This anomaly meant that from late 1916 onwards the Liberals were divided between the Asquithians, who claimed to be the official Liberal Party, and the followers of Lloyd George, the Prime Minister. Their split allowed an overwhelmingly Conservative Coalition Government, under Lloyd George, to win the 'khaki election' of 1918 and later benefited the emerging Labour Party. Never again would the Liberals regain majority power.

After Downing Street, the immediate question for the Asquiths was where to live – 20 Cavendish Square was let. Alice Keppel came to the rescue, inviting them to her large house in Grosvenor Square, where Margot spent much of her time writing letters, mainly at night, for which she demanded fortifying sandwiches (often failing to eat them).

By March the Asquiths were back in Cavendish Square, with weekends spent at The Wharf. Asquith settled well into his life of retirement. He had his books, speeches to write, former colleagues to see and the House of Commons. Margot had no such resources and, filled with rage against the way – as she saw it – her husband had been unfairly hounded from office, she spent much of her time writing furious letters, largely on Lloyd George's iniquities.

She was saved from this self-perpetuating, destructive cycle of recrimination by her son Puffin, now at Oxford, who dragged his mother off to concerts and plays so effectively that these new interests soon absorbed her. Actors, actresses and playwrights, including Noël Coward, Ivor Novello and Frederick Lonsdale, now appeared at The Wharf, along with writers such as Rudyard Kipling; after dinner many of them would play or sing.

In May 1917 Asquith was offered the Lord Chancellorship, with its welcome stipend of £10,000 a year and a pension of £5,000; but as this would have meant serving in a Lloyd George Government he could not bring himself to accept. Margot, of course, heartily agreed with his decision but it left a serious hole in their finances – Asquith no longer had his salary and former prime ministers received no pension, while to Margot the word 'economy' could have been written in Sanskrit for all the effect it had. 'We mean to live very quietly,' Margot had said when Asquith fell from power, 'only seeing the King and a few friends.'

But it was not simply that she was extravagant: her generosity was such that most of those who benefited from it now took it for granted that she would continue either to support or subsidise them as a matter of course. She had helped all her stepchildren with money, paid all medical expenses for the births of Cys's children, kept three servants who had developed tuberculosis in Swiss sanatoria and paid for all her sister Lucy's clothes as well as countless presents and extras for others.

By the end of 1917 Oc, the first of Asquith's sons to volunteer, had fought in major campaigns, winning the DSO and two bars, and had risen to become a Brigadier-General. Four days after this promotion, on 20 December, he was wounded for the fourth time so seriously that his leg had to be amputated. It was the end of his military career, though he served in the Ministry of Munitions as Controller of Trench Warfare. After the war he became a successful businessman.

Restrictions were beginning to bite so deep that the Asquiths were no longer immune. From 1 February 1917 the Germans introduced unrestricted submarine warfare, sinking many ships bringing food from America and Canada.* The Government took over 2.5 million acres of land for farming, mostly worked by the Women's Land Army, since all able-bodied men had been called up. The Government began buying up woods all over the country to cut down – 'think what the wholesale cutting down of coverts will mean to sporting England!' wrote one estate owner – larches were used for pit props in the mines, timber was needed for the railways constructed in France or sometimes sold simply to make a profit.

Petrol was short; in November 1917 Asquith obtained a special white badge that allowed him to motor wherever he liked. Coal was in such limited supply that the house was freezing and Margot dined in a fur coat, hat and with a rug over her knees. In January 1918 food rationing began with sugar; tea, coffee and cocoa were no longer imported; by the end of April meat, butter, cheese and margarine were added (paradoxically, the poor were better nourished than before); and some of the better-off altruistically gave up eating potatoes as they were a staple food of the poor. By February 1918 the butter allowance was 4oz a week, that of bacon 5oz.

In 1918 yet another slur was cast on Margot's name. She had been the target of serious calumny to an extraordinary degree, more than any other prime minister's wife before or since, save possibly Lady Caroline Lamb. In some cases she must have been a surrogate for Asquith, whose moral uprightness, two marriages and six living children were so well known that to accuse him of either treachery or 'unnatural vice' would merely have produced incredulous laughter. Margot, on the other hand, was an easy target: her outspokenness, social visibility and steely loyalty to her friends, especially those in trouble, gave people who wished the Asquiths ill many an opportunity.

On 26 January 1918, the last year of the war which by now seemed to have dragged on for ever, the well-known pilot, inventor and MP Noel Pemberton Billing, of extreme right-wing views, published an article in his magazine *Imperialist* alleging that the

---

* In February 1917 German U-boats sank 230 ships bringing food to Britain and over half a million tons of shipping in March.

Germans had compiled a Black Book containing the names of 47,000 highly placed British subjects who, because of their sexual preferences ('evils which all decent men thought had perished in Sodom and Lesbia'), were being blackmailed into undermining the British war effort. The wives of such men, it was said, were also entangled: 'in Lesbian ecstasy the most sacred secrets of the state were threatened'.

On 9 February Pemberton Billing renamed his journal *Vigilante*. When, the next day, it was announced that the actress Maud Allan was to perform as Salome in Oscar Wilde's play of that name, he struck again, publishing a second article entitled 'The Cult of the Clitoris'. This implied that Maud was a lesbian associate of the conspirators in the Black Book and that all involved, including the audience who went to see *Salome*, were homosexual.

Maud, who had taken London by storm on her arrival ten years earlier, and had remained one of Margot's close women friends, was certainly chiefly known for her twenty-minute solo dance 'The Vision of Salome', a performance so erotic and sensual that she became internationally known as 'the Salome Dancer' (an epithet she hated, as her work was based on years of artistic and musical study). As homosexuality was a criminal offence, Maud sued for libel.

The case, which opened on 18 May 1918, was sensational and appallingly conducted by the judge, who allowed Billing, who defended himself, to smear by implication and innuendo. Maud was forced to admit that her brother was a convicted murderer – Billing was attempting to prove that she had inherited a tendency to 'viciousness'; and when, in answer to his questioning, she revealed that she knew the meaning of the word 'clitoris' (represented in *The Times* report by a row of stars), he asked her if she was aware that out of twenty-four people shown the word only one knew what it meant. (Diana Manners reported to Duff Cooper that Lord Albemarle had walked into the Turf Club and asked who was 'this Greek chap Clitoris they were all talking about?') Maud's acknowledgement that, yes, she knew the meaning of the word, was taken as a sign of moral depravity. In a further attempt to blacken her character great play was made between the 'decadence' of her art and her time in, and by extension sympathy with, Germany, where she had spent several pre-war years studying and performing.

The so-called Black Book was never produced – the two men said to have seen it were both dead. Yet, based on its alleged 'contents', Pemberton Billing and several of his witnesses were allowed to ascribe various perversions to important public figures (among them Asquith, Viscount Haldane and the judge himself), none of whom was allowed the right of reply.

The judge's behaviour was condemned by all newspapers ('lost his head' was the consensus), but although he told Maud that she left the court without a stain on her character, she was ruined. Her work fell off and her friends – except, typically, Margot – deserted her. As for Margot, her daughter-in-law Cynthia thought her 'fairly rational' but Marie Belloc Lowndes (whose husband wrote for *The Times*) said it was the only time she had known Margot 'rattled'. 'She thought (rightly) that [Pemberton Billing] was financed by part of the Press. Of course we waded in the Billing cesspool,' continued Mrs Belloc Lowndes in her diary of 2 June. 'The cruel thing is that, to the public mind, the mere <u>suggestion</u> of such things is in effect the same as though they were proved . . . Margot, of course, attributes the whole thing to a political anti-Asquith plot – to make it impossible for him ever to return to office – and I should think there is a good deal of truth in this theory.'

What was clear was that Margot was aware of the hysterical atmosphere engendered by a war that seemed never-ending, in which conspiracy theories of all sorts could flourish, and that Billing's wild allegations would therefore attract followers. After the case Ottoline Morrell, who sat in the front row of the gallery at Asquith's Romanes Lecture on the Victorian Age at the Sheldonian, Oxford, spotted Margot among the crowds of academics in bright robes, soldiers in khaki, the few women undergraduates in black gowns and the wounded in blue linen. 'She looked as if she had come out of Hell, poor woman,' thought Ottoline, 'so marked and lined by sleepless nights, and the endeavour to keep a brave face in all this libellous story. I felt so sorry for her that I went down and talked to her.'

The long struggle was nearly over. The Battle of the Marne in July 1918 was the last great German effort at victory; on 8 August the Allies hit back so hard that, as the German General Ludendorff put it, this became 'the blackest day in the history of the German Army'.

The Armistice was signed on 11 November 1918, a day of brilliant sunshine. At 11.00 that morning a salute of guns gave the signal for scenes of wild rejoicing. Margot hung flags out of every window of the house; Asquith, at the cremation service of a distant relative that morning, found a telegram from the King awaiting him when he returned to Cavendish Square. 'I look back with gratitude to your wise counsel and calm resolve in the days when great issues had to be decided resulting in our entry into the war.'

After luncheon the Asquiths drove to the House of Commons – where to Margot's delight Asquith was greeted with cheers by the crowds outside – to listen to Lloyd George reading out the terms of the Armistice. Shortly afterwards the Asquiths lunched at Buckingham Palace. The King said to Margot: 'No man ever had a better or wiser friend than I had, and have, in your husband.'

From then on, Asquith's slide down the greasy pole was rapid. He wanted to attend the Versailles Conference where, as the only person from Britain who could both speak French and had a thorough knowledge of international law and finance, his contribution would have been invaluable; and his moderation and dispassionate sense of fair play might easily have mitigated the harshness of the penalties imposed on Germany – which led, though indirectly, to the Second World War. But Lloyd George was impervious to urgings, even from the King, who wrote to him: 'You served for many years in Mr Asquith's Government and know his worth as a lawyer, a statesman and a man of clear, dispassionate judgement,' while Asquith, once rebuffed, was not the man to beg or plead.

In the 'khaki election' of 1918 he lost his seat of East Fife, though he secured another in 1920 in the Paisley, near Glasgow, by-election. During the campaigning Margot and Violet, now on good terms, shared a room in the Station Hotel; during the day, decked out in red rosettes and carnations (red was the Liberal colour) they worked the streets or spoke on platforms.

Violet's campaigning, lovingly describing her father, was very effective. On their last night there was a tribute to Asquith in the Liberal Club. '[It] was one of the most extraordinary things I have ever seen – and is one of the most deeply moving,' wrote Violet in her journal. 'It was a marvellous joy and consummation of my deep and passionate love for Father – a thing born in the marrow of my bones – to feel I had <u>really</u> been able to help him, as I believe I was.

When he said what he owed me and they all stood up and cheered I felt it really too great a joy for my heart to hold.' Their return to London, where they were greeted by a crowd of photographers, press and well-wishers, was a temporary return to the old days of popularity and acclaim.

In 1919, after an abortive engagement to an American ('To marry an American is bad enough, but a poor American!' wrote Cynthia Asquith), Elizabeth became engaged to Prince Antoine Bibesco, a Romanian diplomat stationed in London, who had had his eye on her for some years. Her marriage, on 30 April, was the Society wedding of the year, attended by everyone from the Queen to George Bernard Shaw, and filmed by the newly formed British Moving Picture News organisation. It cost Margot far more than she had bargained for, since many of her relations, accustomed to her free-handed generosity, bought smart clothes to wear to it – and put them on Margot's various dress accounts.

It was the perfect marriage for Elizabeth. She adored her husband, who was twenty-two years older than her, and rich – Elizabeth, like her mother, had no idea how to perform any household tasks. Their home in Paris – an apartment in the Bibesco town house on the Île St Louis, its walls hung with huge Vuillard canvases, and their cultured milieu (Bibesco was a lifelong friend of Marcel Proust) – suited her perfectly.

Her brother Puffin grew up to become the highly successful film-maker Anthony Asquith.

The effect of the war on the sensitive, poetic Beb had been dreadful. He had served in the terrible conditions of the trenches, had had friends killed by his side, been wounded himself, watched attacks fail through lack of ammunition – which engendered a hatred of generals and politicians – and to alleviate his miseries drank too much when on leave. Suffering from shell-shock, he became increasingly withdrawn, often retiring to his room and remaining there for hours, writing poems that were usually about the war. Eventually he was well enough to return to active service, but this barely understood condition blighted his post-war career; it was not the political one for which he had hoped but a fairly minor editorial post working for the publishers Hutchinson.

Cynthia became the family breadwinner through a stroke of

good fortune. Just before the war ended, she had begun working for the well-known playwright J.M. Barrie. Barrie, who had previously befriended a family who had three little boys – who gave him much material for the 1904 play he forever became known for, *Peter Pan, or The Boy Who Wouldn't Grow Up* – now did the same for Cynthia's sons, helping to pay for their upkeep and education.* Beginning in 1927, Cynthia herself went on to write numerous successful books.

Cys, Asquith's clever fourth son, was called to the Bar in 1920 and from then on had a textbook career, with a happy marriage and four children. After eighteen good years at the Chancery Bar he took silk in 1936 and became a judge two years later. In 1948 he was made an Appeal Court judge and Privy Councillor and in 1951 became a Law Lord. He died in 1954, aged sixty-four.

Money was a continuing problem for the Asquiths. They still kept a car, chauffeur, butler, housekeeper, two secretaries and a number of other servants and entertained as much as before – Margot believed this was essential if people were not to forget Asquith. Margot had always been the chief provider and believed that this was still her duty. To earn, she planned to write more of the articles that she had from time to time produced in the past.

Instead, the publisher to whom she was introduced urged her to write her autobiography. Its first part, published on 5 November 1920, became an instant best-seller, receiving castigation and praise in equal amounts. It was a financial success and was followed by a lucrative lecture tour in America. She followed it with a second, equally successful, volume and now, well launched on a literary path, continued to write articles, memoirs and even novels.

All the same, money grew tighter and moving to a smaller, more manageable house became essential. In March 1922 the Asquiths gave their last dinner party at their beautiful old house in Cavendish Square, put on the market at £30,000. They moved to 44 Bedford Square, which they bought from their friend Ottoline Morrell. This too was old and beautiful but much smaller, with a dining room that could only hold ten. Ottoline remained a constant friend, often

---

* When he died in 1937, apart from Great Ormond Street Hospital for Children, which received the royalties from *Peter Pan*, Cynthia was the main beneficiary of his will.

entertaining them at Garsington, and was outraged when Asquith was featured in Aldous Huxley's first novel, *Crome Yellow*. 'Beside him, short and thick-set, stood Mr Callamay, the venerable conservative statesman, with a face like a Roman bust, and short white hair. Young girls didn't much like going for motor drives alone with Mr Callamay,' wrote Huxley.

On one of these weekends, Margot so struck the normally waspish Virginia Woolf that she wrote of her favourably: 'and then there was Mrs Asquith. I was impressed. She is stone white, with the brown veiled eyes of an aged falcon & in them more depth and scrutiny than I expected; a character, with her friendliness, & ease, & decision. Oh if we could have had Shelley's poems, & not Shelley the man! she said. Shelley was quite intolerable, she pronounced; she is a rigid frigid puritan; & in spite of spending thousands on dress. She rides life if you like; & has picked up a thing or two, which I should like to plunder & never shall.'

In the 1922 general election, won by Bonar Law's Conservatives, Asquith managed to hold his seat but with a majority of only 316 ('the tightest fit you ever saw', he said). And when, only six months later, Bonar Law was forced to retire with terminal cancer and his successor, Stanley Baldwin, called a surprise election for December 1923, he still retained it. With Labour now in second place the Liberals held the balance of power in a Conservative government. Asquith's last use of power was to vote them out of office in the New Year and give Liberal support to Labour, so that the first Labour Government took office in January 1924, only to fall eleven months later after rumours of a communist plot forced a general election.

Asquith, now seventy-two, and having campaigned for the fourth time in less than five years, was defeated at Paisley by the Labour candidate, Rosslyn Mitchell. It was the end of his political life.

A week later the King offered him a peerage, largely in order to extend his political career without 'further political contests, with all their attendant turmoil and unpleasantness'. He accepted, requesting that the King revive the ancient title of Earl of Oxford (originally given by Queen Anne to her Prime Minister Robert Harley). This outraged some of the older, more staid aristocrats and the future Lady Salisbury wrote to him saying, 'It is like a suburban villa calling itself Versailles.' Asquith, almost needless to say, was unmoved, but eventually added 'and Asquith' to his title. The suffix made little difference; he and Margot were always known as Lord and Lady Oxford. In the Commons, Lloyd George was now Party leader and, to Margot and Violet, still the enemy.

At about this time the Asquiths met the socially and politically ambitious young diarist Henry ('Chips') Channon, who would visit them at The Wharf. Here is his description of them then: 'Mr Asquith, benign, beautiful and patriarchal, presided at the end of the long table and talked, in his clear bell-like Jacobean English, with a wealth of metaphor. Mrs Asquith, distraite, smoked and read the papers during luncheon, and occasionally said something startling like, apropos of spiritualism, "I always knew the living talked rot but it is nothing to the nonsense the dead talk". She also said she could not help being sorry for ghosts – "Their appearances are so against them."'

Venetia's marriage, after a promising start, did not go well. In 1916 the Montagus had bought Breccles Hall, a huge Tudor house and estate in Norfolk, about a hundred miles from London. It mopped up money: Montagu employed England's best-known architect, Edwin Lutyens, to supervise its restoration, involving new bathrooms, a new kitchen and various structural alterations, as well as complete refurnishing. Montagu, who loved birds and created a bird sanctuary nearby, adored it. But for Venetia, once the initial fun of doing it up had passed, there was the ineluctable fact of a distasteful marriage.

To escape from time alone with Montagu, she organised house parties every weekend. Diana Manners, as one of Venetia's closest women friends, was often there with Duff Cooper. As early as 1918 he was writing: 'The relations of Edwin and Venetia are very distressing. She seems hardly to be able to bear him – she cannot help showing it and he cannot help seeing it.' And again the following year: 'I find I am wrong in supposing Venetia and Edwin happy. He confessed this evening to Diana that he had never been more miserable.'

It was not long before Venetia launched into love affairs. One of the first was with Lord Beaverbrook, Lloyd George's Minister of Information. This gnomelike press lord was a man of huge vitality and compelling charm – with his blend of intense interest, kindness and sharp-edged intelligence, many women found him irresistible. Diana Manners, by now engaged to Duff* and in Paris with her mother on the eve of the Peace Conference, found the Montagus there – Montagu staying in the Majestic Hotel with the rest of the British delegation and, as she wrote to Duff, Venetia and Beaver-brook at the Ritz. 'They are living in open sin at the Ritz in a tall silk suite with a common bath, and unlocked doors between while poor Ted is sardined into the Majestic, unknown and uncared for.'

Montagu became Secretary of State for India, resigning in 1922, and was primarily responsible for the reforms that led, eventually, towards independence. His often-repeated gloomy prediction, 'Of course, I shall be dead by then,' came true. He died in November 1924, aged only forty-five, a year after the birth of Venetia's daughter Judith (although legally and socially known as Montagu's child, Judith was probably fathered by Eric Ward, later Earl of Dudley). On the day of his death, Indians, from the princes and the press to the legislative councils and political leaders of all parties, went into mourning. Venetia lived until 1948.

The Asquiths' money worries were exposed by Margot in the spring of 1927 and a fund was organised by their friends. Violet, whose underlying antipathy to Margot's attitudes and behaviour had never really disappeared, was very upset by this. 'It is monstrous that other people should be made to foot Margot's bridge bills (40£ last Sunday) in his name,' she wrote to her husband on 26 July 1927. 'I mean that he should be made the decoy-duck to induce generous people to defray the cost of her completely irresponsible extravagances . . .

'I am horrified by the publicity because everyone knows how she lives and will think it scandalous that she should be further subsidized in his name to do so. How she has dragged his name through the mud! I can't bear to think of it . . .' Her filial anger completely failed to take into account that it was Margot who had always subsidised everyone and that Asquith enjoyed the good life just as much as Margot.

That Christmas Asquith had a stroke, from which he recovered, but his health was steadily declining. Margot was as cheerful and

* The two married in June 1919.

encouraging as she could be but by the New Year of 1928 she knew there was no real hope. From The Wharf she wrote to Violet:

My dear darling . . . I feel somehow as if I was not equal to what has happened – not good enough, or <u>great</u> enough. I have an old-fashioned feeling that there is some purpose in all this – that life is <u>not</u> a hazard, a throw of dice that anything may turn up: it is firmer & deeper than this. Father has played his part nobly for 75 years – it is for me to play mine.

I don't think I am playing mine well. I've been morbidly <u>afraid</u> of the Press, & of sympathy, but not so much for myself – tho' this sounds sly – but I've long felt that his great brain <u>might</u> go & it would be a humiliation for <u>anyone</u> to know this. That he is ill past recovery was enough – but the other is past all bearing. I see it coming slowly but surely and I am determined <u>no</u> one shall see him again (except all of us) . . . I can stand the truth but don't forget you are young and have everything. I am not young and I am ill: not physically but ill in soul & mind. My heart has a prop – my prop has gone. I shd be on my knees with gratitude that I have had it so long: but I'm not . . . we are crying the same tears, praying at a lost shrine – we must be patient with one another, darling.

Yr Margot.

A week later, on 15 February 1928, Asquith was dead.

Gradually Margot came to terms with widowhood. From 1931 onwards she dressed entirely – and effectively – in black. At the end of 1932 she was forced to sell The Wharf but went on entertaining in Bedford Square and being entertained, if necessary taking matters into her own hands.

There are snapshots of her through these years, her personality as powerful as ever. 'People dined, including Lady Oxford, self-invited as usual,' wrote Chips Channon in March 1937. 'She wore a flowing black dress like a priest and was charmingly cassante, rude, dictatorial and magnificent. She is the cleverest woman I know and is a terrific character. I suppose she must be 75. Her crisp, penetrating phrases are riveting. This evening she played Bridge until 1.30 without a pause, passing judgement on everyone in politics and society the while.'

In 1939 Channon, who, though he often commented on her

rudeness, was always won over by her affectionate nature, celebrated his birthday by lunching with her at Bedford Square: 'she looked like an antique skeleton in black satin with a bright red coat, and received me in her ground floor library, full of books, photographs and bibelots. She had lunched the day before in what was once her old dining room at 10 Downing Street, alone with the Chamberlains, and was full of Neville's praises.'

The summer after the Second World War was declared (in September 1939) a bomb fell so near Margot's house that the authorities made her leave it and she moved to a room on the sixth floor of the Savoy, and later to Thurloe Place, Kensington, where she lived with one servant only. Sometimes she would attend the weekly dinner parties given by Emerald Cunard at the Dorchester (for which all the guests paid a set sum), if only to attack Lady Cunard for 'bunking off' to America to escape the Blitz – the two mutually loathed one another. It was unsurprising: Margot was, thought Channon – who for twenty years was devoted to her – one of the most remarkable, and irritating, women he ever met.

Her great sadness was the separation from her daughter Elizabeth, trapped in Bucharest since the beginning of the war. Margot schemed for her escape but on 7 April 1945 Elizabeth died of pneumonia.

Elizabeth's death crushed Margot completely. She lived only a few months longer, dying on 26 July 1945. Of all the comments made about her, perhaps that of Marie Belloc Lowndes, writing to her daughter after Margot's memorial service that September, comes nearest to defining her: 'The real truth was that she was a child of nature. She could not conceal what she was feeling, and she was wholly lacking in the capacity to behave with what may be called the hypocrisy without which life could scarcely be carried on.'

Or as Frances Horner, her friend for so many years, wrote: 'I only know that we shall never see her like again.'

ACKNOWLEDGEMENTS

First and most importantly I would like to thank Christopher Osborn for his kindness in allowing me unrestricted access to Margot Asquith's diaries. I would like to express great gratitude to all the following for letting me see the manuscripts, letters, diaries and memoirs in their possession, many of which I have quoted from and others have provided invaluable background material: Prue Baillie-Hamilton for the letters of her father Kit Wykeham-Musgrave; Ann Bostock for the memoir of her ancestor George Wyver; Stephen Bourne for the letter from 18 Napper Street; Sir Edward Cazalet for the diaries of his uncles Edward and Victor Cazalet and for permission to use the poem by his step-grandfather P.G. Wodehouse; Christine Gauthier for the letters from her grandfather Corporal Ernest Mansat; Trevor Heath for the memoir written by his father John James Heath; Janet James for the diary of her great-uncle Will Blackwell; Pippa Kay for the journal of her great-grandfather, ship's surgeon John Farrington; Antonia Pulsford for the diary of her grandfather Major Edwin Bedford Steel RAMC; Heather Rickaby for the autobiography of her grandfather; Sylvia Foster for the letter from her great-aunt Florrie to her grandfather George; Margot Grosset for material from the Guiding Archives; David Wiltshire for the story of 'Bon' Dillingham; Lorna Kirk for her copy of *The Freewoman*; Mike McKenna for the letter from his grandfather; Paula Pardoe for the memoir of her grandmother Lottie Martin; Richard Davies for the diaries of his aunt Evie Davies and Jane Wykeham-Musgrave for the diary of her mother Cicely Acland.

I am also deeply grateful to the following for their help, advice, and information about or recollections of the Asquith family circle and environment: Stephen Bourne, Mrs Boothby, Lord Crathorne,

Adam Green of Trinity College Library for his assistance with the Montagu papers, Jill, Duchess of Hamilton, Mark Hichens, Lord Hutchinson, Pauline Lady Rumbold, the Hon Lady Stephenson, Lord Hutchinson, Lord Oxford and Asquith and Arthur Reynolds. I would particularly like to thank Michael Crawcour, whose suggestion of a biography of Margot Asquith encouraged me to write this book; Linden Lawson, who so ably copy-edited it; and of course my incomparable editor Bea Hemming.

BIBLIOGRAPHY

Alsop, Susan Mary, *Lady Sackville* (Doubleday and Co., 1978)

Asquith, Lady Cynthia, *Diaries 1915–18* (Hutchinson, 1968)

Asquith, H.H., ed. Desmond MacCarthy, *Letters to a Friend* (Geoffrey Bles, 1933)

Asquith, Herbert, *Moments of Memory* (Hutchinson, 1938)

Asquith, Margot, *A Little Journey and a Week in Glasgow* (privately printed, 1892)

Asquith, Margot, *Off the Record* (Frederick Muller, 1943)

Asquith, Margot, *More Memories* (Cassell and Co., 1933)

Bailey, Catherine, *The Secret Rooms* (Viking, 2012)

Balfour, Lady Frances, *Ne Obliviscaris* (Hodder and Stoughton, 1930)

Balsan, Consuelo, *The Glitter and the Gold* (Harper and Brothers, 1952)

Bartley, Paula, *Votes for Women 1860–1928* (Bookpoint, 1998)

Beauman, Francesca, *Shapely Ankle Preferr'd* (Chatto and Windus, 2011)

Beauman, Nicola, *Cynthia Asquith* (Hamish Hamilton, 1987)

Begbie, Harold, *The Mirrors of Downing Street* (Mills and Boon, 1920)

Belloc Lowndes, Marie, *Diaries and Letters 1911–47* (Chatto and Windus, 1971)

Benckendorff, Count Constantine, *Half a Life: The Reminiscences of a Russian Gentleman* (The Richmond Press, 1954)

Bennett, Daphne, *Margot: A Life of the Countess of Oxford and Asquith* (Victor Gollancz, 1984)

Benson, E.F., *Dodo – a Detail of the Day* (Donohue, Henneberry, 1893)

Bonham Carter, Violet, ed. Mark Bonham Carter and Mark Potter, *Lantern Slides: The Diaries and Letters of Violet 1904–1914* (Weidenfeld and Nicolson, 1996)

Bonham Carter, Violet, ed. Mark Pottle, *Champion Redoubtable: The Diaries and Letters of Violet Bonham Carter, 1914–1945* (Weidenfeld and Nicolson, 1998)

Brittain, Vera, *Testament of Youth* (Victor Gollancz, 1933)

Brock, Michael and Eleanor, *H.H. Asquith: Letters to Venetia Stanley* (Oxford University Press, 1982)

Brock, Michael and Eleanor, *Margot Asquith's Great War Diary 1914–16: The View from Downing Street*, (Oxford University Press, 2014)

Cassar, George H., *Kitchener: Architect of Victory* (William Kimber, 1977)

Chandos, Viscount, *From Peace to War: A Study in Contrast, 1857–1918* (Bodley Head, 1968)

Chips: The Diaries of Sir Henry Channon, ed. Robert Rhodes James (Weidenfeld and Nicolson, 1967)

Chisholm, Anne, and Davie, Michael, *Beaverbrook: A Life* (Hutchinson, 1992)

Speaking for Themselves: The Personal Letters of Winston and Clementine Churchill, ed. Mary Soames (Doubleday, 1998)

Cooper, Diana, *The Rainbow Comes and Goes* (Rupert Hart-Davis, 1958)

Cooper, Duff, *Old Men Forget* (Rupert Hart-Davis, 1953)

Cooper, Duff, ed. John Julius Norwich, *The Duff Cooper Diaries* (Weidenfeld and Nicolson, 2005)

Cowles, Virginia, *1913: The Defiant Swan Song* (Weidenfeld and Nicolson, 1957)

Curzon, Grace, *Reminiscences* (Hutchinson, 1955)

Dangerfield, George, *The Strange Death of Liberal England* (MacGibbon and Kee, 1966)

Davenport-Hines, Richard, *Ettie: The Intimate Life and Dauntless Spirit of Lady Desborough* (Weidenfeld and Nicolson, 2008)

de Courcy, Anne, *Circe: The Life of Edith, Marchioness of Londonderry* (Sinclair-Stevenson, 1992)

Dugdale, Blanche E., *Arthur James Balfour* (Hutchinson, 1949)

Easton, Laird, M., *Journey to the Abyss: The Diaries of Count Harry Kessler, 1880–1918* (Alfred A. Knopf, 2011)

Fulford, Roger, *Votes for Women* (Faber and Faber, 1957)

Gerzina, Gretchen, *Carrington* (Pimlico, 1995)

Gurney, Samuel, *Isabel, Mrs Gurney, afterwards the Lady Talbot de Malahide, 1851–1932* (Simpkin, Marshall Ltd, 1935)

Hague, Ffion, *The Pain and the Privilege* (HarperPress, 2008)

Hoare, Philip, *Wilde's Last Stand* (Duckworth, 1997)

Holroyd, Michael, *Lytton Strachey* (Heinemann, 1968)

Horner, Frances, *Time Remembered* (Heinemann, 1933)

Hough, Richard, *First Sea Lord* (George Allen and Unwin, 1969)

Huxley, Aldous, *Crome Yellow* (Chatto and Windus, 1921)

Hughes-Hallett, Lucy, *The Pike: Gabrielle d'Annunzio, Poet, Seducer and Preacher of War* (Fourth Estate, 2013)

Hynes, Samuel, *A War Imagined* (The Bodley Head, 1990)

Jenkins, Roy, *Baldwin* (Collins, 1987)

Jephson, Lady Harriet, *A Wartime Journal* (Echo Library, 2009)

Kettle, Michael, *Salome's Last Veil* (Hart-Davis, MacGibbon, 1977)

Lambert, Angela, *Unquiet Souls* (Macmillan, 1984)

Lascelles, Sir Alan, ed. Duff Hart-Davis, *End of an Era: Letters and Journals 1887–1920* (Hamish Hamilton, 1986)

Lee, Georgina, ed. Gavin Roynan, *Home Fires Burning* (Sutton Publishing, 2006)

Lentin, Antony, *Banker, Traitor, Scapegoat, Spy?* (Haus Publishing, 2013)

Levine, Naomi, *Politics, Religion and Love* (New York University Press, 1991)

Lichnowsky, Prince, *My Mission to London* (Cassell and Co., 1918)

Lubbock, Adelaide, *People in Glass Houses* (Hamish Hamilton, 1978)

Lyttelton, Edith, *Alfred Lyttelton: An Account of his Life* (Longmans, Green, 1917)

Lytton, Constance, *Prisons and Prisoners* (William Heinemann, 1914)

Mendes, Valerie and de la Haye, Amy, *Fashion Since 1900* (Thames and Hudson, 1999)

Minney, R.J., *No. 10 Downing Street: A House in History* (Cassell and Co., 1963)

Minney, R.J., *'Puffin' Asquith* (Leslie Frewin, 1973)

Montgomery Hyde, H., *Lord Alfred Douglas* (Methuen, 1984)

Morrell, Ottoline, *Early Memoirs* (Faber and Faber, 1963)

Morrell, Ottoline, *Ottoline at Garsington, 1915–18* (Faber and Faber, 1974)

Mosley, Leonard, *Curzon: The End of an Epoch* (Longmans, 1961)

Nicolson, Nigel, *Mary Curzon* (Weidenfeld and Nicolson, 1977)

Page, Christopher, *Command in the Royal Naval Division* (Spellmount, 1993)

Peel, Mrs C., *How We Lived Then* (John Lane, The Bodley Head, 1929)

Percy, Clayre and Ridley, Jane, *The Letters of Edwin Lutyens to his wife Emily* (Collins, 1985)

Phizackerley, Gerald, ed., *The Diaries of Maria Gyte 1913–20* (Scarthin Books, 1999)

Pimlott, J.A.R., *The Englishman's Holiday* (Faber and Faber, 1947)

Purcell, Hugh, *Lloyd George* (Haus Publishing, 2006)

Repington, Lt-Col. C. à Court, *The First World War 1914–18* (Constable, 1920)

Rose, Kenneth, *Superior Person: A Portrait of Curzon and his Circle in Late Victorian England* (Weidenfeld and Nicolson, 1969)

Rose, Kenneth, *King George V* (Weidenfeld and Nicolson, 1983)

Shelden, Michael, *Young Titan* (Simon and Schuster, 2013)

Soames, Mary, *Clementine Churchill* (Cassell and Co., 1979)

Sykes, Christopher Simon, *The Big House* (HarperCollins, 2004)

Wakehurst, Dame Peggy, *In a Lifetime Full . . .* (privately printed)

Watkin, Pamela, as told to, *A Kingston Lacy Childhood* (Dovecote Press, 1986)

Woolf, Virginia, *Diaries, 1915–19, 1920–24* (The Hogarth Press, 1977 and 1978)

Woolf, Virginia, *Letters* (The Hogarth Press, 1976)

Country Life October 1913 for description of The Wharf, Sutton

1912–14 Anonymous, Home Front Diary, July–Sept 1914, Imperial War Museum 10729

The Asquith papers are at the Bodleian Library, Oxford

Violet Bradby's reminiscences are at the Hampshire Record Office, File no. 46AOB/A11/6

'Journal from a Small Village. William John Brand. Written and compiled by O.C.
   Mayo', the diary of Pampisford's postmaster, can be found at the Imperial War
   Museum, shelf mark 23(=41)/3 [Brand, William John]-2
Duff/Diana Cooper papers are at Churchill Archive Centre, Cambridge
MS 466, Edward Mandell House Papers, Series II, Diaries, Volume 2, Yale
   University Library
Daisy Thorp's diary can be found at the Hampshire Record Office, File no.
   TOP257/3/52

INDEX

Ranks and titles are generally
those applying at the time. The
abbreviations MA and HHA refer to
Margot Asquith and Herbert Henry
Asquith

Aboukir, HMS, 216-17, 239
Acland, Cicely, 234-5
Agadir Crisis (1911), 66-7, 118
aircraft: wartime development and
deployment, 299-300
airships *see* Zeppelins
Albemarle, Arnold Allan Cecil Keppel,
8th Earl of, 345
Albert I, King of the Belgians, 180
alcohol: restrictions on, 252-4, 297
Alderley Hall, Cheshire, 83, 86, 102, 121,
257
Alexandra, Queen of Edward VII, 43,
149, 254, 266, 290
Alexandra Rose Day, 149
Alien Act (1914), 192
Allan, Maud, 9-10, 345
Amery, Leo, 241
Anderson, Dolly (*later* Moore), 98
Anmer (racehorse), 112-14
Anson, Sir Denys, 150
anti-Semitism, 65, 269
Antibes, 131, 137
Anzacs (Australian and New Zealand
forces), 263
Archerfield, Scotland, 72, 86, 129
Argyll, John Douglas Sutherland
Campbell, 9th Duke of, 145n
Arlanza, RMS, 195
Armistice (1918), 347
Army & Navy Stores, London, 204
Asquith, Anthony ('Puffin'; HHA
and MA's son): birth, 20-1; resists
suffragettes, 30; friendship with
Megan Lloyd George, 35-6; leaves for
school, 120; relations with MA, 137;
Christmas present from MA, 215;
plays bridge with MA, 325; takes MA
to concerts and theatre, 343; career as
film-maker, 348
Asquith, Arthur ('Oc'; HHA's son):
relations with MA, 17; career, 199-
200; enlists, 200; Christmas present
from MA, 215; and Violet's feelings
for Rupert Brooke, 244; in Middle
East, 253; wounded, 269, 294; on
Venetia's engagement to Montagu,
272; home leave, 312; on Raymond's
death, 326; leg amputated, 343;
military and civilian career, 343
Asquith, Beb *see* Asquith, Herbert
Asquith, Lady Cynthia (*née* Charteris;
Beb's wife): marriage to Beb, 17, 53;
on HHA's forward sexual behaviour,
82; denigrates MA while accepting
financial support, 146; on 'cuckooing'
in temporary homes, 200; Christmas
present from MA, 215; on rumours
of Kaiser's banning raids on London,
265; on Venetia's defection, 278-9;
praises Haldane, 281; shocked
by unliveried driver, 290; admires
Montagu's lifestyle, 291; on heavy
wartime casualties, 293; on departing
recruits, 297; servants, 298; brother
killed, 302; at Violet's wedding, 304;
on HHA's attitude to war talk, 311;
on HHA's prosperous appearance,
315; on political intrigues, 328; on
MA's obsession with drink, 330;
at Downing Street following HHA's
resignation, 338-9; and Billing's attack
on MA, 346; post-war activities,
348-9; as beneficiary of J.M. Barrie's
will, 349n
Asquith, Cyril ('Cys'; HHA's son): in

family, 12; relations with MA, 17; holiday in Egypt, 131; illness in Egypt, 200; Christmas present from MA, 215; post-war legal career, 349

Asquith, Elizabeth (*later* Bibesco; HHA and MA's daughter): accompanies MA to Switzerland, 105, 130, 137; at Paris finishing school, 130; in Cannes with MA, 137; debutante season, 144-6, 148; suffers social boycott, 144, 155; stays with Mrs Keppel in Holland, 158, 160; summoned home, 164; religious observation, 175; Christmas present from MA, 215; supposed engagement to German, 240, 276; pleaure-seeking, 241-2; on MA's 'thinking with heart', 278; as bridesmaid at Violet's wedding, 304; at Walmer Castle, 311; and death of Raymond, 325; engagement and marriage to Bibesco, 348; trapped in Bucharest and death from pneumonia, 354

Asquith, Emma Alice Margaret *see* Asquith, Margot

Asquith, Helen (HHA's first wife), 75

Asquith, Herbert ('Beb'; HHA's son): at Oxford, 11; in family, 11; marriage, 53; witnesses suffragette attack on Herbert Gladstone, 100; enlists, 200; on conduct of war, 214-15; wounded and suffers shell shock, 292, 348; at Downing Street following HHA's resignarion, 338; post-war career in publishing, 348

Asquith, Herbert Henry (*later* 1st Earl): courtship and marriage to MA, 1-2, 74-80; attacked by suffragettes, 3, 30-1, 95, 127-8; infatuation with Venetia Stanley, 3-4, 87, 89, 96, 102, 119-20, 131, 135-6, 183-4, 197, 210, 222-3, 236-8, 243, 252, 267, 291-2; conduct of World War I, 4-5; premiership, 10, 23; life in Downing Street, 11, 64; background and career, 12, 55; qualities, 12-13; relations with Violet, 17-18, 71, 73, 270-1, 280, 304-5; marital relations end, 21-5, 82; in Downing Street house, 24-5; opposes women's suffrage, 28, 30, 32, 88, 127, 140; golf, 31, 127; unemotional manner, 33, 289-90; drinking, 36, 90, 124, 241, 254, 330;

and building of Dreadnoughts, 41; and Lloyd George's 1909 budget, 42; calls General Election (1910), 43, 49; and Lords crisis (1909-10), 43, 55; and Edward VII's death, 46; opposes power of Lords, 48; shouted down in Commons, 49; social life, 64-5; and industrial unrest, 68-9; relations with MA, 72-4, 81, 121, 127, 285, 306, 317; first marriage, 75; sexual urges, 82; in Sicily with Venetia, 87-8; health, 90-1; speech on Home Rule Bill, 90-1, 93; at Balmoral, 91; letters to Venetia, 92, 122, 129, 131, 135, 154, 161, 197, 202-3, 205, 209, 212, 222, 235, 238, 248, 252; supports Irish Home Rule, 93; at Walmer Castle, 100, 214, 311-12, 332; jealousy of Montagu, 101, 121-2, 249; Churchill invites to cruise on *Enchantress*, 109-10; and Marconi affair, 114; on Lloyd George in Marconi scandal, 115-16; and Puffin's schooling, 120; and MA's depression, 121; good living, 124; on accepting political responsibilities, 137; ignores German threat, 138; on Naval Estimates (1914-15), 138; on Mrs Pankhurst, 141; and 1914 Home Rule Bill, 142, 151; Conservative hostility to, 145; attends opera with MA, 149; on George V, 150; declares love for Venetia, 154; disbelieves war threat, 154; on Austrian ultimatum to Serbia, 160; and outbreak of violence in Dublin, 161-2; attachment ot Ottoline Morrell, 162; predicts war, 165, 168; cancels trip to Penrhos, 169; appeals to Tsar to withdraw mobilisation order, 173; on unpopularity of war with Germany, 174; on Britain's position at outbreak of war, 176; and Kitchener's appointment, 180; addresses Commons on ultimatum to Germany, 181-2; visits to Mells, 183; speech in Parliament on reasons for war, 193, 197; and national unity, 197; physical changes, 197; indifference to popularity, 198; on early wartime measures, 202; on recruitment figures, 208-9; and removal of Frau Heinsius from family, 208; wartime activities, 210; confides wartime secrets to Venetia, 220, 243; wartime speeches,

220-1; consummation with Venetia questioned, 223-4; and Venetia's nursing service, 235; impertubability, 240-1, 266, 289-90; sybaritic life-style, 241, 266; and Venetia's increasing fondness for Montagu, 243; disapproves of Venetia's nursing, 248; letter from MA declaring love, 255, 257; Venetia writes to on intention to marry, 258-9; and Venetia's agreeing to marry Montagu, 263; announces internment policy for enemy aliens, 266n; letter from Venetia telling of marriage to Montagu, 268; unhappiness at losing Venetia to Montagu, 273, 278-9, 285, 287, 294; and Fisher's resignation, 275-6; disregard of press, 276, 310; agrees to formation of coalition government, 277-9, 283; criticised for slackness, 282; private life widely known, 282; Ottoline Morrell on equanimity, 289-90; visits Garsington, 289, 316, 350; ageing, 291; meets Venetia in France, 291; sends wedding present to Venetia, 292; Lord Alfred Douglas attacks, 294-7; and conscription question, 301; accepts conscription, 303; and Violet's engagement and marriage, 303-4; bridge-playing, 310; daily routine, 310; Lloyd George and Northcliffe conspire to remove, 310; rising opposition to, 316, 327; Strachey describes, 317; appoints Lloyd George War Minister, 320; relations with Raymond, 324; visits Western Front, 324; and Raymond's death, 325-6, 330; conspiracy to unseat, 328-9, 333; and proposed War Council, 330, 333-5; sends resignation to King, 336-7; refuses to serve under Lloyd George or Bonar Law, 337; surrenders premiership to Lloyd George, 338; leaves office, 339-40; service and achievements, 340; leads parliamentary Opposition, 342; in retirement, 343; Billing calumniates, 345; King sends telegram of gratitude, 347; loses parliamentary seat (1918) and re-elected (1920), 347; financial difficulties, 349, 352; portrayed in Huxley's *Crome Yellow*, 350; raised to peerage (as Earl of Oxford and Asquith), 350-1; retains parliamentary seat, 350; health decline and death, 352-3

Asquith, Katharine (*née* Horner; Raymond's wife), 16-17, 150, 183, 315

Asquith, Margot (*later* Countess; *née* Tennant): qualities, 1, 10, 13-14, 16, 33-4, 76-7; courtship and marriage, 2, 74-80; social life, 2, 64-6; and HHA's infatuation with Venetia Stanley, 3, 90, 102, 119-20, 131, 135-7, 215, 236-8, 252, 256; invites Maud Allan to Downing Street, 10; life in Downing Street, 11, 25-6, 63; appearance and dress, 13, 15, 71-2, 118, 124-6, 137, 148, 353-4; family background, 14, 55, 64; family responsibilities on marriage, 15-16, 81-2; riding accident, 15; pregnancies and children, 18-21; romances and suitors, 19-20, 78; marital relations end, 21, 82-3; Cavendish Square house, 22-3; letter-writing, 25; supports HHA against women's suffrage, 30, 128; wariness of Lloyd George, 34-5, 277, 281, 284, 287, 320, 335; political meddling, 35; welfare work in East End, 36-7; on 1910 election, 44; and Edward VII's illness and death, 45-6; meets George V, 47-8; and Commons' ill-treatment of HHA, 49; in Souls, 50-2; servants, 57, 63; meets Prince of Wales at Ascot, 64; and Edwin Montagu, 65-6, 210; sympathises with strikers, 70; and Violet's disturbing presence, 70-1, 73, 85, 87, 109, 120; marriage relations, 72-4, 81, 110-11, 120-1, 285, 306, 317; horseriding, 76; and Milner, 76-7; on Venetia Stanley's effect on Violet, 84; emotional-physical reaction to unhappiness, 90; assaults suffragette, 95; friendship with George V, 99-100; Lloyd George entertains, 105; buys and occupies The Wharf, 110, 119; attends Parliament, 116, 165; launches HMS *Collingwood*, 118; depression and health decline, 119-20, 122, 131-2, 313-14; as cultural trendsetter, 124; accused of favouring French fashion, 126; meets Archduke Franz Ferdinand, 130; holiday in Antibes, 131; confides in Montagu, 135-7, 210, 215, 256; suffers from political social differences, 145-7; on Home Rule question, 151; luncheon parties, 155, 164; predicts outbreak of war, 166; disagreement with Benckendorff, 173; friendship with Lichnowskys, 174-6, 181, 193; shocked at outbreak of war, 186; visits wounded, 200-1; at Curzon's entertainment, 211-12; at Walmer Castle, 214-15, 311-12; criticised as unpatriotic, 240; limited war work, 247-8; wartime drinking, 253; on alcohol ban, 254-5; letter to HHA declaring love, 255; reaction to Venetia's engagement to Montagu, 273, 278, 287; on HHA and press, 276; and HHA's acceptance of coalition government, 278; regrets Haldane's downfall, 281; defends HHA, 284; meets Clementine Churchill, 286; criticises Churchill, 287; on HHA's depression, 287; visits Garsington, 289, 317, 350; friendship with Robert Ross, 295-6; on war casualties, 297; on conscription costs, 301; entertains wounded servicemen, 303; and Violet's devotion to father, 304-5; on Violet's marriage, 304; and conspiracy to remove HHA from premiership, 310, 334-6; wartime routine, 314; accused of pro-German sentiments, 312-13, 320; successful libel action against *Globe*, 312-13; defends Churchill, 313-14; and Raymond's death, 325-6; learns of Lloyd George's proposed War Council, 332; attacks Balfour for treachery, 339; leaves Downing Street, 339; on fall of HHA's government, 341; moves to Grosvenor Square, 342; anger at HHA's downfall, 343; extravagance and generosity, 343; returns to Cavendish Square, 343; stands by Maud Allan, 346; campaigns for HHA in 1920 by-election, 347; celebrates war's end, 347; bears cost of Elizabeth's wedding, 348; writing and lecturing, 349; Virginia Woolf describes, 350; on ghosts, 351; title, 351; financial difficulties, 352; on HHA's decline and death, 352-3; bombed out in World War II, 354; death and memorial service, 354; and Elizabeth's death, 354

Asquith, Oc *see* Asquith, Arthur
Asquith, Raymond (HHA's son): at Oxford, 11; in family, 12; brilliance, 16; marriage, 16-17; MA's relations with, 82; in 'Coterie', 83; allowance from MA, 132; present at Thames boat accident, 150; at Mells, 183; letter to Ottoline Morrell, 204; visits wartime London, 207; speaks at recruiting meetings, 221; predicts short war, 224-5; army service, 230, 288, 303; and MA's wartime drinking, 253; on Venetia's engagement to Montagu, 272; son christened, 319; in Battle of Somme, 321; HHA visits in France, 324; HHA's relations with, 324; killed in action, 325-6
Asquith, Violet (*later* Bonham Carter; HHA's daughter): love life, 3; life in Downing Street, 11, 25, 63; in family, 12; on MA's treatment of servants, 16; devotion to father, 17-18, 71, 73, 127, 270-1, 280, 304-5; relations with MA, 17, 270-1; coming-out, 18, 25; on MA's taste, 22; opposes women's suffrage, 30, 88; welcomes Licensing Bill, 37; suffers social ostracism, 55, 146; lady's maid, 56; on acquiring motor car, 58; as disturbing presence for MA, 70-1, 73, 85, 87, 110, 120; on effect of Souls, 84; friendship with Venetia Stanley, 84-5, 146, 256-7; invited by Churchill to *Enchantress* cruise, 109-10; and father's infatuation with Venetia, 121, 287; defends father against suffragette attack, 128; allowance from MA, 132; at Court presentation, 148; infatuation with Rupert Brooke, 200, 244-5; Christmas present from MA, 215; interest in consummated love affairs, 224; courted by Bonham Carter, 242, 278; stays at home in war, 242; and Venetia's move to Wimereux, 268; reaction to Venetia's engagement to Montagu, 269-72; on Venetia's conversion to Judaism, 271-2, 288; and father's unhappiness at losing Venetia, 273; admiration for Churchill, 286, 287; visits Oc in Egypt, 294; and war casualties, 297; engagement and marriage, 304; at Walmer Castle, 311; on effect of

Raymond's death on father, 326; on Lloyd George's appointment to War Office, 341; campaigns for father in 1920 by-election, 347; on MA's financial difficulties, 352

Astor, John Jacob IV and Madeleine, 94

Aubers, Battle of (1915), 265, 274

Austria: Germany supports, 156, 159; ultimatum to Serbia, 156, 159-60; breaks off relations with Serbia, 159

Baden Powell, Agnes, 195

Bailey, Catherine, 289n

Baker, Harold ('Bluetooth'), 328 & n

Bakst, Leon, 124

Baldwin, Stanley, 350

Balfour Act (on secondary education, 1902), 61

Balfour, Alice, 23, 25

Balfour, Arthur James: as prospective husband for MA, 1; in Downing Street, 23; in 1910 election, 43; in Souls, 53-5; signs MA's marriage register, 79-80; on Home Rule question, 142; on munitions shortage, 252; and fall of Haldane, 281; and formation of coalition government, 282; Curzon dislikes, 283; on Lloyd George, 283; replaces Churchill at Admiralty, 285; answers Churchill in Commons, 313; communiqué on Jutland, 318; and U-boat campaign, 323; resigns, 335; and formation of government with Lloyd George as War Council chairman, 337; Lloyd George invites to join government as foreign secretary, 337-8; MA and HHA attack for treachery, 339

Balfour, Betty, 339

Balfour, Frances, 285

Ballets Russes, 124

Balmerino, SS, 144

Balmoral, 91

'Bantam' battalions, 262

Barr, Sir James, 39-40

Barrie, James Matthew, 349

Battenberg, Admiral Louis, Prince of, 211, 221

Battersea, Constance, Lady, 62

Beauchamp, William Lygon, 7th Earl, 214

Beaverbrook, William Maxwell Aitken, 1st Baron, 330, 351-2; Politicians and the War, 1914-1916, 329

Bedford Square, 349

Beecham, Thomas, 87, 140

Begbie, Harold, 198, 241

Behr, Karl, 94

Belfast: demonstration against Home Rule, 92

Belgium: neutrality, 167, 171, 173-4; Germany demands transit rights, 177, 180; German advance through, 180-1; and Schlieffen Plan, 205-6; German atrocities, 206, 211-12; refugees in Britain, 212, 290; relief fund, 250; occupied by Germans, 329

Belloc, Bessie Parkes, 114

Belloc, Hilaire, 114-15

Belridge (tanker), 239

Benckendorff, Alexander, Count, 153, 172-3

Benckendorff, Constantine, 150, 153

Benson, E.F.: Dodo, 78

Berlin: George V and Queen Mary visit, 122; growth, 124; and outbreak of war, 168, 172; anti-British demonstrations, 192-3

Bethmann-Hollweg, Theobald von, 147

Bibesco, Prince Antoine: marriage to Elizabeth, 348

Billing, Noel Pemberton, 344-6

Birmingham, Henry Wakefield, Bishop of, 296

Blomfield, Sara Louisa, Lady, 141

Blunt, Wilfrid Scawen, 12-13, 53, 63, 95-6, 128

Bonham Carter, Maurice ('Bongie'): in Asquith family circle, 10-11; Violet writes to on enlistment, 199; courts Violet, 242, 278; letter from Violet in Egypt, 294; engagement and marriage to Violet, 304; on Lloyd George's appointment to War Office, 341

Bonham Carter, Violet see Asquith, Violet

Boot, Sir Jesse (later 1st Baron Trent), 94

Bottomley, Horatio, 266

Boy Scouts, 233, 250, 323

Bradby, Violet, 207

Brand, William, 231, 265, 281, 288, 318

Brassey, Thomas, 1st Earl, 100n

Breccles Hall, Norfolk, 351

Britain: pre-war industrial unrest, 2-3, 68-70, 112, 126-7; social changes, 10, 290; welfare reforms, 36-8; naval rivalry with Germany, 40-1; agreements with France, 42;

elite aristocracy, 55-6; good living, 124; holidays and festivals, 130-1; high social life and Season, 144-5, 148-9; balance of power policy, 159; unawareness of impending war, 163; financial crisis at outbreak of war, 169; exodus of hotel staff, 170; preparations for war, 171-2, 176, 182; and declaration of war, 185-6, 190, 192; popular euphoria at start of war, 189-92, 204-5; rush to colours, 190; little experience of recent wars, 191; wartime restrictions and measures, 194-6, 220; press power, 198, 261, 267, 278; recruitment and volunteers, 198-9, 221, 230-1; role of post offices, 198; security and confidentiality, 202-3; early effects of war, 206-7; wartime rumours, 211; fear of Zeppelin attacks, 220; hostility to Germany and Germans, 221, 240, 298, 313; spy fever, 222; air raids, 232, 265 & n; German blockade, 239; shipping losses, 240; coalition government, 251, 280-3; civilian life during war, 288-9, 298, 309; privileged classes practise austerity, 314-5; War Council proposed, 330-3; austerity and restrictions, 344; *see also* London

Britannia (royal yacht), 172

British army: recruitment and volunteers, 198-9, 209, 230; strength at outbreak of war, 198; horses, 201-2, 218; discipline and training, 206-7; casualties, 218, 323, 329; conditions, 229-30; and conscription question, 232; minimum height reduced and age limit raised, 262; shell shortage, 274-5; conscription introduced, 303, 309; equipped with respirators, 309

British Expeditionary Force (BEF): French commands, 203; lands in France, 203n; strength, 229

British Summer Time, 314

Brittain, Vera, 150, 246, 291

Broadwood, Lucy, 142, 170

Brockway, Fenner, 218

Brooke, Rupert, 200, 244-5

Brunswick, Ernst Augustus, Duke of, 122

Burnham, Edward Levy-Lawson, 1st Baron, 14

Cambon, Paul, 155

Campbell-Bannerman, Charlotte, Lady, 2, 23-4

Campbell-Bannerman, Sir Henry, 22-3, 128

Carpathia, RMS, 115

Carrington, Dora, 317

Carson, Sir Edward: opposes Home Rule, 92, 99, 141-2, 144, 150; founds Ulster Volunteer Force, 105; insists on Churchill's removal, 281; appointed Attorney-General, 283; resigns, 303; conspires against HHA, 328-9, 331; serves on War Council, 330-1; Bonar Law fears, 335

Cassel, Sir Ernest, 266

Cave, Walter, 110

Cavendish Square, 22-3, 342-3

Cazalet, Edward, 22, 84, 149, 184, 224, 276

Cazalet, Victor, 190, 239, 309, 311

Cecil, Lord Hugh, 66

Chaliapin, Fedor Ivanovich, 155

Chamberlain, Sir Austen, 283

Chamberlain, Joseph, 54

Chamberlain, Neville, 354

Channon, Henry ('Chips'), 351, 353-4

Charteris, Evan, 19-20, 53, 78, 80-1, 109, 317

Charteris, Ivo, 302

children: as strikers, 69; war work, 322-3

Churchill, Clementine, 2, 96, 106, 109, 122, 285-7

Churchill, Lady Gwendoline ('Goonie'), 334

Churchill, Lady Randolph (*née* Jenny Jerome; Winston's mother), 19, 156

Churchill, Lord Randolph (Winston's father), 14

Churchill, Randolph (Winston's son), 286, 304

Churchill, Winston S.: and MA's political influence, 2; on HHA, 12; and Lloyd George, 35; and HHA's drinking, 36; in confrontation with Lords, 43; opposes Home Rule for Ireland, 94; HHA dines with, 95-6; background, 96; as First Lord of Admiralty, 96; Mediterranean cruise with HHA and Violet, 109-10; on strengthening navy, 116, 132; on suffragette attacks on HHA, 128; and Naval Estimates

(1914-15), 132, 138-9; HHA on, 137; favours oil as fuel for navy, 139-40; on Home Rule question, 142, 156; mobilises fleet, 157; on impending war, 165; on pre-war turmoil, 169; bellicosity, 173, 182; in Admiralty building, 185; happiness at outbreak of war, 187; and power of press, 198, 267, 276; favours conscription, 232; plans Dardanelles campaign, 243, 263; on munitions shortage, 252; refuses to give up alcohol, 254; predicts Zeppelin attacks, 265; and Fisher's resignation, 275-6; forced to resign, 280-1; Balfour replaces at Admiralty, 285; blamed for Dardanelles failure, 285; wife appeals to HHA against dismissal, 285-7; active service on Western Front, 286-7; Violet's admiration for, 286; letter from Lord Alfred Douglas, 296; attacks 1916 Naval Estimates, 313; requests release from army, 313-14; conspires for removal of HHA, 328; excluded from Lloyd George's government, 338; on Balfour's joining Lloyd George's government, 339; on Lloyd George's ambitions, 341
class (social): and privilege, 10; and suffragette movement, 29
Cochrane, Thomas, 57
Collingwood, HMS, 118
Conciliation Bill (1910), 31
conscription: debate over, 232, 288, 301-2; introduced (1916), 303, 309, 321
Conservative Party: and aristocratic rule and Society, 55-6; opposes Home Rule for Ireland, 91-3, 144; social hostility to Liberals, 145; favours conscription, 232; supports Lloyd George, 335; in Lloyd George's government, 342; wins 1918 election, 342
contraception, 223
Cooper, Duff, 65, 150, 236, 245, 270, 303, 319, 326, 334, 345, 351-2; Old Men Forget, 319
Corbett, Sir Julian, 117
'Coterie, the', 83-4, 97, 149-50, 223
country houses, 63; as wartime hospitals, 232-3
Country Life (magazine), 231
Coward, Noël, 343
Cowes (Isle of Wight), 159-61, 166-7, 171
Crawford, Major Frederick, 143

Crawford Priory, Fife, 57
Cressy, HMS, 216-17, 239
Crewe-Milnes, Robert Offley Ashburton, Marquess of, 130, 186
Criccieth, north Wales, 105
Cunard, Maud Alice (Emerald), 87, 148, 336, 354
Curragh Mutiny (1914), 142-3
Curzon, George Nathaniel, Earl (later Marquess), 29, 53-5, 78-80, 145-6, 211-12, 281, 283, 318, 337-8
Curzon, Lady Irene, 145, 148
Cust, Sir Charles, 122
Cust, Harry, 14, 53, 84

D'Abernon, Edgar Vincent, Viscount, 165
Daily Chronicle, 330
Daily Mail, 171, 190, 267, 277, 280; Air Race (1911), 299
Daily Mirror, 61
Daily News, 171
Daily Telegraph, 328, 338
Dangerfield, George, 34, 145; The Strange Death of Liberal England, 143
Dardanelles campaign (1915), 243-4, 251, 261, 275-6, 282, 285
Dardanelles Commission (1916), 329
Davies, Evie, 97, 136
Davison, Emily Wilding, 112-14
Defence of the Realm Act (DORA; 1914), 195
Derby, Edward George Villiers Stanley, 17th Earl of, 333
Derby, Edward Henry Stanley, 15th Earl of, 65
Derby (horserace): suffragette killed, 112
Desborough, Ethel (Ettie), Lady: and Evan Charteris, 20, 53; friendship with MA, 66; house parties, 75; and ban on drinking, 253; and daughter Monica's move to Wimereux hospital, 262; sons killed in war, 293
Desborough, William Henry Grenfell, Baron, 66, 75
Diaghilev, Serge, 124, 144, 148
Dickson-Poynder, Sir John and Lady see Islington, 1st Baron and Lady
Dillingham, Rifleman Frederick James ('Bon'), 206, 219, 230
Dillon, E.J., 67, 117
Douglas, Lord Alfred, 294-7
Downing Street (No. 10): life in, 11, 25-6, 63, 164; MA improves, 22-3,

25-6; Asquiths move to, 23; servants, 26; appearance, 27; attacked by suffragettes, 30-1; communications with No.11, 35; Asquiths leave, 341

Downing Street (No.11), 33, 35

Dreadnought, HMS, 117

Dreadnoughts (battleships), 41, 116-17

Dublin: outbreak of violence, 161-3

Duff Gordon, Sir Cosmo and Lucile, Lady, 94

education (secondary), 61

Edward VII, King: and Lloyd George's 1909 Budget, 42; and constitutional crisis (1909-10), 43-4; bronchitis and death, 44-6; Marlborough House set, 52; MA meets at Ascot, 64; and castles, 254

Elcho, Hugo Richard Charteris, Lord, 53, 201

Elcho, Mary, Lady, 17, 53, 124, 201

Elibank, Alexander Murray, Master of, 115

Ellis, Henry Havelock, 162n

Elmwood, Kent, 267

Enchantress (Admiralty yacht), 96, 109

Entente Cordiale, 42, 327

Esher, Reginald Baliol Brett, 2nd Viscount, 138

Eton College: casualties, 302n

eugenics, 39

Ewelme Down, Oxfordshire, 90

Eye-Witness, The (weekly), 114-15

Falkenhayn, Erich von, 164

Fancourt, Mary, 229

FANY (First Aid Nursing Yeomanry), 233

Fawcett, Millicent (*later* Dame), 30

Finance Bill (1909), 42-3, 45, 48

Fisher, Admiral Sir John Arbuthnot ('Jackie'): develops naval strength, 41, 117; on speed of ships, 139; predicts outbreak of war, 158; replaces Battenberg as First Sea Lord, 221; dances with MA, 273; resigns, 275-6; Churchill calls for return, 313

Fitzgerald, Colonel, 298

Fitzroy, Sir Almeric, 168n, 334

Flexner, Abraham: Report, 127

Florence (Downing Street cook), 26

Flower, Peter, 19-20, 78-9, 80-1, 317

Fortescue, Sir John, 99, 130

Fowler, John, 190

France: agreements with Britain, 42; and German war threat, 66; agrees to Belgian neutrality, 167; general mobilisation, 172; Germany plans swift defeat, 177n; Germany invades, 184; army strength, 229; Germans occupy north, 329

Franco-Prussian War (1870), 174, 177n

Franz Ferdinand, Archduke of Austria: at Windsor, 130; assassination, 152, 156-7

Franz Joseph, Emperor of Austro-Hungary, 164

Freeman, Elsa, 250, 261

French, Field Marshal Sir John: commands BEF, 203; friendship with Repington, 274; Haig replaces, 324; visits HHA, 340

Gallipoli, 244, 261, 263, 265, 276

Garsington, Oxfordshire, 289, 316, 350

gas *see* poison gas

General Elections: (1910), 43, 48; (1906), 91; (1918; 'khaki election'), 342, 347; (1922), 350

George V, King: personality and style, 46-7; and Lords crisis (1910), 48, 50; opposes suffragettes, 48, 141; passes over Curzon as PM, 55n; and Home Rule Bill, 91; opposes Home Rule, 99, 150; and 1913 Derby, 112-13; visit to Berlin, 122; seeks conciliation over Home Rule, 155; message from Kaiser denouncing Tsar, 169; and departure of French chefs, 170; and Tsar's mobilisation order, 173; signs general mobilisation order, 184; public appearance on outbreak of war, 185; gives up drinking for duration of war, 253-4; entertains, 254; MA on, 254; changes family name to Windsor, 266; German ancestry, 266; and HHA's resignation, 316, 336; seeks Balfour's advice, 337; telegram of gratitude to HHA, 347

Germany: naval rivalry with Britain, 40-1, 116-18, 158; as war threat, 66-7, 138, 152; and Agadir crisis, 67; militarism, 122-3; warmer relations with Britain, 132, 147; and Irish Home Rule, 143, 151; announces support for Austria, 156, 159; colonial and world power ambitions, 159,

178; Russia declares war on, 167; sends ultimatum to Russia, 167; under martial law, 168; war fever, 169-70; British regard for, 171; declares war on Russia, 172; general mobilisation, 172; invades Luxembourg, 177, 184; war on two fronts, 177n; advance through Belgium, 180; British ultimatum to, 181, 184-7; invades France, 184; and declaration of war with Britain, 185-6; popular enthusiasm for war, 190, 196, 205; as invasion threat, 205; prisoners of war in Britain, 209, 214, 221; army strength, 229; British blockade, 239; submarine warfare, 239, 251, 323, 329; uses poison gas, 260-1; increasing British hostility to, 264, 266, 298, 313; residents in Britain persecuted, 264; and sinking of *Lusitania*, 264 & n; employs flame throwers (*Flammenwerfer*), 292; defeated (1918), 346-7; *see also* Berlin

Gibson, Dorothy, 94
Giesl, Vladimir, Freiherr von, 160
Girl Guides, 233, 250, 322-3
Gladstone, Herbert, 100
Gladstone, Mary, 164
Gladstone, William Ewart, 1, 54, 63, 79-80
Glen, Peebleshire, 24, 51, 63
Glenconner, Edward Tennant, 1st Baron (MA's brother), 55-6, 296
Globe (newspaper), 312-13
Glyn, Elinor, 158-60
Goschen, Sir Edward, 181, 186
Goschen, George Joachim, 1st Viscount, 66
Gosse, Edmund, 192
Graham-Smith, Lucy (MA's sister), 164-5
Granby, Henry Manners, Marquess of (*later* 8th Duke of Rutland), 53, 231
Granby, Violet, Marchioness of, 53
Grant, Duncan, 144
Grant, Lady Sybil, 288
Great Unrest (1912), 68
Great Yarmouth: air raid on, 232
Grenfell, Billy: killed in action, 293, 302
Grenfell, Julian: dies of wounds, 293, 302
Grenfell, Monica, 248, 262
Grey, Sir Edward: as Foreign Secretary, 13, 14; MA appeals to defend HHA

in Commons, 49; opposes Home Rule for Ireland, 94; bridge-playing, 128, 310; HHA on limitations, 137; Colonel House meets, 152; on German war threat, 152, 154; reads out Austrian ultimatum to Serbia, 156; takes fishing holiday, 157; on Kaiser, 159; proposes great powers act for peace, 159, 164; on commitment to war, 180-2; at outbreak of war, 186; on extinguishing lights, 188; on removal of Anna Heinsius from Asquith home, 208; dedication in war, 210

Grosvenor Square, 74-5, 342
Guest, Mrs Freddie, 233
Gurney, John, 151
Gurney, Samuel, 151
Gyte, Maria, 59, 182, 288, 322

Hackwood Park, Hampshire, 211
Haig, General Sir Douglas, 324, 338
Haldane, Richard Burdon, Viscount: army reforms, 35, 180, 198; entertaining, 74; HHA on vagueness, 137; HHA favours as War Minister, 180; bathing at Mells, 183; Beatrice Webb on, 210, 282; warns HHA against drinking, 241; MA writes to over dissolution of Cabinet, 278; accused of pro-German sympathies, 280-1; loses government post, 280; awarded OM, 281; part-educated in Germany, 313; Billing accuses, 348
Hampshire, HMS, 318
Harcourt, Lewis, 1st Viscount, 54, 95
Hardie, Keir, 190
Hardinge, Sir Charles, Baron (of Penshurst), 45, 242
Harte, Bret, 53
Hartington, Spencer Compton Cavendish, Maquess of, 54
Haussonville, Paul Gabriel de Cléron, Count d', 155
Haverfield, Evelina, 219
Heath, John, 206, 322-3
Heath, John James, 61, 72
Heath, William, 57-8, 61
Heinsius, Anna (*later* Meyer; 'Frau'), 26, 208, 214
Helmsley, Charles Duncombe, Viscount, 44
Henderson, Arthur, 337

Henley, Sylvia, the Hon. Mrs (Venetia's
    sister), 233, 269-70, 314, 339
Henn, Second Lieutenant Edward, 293
Henry, Prince of Prussia, 160, 163
Hodges, Rosa, 26
Hogue, HMS, 216-17, 239
Hohenzollern (Kaiser's yacht), 160
Hold, Private John Charles, 230
Home Rule Bills: (1885), 54; (1912),
    90-3, 99, 106, 116; (1914), 92, 138,
    141-3, 150-1, 154-5, 209, 316
Hooge, Battle of, 292-3
Hook, Commander Hereward, 217
Horner, Edward, 253
Horner, Frances, Lady, 16, 45, 75, 183,
    203, 354
Horner, Sir John, 183
horses: in wartime, 201-2, 218; lost, 322
hospitals: British houses converted to,
    232-3; in France, 246
House, Colonel Edward Wendell, 152-3
Howard, Geofrey, 310
Huxley, Aldous: Crome Yellow, 350

income tax: raised in war, 194
Inge, William Ralph, Dean of St Paul's, 319
Ingleby, Holcombe, 182
International Woman Suffrage Alliance,
    127
Ireland: and Home Rule, 3, 32, 43, 54,
    55n, 90-4, 99, 106, 111, 116, 138,
    141-3, 151-2, 154, 163, 207; gun-
    running, 143, 161; threat of armed
    conflict, 150; Buckingham Palace
    Conference on, 155-6; and outbreak
    of war, 165; proclaims Republic
    (1916), 316
Isaacs, Godfrey, 114-15
Isaacs, Sir Rufus (later Viscount, then
    Marquess of Reading), 114-15, 210,
    334, 341
Isis (magazine), 127
Islington, John Dickson-Poynder, 1st
    Baron and Anne, Lady, 66

James, Henry, 18
Japan: naval power, 117
Jekyll, Agnes, Lady, 334
Jenkins, Roy, 241
Jephson, Harriet, Lady, 170, 180, 184,
    207-8 & n
Jews: in Liberal Party, 65; Violet's view
    of, 269

John Bull (magazine), 266
Jones, Herbert, 112-13 & n, 114
Jones, Sir Lawrence, 236
Jones, Leif, 297
Jowett, Benjamin, 1, 15, 79
Jutland, Battle of (1916), 317-18

Kaiser Wilhelm der Grosse, SS, 195
Keppel, Alice: friendship with Margot,
    44; lady's maid, 56; and MA's
    non-invitation to Curzon ball, 146;
    Elizabeth Asquith stays with, 158;
    money management, 194; precautions
    against incendiary bombs, 265; offers
    Grosvenor Square house to Asquiths,
    342
Keppel, Sonia, 194, 219
Kessler, Count Harry: on MA at ballet,
    111; on inevitability of war, 118;
    invites G.B. Shaw to German Embassy,
    138; attends MA luncheon party, 155;
    on failure of Ulster Conference, 156;
    buys personal war equipment, 168;
    welcomes outbreak of war, 172, 178,
    196, 205; reports to regiment, 176
Keswick Evangelical Convention, 167
Keynes, John Maynard, 39, 339
Kiel Canal: widened, 158
King, Hetty, 247
King's Lynn: air raid on, 232
Kinski, Charles, 207
Kipling, Rudyard, 343; 'Ulster' (poem), 99
Kitchener, Field Marshal Horatio
    Herbert, 1st Earl: status, 179; foresees
    long war, 189, 298; reputation
    and popular confidence in, 189;
    as Secretary of State for War, 189-
    90; recruitment drive, 198-9, 209;
    refuses favours to Lady Sackville,
    201; rumours over, 211; disagreement
    with Lloyd George, 222; alienates
    Cabinet, 251, 294; blamed for shell
    shortage and incompetence, 277, 280,
    282; power reduced under coalition
    government, 283; takes pledge against
    alcohol, 297; and conscription
    question, 301; visits Walmer Castle,
    311; drowned, 318-19; visits HHA, 340
Knollys, Francis, 1st Viscount, 45
Krupps, Harry, 166

Labour Party: emergence, 2; first
    government (1924), 350

Lady, The (magazine), 166
Lamb, Lady Caroline, 344
Lang, Cosmo, Archbishop of Canterbury, 42, 154, 165
Lansdowne, Henry Charles Keith Petty-Fitzmaurice, 5th Marquess of, 212, 283, 331, 338; Memorandum on ending war, 327-8, 331, 333, 338 & n
Lansdowne, Maud Evelyn, Marchioness of, 211
Lascelles, (later Sir) Alan ('Tommy'), 177, 186, 195
Laski, Harold, 39
Laurence, Margaret, 127
Lavery, Hazel, 149
Law, Andrew Bonar: successor (1923), 55n; opposes Home Rule for Ireland, 92-3, 151, 154, 209; and postponement of Amending Bill (Ireland), 165; at Hackwood, 212; demands coalition government, 277, 280; and fall of Haldane and Churchill, 281; MA disparages, 283; on appearing active, 310; visits HHA at The Wharf, 320; and conspiracy to unseat HHA, 328, 333; on Lloyd George, 329; serves on War Council, 330-1; fears Carson, 335; as prospective Prime Minister, 336; and formation of new government, 337; retires after winning 1922 election, 352
Lawrence, D.H., 264, 301
Lawson, Frank, 90
Leigh, Mary, 95
Leighton, Roland, 291
Levine, Naomi, 262n
Liberal Party: dominance, 22; social reforms, 36-7; anti-war principles, 40; Jews in, 65; and economic crisis (1912), 68; supports Home Rule, 91-2; and Home Rule Bill, 106; disbelieves German aggression, 140; and Conservative social hostility, 145; opposes conscription, 232; split, 335, 337, 342; MPs support Lloyd George, 342
Liberty (steam yacht), 205
Licensing Bill (1911), 36
Lichnowsky, Karl Max, Prince, 13, 138, 147, 156, 174-5, 181, 186-7, 193
Lichnowsky, Mechtilde, Princess, 174-5, 181, 193
Lister, Charles, 302

Llanelli, Carmarthenshire, 69
Lloyd George, David: political style, 4; as Chancellor of Exchequer, 33-4, 41; MA's wariness of, 34-5, 277, 281, 284, 287, 335; qualities and character, 34, 266; and Licensing Bill, 36; Budget (1909; 'People's Budget'), 41-2, 45, 48; on George V, 47; Mansion House speech warning against war, 67-8, 154; conciliatory acts in industrial unrest, 70; opposes Home Rule for Ireland, 94; MA dines with, 105; relations with Frances Stevenson, 105-6, 342; suffragettes attack house, 107; in Marconi scandal, 114-15, 140; prophesies world peace, 132; on reducing defence spending, 132, 138; HHA on lack of judgment, 137; and 1914 budget, 139, 140; peace views, 173; on German violation of Belgian neutrality, 180; on Churchill's happiness at outbreak of war, 187; HHA sends for, 187; urges non-hoarding of gold, 194; appreciates power of press, 198, 267, 276; dedication in war, 210; wartime speeches, 220-1; favours conscription, 232, 301; Montagu lobbies for appointment as Viceroy of India, 242; forecasts failure of Dardanelles campaign, 244; and formation of coalition government, 251; and alcohol restriction, 252-3, 297; on munitions shortage, 252; blames Kitchener for shell shortage, 277; criticises HHA's conduct of war, 277; demands coalition government, 277, 280, 282; rising popular reputation, 279, 282; Balfour on, 283; as Minister of Munitions, 283-4, 297; conspires for removal of HHA, 310, 328-9, 332, 335, 341; HHA appoints to succeed Kitchener as War Minister, 320-1; and unsatisfactory conduct of war, 324; MA takes to hear Mendelssohn's *Elijah*, 330; proposes War Council, 330-4; Montagu on ambitions for leadership, 332-3; resigns, 335-6; forms government as successor to HHA, 337-8; reforms government, 341-2; ménage à trois, 342; reads out terms of Armistice, 347; as Party leader, 351

Lloyd George, Margaret (David's wife), 35, 105

Lloyd George, Megan (David's daughter): friendship with Puffin Asquith, 35-6; tutored by Frances Stevenson, 105

Lloyd George, Olwen (David's daughter), 124

London: 'pea-souper' fogs, 72-3; war preparations and crowd behaviour, 176, 178-9, 185-8, 191, 194-5; Zeppelin attacks on, 265n, 300; wartime appearance, 297

Londonderry, Theresa Susey Helen, Marchioness of, 154, 165

Long, Walter, 283

Lonsdale, Frederick, 343

Lonsdale, Hugh Cecil Lowther, 5th Earl of, 188

Lords, House of: rejects 1909 Finance Bill, 43, 45; and General Election (1910), 48-9; defeated in 1910 crisis, 50; veto rights over Commons bills, 56; opposes Home Rule for Ireland, 91, 106; powers curtailed, 92

Lourie, Dora Leba, 149, 170, 176, 206

Lowndes, Marie Belloc, 239, 265n, 336, 346, 354

Lowther, Mary (Mrs James William Lowther), 66

Lubbock, Geoffrey, 301

Ludendorff, General Erich von, 346

Lusitania, RMS: sunk, 263-4, 266

Lutyens, Sir Edwin, 62, 95, 192, 351

Lutyens, Lady Emily, 62

Luxembourg: Germany invades, 177, 184

Lympne Castle, Kent, 30

Lyttelton, Alfred, 51, 76

Lyttelton, Laura (née Tennant; MA's sister), 51-2

Lytton, Lady Constance, 29, 31

Lytton, Edward Robert Bulwer Lytton, 1st Earl of, 29

MacCarthy, Desmond, 14

MacDonald, Ramsay, 127

McKenna, Reginald, 283

Mackintosh, Charles Rennie, 222

Man, Isle of: Germans interned in, 266n

Manchester Guardian, 279

Manchester Tramway Workers, 298

Manners, Lady Diana (later Cooper), 84-5, 97, 119, 128, 149-50, 234, 270, 289, 319, 345, 351-2

Manners, Hoppy and Con (i.e. John James and Catherine; Robert's parents), 302

Manners, John, 302

Mansat, Corporal Ernest and Marthe, 251

Marconi affair, 114-16, 140

Marconi, Guglielmo, 114

Marlborough, Consuelo, Duchess of (née Vanderbilt), 126-7

Marne, Battles of the: (first, 1914), 225; (second, 1918), 346

Marshall, Molly, 123

Martin, Lottie, 39, 59-60, 62

Mary, Princess, 185-6

Mary, Queen of George V, 46-7, 112-13, 122, 212, 247, 254, 347

Matrimonial Times, 62

Mells Park, Somerset, 183-4, 207

Mensdorff, Count Albert, 109

Meyer, Rolf, 208

Midleton, St John, 79

Military Service Act (1916), 303

Milner, Alfred, Viscount, 76-7, 329

Minimum Wage Bill (1912), 70

Mitchell, Rosslyn, 350

Mitchison, Naomi, 233

Monday Night Cabal, 329

Mons, Battle of (1914), 211n

Montagu, Edwin: in Asquith family circle, 10-11, 65-6; qualities, 65; attachment to Venetia Stanley, 85-6, 100-1, 121-2, 129-30, 135; wealth, 86, 290-1; in Sicily with HHA, 87-8; on HHA's Home Rule speech, 91; HHA's jealousy of, 101, 121-2; Venetia declines marriage proposal, 101; MA confides in, 135-7, 210, 215, 256; promotion to Treasury, 137, 209; on impending war, 157; letters to Venetia, 209; dedication in war, 210; devotion to Asquiths, 210; and Venetia's attachment to HHA, 215, 258-9; as Chancellor of Duchy of Lancaster, 235-6, 242; appearance, 236; Venetia's growing affection for, 236, 242, 256-8, 262; ambitions, 242; poor health, 242; remains in Britain in war, 245; Venetia visits house, 248-9; Venetia agrees to marry, 262; HHA told of marriage to Venetia, 268; and Violet's reaction to engagement, 272; comforts Mrs Churchill, 286; visits Venetia in France, 290; marriage ceremony, 292; bridge-playing, 310; and Lloyd George's acting to unseat HHA, 332; and Northcliffe's association with Lloyd George, 334; and Lloyd George's propective premiership, 336; as Minister of Munitions under Lloyd George, 338; MA attacks for joining Lloyd George, 339; unhappy married life, 351; at Paris Peace Conference, 352; as Secretary of State for India, 352; death, 352

Moore, Arthur, 98

Morgan, John Pierpont, 110

Morley, John, Viscount, 50

Morning Post, 280, 331

Morocco, 66-8

Morrell, Lady Ottoline: on treatment of conscientious objectors, 31; on Raymond Asquith, 83; salon, 144; visits The Wharf, 157; appearance, 162; HHA's attachment to, 162; letter from Violet, 204; at Garsington, 289; supports Robert Ross, 296; letter from D.H. Lawrence on seeing Zeppelin, 301; on MA's decline, 346; friendship with MA, 349-50

Morrell, Philip, 83, 289, 296

motor cars, 5-8

munitions supply (British), 252, 261, 263; shell shortage, 274, 277; increased under Lloyd George, 284, 297

Nation, The (journal), 171

National Health Insurance Bill (1912), 39

Nationalist Volunteers (Ireland), 161

Naval Estimates: (1914-15), 132, 138; (1916), 313

Neuve Capelle, 274

newspapers *see* press (popular)

Nicholas II, Tsar of Russia: Wilhelm denounces, 169; orders complete mobilisation, 173

Nicolson, Harold, 174, 182, 185-7

Nijinsky, Vaslav, 111, 144

Norman, Florence, Lady, 262

Northcliffe, Alfred Harmsworth, 1st Viscount: influence, 61, 198, 266-7, 277, 280, 301; conspires for removal of HHA, 310, 334, 341; attacks conduct of war, 323

Northumberland, Henry George Percy, 7th Duke of, 34

Novello, Ivor, 343

nursing, 233-5

Nye, Philip, 26

Observer (newspaper), 51

Old Age Pensions Act (1908/9), 38-9

Oliver, Frederick, 141

Ormonde, James Theobald Butler, 3rd Marquess of, 160

Ottoman Empire (Turkey): and Dardanelles/Gallipoli campaign, 242-3, 261, 263

Page, Walter Hines, 302

Paget, General Sir Arthur, 142

Paget, Mary ('Minnie'), Lady, 155

Pals' Battalions, 205

Pankhurst, Christabel, 30

Pankhurst, Emmeline: leads suffragettes, 28, 30, 100, 107-8, 113n, 140-1; wartime truce, 204, 284

Pankhurst, Sylvia, 29-30, 141

Panther (German warship), 67

Paris: threatened at beginning of war, 206

Parliament: women attend, 116, 154, 165; and outbreak of war, 181-2

Parliament Bill and Act (1911), 54-5, 92

Parliamentary Franchise (Women) Bill (1912), 32

Pembroke, George Herbert, 13th Earl of, 13, 53

Pembroke, Gertrude, Countess of, 53

Penrhos, Holyhead, 122, 169

pigs: slaughter, 59-60

Pinfold Manor, Walton-on-the-Hill, 107

Plymouth, Robert George Windsor-Clive, 1st Earl of, 296

Poiret, Paul, 118n, 125

poison gas, 260-1, 309

Ponsonby, Sir Henry, 80

poverty: and welfare reforms, 37-8

Powell, Lynette, 246

press (popular), 61; influence, 198, 261, 267, 276; HHA's indifference to, 276, 310; *see also* Northcliffe, 1st Viscount

Prisoners (Discharge for Ill Health) Act (1913), 108

Queen Alexandra's Royal Army Nursing Corps, 234

Redmond, John, 92-3, 95

Repington, Colonel Charles à Court, 274, 277, 298, 302, 319

Richthofen, Baron Manfred von, 300

Riddell, Sir George, 107

Rimsky-Korsakov, Nikolai Andreevich: *Le Coq d'Or*, 148; *La Légende de Joseph*, 148

Roberts, Field Marshal Frederick Sleigh, 1st Earl, 144

Rosebery, Archibald Philip Primrose, 5th Earl of, 54, 78, 80, 253

Ross, Robert (Robbie), 11, 122, 200, 294-7, 326

Rothenstein, William, 296

Royal Naval Division, 200, 244, 253

Royal Navy: strength, 40, 66, 116-18; Churchill advocates converting to oil, 139-40; and U-boat campaign, 239; in Dardanelles campaign, 251-2; *see also* Naval Estimates

Russell, Bertrand, 39, 190

Russia: and impending war, 153, 161; promises support for Serbia, 159; general mobilisation, 164, 167; war with Germany, 167, 172; seen as enemy in Germany, 176-7; war with Turkey, 242; ban on vodka, 254; defeated, 329

Russo-Japanese war (1904-5), 117

Rutland, Henry John Brinsley Manners, 8th Duke of *see* Granby, Marquess of

Rutland, Marion Margaret Violet, Duchess of, 282

Sackville, Victoria, Lady, 201

St Albans, Grace, Duchess of, 94

Salisbury, Elizabeth Vere, Marchioness of, 350

Salisbury, Robert Arthur Talbot Gascoyne-Cecil, 3rd Marquess of, 54

Samuel, Herbert, 114-15

Sandringham, Norfolk, 130

Sanger, Margaret, 223

Sarajevo, 153

Sassoon, Sir Philip, 239

Saunders, Robert, 176, 202, 204

Savoy Hotel, London, 354

Scapa Flow, 239, 240

Scarborough: shelled, 250

Schlieffen Plan, 177, 205

Scott, Charles Prestwich, 319

Selborne, William Waldegrave Palmer, 2nd Earl of, 283

Serbia: and war threat, 154; Austrian ultimatum to, 156, 159-60; troops accidentally cross into Austrian territory, 164

servants: pre-war, 56-9, 61-3; recruited into services, 231; in wartime, 297-8

Shaw, George Bernard, 39, 138, 347

Shaw Stewart, Patrick, 302

Sheffield, Edward Lyulph Stanley, 4th Baron (Venetia's father), 273

Sheffield, Mary Katharine, Lady (Venetia's mother), 236-7, 273

Sheldon, Derbyshire, 288

shell shortage *see* munitions supply

Sicily, 87-8

Simon, Sir John, 296

Sitwell, Osbert, 148

Smeeton, Trooper Ben, 245

Smith, Frederick Edwin (*later* 1st Earl of Birkenhead), 49

Smyth, Ethel, 140, 296

Somme, Battle of the (1916), 321-2, 324, 329

Sophie, Duchess of Hohenberg (Countess Sophie Chotek; Franz Ferdinand's wife), 152

Souls, the: composition and activities, 50-4, 84; and political differences, 145

Speyer, Sir Edgar, 298-9

Stamfordham, Arthur John Bigge, Baron, 95, 336

Stanley, the Hon. Arthur (Venetia's brother), 237, 269

Stanley, Henry Edward John, 3rd Baron Stanley of Alderley, 83

Stanley, the Hon. Margaret (Venetia's sister-in-law), 237, 269, 290

Stanley, the Hon. Venetia: HHA's infatuation with, 3-4, 87, 89, 96, 102, 119-20, 135-7, 183-4, 197, 210, 222-3, 236-8, 249, 252, 267, 291-2; in Asquith family circle, 10; appearance and character, 83; social life, 83; friendship with Violet Asquith, 84-5, 146, 256; relations with Edwin Montagu, 85-6, 100-1, 121-2, 129, 135; in Sicily with HHA, 87-8; letters from HHA, 92, 122, 129, 131, 135, 154, 161, 183, 197, 202-3, 205, 209, 212, 222, 235, 238, 248, 252; independent-mindedness,

96-7; Montagu proposes marriage, 101-2; effect on MA, 119-20, 137-8, 215, 237; fondness for HHA, 121; and Sarajevo assassination, 153; HHA declares love, 154; and German advance through Belgium, 180; visits Mells, 183; letters from Montagu, 209; HHA confides wartime secrets to, 220; consummation with HHA questioned, 223-4; nursing training, 235, 248, 262; growing fondness for Montagu, 236, 242, 256-8, 262; thoughts of marriage, 242; writes to HHA on intention to marry, 258-9; agrees to marry Montagu, 262; in British Hospital at Wimereux, 262, 267-8, 290; conversion to Judaism, 263, 269, 271-3, 279, 282, 290-1; letter to HHA telling of marriage to Montagu, 268; reactions to engagement, 269-70; relations with HHA widely known, 282; HHA meets in France, 291; marriage ceremony, 292; entertains, 334; unhappy marriage and affairs, 351; birth of daughter, 352; survives until 1948, 352, 354

Stanway, Gloucestershire, 200-1
Stead, William Thomas, 94
Steel, Major Edwin Bedford, 199, 218
Stevenson, Frances, 105-7, 254, 330, 337-8, 342
Strachey, Lytton, 144, 317
strikes (industrial), 68-70, 112
suffragette movement: attacks on HHA, 3, 30-1, 95, 127-8; militancy and direct action, 3, 28, 30-2, 95, 100, 106-7, 127, 140, 141; attack on Lloyd George's house, 107-8; and 'Cat and Mouse Act', 108; and 1913 Derby fatality, 112-14; and restrictions, 149; in war work, 284
Sutherland, Millicent, Duchess of, 53, 246
Swaythling, Louis Samuel Montagu, 2nd Baron (Edwin's brother), 292
Swaythling, Samuel Montagu, 1st Baron (Edwin's father), 86, 269
Switzerland, 105, 131, 170, 176

Talbot de Malahide, Isabel, Lady, 115-16
Taplow Court, 75
Tennant, Sir Charles (MA's father): gives

ball for Violet, 18; career and fortune, 23-4; improves Glen, 51; social status, 64
Tennant, Charlotte ('Charty'; MA's sister), 79
Tennant, Edward, Lord Glenconner, (MA's brother), 64
Tennant, Emma (MA's mother), 14, 77
Tennant, Frances (Marguerite's niece), 18
Tennant, Frank (MA's brother), 72
Tennant, Katharine (K; MA's half-sister), 30
Tennant, Kathleen (MA's niece), 304
Tennant, Marguerite, Lady (née Miles; later Lubbock; MA's stepmother), 14, 18, 301
Tennyson, Alfred, 1st Baron: Maud, 54
Tennyson, Lionel, 53
Thornhill, Sir James, 22
Thorp, Daisy, 131
Thurloe Place, Kensington, 354
Times, The: Northcliffe owns, 61; and outbreak of war, 171; on rush to colours, 190; readership, 267; on shell shortage, 274; refuses to print Lansdowne Memorandum, 328
Titanic, RMS, 93-4, 115
Tower, Winifred, 161, 163, 166, 171, 177, 192, 211, 309
Trades Union Congress, 130
transport (public), 60-1
Tredegar, Courtenay Morgan, 3rd Baron, 205
Trefusis, Beatrice, 191, 210, 264
Trott, Madeleine, 26
Tsushima, Battle of (1905), 117
Tuckwell, Gertrude, 127
Turkey see Ottoman Empire
Tyrrell, Sir William, 173

U-boats: as threat, 217; campaign against shipping, 239-40, 251, 323, 329; individual: U-9, 216-17; U-18, 240; U-75, 319, 344
Ulster (Northern Ireland): opposes Irish Home Rule, 92-4, 99, 106, 138; and Curragh mutiny, 142-3; gun-running, 143-4; excluded from Home Rule Bill, 150-1
Ulster Volunteer Force, 106, 143, 144
United States of America: and sinking of Lusitania, 264

Velasquez, Diego: *The Rokeby Venus*, 140-1
Versailles Conference (1918-19), 374
Victoria, Queen, 80, 266
Victoria Louise, Princess of Prussia, 122
Victoria Station, London, 250
Vigilante (journal), 345
Voluntary Aid Detachment (VAD), 233-5, 246-8

Wakefield, Henry *see* Birmingham, Bishop of
Wakes (celebrations), 60
Walmer Castle, Kent, 100, 214, 311-12, 332
Walpole, Sir Robert, 25n
War Council (British), proposed, 330-5
Ward, Eric (*later* Earl of Dudley), 352
Webb, Beatrice: supports eugenics, 39; on MA's dinner parties, 66; diary, 94, 145; on governing classes' talk of revolution, 94, 145; complains of rowdy party, 167; attends anti-war demonstration, 176; on effect of Grey's speech, 181; on hard-working Cabinet members, 210; on new Coalition, 282; on Zeppelins, 300
Webb, Sidney, 39, 300
Welfare State: beginnings, 2
Wells, H.G.: on suffragettes, 32; on war threat, 138; supports Robert Ross, 296
West, Gabrielle, 194, 206, 212, 222
Westminster, Constance, Duchess of, 246
Wharf, The, Sutton Courtenay, 19, 109-10, 119, 157, 162, 273, 317, 325, 353
White Feather Campaign, 218
Wilde, Oscar, 1, 14, 294, 295
Wilhelm II, Kaiser of Germany: develops navy, 40, 117; militarism, 123; popularity, 124; Grey describes, 158; on summer cruise (1914), 160; returns to Germany, 163; on outbreak of war, 168; public appearance at outbreak of war, 172; Lichnowskys denounce, 175-6; protects English church in Berlin, 185; returns British insignia and medals, 185; predicts short war, 190; agrees to air raids on Britain, 232; opposes Zeppelin attacks on London, 265; MA believes responsible for war, 313
Williams, Revd Harold, 123, 160, 163, 172, 185

Wimborne, Alice, Viscountess, 334
Wimereux, near Boulogne, 262, 267-8, 290
Windsor Castle, 47, 130, 214, 252, 254
Wodehouse, P.G., 9
women: status of, 3; as domestic servants, 56, 298; employment, 60; fashion, 61-2, 118n, 125; 'followers' and marriage prospects, 62-3; surplus numbers, 62; chaperonage and restraints, 97; sexual innocence, 97-8, 162; Almroth Wright disparages, 106; education, 127; wartime voluntary activities, 204; press white feathers on men, 218; war work, 219, 231, 233-4, 284, 290, 298; *see also* suffragette movement
Women's Emergency Corps, 219
Women's Institute, 190
Women's Land Army, 344
Women's Social and Political Union, 28, 30
Woolf, Virginia, 245, 299, 339, 350
Work for Women Fund, 290
Workers' Union, 112
workhouses, 37-8
World War I: early conduct, 4-5; volunteer workers, 4, 232, 250; outbreak, 158-9, 185-90, 192; preparations for, 166-7; popular enthusiasm for, 190-2, 204; expected duration, 218-19, 224, 239, 298; life on home front, 220; Christmas truce (1914), 225; medical facilities and conditions, 232-3, 245-6; Western Front, 245; poison gas in, 260-1, 309; casualties, 261 & n, 293, 297, 302, 322; Allied reverses, 265, 294, 323; cost, 302, 327; Lansdowne urges discontinuation, 327; ends, 346-7
Worth, Charles, 125-6
Wortley, Rothesay Stuart, 289n
Wright, Sir Almroth, 106
Wykeham-Musgrave, Kit, 216-17
Wyndham, George, 53
Wyver, George, 30, 37, 126, 302
Wyver, John, 37

Ypres, Battle of (first, 1915), 260, 276

Zeppelins, 220, 232, 265, 300-1, 311